Living with Christ

SUNDAY MISSAL

2015-2016

with Prayers and Hymns

Approved for use in Canada

NOVALIS

NOVALIS

Novalis Publishing Inc.
10 Lower Spadina Ave., Suite 400
Toronto, ON M5V 2Z2
Canada

Telephone: 1-800-387-7164
Fax: 1-800-204-4140
Email: books@novalis.ca

www.novalis.ca

Novalis has dedicated itself since 1936 to the development of pastoral resources which assist the People of God in preparing for and participating in the liturgy.

Please write, phone, or visit us for further information on our publications, or visit our website at www.novalis.ca.

For more suggested intentions for the Prayer of the Faithful, please visit: www.livingwithchrist.ca.

Editor-in-chief: Natalia Kononenko, email: LWC@novalis.ca

Associate editor: Nancy Keyes

Music: All credits accompany the music texts.

Cover design & layout: Jessica AuCoin

ISBN: 978-2-89688-119-2

ISSN: 0832-5324

Printed in Canada

We acknowledge the financial support of the Government of Canada through the Book Publishing Industry Development Program (BPIDP) for our publishing activities.

Contents

Liturgical Calendar............inside front cover
Order of Mass.................................5
Sunday Readings and Prayer...................72

PRAYER

Year C: The Year of Luke....................606
Papal Prayer Intentions 2016................608
Traditional Prayers.........................611
The Rosary..................................614
The Way of the Cross........................616
Praying with the Eucharist..................623
Inspiration from the Saints.................625
Prayers for Cemetery Visits.................629
When to Pray................................631
Prayer in the Morning.......................633
Prayer in the Evening.......................637
Celebrating the Sacrament
of Reconciliation...........................641

MUSIC

Eucharistic Chants..........................644
Hymns.......................................652
Music Index.................................672

From the Eucharist,
this sacrament of love,
flows every authentic
journey of faith,
of communion,
and of witness.

Pope Francis

Introductory Rites

ENTRANCE CHANT

(or Entrance Antiphon – ▶ The appropriate day)

GREETING

In the name of the Father, and of the Son, and of the Holy Spirit. **Amen.**

1 The grace of our Lord Jesus Christ, and the love of God, and the communion of the Holy Spirit be with you all.

2 Grace to you and peace from God our Father and the Lord Jesus Christ.

3 The Lord be with you.

And with your spirit.

PENITENTIAL ACT

(or Rite for the Blessing and Sprinkling of Water, p. 7)

Brothers and sisters, let us acknowledge our sins, and so prepare ourselves to celebrate the sacred mysteries. *(Pause)*

1 **I confess to almighty God**
and to you, my brothers and sisters,
that I have greatly sinned,
in my thoughts and in my words,
in what I have done and in what I have failed to do,
through my fault, through my fault,
through my most grievous fault;
therefore I ask blessed Mary ever-Virgin,
all the Angels and Saints,

and you, my brothers and sisters,
to pray for me to the Lord our God.

May almighty God have mercy on us, forgive us our sins, and bring us to everlasting life.
Amen.

Lord, have mercy. **Lord, have mercy.**
or Kyrie, eleison. **Kyrie, eleison.**

Christ, have mercy. **Christ, have mercy.**
or Christe, eleison. **Christe, eleison.**

Lord, have mercy. **Lord, have mercy.**
or Kyrie, eleison. **Kyrie, eleison.**

2 Have mercy on us, O Lord.
For we have sinned against you.

Show us, O Lord, your mercy.
And grant us your salvation.

May almighty God have mercy on us, forgive us our sins, and bring us to everlasting life.
Amen.

Lord, have mercy. **Lord, have mercy.**
or Kyrie, eleison. **Kyrie, eleison.**

Christ, have mercy. **Christ, have mercy.**
or Christe, eleison. **Christe, eleison.**

Lord, have mercy. **Lord, have mercy.**
or Kyrie, eleison. **Kyrie, eleison.**

3 You were sent to heal the contrite of heart:

Lord, have mercy. **Lord, have mercy.**
or Kyrie, eleison. **Kyrie, eleison.**

You came to call sinners:

Christ, have mercy. **Christ, have mercy.**
or Christe, eleison. **Christe, eleison.**

You are seated at the right hand of the Father to intercede for us:

Lord, have mercy. **Lord, have mercy.**
or Kyrie, eleison. **Kyrie, eleison.**

May almighty God have mercy on us, forgive us our sins, and bring us to everlasting life. **Amen.**

(▶ *Glory to God, p. 10)*

RITE FOR THE BLESSING AND SPRINKLING OF WATER

Dear brothers and sisters, let us humbly beseech the Lord our God to bless this water he has created, which will be sprinkled on us as a memorial of our Baptism. May he help us by his grace to remain faithful to the Spirit we have received. *(Pause)*

1 Almighty ever-living God, who willed that through water, the fountain of life and the source of purification, even souls should be cleansed and receive the gift of eternal life; be pleased, we pray, to bless this water, by which we seek protection on this your day, O Lord. Renew the living spring of your grace within us and grant that by this water we may be defended from all ills of spirit and body, and so approach you with hearts made clean and worthily receive your salvation. Through Christ our Lord. **Amen.**

2 Almighty Lord and God, who are the source and origin of all life, whether of body or soul, we ask you to bless this water, which we use in confidence to implore forgiveness for our sins and to obtain the protection of your grace against all illness and every snare of the enemy. Grant, O Lord, in your mercy, that living waters may always spring up for our salvation, and so may we approach you with a pure heart and avoid all danger to body and soul. Through Christ our Lord. **Amen.**

3 *During Easter Time:*
Lord our God, in your mercy be present to your people's prayers, and, for us who recall the wondrous work of our creation and the still greater work of our redemption, graciously bless this water. For you created water to make the fields fruitful and to refresh and cleanse our bodies. You also made water the instrument of your mercy: for through water you freed your people from slavery and quenched their thirst in the desert; through water the Prophets proclaimed the new covenant you were to enter upon with the human race; and last of all, through water, which Christ made holy in the Jordan, you have renewed our corrupted nature in the bath of regeneration. Therefore, may this water be for us a memorial of the Baptism we have received, and grant that we may share in the gladness of our brothers and sisters who at Easter have received their Baptism. Through Christ our Lord. **Amen.**

Where it is customary to bless salt also, add:

We humbly ask you, almighty God: be pleased in your faithful love to bless this salt you have created, for it was you who commanded the prophet Elisha to cast salt into water, that impure water might be purified. Grant, O Lord, we pray, that, wherever this mixture of salt and water is sprinkled, every attack of the enemy may be repulsed and your Holy Spirit may be present to keep us safe at all times. Through Christ our Lord. **Amen.**

During the sprinkling, an appropriate song may be sung.

May almighty God cleanse us of our sins, and through the celebration of this Eucharist make us worthy to share at the table of his Kingdom. **Amen.**

GLORY TO GOD

Omitted during Advent and Lent.

**Glory to God in the highest,
and on earth peace to people of good will.**

**We praise you,
we bless you,
we adore you,
we glorify you,
we give you thanks for your great glory,
Lord God, heavenly King,
O God, almighty Father.**

**Lord Jesus Christ, Only Begotten Son,
Lord God, Lamb of God, Son of the Father,
you take away the sins of the world,
have mercy on us;
you take away the sins of the world,
receive our prayer;
you are seated at the right hand of the Father,
have mercy on us.**

**For you alone are the Holy One,
you alone are the Lord,
you alone are the Most High,
Jesus Christ,
with the Holy Spirit,
in the glory of God the Father.
Amen.**

COLLECT *(▶ The appropriate day)*

Liturgy of the Word

READINGS (▶ *The appropriate day*)

HOMILY

PROFESSION OF FAITH

1 Nicene Creed
All bow at the words in italics.

**I believe in one God,
the Father almighty,
maker of heaven and earth,
of all things visible and invisible.**

**I believe in one Lord Jesus Christ,
the Only Begotten Son of God,
born of the Father before all ages.
God from God, Light from Light,
true God from true God,
begotten, not made,
consubstantial with the Father;
through him all things were made.
For us men and for our salvation
he came down from heaven,
*and by the Holy Spirit was incarnate
of the Virgin Mary,
and became man.*
For our sake he was crucified under
Pontius Pilate,
he suffered death and was buried,
and rose again on the third day
in accordance with the Scriptures.
He ascended into heaven**

and is seated at the right hand of the Father.
He will come again in glory
to judge the living and the dead
and his kingdom will have no end.

I believe in the Holy Spirit, the Lord,
the giver of life,
who proceeds from the Father and the Son,
who with the Father and the Son is adored
and glorified,
who has spoken through the prophets.

I believe in one, holy, catholic and
apostolic Church.
I confess one Baptism for the forgiveness
of sins
and I look forward to the resurrection of
the dead
and the life of the world to come. Amen.

2 Apostles' Creed
All bow at the words in italics.

I believe in God,
the Father almighty,
Creator of heaven and earth,
and in Jesus Christ, his only Son, our Lord,
who was conceived by the Holy Spirit,
born of the Virgin Mary,
suffered under Pontius Pilate,
was crucified, died and was buried;
he descended into hell;
on the third day he rose again from the dead;
he ascended into heaven,
and is seated at the right hand of God
the Father almighty;
from there he will come to judge
the living and the dead.

I believe in the Holy Spirit,
the holy catholic Church,
the communion of saints,
the forgiveness of sins,
the resurrection of the body,
and life everlasting. Amen.

PRAYER OF THE FAITHFUL (▶ *The appropriate day*)

Liturgy of the Eucharist

PREPARATION OF THE GIFTS

Blessed are you, Lord God of all creation, for through your goodness we have received the bread we offer you: fruit of the earth and work of human hands, it will become for us the bread of life. **Blessed be God for ever.**

By the mystery of this water and wine may we come to share in the divinity of Christ who humbled himself to share in our humanity.

Blessed are you, Lord God of all creation, for through your goodness we have received the wine we offer you: fruit of the vine and work of human hands, it will become our spiritual drink. **Blessed be God for ever.**

With humble spirit and contrite heart may we be accepted by you, O Lord, and may our sacrifice in your sight this day be pleasing to you, Lord God.

Wash me, O Lord, from my iniquity and cleanse me from my sin.

Pray, brothers and sisters, that my sacrifice and yours may be acceptable to God, the almighty Father.
May the Lord accept the sacrifice at your hands for the praise and glory of his name, for our good and the good of all his holy Church.

PRAYER OVER THE OFFERINGS

(The appropriate day)

THE EUCHARISTIC PRAYER

The Lord be with you. **And with your spirit.**
Lift up your hearts. **We lift them up to the Lord.**
Let us give thanks to the Lord our God.
It is right and just.

The Priest selects an appropriate Preface, which concludes with the Holy, Holy.

PREFACE I OF ADVENT

It is truly right and just, our duty and our salvation, always and everywhere to give you thanks, Lord, holy Father, almighty and eternal God, through Christ our Lord.

For he assumed at his first coming the lowliness of human flesh, and so fulfilled the design you formed long ago, and opened for us the way to eternal salvation, that, when he comes again in glory and majesty and all is at last made manifest, we who watch for that day may inherit the great promise in which now we dare to hope.

And so, with Angels and Archangels, with Thrones and Dominions, and with all the hosts and Powers of heaven, we sing the hymn of your glory, as without end we acclaim: **Holy, Holy** *(p. 37)*

PREFACE II OF ADVENT

It is truly right and just, our duty and our salvation, always and everywhere to give you thanks, Lord, holy Father, almighty and eternal God, through Christ our Lord.

For all the oracles of the prophets foretold him, the Virgin Mother longed for him with love beyond all telling, John the Baptist sang of his coming and proclaimed his presence when he came.

It is by his gift that already we rejoice at the mystery of his Nativity, so that he may find us watchful in prayer and exultant in his praise.

And so, with Angels and Archangels, with Thrones and Dominions, and with all the hosts and Powers of heaven, we sing the hymn of your glory, as without end we acclaim: **Holy, Holy** *(p. 37)*

PREFACE I OF THE NATIVITY OF THE LORD

It is truly right and just, our duty and our salvation, always and everywhere to give you thanks, Lord, holy Father, almighty and eternal God.

For in the mystery of the Word made flesh a new light of your glory has shone upon the eyes of our mind, so that, as we recognize in him God made visible, we may be caught up through him in love of things invisible.

And so, with Angels and Archangels, with Thrones and Dominions, and with all the hosts and Powers of heaven, we sing the hymn of your glory, as without end we acclaim: **Holy, Holy** *(p. 37)*

PREFACE II OF THE NATIVITY OF THE LORD

It is truly right and just, our duty and our salvation, always and everywhere to give you thanks, Lord, holy Father, almighty and eternal God, through Christ our Lord.

For on the feast of this awe-filled mystery, though invisible in his own divine nature, he has appeared visibly in ours; and begotten before all ages, he has begun to exist in time; so that, raising up in himself all that was cast down, he might restore unity to all creation and call straying humanity back to the heavenly Kingdom.

And so, with all the Angels, we praise you, as in joyful celebration we acclaim: **Holy, Holy** *(p. 37)*

PREFACE III OF THE NATIVITY OF THE LORD

It is truly right and just, our duty and our salvation, always and everywhere to give you thanks, Lord, holy Father, almighty and eternal God, through Christ our Lord.

For through him the holy exchange that restores our life has shone forth today in splendour: when our frailty is assumed by your Word not only does human mortality receive unending honour but by this wondrous union we, too, are made eternal.

And so, in company with the choirs of Angels, we praise you, and with joy we proclaim: **Holy, Holy** *(p. 37)*

PREFACE I OF THE BLESSED VIRGIN MARY

It is truly right and just, our duty and our salvation, always and everywhere to give you thanks, Lord, holy Father, almighty and eternal God, and to praise, bless, and glorify your name on the Solemnity of the Motherhood of the Blessed ever-Virgin Mary.

For by the overshadowing of the Holy Spirit she conceived your Only Begotten Son, and without losing the glory of virginity, brought forth into the world the eternal Light, Jesus Christ our Lord.

Through him the Angels praise your majesty, Dominions adore and Powers tremble before you. Heaven and the Virtues of heaven and the blessed Seraphim worship together with exultation. May our voices, we pray, join with theirs in humble praise, as we acclaim: **Holy, Holy** *(p. 37)*

PREFACE OF THE EPIPHANY OF THE LORD

It is truly right and just, our duty and our salvation, always and everywhere to give you thanks, Lord, holy Father, almighty and eternal God.

For today you have revealed the mystery of our salvation in Christ as a light for the nations, and, when he appeared in our mortal nature, you made us new by the glory of his immortal nature.

And so, with Angels and Archangels, with Thrones and Dominions, and with all the hosts and Powers of heaven, we sing the hymn of your glory, as without end we acclaim: **Holy, Holy** *(p. 37)*

PREFACE OF THE BAPTISM OF THE LORD

It is truly right and just, our duty and our salvation, always and everywhere to give you thanks, Lord, holy Father, almighty and eternal God.

For in the waters of the Jordan you revealed with signs and wonders a new Baptism, so that through the voice that came down from heaven we might come to believe in your Word dwelling among us, and by the Spirit's descending in the likeness of a dove we might know that Christ your Servant has been anointed with the oil of gladness and sent to bring the good news to the poor.

And so, with the Powers of heaven, we worship you constantly on earth, and before your majesty without end we acclaim: **Holy, Holy** *(p. 37)*

PREFACE I OF LENT

It is truly right and just, our duty and our salvation, always and everywhere to give you thanks, Lord, holy Father, almighty and eternal God, through Christ our Lord.

For by your gracious gift each year your faithful await the sacred paschal feasts with the joy of minds made pure, so that, more eagerly intent on prayer and on the works of charity, and participating in the mysteries by which they have been reborn, they may be led to the fullness of grace that you bestow on your sons and daughters.

And so, with Angels and Archangels, with Thrones and Dominions, and with all the hosts and Powers of heaven, we sing the hymn of your glory, as without end we acclaim: **Holy, Holy** *(p. 37)*

PREFACE II OF LENT

It is truly right and just, our duty and our salvation, always and everywhere to give you thanks, Lord, holy Father, almighty and eternal God.

For you have given your children a sacred time for the renewing and purifying of their hearts, that, freed from disordered affections, they may so deal with the things of this passing world as to hold rather to the things that eternally endure.

And so, with all the Angels and Saints, we praise you, as without end we acclaim: **Holy, Holy** *(p. 37)*

PREFACE III OF LENT

It is truly right and just, our duty and our salvation, always and everywhere to give you thanks, Lord, holy Father, almighty and eternal God.

For you will that our self-denial should give you thanks, humble our sinful pride, contribute to the feeding of the poor, and so help us imitate you in your kindness.

And so we glorify you with countless Angels, as with one voice of praise we acclaim: **Holy, Holy** *(p. 37)*

PREFACE IV OF LENT

It is truly right and just, our duty and our salvation, always and everywhere to give you thanks, Lord, holy Father, almighty and eternal God.

For through bodily fasting you restrain our faults, raise up our minds, and bestow both virtue and its rewards, through Christ our Lord.

Through him the Angels praise your majesty, Dominions adore and Powers tremble before you. Heaven and the Virtues of heaven and the blessed Seraphim worship together with exultation. May our voices, we pray, join with theirs in humble praise, as we acclaim: **Holy, Holy** *(p. 37)*

PREFACE OF 1ST SUNDAY OF LENT

It is truly right and just, our duty and our salvation, always and everywhere to give you thanks, Lord, holy Father, almighty and eternal God, through Christ our Lord.

By abstaining forty long days from earthly food, he consecrated through his fast the pattern of our Lenten observance and, by overturning all the snares of the ancient serpent, taught us to cast out the leaven of malice, so that, celebrating worthily the Paschal Mystery, we might pass over at last to the eternal paschal feast.

And so, with the company of Angels and Saints, we sing the hymn of your praise, as without end we acclaim: **Holy, Holy** *(p. 37)*

PREFACE OF 2ND SUNDAY OF LENT

It is truly right and just, our duty and our salvation, always and everywhere to give you thanks, Lord, holy Father, almighty and eternal God, through Christ our Lord.

For after he had told the disciples of his coming Death, on the holy mountain he manifested to them his glory, to show, even by the testimony of the law and the prophets, that the Passion leads to the glory of the Resurrection.

And so, with the Powers of heaven, we worship you constantly on earth, and before your majesty without end we acclaim: **Holy, Holy** *(p. 37)*

PREFACE OF 3RD SUNDAY OF LENT

It is truly right and just, our duty and our salvation, always and everywhere to give you thanks, Lord, holy Father, almighty and eternal God, through Christ our Lord.

For when he asked the Samaritan woman for water to drink, he had already created the gift of faith within her and so ardently did he thirst for her faith, that he kindled in her the fire of divine love.

And so we, too, give you thanks and with the Angels praise your mighty deeds, as we acclaim: **Holy, Holy** *(p. 37)*

PREFACE OF 4TH SUNDAY OF LENT

It is truly right and just, our duty and our salvation, always and everywhere to give you thanks, Lord, holy Father, almighty and eternal God, through Christ our Lord.

By the mystery of the Incarnation, he has led the human race that walked in darkness into the radiance of the faith and has brought those born in slavery to ancient sin through the waters of regeneration to make them your adopted children.

Therefore, all creatures of heaven and earth sing a new song in adoration, and we, with all the host of Angels, cry out, and without end acclaim: **Holy, Holy** *(p. 37)*

PREFACE OF 5TH SUNDAY OF LENT

It is truly right and just, our duty and our salvations, always and everywhere to give you thanks, Lord, holy Father, almighty and eternal God, through Christ our Lord.

For as true man he wept for Lazarus his friend and as eternal God raised him from the tomb, just as, taking pity on the human race, he leads us by sacred mysteries to new life.

Through him the host of Angels adores your majesty and rejoices in your presence for ever. May our voices, we pray, join with theirs in one chorus of exultant praise, as we acclaim: **Holy, Holy** *(p. 37)*

PREFACE OF THE PASSION OF THE LORD

(Palm Sunday)

It is truly right and just, our duty and our salvation, always and everywhere to give you thanks,

Lord, holy Father, almighty and eternal God, through Christ our Lord.

For, though innocent, he suffered willingly for sinners and accepted unjust condemnation to save the guilty. His Death has washed away our sins, and his Resurrection has purchased our justification.

And so, with all the Angels, we praise you, as in joyful celebration we acclaim: **Holy, Holy** *(p. 37)*

PREFACE I OF EASTER

It is truly right and just, our duty and our salvation, at all times to acclaim you, O Lord, but

Easter Vigil: on this night
Easter Sunday and Octave: on this day
rest of Easter Time: in this time

above all to laud you yet more gloriously, when Christ our Passover has been sacrificed.

For he is the true Lamb who has taken away the sins of the world; by dying he has destroyed our death, and by rising, restored our life.

Therefore, overcome with paschal joy, every land, every people exults in your praise and even the heavenly Powers, with the angelic hosts, sing together the unending hymn of your glory, as they acclaim: **Holy, Holy** *(p. 37)*

PREFACE II OF EASTER

It is truly right and just, our duty and our salvation, at all times to acclaim you, O Lord, but in this time above all to laud you yet more gloriously, when Christ our Passover has been sacrificed.

Through him the children of light rise to eternal life and the halls of the heavenly Kingdom are thrown open to the faithful; for his Death is our ransom from death, and in his rising the life of all has risen.

Therefore, overcome with paschal joy, every land, every people exults in your praise and even the heavenly Powers, with the angelic hosts, sing together the unending hymn of your glory, as they acclaim: **Holy, Holy** *(p. 37)*

PREFACE III OF EASTER

It is truly right and just, our duty and our salvation, at all times to acclaim you, O Lord, but in this time above all to laud you yet more gloriously, when Christ our Passover has been sacrificed.

He never ceases to offer himself for us but defends us and ever pleads our cause before you: he is the sacrificial Victim who dies no more, the Lamb, once slain, who lives for ever.

Therefore, overcome with paschal joy, every land, every people exults in your praise and even the heavenly Powers, with the angelic hosts, sing together the unending hymn of your glory, as they acclaim: **Holy, Holy** *(p. 37)*

PREFACE IV OF EASTER

It is truly right and just, our duty and our salvation, at all times to acclaim you, O Lord, but in this time above all to laud you yet more gloriously, when Christ our Passover has been sacrificed.

For, with the old order destroyed, a universe cast down is renewed, and integrity of life is restored to us in Christ.

Therefore, overcome with paschal joy, every land, every people exults in your praise and even the heavenly Powers, with the angelic hosts, sing together the unending hymn of your glory, as they acclaim: **Holy, Holy** *(p. 37)*

PREFACE V OF EASTER

It is truly right and just, our duty and our salvation, at all times to acclaim you, O Lord, but in this time above all to laud you yet more gloriously, when Christ our Passover has been sacrificed.

By the oblation of his Body, he brought the sacrifices of old to fulfillment in the reality of the Cross and, by commending himself to you for our salvation, showed himself the Priest, the Altar, and the Lamb of sacrifice.

Therefore, overcome with paschal joy, every land, every people exults in your praise and even the heavenly Powers, with the angelic hosts, sing together the unending hymn of your glory, as they acclaim: **Holy, Holy** *(p. 37)*

PREFACE I OF THE ASCENSION OF THE LORD

It is truly right and just, our duty and our salvation, always and everywhere to give you thanks, Lord, holy Father, almighty and eternal God.

For the Lord Jesus, the King of glory, conqueror of sin and death, ascended (today) to the highest heavens, as the Angels gazed in wonder.

Mediator between God and man, judge of the world and Lord of hosts, he ascended, not to distance himself from our lowly state but that we, his members, might be confident of following where he, our Head and Founder, has gone before.

Therefore, overcome with paschal joy, every land, every people exults in your praise and even the heavenly Powers, with the angelic hosts, sing together the unending hymn of your glory, as they acclaim: **Holy, Holy** *(p. 37)*

PREFACE II OF THE ASCENSION OF THE LORD

It is truly right and just, our duty and our salvation, always and everywhere to give you thanks, Lord, holy Father, almighty and eternal God, through Christ our Lord.

For after his Resurrection he plainly appeared to all his disciples and was taken up to heaven in their sight, that he might make us sharers in his divinity.

Therefore, overcome with paschal joy, every land, every people exults in your praise and even the heavenly Powers, with the angelic hosts, sing together the unending hymn of your glory, as they acclaim: **Holy, Holy** *(p. 37)*

PREFACE OF PENTECOST

It is truly right and just, our duty and our salvation, always and everywhere to give you thanks, Lord, holy Father, almighty and eternal God.

For, bringing your Paschal Mystery to completion, you bestowed the Holy Spirit today on those you made your adopted children by uniting them to your Only Begotten Son.

This same Spirit, as the Church came to birth, opened to all peoples the knowledge of God and brought together the many languages of the earth in profession of the one faith.

Therefore, overcome with paschal joy, every land, every people exults in your praise and even the heavenly Powers, with the angelic hosts, sing together the unending hymn of your glory, as they acclaim: **Holy, Holy** *(p. 37)*

PREFACE OF HOLY TRINITY

It is truly right and just, our duty and our salvation, always and everywhere to give you thanks, Lord, holy Father, almighty and eternal God.

For with your Only Begotten Son and the Holy Spirit you are one God, one Lord: not in the unity of a single person, but in a Trinity of one substance.

For what you have revealed to us of your glory we believe equally of your Son and of the Holy Spirit, so that, in the confessing of the true and eternal Godhead, you might be adored in what is proper to each Person, their unity in substance, and their equality in majesty.

For this is praised by Angels and Archangels, Cherubim, too, and Seraphim, who never cease to cry out each day, as with one voice they acclaim: **Holy, Holy** *(p. 37)*

PREFACE I OF THE MOST HOLY EUCHARIST

It is truly right and just, our duty and our salvation, always and everywhere to give you thanks, Lord, holy Father, almighty and eternal God, through Christ our Lord.

For he is the true and eternal Priest, who instituted the pattern of an everlasting sacrifice and was the first to offer himself as the saving Victim, commanding us to make this offering as his memorial.

As we eat his flesh that was sacrificed for us, we are made strong, and, as we drink his Blood that was poured out for us, we are washed clean.

And so, with Angels and Archangels, with Thrones and Dominions, and with all the hosts and Powers of heaven, we sing the hymn of your glory, as without end we acclaim: **Holy, Holy** *(p. 37)*

PREFACE II OF THE MOST HOLY EUCHARIST

It is truly right and just, our duty and our salvation, always and everywhere to give you thanks, Lord, holy Father, almighty and eternal God, through Christ our Lord.

For at the Last Supper with his Apostles, establishing for the ages to come the saving memorial of the Cross, he offered himself to you as the unblemished Lamb, the acceptable gift of perfect praise.

Nourishing your faithful by this sacred mystery, you make them holy, so that the human race, bounded by one world, may be enlightened by one faith and united by one bond of charity.

And so, we approach the table of this wondrous Sacrament, so that, bathed in the sweetness of your grace, we may pass over to the heavenly realities here foreshadowed.

Therefore, all creatures of heaven and earth sing a new song in adoration, and we, with all the host of Angels, cry out, and without end we acclaim: **Holy, Holy** *(p. 37)*

PREFACE I OF SUNDAYS IN ORDINARY TIME

It is truly right and just, our duty and our salvation, always and everywhere to give you thanks, Lord, holy Father, almighty and eternal God, through Christ our Lord.

For through his Paschal Mystery, he accomplished the marvellous deed, by which he has freed us from the yoke of sin and death, summoning us to the glory of being now called a chosen race, a royal priesthood, a holy nation, a people for your own possession, to proclaim everywhere your mighty works, for you have called us out of darkness into your own wonderful light.

And so, with Angels and Archangels, with Thrones and Dominions, and with all the hosts and Powers of heaven, we sing the hymn of your glory, as without end we acclaim: **Holy, Holy** *(p. 37)*

PREFACE II OF SUNDAYS IN ORDINARY TIME

It is truly right and just, our duty and our salvation, always and everywhere to give you thanks, Lord, holy Father, almighty and eternal God, through Christ our Lord.

For out of compassion for the waywardness that is ours, he humbled himself and was born of the Virgin; by the passion of the Cross he freed us from unending death, and by rising from the dead he gave us life eternal.

And so, with Angels and Archangels, with Thrones and Dominions, and with all the hosts and Powers of heaven, we sing the hymn of your glory, as without end we acclaim: **Holy, Holy** *(p. 37)*

PREFACE III OF SUNDAYS IN ORDINARY TIME

It is truly right and just, our duty and our salvation, always and everywhere to give you thanks, Lord, holy Father, almighty and eternal God.

For we know it belongs to your boundless glory, that you came to the aid of mortal beings with your divinity and even fashioned for us a remedy out of mortality itself, that the cause of our downfall might become the means of our salvation, through Christ our Lord.

Through him the host of Angels adores your majesty and rejoices in your presence for ever. May our voices, we pray, join with theirs in one chorus of exultant praise, as we acclaim: **Holy, Holy** *(p. 37)*

PREFACE IV OF SUNDAYS IN ORDINARY TIME

It is truly right and just, our duty and our salvation, always and everywhere to give you thanks, Lord, holy Father, almighty and eternal God, through Christ our Lord.

For by his birth he brought renewal to humanity's fallen state, and by his suffering, cancelled out our sins; by his rising from the dead he has opened the way to eternal life, and by ascending to you, O Father, he has unlocked the gates of heaven.

And so, with the company of Angels and Saints, we sing the hymn of your praise, as without end we acclaim: **Holy, Holy** *(p. 37)*

PREFACE V OF SUNDAYS IN ORDINARY TIME

It is truly right and just, our duty and our salvation, always and everywhere to give you thanks, Lord, holy Father, almighty and eternal God.

For you laid the foundations of the world and have arranged the changing of times and seasons; you formed man in your own image and set humanity over the whole world in all its wonder, to rule in your name over all you have made and for ever praise you in your mighty works, through Christ our Lord.

And so, with all the Angels, we praise you, as in joyful celebration we acclaim: **Holy, Holy** *(p. 37)*

PREFACE VI OF SUNDAYS IN ORDINARY TIME

It is truly right and just, our duty and our salvation, always and everywhere to give you thanks, Lord, holy Father, almighty and eternal God.

For in you we live and move and have our being, and while in this body we not only experience the daily effects of your care, but even now possess the pledge of life eternal.

For, having received the first fruits of the Spirit, through whom you raised up Jesus from the dead, we hope for an everlasting share in the Paschal Mystery.

And so, with all the Angels, we praise you, as in joyful celebration we acclaim: **Holy, Holy** *(p. 37)*

PREFACE VII OF SUNDAYS IN ORDINARY TIME

It is truly right and just, our duty and our salvation, always and everywhere to give you thanks, Lord, holy Father, almighty and eternal God.

For you so loved the world that in your mercy you sent us the Redeemer, to live like us in all things but sin, so that you might love in us what you loved in your Son, by whose obedience we have been restored to those gifts of yours that, by sinning, we had lost in disobedience.

And so, Lord, with all the Angels and Saints, we, too, give you thanks, as in exultation we acclaim: **Holy, Holy** *(p. 37)*

PREFACE VIII OF SUNDAYS IN ORDINARY TIME

It is truly right and just, our duty and our salvation, always and everywhere to give you thanks, Lord, holy Father, almighty and eternal God.

For, when your children were scattered afar by sin, through the Blood of your Son and the power of the Spirit, you gathered them again to yourself, that a people, formed as one by the unity of the Trinity, made the body of Christ and the temple of the Holy Spirit, might, to the praise of your manifold wisdom, be manifest as the Church.

And so, in company with the choirs of Angels, we praise you, and with joy we proclaim: **Holy, Holy** *(p. 37)*

PREFACE OF OUR LORD JESUS CHRIST, KING OF THE UNIVERSE

It is truly right and just, our duty and our salvation, always and everywhere to give you thanks, Lord, holy Father, almighty and eternal God.

For you anointed your Only Begotten Son, our Lord Jesus Christ, with the oil of gladness as eternal Priest and King of all creation, so that, by offering himself on the altar of the Cross as a spotless sacrifice to bring us peace, he might accomplish the mysteries of human redemption and, making all created things subject to his rule, he might present to the immensity of your majesty an eternal and universal kingdom, a kingdom of truth and life, a kingdom of holiness and grace, a kingdom of justice, love and peace.

And so, with Angels and Archangels, with Thrones and Dominions, and with all the hosts and Powers of heaven, we sing the hymn of your glory, as without end we acclaim: **Holy, Holy** *(p. 37)*

PREFACE OF RECONCILIATION I

It is truly right and just that we should always give you thanks, Lord, holy Father, almighty and eternal God.

For you do not cease to spur us on to possess a more abundant life and, being rich in mercy, you constantly offer pardon and call on sinners to trust in your forgiveness alone.

Never did you turn away from us, and, though time and again we have broken your covenant, you have bound the human family to yourself through Jesus your Son, our Redeemer, with a new bond of love so tight that it can never be undone.

Even now you set before your people a time of grace and reconciliation, and, as they turn back to you in spirit, you grant them hope in Christ Jesus and a desire to be of service to all, while they entrust themselves more fully to the Holy Spirit.

And so, filled with wonder, we extol the power of your love, and, proclaiming our joy at the salvation that comes from you, we join in the heavenly hymn of countless hosts, as without end we acclaim: **Holy, Holy** *(p. 37)*

PREFACE OF RECONCILIATION II

It is truly right and just that we should give you thanks and praise, O God, almighty Father, for all you do in this world, through our Lord Jesus Christ.

For though the human race is divided by dissension and discord, yet we know that by testing us you change our hearts to prepare them for reconciliation.

Even more, by your Spirit you move human hearts that enemies may speak to each other again, adversaries join hands, and peoples seek to meet together.

By the working of your power it comes about, O Lord, that hatred is overcome by love, revenge gives way to forgiveness, and discord is changed to mutual respect.

Therefore, as we give you ceaseless thanks with the choirs of heaven, we cry out to your majesty on earth, and without end we acclaim: **Holy, Holy** *(p. 37)*

PREFACE OF VARIOUS NEEDS I

It is truly right and just to give you thanks and raise to you a hymn of glory and praise, O Lord, Father of infinite goodness.

For by the word of your Son's Gospel you have brought together one Church from every people, tongue, and nation, and, having filled her with life by the power of your Spirit, you never cease through her to gather the whole human race into one.

Manifesting the covenant of your love, she dispenses without ceasing the blessed hope of your Kingdom and shines bright as the sign of your faithfulness, which in Christ Jesus our Lord you promised would last for eternity.

And so, with all the Powers of heaven, we worship you constantly on earth, while, with all the Church, as one voice we acclaim: **Holy, Holy** *(p. 37)*

PREFACE OF VARIOUS NEEDS II

It is truly right and just, our duty and our salvation, always and everywhere to give you thanks, Lord, holy Father, creator of the world and source of all life.

For you never forsake the works of your wisdom, but by your providence are even now at work in our midst. With mighty hand and outstretched arm you led your people Israel through the desert. Now, as your Church makes her pilgrim journey in the world, you always accompany her by the power of the Holy Spirit and lead her along the paths of time to the eternal joy of your Kingdom, through Christ our Lord.

And so, with the Angels and Saints, we, too, sing the hymn of your glory, as without end we acclaim: **Holy, Holy** *(p. 37)*

PREFACE OF VARIOUS NEEDS III

It is truly right and just, our duty and our salvation, always and everywhere to give you thanks, holy Father, Lord of heaven and earth, through Christ our Lord.

For by your Word you created the world and you govern all things in harmony. You gave us the same Word made flesh as Mediator, and he has spoken your words to us and called us to follow him. He is the way that leads us to you, the truth that sets us free, the life that fills us with gladness.

Through your Son you gather men and women, whom you made for the glory of your name, into one family, redeemed by the Blood of his Cross and signed with the seal of the Spirit.

Therefore, now and for ages unending, with all the Angels, we proclaim your glory, as in joyful celebration we acclaim: **Holy, Holy** *(p. 37)*

PREFACE OF VARIOUS NEEDS IV

It is truly right and just, our duty and our salvation, always and everywhere to give you thanks, Father of mercies and faithful God.

For you have given us Jesus Christ, your Son, as our Lord and Redeemer.

He always showed compassion for children and for the poor, for the sick and for sinners, and he became a neighbour to the oppressed and the afflicted.

By word and deed he announced to the world that you are our Father and that you care for all your sons and daughters.

And so, with all the Angels and Saints, we exalt and bless your name and sing the hymn of your glory, as without end we acclaim: **Holy, Holy** *(p. 37)*

PREFACE OF EUCHARISTIC PRAYER II

It is truly right and just, our duty and our salvation, always and everywhere to give you thanks, Father most holy, through your beloved Son, Jesus Christ, your Word through whom you made all things, whom you sent as our Saviour and Redeemer, incarnate by the Holy Spirit and born of the Virgin.

Fulfilling your will and gaining for you a holy people, he stretched out his hands as he endured his Passion, so as to break the bonds of death and manifest the resurrection.

And so, with the Angels and all the Saints we declare your glory, as with one voice we acclaim: **Holy, Holy** *(p. 37)*

PREFACE OF EUCHARISTIC PRAYER IV

It is truly right to give you thanks, truly just to give you glory, Father most holy, for you are the one God living and true, existing before all ages and abiding for all eternity, dwelling in unapproachable light; yet you, who alone are good, the source of life, have made all that is, so that you might fill your creatures with blessings and bring joy to many of them by the glory of your light.

And so, in your presence are countless hosts of Angels, who serve you day and night and, gazing upon the glory of your face, glorify you without ceasing.

With them we, too, confess your name in exultation, giving voice to every creature under heaven, as we acclaim:

HOLY, HOLY

Holy, Holy, Holy Lord God of hosts.
Heaven and earth are full of your glory.
Hosanna in the highest.
Blessed is he who comes in the name of the Lord.
Hosanna in the highest.

The Eucharistic Prayer continues:

Eucharistic Prayer I *p. 39*
To you, therefore

Eucharistic Prayer II *p. 44*
You are indeed Holy, O Lord, the fount

Eucharistic Prayer III *p. 46*
You are indeed Holy, O Lord, and all you

Eucharistic Prayer IV *p. 49*
We give you praise

Reconciliation I *p. 52*
You are indeed Holy, O Lord, and from

Reconciliation II *p. 54*
You, therefore, almighty Father

Various Needs I *p. 57*
You are indeed Holy and to be glorified

Various Needs II *p. 59*
You are indeed Holy and to be glorified

Various Needs III *p. 62*
You are indeed Holy and to be glorified

Various Needs IV *p. 65*
You are indeed Holy and to be glorified

EUCHARISTIC PRAYER I

To you, therefore, most merciful Father, we make humble prayer and petition through Jesus Christ, your Son, our Lord: that you accept and bless these gifts, these offerings, these holy and unblemished sacrifices, which we offer you firstly for your holy catholic Church. Be pleased to grant her peace, to guard, unite and govern her throughout the whole world, together with your servant N. our Pope and N. our Bishop, and all those who, holding to the truth, hand on the catholic and apostolic faith.

Remember, Lord, your servants

Christian Initiation (Scrutinies):
who are to present your chosen ones for the holy grace of your Baptism,

N. and N. and all gathered here, whose faith and devotion are known to you. For them, we offer you this sacrifice of praise or they offer it for themselves and all who are dear to them: for the redemption of their souls, in hope of health and well-being, and paying their homage to you, the eternal God, living and true.

Nativity of the Lord and Octave of the Nativity:
Celebrating the most sacred night (day) on which blessed Mary the immaculate Virgin brought forth the Saviour for this world, and

Epiphany of the Lord:
Celebrating the most sacred day on which your Only Begotten Son, eternal with you in your glory, appeared in a human body, truly sharing our flesh, and

Holy Thursday:
Celebrating the most sacred day on which our Lord Jesus Christ was handed over for our sake, and

Easter Vigil to Second Sunday of Easter:
Celebrating the most sacred night (day) of the Resurrection of our Lord Jesus Christ in the flesh, and

Ascension of the Lord:
Celebrating the most sacred day on which your Only Begotten Son, our Lord, placed at the right hand of your glory our weak human nature, which he had united to himself, and

Pentecost Sunday:
Celebrating the most sacred day of Pentecost, on which the Holy Spirit appeared to the Apostles in tongues of fire, and

In communion with those whose memory we venerate, especially the glorious ever-Virgin Mary, Mother of our God and Lord, Jesus Christ, and blessed Joseph, her Spouse, your blessed Apostles and Martyrs, Peter and Paul, Andrew,

James, John, Thomas, James, Philip, Bartholomew, Matthew, Simon and Jude; Linus, Cletus, Clement, Sixtus, Cornelius, Cyprian, Lawrence, Chrysogonus, John and Paul, Cosmas and Damian

and all your Saints; we ask that through their merits and prayers, in all things we may be defended by your protecting help. (Through Christ our Lord. Amen.)

Therefore, Lord, we pray: graciously accept this oblation of our service, that of your whole family;

Christian Initiation (Scrutinies):
which we make to you for your servants, whom you have been pleased to enroll, choose and call for eternal life and for the blessed gift of your grace. (Through Christ our Lord. Amen.)

Holy Thursday:
which we make to you as we observe the day on which our Lord Jesus Christ handed on the mysteries of his Body and Blood for his disciples to celebrate;

Easter Vigil to Second Sunday of Easter:
which we make to you also for those to whom you have been pleased to give the new birth of water and the Holy Spirit, granting them forgiveness of all their sins;

order our days in your peace, and command that we be delivered from eternal damnation and counted among the flock of those you have chosen. (Through Christ our Lord. Amen.)

Be pleased, O God, we pray, to bless, acknowledge, and approve this offering in every respect; make it spiritual and acceptable, so that it may become for us the Body and Blood of your most beloved Son, our Lord Jesus Christ.

On the day before he was to suffer,

Holy Thursday:
for our salvation and the salvation of all, that is today,

he took bread in his holy and venerable hands, and with eyes raised to heaven to you, O God, his almighty Father, giving you thanks, he said the blessing, broke the bread and gave it to his disciples, saying:

Take this, all of you, and eat of it,
for this is my Body
which will be given up for you.

In a similar way, when supper was ended, he took this precious chalice in his holy and venerable hands, and once more giving you thanks, he said the blessing and gave the chalice to his disciples, saying:

Take this, all of you, and drink from it,
for this is the chalice of my Blood,
the Blood of the new and eternal covenant,
which will be poured out for you and for many
for the forgiveness of sins.
Do this in memory of me.

The mystery of faith.

1 **We proclaim your Death, O Lord, and profess your Resurrection until you come again.**

2 **When we eat this Bread and drink this Cup, we proclaim your Death, O Lord, until you come again.**

3 **Save us, Saviour of the world, for by your Cross and Resurrection you have set us free.**

Therefore, O Lord, as we celebrate the memorial of the blessed Passion, the Resurrection from the dead, and the glorious Ascension into heaven of Christ, your Son, our Lord, we, your servants and your holy people, offer to your glorious majesty from the gifts that you have given us, this pure victim, this holy victim, this spotless victim, the holy Bread of eternal life and the Chalice of everlasting salvation.

Be pleased to look upon these offerings with a serene and kindly countenance, and to accept them, as once you were pleased to accept the gifts of your servant Abel the just, the sacrifice of Abraham, our father in faith, and the offering of your high priest Melchizedek, a holy sacrifice, a spotless victim.

In humble prayer we ask you, almighty God: command that these gifts be borne by the hands of your holy Angel to your altar on high in the sight of your divine majesty, so that all of us, who through this participation at the altar receive the most holy Body and Blood of your Son, may be filled with every grace and heavenly blessing. (Through Christ our Lord. Amen.)

Remember also, Lord, your servants N. and N., who have gone before us with the sign of faith and rest in the sleep of peace. *(Pause)* Grant them, O Lord, we pray, and all who sleep in Christ, a place of refreshment, light and peace. (Through Christ our Lord. Amen.)

To us, also, your servants, who, though sinners, hope in your abundant mercies, graciously grant some share and fellowship with your holy Apostles and Martyrs: with John the Baptist, Stephen, Matthias, Barnabas,

Ignatius, Alexander, Marcellinus, Peter, Felicity, Perpetua, Agatha, Lucy, Agnes, Cecilia, Anastasia

and all your Saints; admit us, we beseech you, into their company, not weighing our merits, but granting us your pardon, through Christ our Lord.

Through whom you continue to make all these good things, O Lord; you sanctify them, fill them with life, bless them, and bestow them upon us.

Through him, and with him, and in him, O God, almighty Father, in the unity of the Holy Spirit, all glory and honour is yours, for ever and ever. **Amen.**

(▶ Communion Rite, p. 68)

EUCHARISTIC PRAYER II

You are indeed Holy, O Lord, the fount of all holiness. Make holy, therefore, these gifts, we pray, by sending down your Spirit upon them like the dewfall, so that they may become for us the Body and Blood of our Lord Jesus Christ.

At the time he was betrayed and entered willingly into his Passion, he took bread and, giving thanks, broke it, and gave it to his disciples, saying:

Take this, all of you, and eat of it,
for this is my Body
which will be given up for you.

In a similar way, when supper was ended, he took the chalice and, once more giving thanks, he gave it to his disciples, saying:

Take this, all of you, and drink from it,
for this is the chalice of my Blood,
the Blood of the new and eternal covenant,
which will be poured out for you and for many
for the forgiveness of sins.
Do this in memory of me.

The mystery of faith.

1 **We proclaim your Death, O Lord, and profess your Resurrection until you come again.**

2 **When we eat this Bread and drink this Cup, we proclaim your Death, O Lord, until you come again.**

3 **Save us, Saviour of the world, for by your Cross and Resurrection you have set us free.**

Therefore, as we celebrate the memorial of his Death and Resurrection, we offer you, Lord, the Bread of life and the Chalice of salvation, giving thanks that you have held us worthy to be in your presence and minister to you.

Humbly we pray that, partaking of the Body and Blood of Christ, we may be gathered into one by the Holy Spirit.

Remember, Lord, your Church, spread throughout the world, and bring her to the fullness of charity, together with N. our Pope and N. our Bishop and all the clergy.

Christian Initiation (Scrutinies):
Remember also, Lord, your servants who are to present these chosen ones at the font of rebirth.

Remember also our brothers and sisters who have fallen asleep in the hope of the resurrection, and all who have died in your mercy: welcome them into the light of your face. Have mercy on us all, we pray, that with the Blessed Virgin Mary, Mother of God, with blessed Joseph, her Spouse, with the blessed Apostles, and all the Saints who have pleased you throughout the ages, we may merit to be co-heirs to eternal life, and may praise and glorify you through your Son, Jesus Christ.

Through him, and with him, and in him, O God, almighty Father, in the unity of the Holy Spirit, all glory and honour is yours, for ever and ever. **Amen.**

(▶ *Communion Rite, p. 68*)

EUCHARISTIC PRAYER III

You are indeed Holy, O Lord, and all you have created rightly gives you praise, for through your Son our Lord Jesus Christ, by the power and working of the Holy Spirit, you give life to all things and make them holy, and you never cease to gather a people to yourself, so that from the rising of the sun to its setting a pure sacrifice may be offered to your name.

Therefore, O Lord, we humbly implore you: by the same Spirit graciously make holy these gifts we have brought to you for consecration, that they may become the Body and Blood of your Son our Lord Jesus Christ, at whose command we celebrate these mysteries.

For on the night he was betrayed he himself took bread, and, giving you thanks, he said the blessing, broke the bread and gave it to his disciples, saying:

> Take this, all of you, and eat of it,
> for this is my Body
> which will be given up for you.

In a similar way, when supper was ended, he took the chalice, and, giving you thanks, he said the blessing, and gave the chalice to his disciples, saying:

Take this, all of you, and drink from it,
for this is the chalice of my Blood,
the Blood of the new and eternal covenant,
which will be poured out for you and for many
for the forgiveness of sins.
Do this in memory of me.

The mystery of faith.

1 **We proclaim your Death, O Lord, and profess your Resurrection until you come again.**

2 **When we eat this Bread and drink this Cup, we proclaim your Death, O Lord, until you come again.**

3 **Save us, Saviour of the world, for by your Cross and Resurrection you have set us free.**

Therefore, O Lord, as we celebrate the memorial of the saving Passion of your Son, his wondrous Resurrection and Ascension into heaven, and as we look forward to his second coming, we offer you in thanksgiving this holy and living sacrifice.

Look, we pray, upon the oblation of your Church and, recognizing the sacrificial Victim by whose death you willed to reconcile us to yourself, grant that we, who are nourished by the Body and Blood of your Son and filled with his Holy Spirit, may become one body, one spirit in Christ.

May he make of us an eternal offering to you, so that we may obtain an inheritance with your elect, especially with the most Blessed Virgin Mary, Mother of God, with blessed Joseph, her

Spouse, with your blessed Apostles and glorious Martyrs, (with Saint N.) and with all the Saints, on whose constant intercession in your presence we rely for unfailing help.

May this Sacrifice of our reconciliation, we pray, O Lord, advance the peace and salvation of all the world. Be pleased to confirm in faith and charity your pilgrim Church on earth, with your servant N. our Pope and N. our Bishop, the Order of Bishops, all the clergy, and the entire people you have gained for your own.

Christian Initiation (Scrutinies):
Assist your servants with your grace, O Lord, we pray, that they may lead these chosen ones by word and example to new life in Christ, our Lord.

Listen graciously to the prayers of this family, whom you have summoned before you: in your compassion, O merciful Father, gather to yourself all your children scattered throughout the world. To our departed brothers and sisters and to all who were pleasing to you at their passing from this life, give kind admittance to your kingdom. There we hope to enjoy for ever the fullness of your glory through Christ our Lord, through whom you bestow on the world all that is good.

Through him, and with him, and in him, O God, almighty Father, in the unity of the Holy Spirit, all glory and honour is yours, for ever and ever. **Amen.**

(▶ *Communion Rite, p. 68)*

EUCHARISTIC PRAYER IV

We give you praise, Father most holy, for you are great and you have fashioned all your works in wisdom and in love. You formed man in your own image and entrusted the whole world to his care, so that in serving you alone, the Creator, he might have dominion over all creatures. And when through disobedience he had lost your friendship, you did not abandon him to the domain of death. For you came in mercy to the aid of all, so that those who seek might find you. Time and again you offered them covenants and through the prophets taught them to look forward to salvation.

And you so loved the world, Father most holy, that in the fullness of time you sent your Only Begotten Son to be our Saviour. Made incarnate by the Holy Spirit and born of the Virgin Mary, he shared our human nature in all things but sin. To the poor he proclaimed the good news of salvation, to prisoners, freedom, and to the sorrowful of heart, joy. To accomplish your plan, he gave himself up to death, and, rising from the dead, he destroyed death and restored life.

And that we might live no longer for ourselves but for him who died and rose again for us, he sent the Holy Spirit from you, Father, as the first fruits for those who believe, so that, bringing to perfection his work in the world, he might sanctify creation to the full.

Therefore, O Lord, we pray: may this same Holy Spirit graciously sanctify these offerings, that they may become the Body and Blood of our Lord Jesus

Christ for the celebration of this great mystery, which he himself left us as an eternal covenant.

For when the hour had come for him to be glorified by you, Father most holy, having loved his own who were in the world, he loved them to the end: and while they were at supper, he took bread, blessed and broke it, and gave it to his disciples, saying:

Take this, all of you, and eat of it,
for this is my Body
which will be given up for you.

In a similar way, taking the chalice filled with the fruit of the vine, he gave thanks, and gave the chalice to his disciples, saying:

Take this, all of you, and drink from it,
for this is the chalice of my Blood,
the Blood of the new and eternal covenant,
which will be poured out for you and for many
for the forgiveness of sins.
Do this in memory of me.

The mystery of faith.

1 **We proclaim your Death, O Lord, and profess your Resurrection until you come again.**

2 **When we eat this Bread and drink this Cup, we proclaim your Death, O Lord, until you come again.**

3 **Save us, Saviour of the world, for by your Cross and Resurrection you have set us free.**

Therefore, O Lord, as we now celebrate the memorial of our redemption, we remember Christ's Death and his descent to the realm of the dead, we proclaim his

Resurrection and his Ascension to your right hand, and, as we await his coming in glory, we offer you his Body and Blood, the sacrifice acceptable to you which brings salvation to the whole world.

Look, O Lord, upon the Sacrifice which you yourself have provided for your Church, and grant in your loving kindness to all who partake of this one Bread and one Chalice that, gathered into one body by the Holy Spirit, they may truly become a living sacrifice in Christ to the praise of your glory.

Therefore, Lord, remember now all for whom we offer this sacrifice: especially your servant N. our Pope, N. our Bishop, and the whole Order of Bishops, all the clergy, those who take part in this offering, those gathered here before you, your entire people, and all who seek you with a sincere heart.

Remember also those who have died in the peace of your Christ and all the dead, whose faith you alone have known.

To all of us, your children, grant, O merciful Father, that we may enter into a heavenly inheritance with the Blessed Virgin Mary, Mother of God, with blessed Joseph, her Spouse, and with your Apostles and Saints in your kingdom. There, with the whole of creation, freed from the corruption of sin and death, may we glorify you through Christ our Lord, through whom you bestow on the world all that is good.

Through him, and with him, and in him, O God, almighty Father, in the unity of the Holy Spirit, all glory and honour is yours, for ever and ever. **Amen.**

(▶ Communion Rite, p. 68)

EUCHARISTIC PRAYER FOR RECONCILIATION I

You are indeed Holy, O Lord, and from the world's beginning are ceaselessly at work, so that the human race may become holy, just as you yourself are holy.

Look, we pray, upon your people's offerings and pour out on them the power of your Spirit, that they may become the Body and Blood of your beloved Son, Jesus Christ, in whom we, too, are your sons and daughters. Indeed, though we once were lost and could not approach you, you loved us with the greatest love: for your Son, who alone is just, handed himself over to death, and did not disdain to be nailed for our sake to the wood of the Cross.

But before his arms were outstretched between heaven and earth, to become the lasting sign of your covenant, he desired to celebrate the Passover with his disciples.

As he ate with them, he took bread and, giving you thanks, he said the blessing, broke the bread and gave it to them, saying:

Take this, all of you, and eat of it,
for this is my Body
which will be given up for you.

In a similar way, when supper was ended, knowing that he was about to reconcile all things in himself through his Blood to be shed on the Cross, he took the chalice, filled with the fruit of the vine, and once more giving you thanks, handed the chalice to his disciples, saying:

Take this, all of you, and drink from it,
for this is the chalice of my Blood,
the Blood of the new and eternal covenant,
which will be poured out for you and for many
for the forgiveness of sins.
Do this in memory of me.

The mystery of faith.

1 **We proclaim your Death, O Lord, and profess your Resurrection until you come again.**

2 **When we eat this Bread and drink this Cup, we proclaim your Death, O Lord, until you come again.**

3 **Save us, Saviour of the world, for by your Cross and Resurrection you have set us free.**

Therefore, as we celebrate the memorial of your Son Jesus Christ, who is our Passover and our surest peace, we celebrate his Death and Resurrection from the dead, and looking forward to his blessed Coming, we offer you, who are our faithful and merciful God, this sacrificial Victim who reconciles to you the human race.

Look kindly, most compassionate Father, on those you unite to yourself by the Sacrifice of your Son, and grant that, by the power of the Holy Spirit, as they partake of this one Bread and one Chalice, they may be gathered into one Body in Christ, who heals every division.

Be pleased to keep us always in communion of mind and heart, together with N. our Pope and N. our Bishop. Help us to work together for the coming of your Kingdom, until the hour when we stand before you, Saints among the Saints in the halls of heaven, with the Blessed Virgin Mary, Mother of God, the blessed Apostles and all the Saints, and with our deceased brothers and sisters, whom we humbly commend to your mercy.

Then, freed at last from the wound of corruption and made fully into a new creation, we shall sing to you with gladness the thanksgiving of Christ, who lives for all eternity.

Through him, and with him, and in him, O God, almighty Father, in the unity of the Holy Spirit, all glory and honour is yours, for ever and ever. **Amen.**

(▶ Communion Rite, p. 68)

EUCHARISTIC PRAYER FOR RECONCILIATION II

You, therefore, almighty Father, we bless through Jesus Christ your Son, who comes in your name. He himself is the Word that brings salvation, the hand you extend to sinners, the way by which your peace is offered to us. When we ourselves had turned away from you on account of our sins, you brought us back to be reconciled, O Lord, so that, converted at last to you, we might love one another through your Son, whom for our sake you handed over to death.

And now, celebrating the reconciliation Christ has brought us, we entreat you: sanctify these gifts by the outpouring of your Spirit, that they may become the Body and Blood of your Son, whose command we fulfill when we celebrate these mysteries.

For when about to give his life to set us free, as he reclined at supper, he himself took bread into his hands, and, giving you thanks, he said the blessing, broke the bread and gave it to his disciples, saying:

Take this, all of you, and eat of it,
for this is my Body
which will be given up for you.

In a similar way, on that same evening, he took the chalice of blessing in his hands, confessing your mercy, and gave the chalice to his disciples, saying:

Take this, all of you, and drink from it,
for this is the chalice of my Blood,
the Blood of the new and eternal covenant,
which will be poured out for you and for many
for the forgiveness of sins.
Do this in memory of me.

The mystery of faith.

1 **We proclaim your Death, O Lord, and profess your Resurrection until you come again.**

2 **When we eat this Bread and drink this Cup, we proclaim your Death, O Lord, until you come again.**

3 **Save us, Saviour of the world, for by your Cross and Resurrection you have set us free.**

Celebrating, therefore, the memorial of the Death and Resurrection of your Son, who left us this pledge of his love, we offer you what you have bestowed on us, the Sacrifice of perfect reconciliation.

Holy Father, we humbly beseech you to accept us also, together with your Son, and in this saving banquet graciously to endow us with his very Spirit, who takes away everything that estranges us from one another.

May he make your Church a sign of unity and an instrument of your peace among all people and may he keep us in communion with N. our Pope and N. our Bishop and all the Bishops and your entire people.

Just as you have gathered us now at the table of your Son, so also bring us together, with the glorious Virgin Mary, Mother of God, with your blessed Apostles and all the Saints, with our brothers and sisters and those of every race and tongue who have died in your friendship. Bring us to share with them the unending banquet of unity in a new heaven and a new earth, where the fullness of your peace will shine forth in Christ Jesus our Lord.

Through him, and with him, and in him, O God, almighty Father, in the unity of the Holy Spirit, all glory and honour is yours, for ever and ever. **Amen.**

(▶ Communion Rite, p. 68)

EUCHARISTIC PRAYER FOR MASS FOR VARIOUS NEEDS I

The Church on the Path of Unity

You are indeed Holy and to be glorified, O God, who love the human race and who always walk with us on the journey of life. Blessed indeed is your Son, present in our midst when we are gathered by his love, and when, as once for the disciples, so now for us, he opens the Scriptures and breaks the bread.

Therefore, Father most merciful, we ask that you send forth your Holy Spirit to sanctify these gifts of bread and wine, that they may become for us the Body and Blood of our Lord Jesus Christ.

On the day before he was to suffer, on the night of the Last Supper, he took bread and said the blessing, broke the bread and gave it to his disciples, saying:

Take this, all of you, and eat of it,
for this is my Body
which will be given up for you.

In a similar way, when supper was ended, he took the chalice, gave you thanks and gave the chalice to his disciples, saying:

Take this, all of you, and drink from it,
for this is the chalice of my Blood,
the Blood of the new and eternal covenant,
which will be poured out for you and for many
for the forgiveness of sins.
Do this in memory of me.

The mystery of faith.

1 **We proclaim your Death, O Lord, and profess your Resurrection until you come again.**

2 **When we eat this Bread and drink this Cup, we proclaim your Death, O Lord, until you come again.**

3 **Save us, Saviour of the world, for by your Cross and Resurrection you have set us free.**

Therefore, holy Father, as we celebrate the memorial of Christ your Son, our Saviour, whom you led through his Passion and Death on the Cross to the glory of the Resurrection, and whom you have seated at your right hand, we proclaim the work of your love until he comes again and we offer you the Bread of life and the Chalice of blessing.

Look with favour on the oblation of your Church, in which we show forth the paschal Sacrifice of Christ that has been handed on to us, and grant that, by the power of the Spirit of your love, we may be counted now and until the day of eternity among the members of your Son, in whose Body and Blood we have communion.

Lord, renew your Church (which is in N.) by the light of the Gospel. Strengthen the bond of unity between the faithful and the pastors of your people, together with N. our Pope, N. our Bishop, and the whole Order of Bishops, that in a world torn by strife your people may shine forth as a prophetic sign of unity and concord.

Remember our brothers and sisters (N. and N.), who have fallen asleep in the peace of your Christ, and all the dead, whose faith you alone have known. Admit them to rejoice in the light of your face, and in the resurrection give them the fullness of life.

Grant also to us, when our earthly pilgrimage is done, that we may come to an eternal dwelling place and live with you for ever; there, in communion with the Blessed Virgin Mary, Mother of God, with the Apostles and Martyrs, (with Saint N.) and with all the Saints, we shall praise and exalt you through Jesus Christ, your Son.

Through him, and with him, and in him, O God, almighty Father, in the unity of the Holy Spirit, all glory and honour is yours, for ever and ever. **Amen.**

(▶ Communion Rite, p. 68)

EUCHARISTIC PRAYER FOR MASS FOR VARIOUS NEEDS II

God Guides His Church along the Way of Salvation

You are indeed Holy and to be glorified, O God, who love the human race and who always walk with us on the journey of life. Blessed indeed is your Son, present in our midst when we are gathered by his love and when, as once for the disciples, so now for us, he opens the Scriptures and breaks the bread.

Therefore, Father most merciful, we ask that you send forth your Holy Spirit to sanctify these gifts of bread and wine, that they may become for us the Body and Blood of our Lord Jesus Christ.

On the day before he was to suffer, on the night of the Last Supper, he took bread and said the blessing, broke the bread and gave it to his disciples, saying:

Take this, all of you, and eat of it,
for this is my Body
which will be given up for you.

In a similar way, when supper was ended, he took the chalice, gave you thanks and gave the chalice to his disciples, saying:

Take this, all of you, and drink from it,
for this is the chalice of my Blood,
the Blood of the new and eternal covenant,
which will be poured out for you and for many
for the forgiveness of sins.
Do this in memory of me.

The mystery of faith.

1 **We proclaim your Death, O Lord, and profess your Resurrection until you come again.**

2 **When we eat this Bread and drink this Cup, we proclaim your Death, O Lord, until you come again.**

3 **Save us, Saviour of the world, for by your Cross and Resurrection you have set us free.**

Therefore, holy Father, as we celebrate the memorial of Christ your Son, our Saviour, whom you led through his Passion and Death on the Cross to the glory of the Resurrection, and whom you have seated at your right hand, we proclaim the work of your love until he comes again and we offer you the Bread of life and the Chalice of blessing.

Look with favour on the oblation of your Church, in which we show forth the paschal Sacrifice of Christ that has been handed on to us, and grant that, by the power of the Spirit of your love, we may be counted now and until the day of eternity among the members of your Son, in whose Body and Blood we have communion.

And so, having called us to your table, Lord, confirm us in unity, so that, together with N. our Pope and N. our Bishop, with all Bishops, Priests and Deacons, and your entire people, as we walk your ways with faith and hope, we may strive to bring joy and trust into the world.

Remember our brothers and sisters (N. and N.), who have fallen asleep in the peace of your Christ, and all the dead, whose faith you alone have known. Admit them to rejoice in the light of your face, and in the resurrection give them the fullness of life.

Grant also to us, when our earthly pilgrimage is done, that we may come to an eternal dwelling place and live with you for ever; there, in communion with the Blessed Virgin Mary, Mother of God, with the Apostles and Martyrs, (with Saint N.) and with all the Saints, we shall praise and exalt you through Jesus Christ, your Son.

Through him, and with him, and in him, O God, almighty Father, in the unity of the Holy Spirit, all glory and honour is yours, for ever and ever. **Amen.**

(▶ Communion Rite, p. 68)

EUCHARISTIC PRAYER FOR MASS FOR VARIOUS NEEDS III

Jesus, the Way to the Father

You are indeed Holy and to be glorified, O God, who love the human race and who always walk with us on the journey of life. Blessed indeed is your Son, present in our midst when we are gathered by his love and when, as once for the disciples, so now for us, he opens the Scriptures and breaks the bread.

Therefore, Father most merciful, we ask that you send forth your Holy Spirit to sanctify these gifts of bread and wine, that they may become for us the Body and Blood of our Lord Jesus Christ.

On the day before he was to suffer, on the night of the Last Supper, he took bread and said the blessing, broke the bread and gave it to his disciples, saying:

Take this, all of you, and eat of it,
for this is my Body
which will be given up for you.

In a similar way, when supper was ended, he took the chalice, gave you thanks and gave the chalice to his disciples, saying:

Take this, all of you, and drink from it,
for this is the chalice of my Blood,
the Blood of the new and eternal covenant,
which will be poured out for you and for many
for the forgiveness of sins.
Do this in memory of me.

The mystery of faith.

1 We proclaim your Death, O Lord, and profess your Resurrection until you come again.

2 When we eat this Bread and drink this Cup, we proclaim your Death, O Lord, until you come again.

3 Save us, Saviour of the world, for by your Cross and Resurrection you have set us free.

Therefore, holy Father, as we celebrate the memorial of Christ your Son, our Saviour, whom you led through his Passion and Death on the Cross to the glory of the Resurrection, and whom you have seated at your right hand, we proclaim the work of your love until he comes again and we offer you the Bread of life and the Chalice of blessing.

Look with favour on the oblation of your Church, in which we show forth the paschal Sacrifice of Christ that has been handed on to us, and grant that, by the power of the Spirit of your love, we may be counted now and until the day of eternity among the members of your Son, in whose Body and Blood we have communion.

By our partaking of this mystery, almighty Father, give us life through your Spirit, grant that we may be conformed to the image of your Son, and confirm us in the bond of communion, together with N. our Pope and N. our Bishop, with all other Bishops, with Priests and Deacons, and with your entire people.

Grant that all the faithful of the Church, looking into the signs of the times by the light of faith, may constantly devote themselves to the service of the Gospel.

Keep us attentive to the needs of all that, sharing their grief and pain, their joy and hope, we may faithfully bring them the good news of salvation and go forward with them along the way of your Kingdom.

Remember our brothers and sisters (N. and N.), who have fallen asleep in the peace of your Christ, and all the dead, whose faith you alone have known. Admit them to rejoice in the light of your face, and in the resurrection give them the fullness of life.

Grant also to us, when our earthly pilgrimage is done, that we may come to an eternal dwelling place and live with you for ever; there, in communion with the Blessed Virgin Mary, Mother of God, with the Apostles and Martyrs, (with Saint N.) and with all the Saints, we shall praise and exalt you through Jesus Christ, your Son.

Through him, and with him, and in him, O God, almighty Father, in the unity of the Holy Spirit, all glory and honour is yours, for ever and ever. **Amen.**

(▶ Communion Rite, p. 68)

EUCHARISTIC PRAYER FOR MASS FOR VARIOUS NEEDS IV

Jesus, Who Went About Doing Good

You are indeed Holy and to be glorified, O God, who love the human race and who always walk with us on the journey of life. Blessed indeed is your Son, present in our midst when we are gathered by his love and when, as once for the disciples, so now for us, he opens the Scriptures and breaks the bread.

Therefore, Father most merciful, we ask that you send forth your Holy Spirit to sanctify these gifts of bread and wine, that they may become for us the Body and Blood of our Lord Jesus Christ.

On the day before he was to suffer, on the night of the Last Supper, he took bread and said the blessing, broke the bread and gave it to his disciples, saying:

Take this, all of you, and eat of it,
for this is my Body
which will be given up for you.

In a similar way, when supper was ended, he took the chalice, gave you thanks and gave the chalice to his disciples, saying:

Take this, all of you, and drink from it,
for this is the chalice of my Blood,
the Blood of the new and eternal covenant,
which will be poured out for you and for many
for the forgiveness of sins.
Do this in memory of me.

The mystery of faith.

1 **We proclaim your Death, O Lord, and profess your Resurrection until you come again.**

2 **When we eat this Bread and drink this Cup, we proclaim your Death, O Lord, until you come again.**

3 **Save us, Saviour of the world, for by your Cross and Resurrection you have set us free.**

Therefore, holy Father, as we celebrate the memorial of Christ your Son, our Saviour, whom you led through his Passion and Death on the Cross to the glory of the Resurrection, and whom you have seated at your right hand, we proclaim the work of your love until he comes again and we offer you the Bread of life and the Chalice of blessing.

Look with favour on the oblation of your Church, in which we show forth the paschal Sacrifice of Christ that has been handed on to us, and grant that, by the power of the Spirit of your love, we may be counted now and until the day of eternity among the members of your Son, in whose Body and Blood we have communion.

Bring your Church, O Lord, to perfect faith and charity, together with N. our Pope and N. our Bishop, with all Bishops, Priests and Deacons, and the entire people you have made your own.

Open our eyes to the needs of our brothers and sisters; inspire in us words and actions to comfort those who labour and are burdened. Make us serve them truly, after the example of Christ and at his command. And may your Church stand as a living witness to truth and freedom, to peace and justice, that all people may be raised up to a new hope.

Remember our brothers and sisters (N. and N.), who have fallen asleep in the peace of your Christ, and all the dead, whose faith you alone have known. Admit them to rejoice in the light of your face, and in the resurrection give them the fullness of life.

Grant also to us, when our earthly pilgrimage is done, that we may come to an eternal dwelling place and live with you for ever; there, in communion with the Blessed Virgin Mary, Mother of God, with the Apostles and Martyrs, (with Saint N.) and with all the Saints, we shall praise and exalt you through Jesus Christ, your Son.

Through him, and with him, and in him, O God, almighty Father, in the unity of the Holy Spirit, all glory and honour is yours, for ever and ever. **Amen.**

The Communion Rite

At the Saviour's command and formed by divine teaching, we dare to say:

**Our Father, who art in heaven,
hallowed be thy name;
thy kingdom come,
thy will be done
on earth as it is in heaven.
Give us this day our daily bread,
and forgive us our trespasses,
as we forgive those who trespass against us;
and lead us not into temptation,
but deliver us from evil.**

Deliver us, Lord, we pray, from every evil, graciously grant peace in our days, that, by the help of your mercy, we may be always free from sin and safe from all distress, as we await the blessed hope and the coming of our Saviour, Jesus Christ.

**For the kingdom,
the power and the glory are yours
now and for ever.**

Lord Jesus Christ, who said to your Apostles: Peace I leave you, my peace I give you, look not on our sins, but on the faith of your Church, and graciously grant her peace and unity in accordance with your will. Who live and reign for ever and ever. **Amen.**

The peace of the Lord be with you always. **And with your spirit.**

Let us offer each other the sign of peace.

May this mingling of the Body and Blood of our Lord Jesus Christ bring eternal life to us who receive it.

Lamb of God, you take away the sins of the world, have mercy on us.

Lamb of God, you take away the sins of the world, have mercy on us.

Lamb of God, you take away the sins of the world, grant us peace.

1 Lord Jesus Christ, Son of the living God, who, by the will of the Father and the work of the Holy Spirit, through your Death gave life to the world, free me by this, your most holy Body and Blood, from all my sins and from every evil; keep me always faithful to your commandments, and never let me be parted from you.

2 May the receiving of your Body and Blood, Lord Jesus Christ, not bring me to judgment and condemnation, but through your loving mercy be for me protection in mind and body and a healing remedy.

Behold the Lamb of God, behold him who takes away the sins of the world. Blessed are those called to the supper of the Lamb.

Lord, I am not worthy that you should enter under my roof, but only say the word and my soul shall be healed.

May the Body (Blood) of Christ keep me safe for eternal life.

COMMUNION CHANT

(or Communion Antiphon — ▶ The appropriate day)

PRAYER AFTER COMMUNION

(▶ The appropriate day)

Concluding Rites

ANNOUNCEMENTS *(Optional)*

BLESSING *(or Solemn Blessing – Optional)*

The Lord be with you. **And with your spirit.**
May almighty God bless you, the Father, and the Son, and the Holy Spirit. **Amen.**

DISMISSAL
During Easter Octave, add the double alleluia.

1 Go forth, the Mass is ended.

2 Go and announce the Gospel of the Lord.

3 Go in peace, glorifying the Lord by your life.

4 Go in peace.

Thanks be to God.

December Saints' Days

The following saints are traditionally remembered in December in Canada.

3 Saint Francis Xavier
4 Saint John Damascene
6 Saint Nicholas
7 Saint Ambrose
9 Saint Juan Diego Cuauhtlatoatzin
11 Saint Damasus I
12 Our Lady of Guadalupe, Patroness of the Americas
13 Saint Lucy
14 Saint John of the Cross
21 Saint Peter Canisius
23 Saint John of Kanty
26 Saint Stephen
27 Saint John
28 The Holy Innocents
29 Saint Thomas Becket
31 Saint Sylvester I

November 29

Advent calls us to prepare for the two comings of Christ: at the Incarnation and at the end of time. The gospel on the first Sunday of the new liturgical year urges us to be ready to greet the Son of Man. We are to be awake and aware of our surroundings and concerns.

A quick reading of this gospel may lead us to long for a gentler time. The images of roaring seas and waves can cause turmoil, fear or unease. This time of year can be busy with demands on our energy, time and resources, demands that may trap and weigh us down. We wonder how we can be ready to greet Christ at the end of time when our hearts and minds are trapped in the demands of today. But as we learn to recognize Christ in the present, we will be ready to stand before the Son of Man.

Jesus calls us to be alert and raise our heads, recognizing salvation is near. Advent is a time to refocus and put worry away, for our God has come to us. Today as we celebrate Eucharist, may we come with hearts ready to encounter Christ in the Word, in the people among us and in the breaking of the bread so that, nourished, we may be sent, ready to greet Christ in our midst.

Catherine Ecker, Barrie, ON

ENTRANCE ANTIPHON *(Cf. Psalm 24.1-3)*
To you, I lift up my soul, O my God. In you, I have trusted; let me not be put to shame. Nor let my enemies exult over me; and let none who hope in you be put to shame.

INTRODUCTORY RITES *(p. 5)*

COLLECT
Grant your faithful, we pray, almighty God, the resolve to run forth to meet your Christ with righteous deeds at his coming, so that, gathered at his right hand, they may be worthy to possess the heavenly Kingdom. Through our Lord Jesus Christ, your Son, who lives and reigns with you in the unity of the Holy Spirit, one God, for ever and ever. **Amen.**

FIRST READING *(Jeremiah 33.14-16)*
The days are surely coming, says the Lord, when I will fulfill the promise I made to the house of Israel and the house of Judah.

In those days and at that time I will cause a righteous Branch to spring up for David; and he shall execute justice and righteousness in the land.

In those days Judah will be saved and Jerusalem will live in safety. And this is the name by which it will be called: "The Lord is our righteousness."

The word of the Lord. **Thanks be to God.**

RESPONSORIAL PSALM *(Psalm 25)*

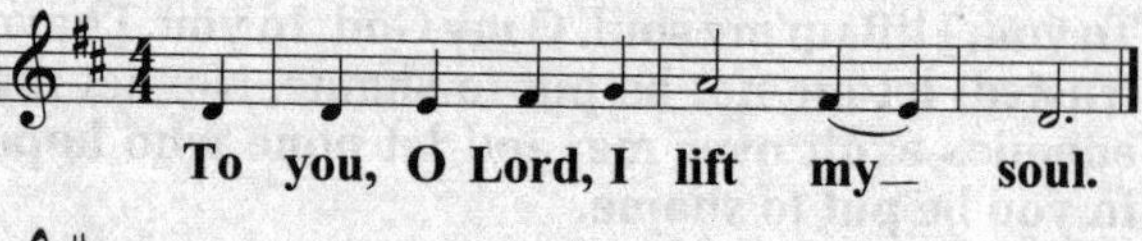

℟. **To you, O Lord, I lift my soul.**

Make me to know your ways, O · **Lord**,
teach me your · **paths.**
Lead me in your truth and · **teach_me**,
for you are the God of my · **sal**-vation. ℟.

Good and upright is the · **Lord**,
therefore he instructs sinners in the · **way.**
He leads the humble in what is · **right**,
and teaches the humble · **his** way. ℟.

All the paths of the Lord are steadfast love
  and · **faithfulness**,
for those who keep his covenant
  and his de·-**crees.**
The friendship of the Lord is for those
  who · **fear_him**,
and he makes his covenant known · **to** them. ℟.

To hear the Sunday Psalms, go to www.livingwithchrist.ca and select the psalm button at the bottom of the home page.

SECOND READING *(1 Thessalonians 3.12 – 4.2)*

Brothers and sisters: May the Lord make you increase and abound in love for one another and for all, just as we abound in love for you. And may he so strengthen your hearts in holiness that you may be blameless before our God and Father at the coming of our Lord Jesus with all his saints.

Finally, brothers and sisters, we ask and urge you in the Lord Jesus that, as you learned from us how you ought to live and to please God, as, in fact, you are doing, you should do so more and more. For you know what instructions we gave you through the Lord Jesus.

The word of the Lord. **Thanks be to God.**

GOSPEL ACCLAMATION *(Psalm 85.7)*

Alleluia. Alleluia. Show us your steadfast love, O Lord, and grant us your salvation. **Alleluia.**

GOSPEL *(Luke 21.25-28, 34-36)*

The Lord be with you. **And with your spirit.** A reading from the holy Gospel according to Luke. **Glory to you, O Lord.**

Jesus spoke to his disciples: "There will be signs in the sun, the moon, and the stars and on the earth distress among nations confused by the roaring of the sea and the waves. People will faint from fear and foreboding of what is coming upon the world, for the powers of the heavens will be shaken.

"Then they will see 'the Son of Man coming in a cloud' with power and great glory. Now when these things begin to take place, stand up and raise your heads, because your redemption is drawing near.

"Be on guard so that your hearts are not weighed down with dissipation and drunkenness and the worries of this life, and that day catch you unexpectedly, like a trap. For it will come upon all who live on the face of the whole earth. Be alert at all times, praying that you may have the strength to escape all these things that will take place, and to stand before the Son of Man."

The Gospel of the Lord. **Praise to you, Lord Jesus Christ.**

PROFESSION OF FAITH *(p. 11)*

PRAYER OF THE FAITHFUL

The following intentions are suggestions only. There are more suggestions at www.livingwithchrist.ca

℟. **Lord, hear our prayer.**

For the Church, called to see with the eyes of faith God's living presence in our midst, we pray to the Lord: ℟.

For leaders who seek to build a world of justice for all people, we pray to the Lord: ℟.

For people who walk in darkness, loneliness and despair in this season of joyful light, we pray to the Lord: ℟.

For renewed strength and commitment to Christ in our parish families as we begin this Advent, we pray to the Lord: ℟.

PREPARATION OF THE GIFTS *(p. 14)*

PRAYER OVER THE OFFERINGS

Accept, we pray, O Lord, these offerings we make, gathered from among your gifts to us, and may what you grant us to celebrate devoutly here below gain for us the prize of eternal redemption. Through Christ our Lord. **Amen.**

PREFACE *(Advent I, p. 15)*

COMMUNION ANTIPHON *(Psalm 84.13)*
The Lord will bestow his bounty, and our earth shall yield its increase.

PRAYER AFTER COMMUNION
May these mysteries, O Lord, in which we have participated, profit us, we pray, for even now, as we walk amid passing things, you teach us by them to love the things of heaven and hold fast to what endures. Through Christ our Lord. **Amen.**

SOLEMN BLESSING – ADVENT *(Optional)*
Bow down for the blessing.

May the almighty and merciful God, by whose grace you have placed your faith in the First Coming of his Only Begotten Son and yearn for his coming again, sanctify you by the radiance of Christ's Advent and enrich you with his blessing. **Amen.**

As you run the race of this present life, may he make you firm in faith, joyful in hope and active in charity. **Amen.**

So that, rejoicing now with devotion at the Redeemer's coming in the flesh, you may be endowed with the rich reward of eternal life when he comes again in majesty. **Amen.**

And may the blessing of almighty God, the Father, and the Son, and the Holy Spirit, come down on you and remain with you for ever. **Amen.**

DISMISSAL *(p. 70)*

December 6

Prophets of old like Isaiah and John the Baptist remain meaningful and powerful voices for our time. Together with Jesus, they stood up and cried out in all possible ways to challenge any type of oppression or injustice as well as the unfaithfulness of their people. Yet they were also exceptional agents of change, tireless preachers of conversion and bearers of good news.

Who would deny that there are paths that need to be made straight and ways to be made smooth everywhere in today's world? Humankind is dying for hope and reconciliation, which seem so elusive, while political powers and leaders fall short of solutions to straighten what goes wrong on this planet and between nations.

We badly need the courage, hope and sense of justice displayed by the prophets. They keep telling us about the ways of the Lord, ways that lead humankind towards peace and lasting joy. May we all open up our hearts to the voices of these prophets, so that we straighten our own ways and become true agents of change in the world. May we too become genuine voices evermore dedicated to the good news brought about by Jesus, voices grounded in love, compassion, justice and joy.

Jean-Pierre Prévost, Chénéville, QC

ENTRANCE ANTIPHON *(Cf. Isaiah 30.19, 30)*
O people of Sion, behold, the Lord will come to save the nations, and the Lord will make the glory of his voice heard in the joy of your heart.

INTRODUCTORY RITES *(p. 5)*

COLLECT
Almighty and merciful God, may no earthly undertaking hinder those who set out in haste to meet your Son, but may our learning of heavenly wisdom gain us admittance to his company. Who lives and reigns with you in the unity of the Holy Spirit, one God, for ever and ever. **Amen.**

FIRST READING *(Baruch 5.1-9)*
Take off the garment of your sorrow
  and affliction, O Jerusalem,
and put on forever the beauty of the glory
  from God.
Put on the robe of the righteousness that comes
  from God;
put on your head the diadem of the glory
  of the Everlasting;
for God will show your splendour everywhere
  under heaven.
For God will give you evermore the name,
"Righteous Peace, Godly Glory."

Arise, O Jerusalem, stand upon the height;
look toward the east,
and see your children gathered
  from west and east
at the word of the Holy One,

rejoicing that God has remembered them.
For they went out from you on foot,
led away by their enemies;
but God will bring them back to you,
carried in glory, as on a royal throne.

For God has ordered that every high mountain
and the everlasting hills be made low
and the valleys filled up, to make level ground,
so that Israel may walk safely in the glory of God.
The woods and every fragrant tree
have shaded Israel at God's command.
For God will lead Israel with joy,
in the light of his glory,
with the mercy and righteousness that
come from him.

The word of the Lord. **Thanks be to God.**

RESPONSORIAL PSALM *(Psalm 126)*

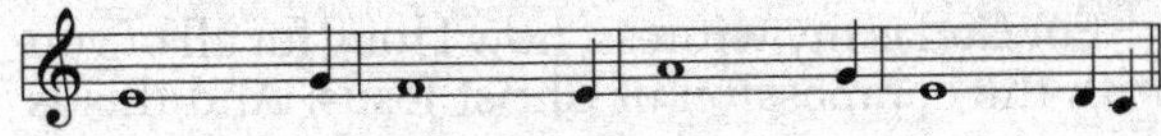

℟. **The Lord has done great things for us;**
we are filled with joy.

When the Lord restored the fortunes of · **Zion,**
we were like those who · **dream.**
Then our mouth was filled with · **laughter,**
and our tongue with shouts · **of** joy. ℟.

Then it was said among the · **nations,**
"The Lord has done great things for · **them.**"
The Lord has done great things for · **us,**
and we · **re**-joiced. ℟.

Restore our fortunes, O · **Lord,**
like the watercourses in the desert
of the · **Negev.**
May those who sow in · **tears**
reap with shouts · **of** joy. ℟.

Those who go out · **weeping,**
bearing the seed for · **sowing,**
shall come home with shouts of · **joy,**
carrying · **their** sheaves. ℟.

SECOND READING *(Philippians 1.3-6, 8-11)*
Brothers and sisters, I thank my God every time I remember you, constantly praying with joy in every one of my prayers for all of you, because of your sharing in the Gospel from the first day until now.

I am confident of this, that the one who began a good work among you will bring it to completion by the day of Jesus Christ.

For God is my witness, how I long for all of you with the compassion of Christ Jesus. And this is my prayer, that your love may overflow more and more with knowledge and full insight to help you determine what is best, so that in the day of Christ you may be pure and blameless, having produced the harvest of righteousness that comes through Jesus Christ for the glory and praise of God.

The word of the Lord. **Thanks be to God.**

GOSPEL ACCLAMATION *(Luke 3.4, 6)*
Alleluia. Alleluia. Prepare the way of the Lord, make straight his paths: all flesh shall see the salvation of God. **Alleluia.**

GOSPEL *(Luke 3.1-6)*
The Lord be with you. **And with your spirit.** A reading from the holy Gospel according to Luke. **Glory to you, O Lord.**

In the fifteenth year of the reign of Emperor Tiberius, when Pontius Pilate was governor of Judea, and Herod was ruler of Galilee, and his brother Philip ruler of the region of Ituraea and Trachonitis, and Lysanias ruler of Abilene, during the high priesthood of Annas and Caiaphas, the word of God came to John son of Zechariah in the wilderness.

He went into all the region around the Jordan, proclaiming a baptism of repentance for the forgiveness of sins, as it is written in the book of the words of the Prophet Isaiah, "The voice of one crying out in the wilderness: 'Prepare the way of the Lord, make his paths straight. Every valley shall be filled, and every mountain and hill shall be made low, and the crooked shall be made straight, and the rough ways made smooth; and all flesh shall see the salvation of God.'"

The Gospel of the Lord. **Praise to you, Lord Jesus Christ.**

PROFESSION OF FAITH *(p. 11)*

PRAYER OF THE FAITHFUL

The following intentions are suggestions only. There are more suggestions at www.livingwithchrist.ca

℟. **Lord, hear our prayer.**

For the Church, called to prepare the way for God's coming among us, we pray to the Lord: ℟.

For trustworthy leaders whose lives are rooted in integrity and justice, we pray to the Lord: ℟.

For the hungry, the homeless and the rejected, we pray to the Lord: ℟.

For hearts that are quiet enough, still enough and humble enough to hear God's Word to us this Advent, we pray to the Lord: ℟.

PREPARATION OF THE GIFTS *(p. 14)*

PRAYER OVER THE OFFERINGS

Be pleased, O Lord, with our humble prayers and offerings, and, since we have no merits to plead our cause, come, we pray, to our rescue with the protection of your mercy. Through Christ our Lord. **Amen.**

PREFACE *(Advent I, p. 15)*

COMMUNION ANTIPHON *(Baruch 5.5; 4.36)*

Jerusalem, arise and stand upon the heights, and behold the joy which comes to you from God.

PRAYER AFTER COMMUNION

Replenished by the food of spiritual nourishment, we humbly beseech you, O Lord, that, through our partaking in this mystery, you may teach us to judge wisely the things of earth and hold firm to the things of heaven. Through Christ our Lord. **Amen.**

SOLEMN BLESSING AND DISMISSAL *(p. 77)*

December 13

How amazing it is to think that in today's second reading, Paul was actually writing from prison. While we may not know his exact circumstances, we can imagine that imprisonment in the first century undoubtedly meant horrible living conditions, likely in darkness, with very little to eat. In spite of this, however, Paul exudes a profound sense of joy and peace and gratitude in his Letter to the Philippians. How is that even possible?

It is possible because Paul knew to the very core of his being that God was with him, as real as the chains that bound him. Knowing that God was present sustained Paul and filled him with joy, even in the very midst of suffering.

God is just as real and as present in our world today as he was for Paul. In today's gospel, however, John the Baptist challenges us to make that presence known and felt in very concrete ways. Share everything you have, he tells us. Be fair and honest in everything you do. Be satisfied with what you have, not always grasping for more.

In less than two weeks, we celebrate the coming of Emmanuel. In a world much in need of joy and peace, our lives must be the witness that God is with us, here and now. Rejoice in the Lord always; again I say, rejoice!

Teresa Whalen Lux, Regina, SK

ENTRANCE ANTIPHON *(Philippians 4.4-5)*
Rejoice in the Lord always; again I say, rejoice. Indeed, the Lord is near.

INTRODUCTORY RITES *(p. 5)*

COLLECT
O God, who see how your people faithfully await the feast of the Lord's Nativity, enable us, we pray, to attain the joys of so great a salvation and to celebrate them always with solemn worship and glad rejoicing. Through our Lord Jesus Christ, your Son, who lives and reigns with you in the unity of the Holy Spirit, one God, for ever and ever. **Amen.**

FIRST READING *(Zephaniah 3.14-18a)*
Sing aloud, O daughter Zion; shout, O Israel!
Rejoice and exult with all your heart,
O daughter of Jerusalem!
The Lord has taken away the judgments against you,
he has turned away your enemies.
The king of Israel, the Lord, is in your midst;
you shall fear disaster no more.
On that day it shall be said to Jerusalem:
Do not fear, O Zion;
do not let your hands grow weak.
The Lord, your God, is in your midst,
a warrior who gives victory;
he will rejoice over you with gladness,
he will renew you in his love.
The Lord, your God, will exult over you
with loud singing
as on a day of festival.

The word of the Lord. **Thanks be to God.**

RESPONSORIAL PSALM *(Isaiah 12)*

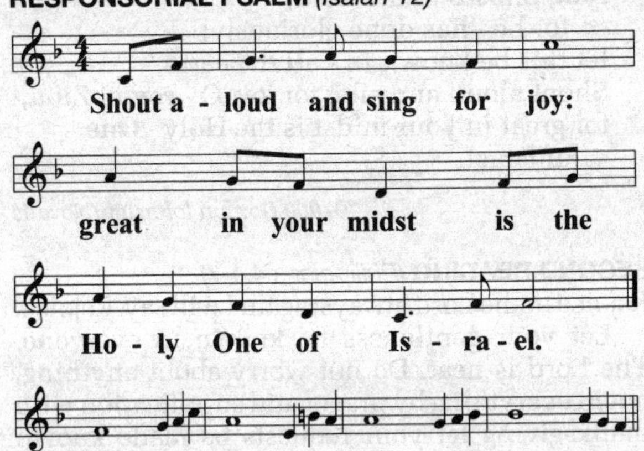

℟. **Shout aloud and sing for joy:**
great in your midst is the Holy One of Israel.

Surely God is my salvation; I will trust,
and will not · **be** a-fraid,
for the Lord God is my strength and my might;
he has be-·**come_my** sal-vation.
With joy · **you_will** draw water
from the wells · **of** sal-vation. ℟.

Give thanks · **to** the Lord,
call · **on** his name;
make known his deeds a-·**mong** the nations;
proclaim that his · **name_is** ex-alted. ℟.

Sing praises to the Lord,
for he · **has** done gloriously;
let this be known in · **all** the earth.
Shout aloud and sing for joy, O · **roy**-al Zion,
for great in your midst is the Holy · **One**
of Israel. R.

SECOND READING *(Philippians 4.4-7)*
Rejoice in the Lord always; again I will say, Rejoice.
Let your gentleness be known to everyone. The Lord is near. Do not worry about anything, but in everything by prayer and supplication with thanksgiving let your requests be made known to God.

And the peace of God, which surpasses all understanding, will guard your hearts and your minds in Christ Jesus.

The word of the Lord. **Thanks be to God.**

GOSPEL ACCLAMATION *(Luke 4.18 [Isaiah 61.1])*
Alleluia. Alleluia. The Spirit of the Lord is upon me; he has sent me to bring good news to the poor. **Alleluia.**

GOSPEL *(Luke 3.10-18)*
The Lord be with you. **And with your spirit.** A reading from the holy Gospel according to Luke. **Glory to you, O Lord.**

The crowds, who were gathering to be baptized by John, asked him, "What should we do?" In reply John said to them, "Whoever has two coats must share with anyone who has none; and whoever has food must do likewise."

Even tax collectors came to be baptized, and they asked him, "Teacher, what should we do?" He said to them, "Collect no more than the amount prescribed for you." Soldiers also asked him, "And we, what should we do?" He said to them, "Do not extort money from anyone by threats or false accusation, and be satisfied with your wages."

As the people were filled with expectation, and all were questioning in their hearts concerning John, whether he might be the Messiah, John answered all of them by saying, "I baptize you with water; but one who is more powerful than I is coming; I am not worthy to untie the thong of his sandals. He will baptize you with the Holy Spirit and fire. His winnowing fork is in his hand, to clear his threshing floor and to gather the wheat into his granary; but the chaff he will burn with unquenchable fire."

So, with many other exhortations, John proclaimed the good news to the people.

The Gospel of the Lord. **Praise to you, Lord Jesus Christ.**

PROFESSION OF FAITH *(p. 11)*

PRAYER OF THE FAITHFUL

The following intentions are suggestions only. There are more suggestions at www.livingwithchrist.ca

℟. **Lord, hear our prayer.**

For religious leaders called to teach and guide in the practice of the faith, we pray to the Lord: ℟.

For deepening respect among people of all races, cultures and religions, we pray to the Lord: ℟.

For those whose hearts are filled with fear and anxiety, we pray to the Lord: ℟.

For the special needs of the community gathered here today, we pray to the Lord: ℟.

PREPARATION OF THE GIFTS *(p. 14)*

PRAYER OVER THE OFFERINGS
May the sacrifice of our worship, Lord, we pray, be offered to you unceasingly, to complete what was begun in sacred mystery and powerfully accomplish for us your saving work. Through Christ our Lord. **Amen.**

PREFACE *(Advent I, p. 15)*

COMMUNION ANTIPHON *(Cf. Isaiah 35.4)*
Say to the faint of heart: Be strong and do not fear. Behold, our God will come, and he will save us.

PRAYER AFTER COMMUNION
We implore your mercy, Lord, that this divine sustenance may cleanse us of our faults and prepare us for the coming feasts. Through Christ our Lord. **Amen.**

SOLEMN BLESSING AND DISMISSAL *(p. 77)*

December 20

Sometimes I feel I have so much to be thankful for, while at other times — less so. Life is filled with ups and downs: what I need to remember is that God is here with me through good times and bad.

I remember times when I felt like I'd hit bottom, and I imagine similar times are ahead. At the moment, I feel as though I am on top. God was there with me when I felt down and low, and I turned to him. Now, feeling up and on top, I turn to him less. Clearly this is not what he or I want.

In the first reading today, Micah reminds us of how tough times will come to pass, and how God will be there to provide a sense of peace. Then, in the Letter to the Hebrews, the author writes about sacrifice. Ours no longer being sufficient, Christ makes the ultimate sacrifice for all of us. In the gospel, Luke's portrait of Elizabeth reflects her mindfulness of the highs and lows of life: we learn she has patiently waited for a child and now, being with child, she does not lose sight of God. Instead she gives him praise and glory, just as we should remember to do, in both good times and bad.

Dana Kenny, Charlottetown, PE

ENTRANCE ANTIPHON *(Cf. Isaiah 45.8)*
Drop down dew from above, you heavens, and let the clouds rain down the Just One; let the earth be opened and bring forth a Saviour.

INTRODUCTORY RITES *(p. 5)*

COLLECT
Pour forth, we beseech you, O Lord, your grace into our hearts, that we, to whom the Incarnation of Christ your Son was made known by the message of an Angel, may by his Passion and Cross be brought to the glory of his Resurrection. Who lives and reigns with you in the unity of the Holy Spirit, one God, for ever and ever. **Amen.**

FIRST READING *(Micah 5.2-5a)*
The Lord says to his people:
"You, O Bethlehem of Ephrathah,
who are one of the little clans of Judea,
from you shall come forth for me
one who is to rule in Israel,
whose origin is from of old, from ancient days."
Therefore he shall give them up until the time
when she who is in labour has brought forth;
then the rest of his kindred
shall return to the children of Israel.
And he shall stand and feed his flock
in the strength of the Lord,
in the majesty of the name of the Lord his God.
And they shall live secure,
for now he shall be great to the ends of the earth;
and he shall be peace.

The word of the Lord. **Thanks be to God.**

RESPONSORIAL PSALM *(Psalm 80)*

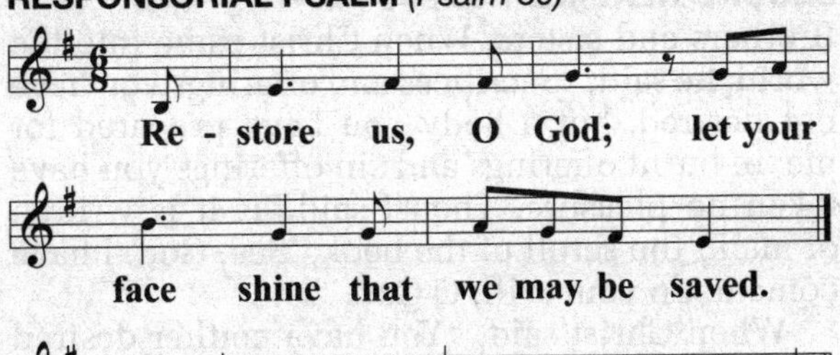

℟. **Restore us, O God;**
let your face shine, that we may be saved.

Give ear, O Shepherd · **of** Israel,
you who are enthroned upon the cherubim,
shine · **forth.**
Stir up your · **might,**
and come to · **save_us.** ℟.

Turn again, O God · **of** hosts;
look down from heaven, and · **see;**
have regard for this · **vine,**
the stock that your right hand has · **planted.** ℟.

But let your hand be upon the man
at · **your** right,
the son of man you have made strong
for your · **-self.**
Then we will never turn · **back_from_you;**
give us life, and we will call
on your · **name.** ℟.

SECOND READING *(Hebrews 10.5-10)*
Brothers and sisters: When Christ came into the world, he said, "Sacrifices and offerings you have not desired, but a body you have prepared for me; in burnt offerings and sin offerings you have taken no pleasure. Then I said, as it is written of me in the scroll of the book, 'See, God, I have come to do your will, O God.'"

When Christ said, "You have neither desired nor taken pleasure in sacrifices and offerings and burnt offerings and sin offerings" (these are offered according to the Law), then he added, "See, I have come to do your will." He abolishes the first in order to establish the second.

And it is by God's will that we have been sanctified through the offering of the body of Jesus Christ once for all.

The word of the Lord. **Thanks be to God.**

GOSPEL ACCLAMATION *(Luke 1.38)*
Alleluia. Alleluia. Here am I, the servant of the Lord: let it be done to me according to your word. **Alleluia.**

GOSPEL *(Luke 1.39-45)*
The Lord be with you. **And with your spirit.** A reading from the holy Gospel according to Luke. **Glory to you, O Lord.**

Mary set out and went with haste to a Judean town in the hill country, where she entered the house of Zechariah and greeted Elizabeth.

When Elizabeth heard Mary's greeting, the child leaped in her womb. And Elizabeth was filled with the Holy Spirit and exclaimed with a loud cry, "Blessed are you among women, and blessed is the fruit of your womb. And why has this happened to me, that the mother of my Lord comes to me? For as soon as I heard the sound of your greeting, the child in my womb leaped for joy. And blessed is she who believed that there would be a fulfillment of what was spoken to her by the Lord."

The Gospel of the Lord. **Praise to you, Lord Jesus Christ.**

PROFESSION OF FAITH *(p. 11)*

PRAYER OF THE FAITHFUL

The following intentions are suggestions only. There are more suggestions at www.livingwithchrist.ca

℟. **Lord, hear our prayer.**

For the Church, a sign of openness to the Holy Spirit, we pray to the Lord: ℟.

For discerning hearts in our world leaders, we pray to the Lord: ℟.

For all whose joy this season is diminished by suffering in mind or body, we pray to the Lord: ℟.

For our faith community, called to wait in joyful hope for the coming of our Saviour, we pray to the Lord: ℟.

PREPARATION OF THE GIFTS *(p. 14)*

PRAYER OVER THE OFFERINGS

May the Holy Spirit, O Lord, sanctify these gifts laid upon your altar, just as he filled with his power the womb of the Blessed Virgin Mary. Through Christ our Lord. **Amen.**

PREFACE *(Advent II, p. 15)*

COMMUNION ANTIPHON *(Isaiah 7.14)*

Behold, a Virgin shall conceive and bear a son; and his name will be called Emmanuel.

PRAYER AFTER COMMUNION

Having received this pledge of eternal redemption, we pray, almighty God, that, as the feast day of our salvation draws ever nearer, so we may press forward all the more eagerly to the worthy celebration of the mystery of your Son's Nativity. Who lives and reigns for ever and ever. **Amen.**

SOLEMN BLESSING AND DISMISSAL *(p. 77)*

December 25

Moth-like, I am instinctively attracted to light. My inner child is enchanted by the kaleidoscope of colours displayed in Christmas neighbourhoods, by twinkling fireflies on a summer evening, or by festive fireworks displays. My spirit is soothed by candle glow and firelight, by shimmering moonbeams on new snow, by dappled sunlight through the trees. On a practical level, I am thankful for flashlights and lanterns to light my way during a power blackout. Light is an essential, uplifting and transformative element in our lives.

The Nativity readings glow with images of light. Isaiah proclaims: "The people who walked in darkness have seen a great light." Psalm 97 exults in the light that will "shine on us this day." John's Gospel, too, speaks of a light shining in the darkness, "and the darkness did not overcome it." What we celebrate today is Jesus as the radiance of God bursting forth into our darkened world.

But it is not enough for us to be merely passive recipients of that light. We are called to become, each of us, a light for others. Often the darkness surrounding us may seem to be impenetrable. Alone, we each may be only a tiny firefly or a wavering candle flame. Joined together in the light of Christ, however, we can illuminate and transform our world.

Krystyna Higgins, Fredericton, NB

MASS DURING THE NIGHT

ENTRANCE ANTIPHON *(Psalm 2.7)*
The Lord said to me: You are my Son. It is I who have begotten you this day.

or

Let us all rejoice in the Lord, for our Saviour has been born in the world. Today true peace has come down to us from heaven.

INTRODUCTORY RITES *(p. 5)*

COLLECT
O God, who have made this most sacred night radiant with the splendour of the true light, grant, we pray, that we, who have known the mysteries of his light on earth, may also delight in his gladness in heaven. Who lives and reigns with you in the unity of the Holy Spirit, one God, for ever and ever. **Amen.**

FIRST READING *(Isaiah 9.2-4, 6-7)*
The people who walked in darkness have seen
a great light;
those who lived in a land of deep darkness —
on them light has shone.
You have multiplied the nation,
you have increased its joy;
they rejoice before you
as with joy at the harvest,
as people exult when dividing plunder.

For the yoke of their burden,
and the bar across their shoulders,
the rod of their oppressor,
you have broken as on the day of Midian.

For a child has been born for us,
a son given to us;
authority rests upon his shoulders;
and he is named
Wonderful Counsellor, Mighty God,
Everlasting Father, Prince of Peace.

His authority shall grow continually,
and there shall be endless peace
for the throne of David and his kingdom.
He will establish and uphold it
with justice and with righteousness
from this time onward and forevermore.
The zeal of the Lord of hosts will do this.

The word of the Lord. **Thanks be to God.**

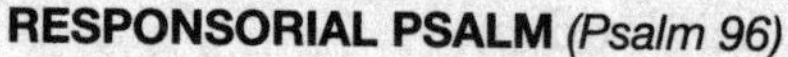

RESPONSORIAL PSALM *(Psalm 96)*

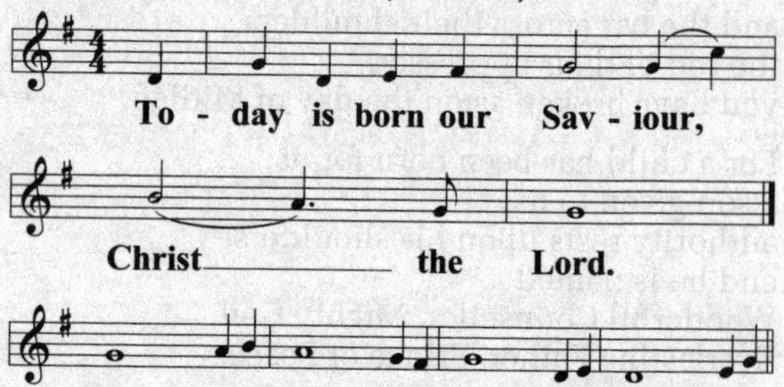

℟. **Today is born our Saviour, Christ the Lord.**

O sing to the Lord a · **new** song;
sing to the Lord, · **all_the** earth.
Sing to the Lord, · **bless_his** name;
tell of his salvation from day · **to** day. ℟.

Declare his glory among · **the** nations,
his marvellous works among all · **the** peoples.
For great is the Lord, and greatly · **to_be** praised;
he is to be revered above · **all** gods. ℟.

Let the heavens be glad, and let the earth ·
  re-joice;
let the sea roar, and all · **that** fills_it;
let the field exult, and every·-**thing** in_it.
Then shall all the trees of the forest sing ·
  for joy. ℟.

Rejoice before the Lord; for · **he_is** coming,
for he is coming to judge · **the** earth.
He will judge the world · **with** righteousness,
and the peoples · **with_his** truth. ℟.

SECOND READING *(Titus 2.11-14)*
Beloved: The grace of God has appeared, bringing salvation to all, training us to renounce impiety and worldly passions, and in the present age to live lives that are self-controlled, upright, and godly, while we wait for the blessed hope and the manifestation of the glory of our great God and Saviour, Jesus Christ.

He it is who gave himself for us that he might redeem us from all iniquity and purify for himself a people of his own who are zealous for good deeds.

The word of the Lord. **Thanks be to God.**

GOSPEL ACCLAMATION *(Luke 2.10-11)*
Alleluia. Alleluia. Good news and great joy to all the world: today is born our Saviour, Christ the Lord. **Alleluia.**

GOSPEL *(Luke 2.1-16)*
The Lord be with you. **And with your spirit.** A reading from the holy Gospel according to Luke. **Glory to you, O Lord.**

In those days a decree went out from Caesar Augustus that all the world should be registered. This was the first registration and was taken while Quirinius was governor of Syria. All went to their own towns to be registered. Joseph also went from the town of Nazareth in Galilee to Judea, to the city of David called Bethlehem, because he was descended from the house and family of David. He went to be registered with Mary, to whom he was engaged and who was expecting a child.

While they were there, the time came for her to deliver her child. And she gave birth to her firstborn son and wrapped him in swaddling clothes, and laid him in a manger, because there was no place for them in the inn.

In that region there were shepherds living in the fields, keeping watch over their flock by night. Then an Angel of the Lord stood before them, and the glory of the Lord shone around them, and they were terrified. But the Angel said to them, "Do not be afraid; for see — I am bringing you good news of great joy for all the people: to you is born this day in the city of David a Saviour, who is the Christ, the Lord. This will be a sign for you: you will find a child wrapped in swaddling clothes and lying in a manger."

And suddenly there was with the Angel a multitude of the heavenly host, praising God and saying, "Glory to God in the highest heaven, and on earth peace among those whom he favours!"

When the Angels had left them and gone into heaven, the shepherds said to one another, "Let us go now to Bethlehem and see this thing that has taken place, which the Lord has made known to us." So they went with haste and found Mary and Joseph, and the child lying in the manger.

The Gospel of the Lord. **Praise to you, Lord Jesus Christ.**

PROFESSION OF FAITH *(p. 11. All kneel at the words "and by the Holy Spirit was incarnate.")*

PRAYER OF THE FAITHFUL

The following intentions are suggestions only. There are more suggestions at www.livingwithchrist.ca

℟. **Lord, hear our prayer.**

For Christians everywhere, striving to bear witness to God's unfathomable love for the world, we pray to the Lord: ℟.

For governments and citizens' groups working to build peace among nations and peoples, we pray to the Lord: ℟.

For families everywhere, where we first encounter the joy and love of God's presence, we pray to the Lord: ℟.

For this community, called to proclaim God's love to the world, we pray to the Lord: ℟.

PREPARATION OF THE GIFTS *(p. 14)*

PRAYER OVER THE OFFERINGS

May the oblation of this day's feast be pleasing to you, O Lord, we pray, that through this most holy exchange we may be found in the likeness of Christ, in whom our nature is united to you. Who lives and reigns for ever and ever. **Amen.**

PREFACE *(Nativity, p. 16)*

COMMUNION ANTIPHON *(John 1.14)*

The Word became flesh, and we have seen his glory.

PRAYER AFTER COMMUNION
Grant us, we pray, O Lord our God, that we, who are gladdened by participation in the feast of our Redeemer's Nativity, may through an honourable way of life become worthy of union with him. Who lives and reigns for ever and ever. **Amen.**

SOLEMN BLESSING – NATIVITY *(Optional)*
Bow down for the blessing.

May the God of infinite goodness, who by the Incarnation of his Son has driven darkness from the world and by that glorious Birth has illumined this most holy night (day), drive far from you the darkness of vice and illumine your hearts with the light of virtue. **Amen.**

May God, who willed that the great joy of his Son's saving Birth be announced to shepherds by the Angel, fill your minds with the gladness he gives and make you heralds of his Gospel. **Amen.**

And may God, who by the Incarnation brought together the earthly and heavenly realm, fill you with the gift of his peace and favour and make you sharers with the Church in heaven. **Amen.**

And may the blessing of almighty God, the Father, and the Son, and the Holy Spirit, come down on you and remain with you for ever. **Amen.**

DISMISSAL *(p. 70)*

MASS AT DAWN

ENTRANCE ANTIPHON *(Cf. Isaiah 9.1, 5; Luke 1.33)*
Today a light will shine upon us, for the Lord is born for us; and he will be called Wondrous God, Prince of peace, Father of future ages: and his reign will be without end.

INTRODUCTORY RITES *(p. 5)*

COLLECT
Grant, we pray, almighty God, that, as we are bathed in the new radiance of your incarnate Word, the light of faith, which illumines our minds, may also shine through in our deeds. Through our Lord Jesus Christ, your Son, who lives and reigns with you in the unity of the Holy Spirit, one God, for ever and ever. **Amen.**

FIRST READING *(Isaiah 62.11-12)*
The Lord has proclaimed to the end of the earth:
"Say to daughter Zion,
See, your salvation comes;
his reward is with him,
and his recompense before him.

"They shall be called 'The Holy People,'
'The Redeemed of the Lord';
and you shall be called 'Sought Out,'
'A City Not Forsaken.'"

The word of the Lord. **Thanks be to God.**

RESPONSORIAL PSALM *(Psalm 97)*

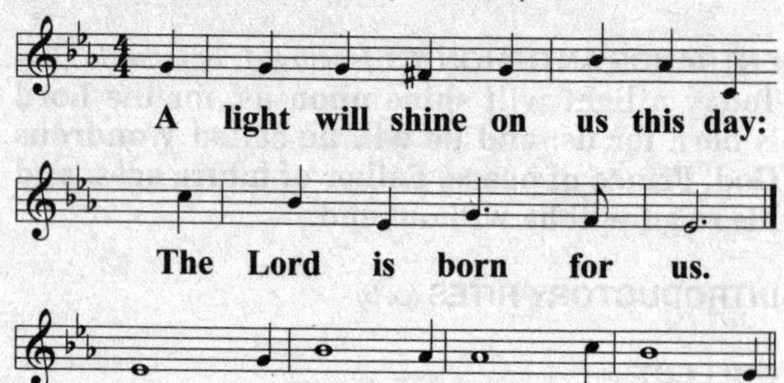

℟. **A light will shine on us this day:**
The Lord is born for us.

The Lord is king! Let the earth re··**joice;**
let the many coastlands be · **glad!**
Clouds and thick darkness are all a··**round_him;**
righteousness and justice are the foundation
of his · **throne.** ℟.

The mountains melt like wax before the · **Lord,**
before the Lord of all the · **earth.**
The heavens proclaim his · **righteousness;**
and all the peoples behold his · **glory.** ℟.

Light dawns for the · **righteous,**
and joy for the upright in · **heart.**
Rejoice in the Lord, O you · **righteous,**
and give thanks to his holy · **name!** ℟.

To hear the Sunday Psalms, go to www.livingwithchrist.ca and select the psalm button at the bottom of the home page.

SECOND READING *(Titus 3.4-7)*
When the goodness and loving kindness of God our Saviour appeared, he saved us, not because of any works of righteousness that we had done, but according to his mercy, through the water of rebirth and renewal by the Holy Spirit. This Spirit he poured out on us richly through Jesus Christ our Saviour, so that, having been justified by his grace, we might become heirs according to the hope of eternal life.
The word of the Lord. **Thanks be to God.**

GOSPEL ACCLAMATION *(Luke 2.14)*
Alleluia. Alleluia. Glory to God in the highest heaven; peace on earth to people of good will. **Alleluia.**

GOSPEL *(Luke 2.15-20)*
The Lord be with you. **And with your spirit.** A reading from the holy Gospel according to Luke. **Glory to you, O Lord.**

When the Angels had left them and gone into heaven, the shepherds said to one another, "Let us go now to Bethlehem and see this thing that has taken place, which the Lord has made known to us."

So they went with haste and found Mary and Joseph, and the child lying in the manger. When they saw this, they made known what had been told them about this child; and all who heard it were amazed at what the shepherds told them.

But Mary treasured all these words and pondered them in her heart. The shepherds returned, glorifying and praising God for all they had heard and seen, as it had been told them.

The Gospel of the Lord. **Praise to you, Lord Jesus Christ.**

PROFESSION OF FAITH *(p. 11. All kneel at the words "and by the Holy Spirit was incarnate.")*

PRAYER OF THE FAITHFUL *(p. 103)*

PREPARATION OF THE GIFTS *(p. 14)*

PRAYER OVER THE OFFERINGS
May our offerings be worthy, we pray, O Lord, of the mysteries of the Nativity this day, that, just as Christ was born a man and also shone forth as God, so these earthly gifts may confer on us what is divine. Through Christ our Lord. **Amen.**

PREFACE *(Nativity, p. 16)*

COMMUNION ANTIPHON *(Cf. Zechariah 9.9)*
Rejoice, O Daughter Sion; lift up praise, Daughter Jerusalem: Behold, your King will come, the Holy One and Saviour of the world.

PRAYER AFTER COMMUNION
Grant us, Lord, as we honour with joyful devotion the Nativity of your Son, that we may come to know with fullness of faith the hidden depths of this mystery and to love them ever more and more. Through Christ our Lord. **Amen.**

SOLEMN BLESSING AND DISMISSAL *(p. 104)*

MASS DURING THE DAY

ENTRANCE ANTIPHON *(Cf. Isaiah 9.5)*
A child is born for us, and a son is given to us; his sceptre of power rests upon his shoulder, and his name will be called Messenger of great counsel.

INTRODUCTORY RITES *(p. 5)*

COLLECT
O God, who wonderfully created the dignity of human nature and still more wonderfully restored it, grant, we pray, that we may share in the divinity of Christ, who humbled himself to share in our humanity. Who lives and reigns with you in the unity of the Holy Spirit, one God, for ever and ever. **Amen.**

FIRST READING *(Isaiah 52.7-10)*
How beautiful upon the mountains are the feet of the messenger who announces peace, who brings good news, who announces salvation, who says to Zion, "Your God reigns."

Listen! Your watchmen lift up their voices, together they sing for joy; for in plain sight they see the return of the Lord to Zion.

Break forth together into singing, you ruins of Jerusalem; for the Lord has comforted his people, he has redeemed Jerusalem. The Lord has bared his holy arm before the eyes of all the nations; and all the ends of the earth shall see the salvation of our God.

The word of the Lord. **Thanks be to God.**

RESPONSORIAL PSALM *(Psalm 98)*

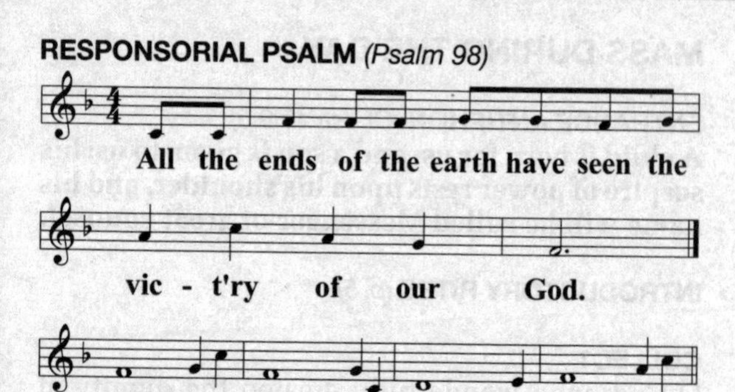

℟. **All the ends of the earth have seen the victory of our God.**

O sing to the Lord a · **new** song,
for he has done · **marvellous** things.
His right hand and his holy · **arm**
have brought · **him** victory. ℟.

The Lord has made known · **his** victory;
he has revealed his vindication in the sight
of · **the** nations.
He has remembered his steadfast love and
· **faithfulness**
to the house · **of** Israel. ℟.

All the ends of the earth · **have** seen
the victory of · **our** God.
Make a joyful noise to the Lord, all the · **earth;**
break forth into joyous song and · **sing**
praises. ℟.

Sing praises to the Lord with · **the** lyre,
with the lyre and the sound · **of** melody.
With trumpets and the sound of the · **horn**
make a joyful noise before the King,
· **the** Lord. ℟.

To hear the Sunday Psalms, go to www.livingwithchrist.ca and select the psalm button at the bottom of the home page.

SECOND READING *(Hebrews 1.1-6)*
Long ago God spoke to our ancestors in many and various ways by the Prophets, but in these last days he has spoken to us by the Son, whom he appointed heir of all things, through whom he also created the ages.

He is the reflection of God's glory and the exact imprint of God's very being, and he sustains all things by his powerful word. When he had made purification for sins, he sat down at the right hand of the Majesty on high, having become as much superior to Angels as the name he has inherited is more excellent than theirs.

For to which of the Angels did God ever say, "You are my Son; today I have begotten you"? Or again, "I will be his Father, and he will be my Son"? And again, when he brings the firstborn into the world, he says, "Let all God's Angels worship him."

The word of the Lord. **Thanks be to God.**

GOSPEL ACCLAMATION

Alleluia. Alleluia. A holy day has dawned upon us. Come you nations and adore the Lord. Today a great light has come down upon the earth. **Alleluia.**

GOSPEL *(John 1.1-18)*

For the shorter version, omit the indented parts.

The Lord be with you. **And with your spirit.**
A reading from the holy Gospel according to John.
Glory to you, O Lord.

In the beginning was the Word, and the Word was with God, and the Word was God. He was in the beginning with God. All things came into being through him, and without him not one thing came into being. What has come into being in him was life, and the life was the light of the human race.

The light shines in the darkness, and the darkness did not overcome it.

> There was a man sent from God, whose name was John. He came as a witness to testify to the light, so that all might believe through him. He himself was not the light, but he came to testify to the light.

The true light, which enlightens everyone, was coming into the world. He was in the world, and the world came into being through him; yet the world did not know him. He came to what was his own, and his own people did not accept him. But to all who received him, who believed in his name, he gave power to become children of God, who were born, not of blood or of the will of the flesh or of the will of man, but of God.

And the Word became flesh and lived among us, and we have seen his glory, the glory as of a father's only-begotten son, full of grace and truth.

> John testified to him and cried out, "This was he of whom I said, 'He who comes after me ranks ahead of me because he was before me.'" From his fullness we have all received, grace upon grace. The law indeed was given through Moses; grace and truth came through Jesus Christ. No one has ever seen God. It is God the only-begotten Son, who is close to the Father's heart, who has made him known.

The Gospel of the Lord. **Praise to you, Lord Jesus Christ.**

PROFESSION OF FAITH *(p. 11. All kneel at the words "and by the Holy Spirit was incarnate.")*

PRAYER OF THE FAITHFUL *(p. 103)*

PREPARATION OF THE GIFTS *(p. 14)*

PRAYER OVER THE OFFERINGS
Make acceptable, O Lord, our oblation on this solemn day, when you manifested the reconciliation that makes us wholly pleasing in your sight and inaugurated for us the fullness of divine worship. Through Christ our Lord. **Amen.**

PREFACE *(Nativity, p. 16)*

COMMUNION ANTIPHON *(Cf. Psalm 97.3)*
All the ends of the earth have seen the salvation of our God.

PRAYER AFTER COMMUNION
Grant, O merciful God, that, just as the Saviour of the world, born this day, is the author of divine generation for us, so he may be the giver even of immortality. Who lives and reigns for ever and ever. **Amen.**

SOLEMN BLESSING AND DISMISSAL *(p. 104)*

December 27

For generations the Church has held up the Holy Family as the model for all Christian families. Some people in recent years have claimed that such an ideal is impossible — a virgin mother, a silent father, and a son who is both divine and human — but this claim is missing the point completely. The ideal of the Holy Family is found in their total faithfulness to God, their love for one another, and their desire to live in the world as true children of God.

Their humility, simplicity and prayerful devotion are reflected in their annual pilgrimage to the Temple of the Lord. Their desire to live in right relationship with God sets an example for us all. They are a faith-filled, loving family who will not be spared the sufferings and challenges of life, yet who place their complete trust in God.

Losing the young boy in Jerusalem must have caused fierce anxiety for Mary and Joseph. Rushing back to search for him, they found him in the Temple, his Father's house: another aspect of his life upon which Mary would ponder and reflect.

The Holy Family is not distant from us. They stand with each of us as we seek to live in right relationship with God and neighbour.

Fr. John Reddy, CSB, Toronto, ON

ENTRANCE ANTIPHON *(Luke 2.16)*
The shepherds went in haste, and found Mary and Joseph and the Infant lying in a manger.

INTRODUCTORY RITES *(p. 5)*

COLLECT
O God, who were pleased to give us the shining example of the Holy Family, graciously grant that we may imitate them in practising the virtues of family life and in the bonds of charity, and so, in the joy of your house, delight one day in eternal rewards. Through our Lord Jesus Christ, your Son, who lives and reigns with you in the unity of the Holy Spirit, one God, for ever and ever. **Amen.**

These readings may be used in Year C. Alternate readings can be found on p. 120.

FIRST READING *(1 Samuel 1.20-22, 24-28)*
In due time Hannah conceived and bore a son. She named him Samuel, for she said, "I have asked him of the Lord." Elkanah and all his household went up to offer to the Lord the yearly sacrifice, and to pay his vow. But Hannah did not go up, for she said to her husband, "As soon as the child is weaned, I will bring him, that he may appear in the presence of the Lord, and remain there forever; I will offer him as a nazirite for all time."

When she had weaned him, she took him up with her, along with a three-year-old bull, a measure of flour, and a skin of wine. She brought him to the house of the Lord at Shiloh; and the child was young. Then they slaughtered the bull, and they brought the child to Eli. And she said, "Oh, my lord! As you live, my lord, I am the woman who was standing here in your presence, praying to the Lord. For this child I prayed; and the Lord has granted me the petition that I made to him. Therefore I have lent him to the Lord; as long as he lives, he is given to the Lord." She left him there for the Lord.

The word of the Lord. **Thanks be to God.**

RESPONSORIAL PSALM *(Psalm 84)*

℟. **Blessed are those who live in your house, O Lord.**

How lovely is · your **dwelling_place,**
O Lord · **of** hosts!
My soul longs, indeed it faints for the courts
of · **the** Lord;
my heart and my flesh sing for joy
to the · **liv**-ing God. ℟.

Blessed are those who live in · **your** house,
ever singing · **your** praise.
Blessed are those whose strength is · **in** you,
in whose heart are the · **highways** to Zion. ℟.

O Lord God of hosts, hear · **my** prayer;
give ear, O God · **of** Jacob!
Behold our shield, · **O** God;
look on the face of · **your** a-nointed. ℟.

For a day in your courts · **is** better
than a thou·-**sand** elsewhere.
I would rather be a doorkeeper in the house
of · **my** God
than live in the · **tents** of wickedness. ℟.

To hear the Sunday Psalms, go to www.livingwithchrist.ca and select the psalm button at the bottom of the home page.

SECOND READING *(1 John 3.1-2, 21-24)*

Beloved: See what love the Father has given us, that we should be called children of God; and that is what we are. The reason the world does not know us is that it did not know him. Beloved, we are God's children now; what we will be has not yet been revealed. What we do know is this: when he is revealed, we will be like him, for we will see him as he is.

Beloved, if our hearts do not condemn us, we have boldness before God; and we receive from him whatever we ask, because we obey his commandments and do what pleases him. And this is his commandment, that we should believe in the name of his Son Jesus Christ and love one another, just as he has commanded us. Whoever obeys his commandments abides in him, and he abides in them. And by this we know that he abides in us, by the Spirit that he has given us.

The word of the Lord. **Thanks be to God.**

GOSPEL ACCLAMATION *(See Acts 16.14)*
Alleluia. Alleluia. Open our hearts, O Lord, to listen to the words of your Son. **Alleluia.**

GOSPEL *(Luke 2.41-52)*
The Lord be with you. **And with your spirit.** A reading from the holy Gospel according to Luke. **Glory to you, O Lord.**

Every year the parents of Jesus went to Jerusalem for the festival of the Passover. And when he was twelve years old, they went up as usual for the festival.

When the festival was ended and they started to return, the boy Jesus stayed behind in Jerusalem, but his parents did not know it. Assuming that he was in the group of travellers, they went a day's journey. Then they started to look for him among their relatives and friends. When they did not find him, they returned to Jerusalem to search for him.

After three days they found him in the temple, sitting among the teachers, listening to them and asking them questions. And all who heard him were amazed at his understanding and his answers. When his parents saw him they were astonished; and his mother said to him, "Child, why have you treated us like this? Look, your father and I have been searching for you in great anxiety." He said to them, "Why were you searching for me? Did you not know that I must be in my Father's house?" But they did not understand what he said to them.

Then he went down with them and came to Nazareth, and was obedient to them. His mother treasured all these things in her heart. And Jesus increased in wisdom and in years, and in favour with God and human beings.

The Gospel of the Lord. **Praise to you, Lord Jesus Christ.**

Mass resumes on p. 124.

Alternate readings:

FIRST READING *(Sirach 3.2-6, 12-14)*

The Lord honours a father above his children,
and he confirms a mother's rights over her sons.
Whoever honours their father atones for sins
and gains preservation from them;
when they pray, they will be heard.
Whoever respects their mother
is like one who lays up treasure.
The person who honours their father
will have joy in their own children,
and when they pray they will be heard.
Whoever respects their father will have a long life,
and whoever honours their mother
obeys the Lord.

My child, help your father in his old age,
and do not grieve him as long as he lives.
Even if his mind fails, be patient with him;
because you have all your faculties,
do not despise him all the days of his life.
For kindness to your father will not be forgotten,
and will be credited to you against your sins —
a house raised in justice for you.

The word of the Lord. **Thanks be to God.**

RESPONSORIAL PSALM *(Psalm 128)*

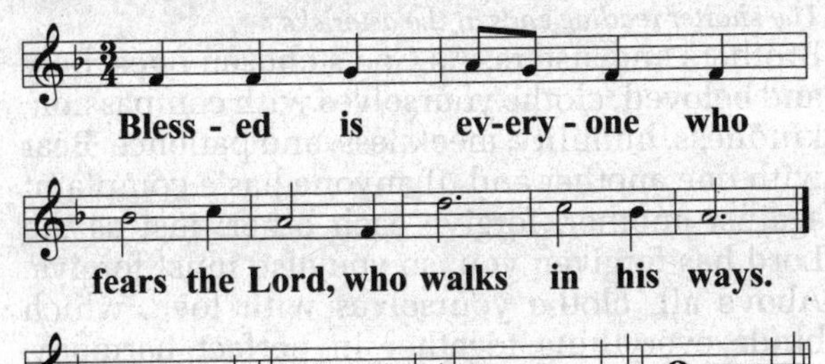

℟. **Blessed is everyone who fears the Lord.**

or **Blessed is everyone who fears the Lord, who walks in his ways.**

Blessed is everyone who fears · **the** Lord,
who walks in · **his** ways.
You shall eat the fruit of the labour of · **your** hands;
you shall be happy, and it shall go well · **with** you. ℟.

Your wife will be like a fruit·-**ful** vine
within · **your** house;
your children will be · **like** olive_shoots
around · **your** table. ℟.

Thus shall the man be blessed who fears · **the** Lord.
The Lord bless you · **from** Zion.
May you see the prosperity of · **Je**-rusalem
ll the days of · **your** life. ℟.

SECOND READING *(Colossians 3.12-21)*

The shorter reading ends at the asterisks.

Brothers and sisters: As God's chosen ones, holy and beloved, clothe yourselves with compassion, kindness, humility, meekness, and patience. Bear with one another and, if anyone has a complaint against another, forgive each other; just as the Lord has forgiven you, so you also must forgive. Above all, clothe yourselves with love, which binds everything together in perfect harmony. And let the peace of Christ rule in your hearts, to which indeed you were called in the one body. And be thankful.

Let the word of Christ dwell in you richly; teach and admonish one another in all wisdom; and with gratitude in your hearts sing Psalms, hymns, and spiritual songs to God. And whatever you do, in word or deed, do everything in the name of the Lord Jesus, giving thanks to God the Father through him.

***

Wives, be subject to your husbands, as is fitting in the Lord. Husbands, love your wives and never treat them harshly. Children, obey your parents in everything, for this is your acceptable duty in the Lord. Fathers, do not provoke your children, or they may lose heart.

The word of the Lord. **Thanks be to God.**

GOSPEL ACCLAMATION *(Colossians 3.15, 16)*

Alleluia. Alleluia. Let the peace of Christ rule in your hearts, and the word of Christ dwell in you richly. **Alleluia.**

GOSPEL *(Matthew 2.13-15, 19-23)*
The Lord be with you. **And with your spirit.**
A reading from the holy Gospel according to Matthew. **Glory to you, O Lord.**

After the wise men had left, an Angel of the Lord appeared to Joseph in a dream and said, "Get up, take the child and his mother, and flee to Egypt, and remain there until I tell you; for Herod is about to search for the child, to destroy him." Then Joseph got up, took the child and his mother by night, and went to Egypt, and remained there until the death of Herod. This was to fulfill what had been spoken by the Lord through the Prophet, "Out of Egypt I have called my son."

When Herod died, an Angel of the Lord suddenly appeared in a dream to Joseph in Egypt and said, "Get up, take the child and his mother, and go to the land of Israel, for those who were seeking the child's life are dead." Then Joseph got up, took the child and his mother, and went to the land of Israel.

But when he heard that Archelaus was ruling over Judea in place of his father Herod, he was afraid to go there. And after being warned in a dream, he went away to the district of Galilee. There he made his home in a town called Nazareth, so that what had been spoken through the Prophets might be fulfilled, "He will be called a Nazorean."

The Gospel of the Lord. **Praise to you, Lord Jesus Christ.**

PROFESSION OF FAITH *(p. 11)*

PRAYER OF THE FAITHFUL

The following intentions are suggestions only. There are more suggestions at www.livingwithchrist.ca

℟. **Lord, hear our prayer.**

For the Church, instrument of God's compassionate hospitality, we pray to the Lord: ℟.

For peace in every heart and in every home, we pray to the Lord: ℟.

For the needs of families in this parish and around the world, we pray to the Lord: ℟.

For us, God's people gathered here, called to recognize God's presence in all things, we pray to the Lord: ℟.

PREPARATION OF THE GIFTS *(p. 14)*

PRAYER OVER THE OFFERINGS

We offer you, Lord, the sacrifice of conciliation, humbly asking that, through the intercession of the Virgin Mother of God and Saint Joseph, you may establish our families firmly in your grace and your peace. Through Christ our Lord. **Amen.**

PREFACE *(Nativity, p. 16)*

COMMUNION ANTIPHON *(Baruch 3.38)*

Our God has appeared on the earth, and lived among us.

PRAYER AFTER COMMUNION

Bring those you refresh with this heavenly Sacrament, most merciful Father, to imitate constantly the example of the Holy Family, so that, after the trials of this world, we may share their company for ever. Through Christ our Lord. **Amen.**

BLESSING AND DISMISSAL *(p. 70)*

January Saints' Days

The following saints are traditionally remembered in January in Canada.

1 Solemnity of Mary, the Holy Mother of God
2 Saints Basil and Gregory Nazianzen
7 Saint André Bessette
8 Saint Raymond of Penyafort
12 Saint Marguerite Bourgeoys
13 Saint Hilary
17 Saint Anthony
20 Saint Fabian
Saint Sebastian
21 Saint Agnes
22 Saint Vincent
24 Saint Francis de Sales
26 Saints Timothy and Titus
27 Saint Angela Merici
28 Saint Thomas Aquinas
31 Saint John Bosco

January 1

World Day of Peace

Today we honour Mary as the Mother of God, while also marking World Day of Peace. At first glance, this feast and the theme might appear to be in competition with each other. Their connections, however, run deep within our tradition. For example, Mary carries, among others, the title Queen of Peace. In today's gospel passage, Mary has just given birth to the Prince of Peace. Being at peace and bringing peace are central to Mary's life and the example as the First Disciple that she sets for all of us.

By her example, Mary shows us how choosing to be open to God's will brings her the peace in her heart necessary for her to reflect and ponder on her life. It is in peace that she listens to the angel and the shepherds, both of whom share with her what the Lord had made known to them, further adding to her sense of peace over the choice she has made.

To be at peace should be the goal of all nations and all peoples. Only when there is peace can we grow, develop and prosper. If we follow Mary's example of faithfulness and say yes to God's will for us, then we will allow that same peace to take root in our hearts.

Connie Paré, London, ON

ENTRANCE ANTIPHON

Hail, Holy Mother, who gave birth to the King who rules heaven and earth for ever.

or (Cf. Isaiah 9.1, 5; Luke 1.33)

Today a light will shine upon us, for the Lord is born for us; and he will be called Wondrous God, Prince of peace, Father of future ages: and his reign will be without end.

INTRODUCTORY RITES *(p. 5)*

COLLECT

O God, who through the fruitful virginity of Blessed Mary bestowed on the human race the grace of eternal salvation, grant, we pray, that we may experience the intercession of her, through whom we were found worthy to receive the author of life, our Lord Jesus Christ, your Son. Who lives and reigns with you in the unity of the Holy Spirit, one God, for ever and ever. **Amen.**

FIRST READING *(Numbers 6.22-27)*

The Lord spoke to Moses: Speak to Aaron and his sons, saying, Thus you shall bless the children of Israel: You shall say to them,

The Lord bless you and keep you;
the Lord make his face to shine upon you,
and be gracious to you;
the Lord lift up his countenance upon you,
and give you peace.

So they shall put my name on the children of Israel, and I will bless them.

The word of the Lord. **Thanks be to God.**

RESPONSORIAL PSALM *(Psalm 67)*

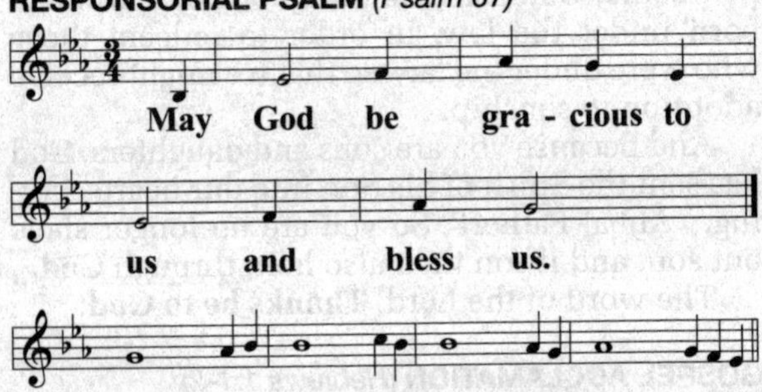

℟. **May God be gracious to us and bless us.**

May God be gracious to us · **and** bless_us
and make his face to shine · **up**-on_us,
that your way may be known up·-**on** earth,
your saving power a·-**mong** all nations. ℟.

Let the nations be glad and sing · **for** joy,
for you judge the peoples with equity
and guide the nations up·-**on** earth.
Let the peoples praise you, · **O** God;
let all the · **peo**-ples praise_you. ℟.

The earth has yielded · **its** increase;
God, our God, · **has** blessed_us.
May God continue · **to** bless_us;
let all the ends of the · **earth** re-vere_him. ℟.

To hear the Sunday Psalms, go to www.livingwithchrist.ca and select the psalm button at the bottom of the home page.

SECOND READING *(Galatians 4.4-7)*
Brothers and sisters: When the fullness of time had come, God sent his Son, born of a woman, born under the law, in order to redeem those who were under the law, so that we might receive adoption to sonship.

And because you are sons and daughters, God has sent the Spirit of his Son into our hearts, crying, "Abba! Father!" So you are no longer slave but son, and if son then also heir, through God.

The word of the Lord. **Thanks be to God.**

GOSPEL ACCLAMATION *(Hebrews 1.1-2)*
Alleluia. Alleluia. Long ago God spoke to our ancestors by the Prophets; in these last days he has spoken to us by the Son. **Alleluia.**

GOSPEL *(Luke 2.16-21)*
The Lord be with you. **And with your spirit.** A reading from the holy Gospel according to Luke. **Glory to you, O Lord.**

The shepherds went with haste to Bethlehem and found Mary and Joseph, and the child lying in the manger. When they saw this, they made known what had been told them about this child; and all who heard it were amazed at what the shepherds told them.

But Mary treasured all these words and pondered them in her heart.

The shepherds returned, glorifying and praising God for all they had heard and seen, as it had been told them.

After eight days had passed, it was time to circumcise the child; and he was called Jesus, the name given by the Angel before he was conceived in the womb.

The Gospel of the Lord. **Praise to you, Lord Jesus Christ.**

PROFESSION OF FAITH *(p. 11)*

PRAYER OF THE FAITHFUL

The following intentions are suggestions only. There are more suggestions at www.livingwithchrist.ca

℟. **Lord, hear our prayer.**

For the Church, called to be a sign of God's presence in the world, we pray to the Lord: ℟.

For leaders of nations and religions intent on building the kingdom of peace, we pray to the Lord: ℟.

For the gift of trust in God's promises, even in adverse circumstances, we pray to the Lord: ℟.

For hearts that welcome the poor as 'bearers of God,' we pray to the Lord: ℟.

PREPARATION OF THE GIFTS *(p. 14)*

PRAYER OVER THE OFFERINGS

O God, who in your kindness begin all good things and bring them to fulfillment, grant to us, who find joy in the Solemnity of the holy Mother of God, that, just as we glory in the beginnings of your grace, so one day we may rejoice in its completion. Through Christ our Lord. **Amen.**

PREFACE *(BVM I, p. 17)*

COMMUNION ANTIPHON *(Hebrews 13.8)*
Jesus Christ is the same yesterday, today, and for ever.

PRAYER AFTER COMMUNION
We have received this heavenly Sacrament with joy, O Lord: grant, we pray, that it may lead us to eternal life, for we rejoice to proclaim the blessed ever-Virgin Mary Mother of your Son and Mother of the Church. Through Christ our Lord. **Amen.**

SOLEMN BLESSING – NEW YEAR *(Optional)*
Bow down for the blessing.

May God, the source and origin of all blessing, grant you grace, pour out his blessing in abundance, and keep you safe from harm throughout the year. **Amen.**

May he give you integrity in the faith, endurance in hope, and perseverance in charity with holy patience to the end. **Amen.**

May he order your days and your deeds in his peace, grant your prayers in this and in every place, and lead you happily to eternal life. **Amen.**

And may the blessing of almighty God, the Father, and the Son, and the Holy Spirit, come down on you and remain with you for ever. **Amen.**

DISMISSAL *(p. 70)*

January 3

Epiphania: A revelation, a proclamation, a broadcast. Such is the meaning of the feast of the Epiphany, usually understood as the revelation of the Incarnation to the world beyond the Chosen People, a revelation to the Gentiles.

It is a story full of the exotic: heavenly portents, mysterious wise men, precious gifts, dreams and visions, all leading the world to the astonishing mystery of God-made-flesh. The curious thing in this story is that these strange visitors from the East do not seem in the least dismayed by the discovery that this supposed king of the Jews is born in poverty. Undeterred by the humble circumstances, they pay him homage and offer their gifts.

This is an encounter replete with symbolism and meaning. What stands out is the fact that these wise men discovered the birth of the king by interpreting the signs they had observed. Not limited by presuppositions, false expectations or jealousy, they could see the truth and accept it, where others could not.

Let us pray with grateful hearts for the wisdom to see Christ revealed in the world around us, even when that revelation challenges our preconceptions and invites us to find him where we least expect him.

Fr. Len Altilia, SJ, Winnipeg, MB

ENTRANCE ANTIPHON
(Cf. Malachi 3.1; 1 Chronicles 29.12)
Behold, the Lord, the Mighty One, has come; and kingship is in his grasp, and power and dominion.

INTRODUCTORY RITES *(p. 5)*

COLLECT
O God, who on this day revealed your Only Begotten Son to the nations by the guidance of a star, grant in your mercy that we, who know you already by faith, may be brought to behold the beauty of your sublime glory. Through our Lord Jesus Christ, your Son, who lives and reigns with you in the unity of the Holy Spirit, one God, for ever and ever. **Amen.**

FIRST READING *(Isaiah 60.1-6)*
Arise, shine, for your light has come,
and the glory of the Lord has risen upon you!
For darkness shall cover the earth,
and thick darkness the peoples;
but the Lord will arise upon you,
and his glory will appear over you.
Nations shall come to your light,
and kings to the brightness of your dawn.
Lift up your eyes and look around;
they all gather together, they come to you;
your sons shall come from far away,
and your daughters shall be carried
on their nurses' arms.

Then you shall see and be radiant;
your heart shall thrill and rejoice,
because the abundance of the sea
  shall be brought to you,
the wealth of the nations shall come to you.
A multitude of camels shall cover you,
the young camels of Midian and Ephah;
all those from Sheba shall come.
They shall bring gold and frankincense,
and shall proclaim the praise of the Lord.

The word of the Lord. **Thanks be to God.**

RESPONSORIAL PSALM *(Psalm 72)*

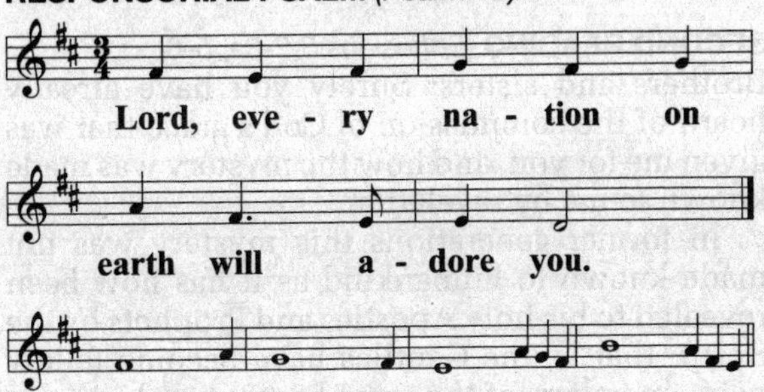

℟. **Lord, every nation on earth will adore you.**

Give the king your justice, O · **God,**
and your righteousness to a king's · **son.**
May he judge your · **people** with righteousness,
and your · **poor** with justice. ℟.

In his days may righteousness · **flourish**
and peace abound, until the moon is no · **more.**
May he have dominion from · **sea** to sea,
and from the River to the · **ends_of** the earth. ℟.

May the kings of Tarshish and of the isles
render him · **tribute,**
may the kings of Sheba and Seba bring · **gifts.**
May all kings fall · **down** be-fore_him,
all nations · **give** him service. ℟.

For he delivers the needy one who · **calls,**
the poor and the one who has no · **helper.**
He has pity on the · **weak_and** the needy,
and saves the · **lives_of** the needy. ℟.

To hear the Sunday Psalms, go to www.livingwithchrist.ca and select the psalm button at the bottom of the home page.

SECOND READING *(Ephesians 3.2-3a, 5-6)*

Brothers and sisters: Surely you have already heard of the commission of God's grace that was given me for you, and how the mystery was made known to me by revelation.

In former generations this mystery was not made known to humankind as it has now been revealed to his holy Apostles and Prophets by the Spirit: that is, the Gentiles have become fellow heirs, members of the same body, and sharers in the promise in Christ Jesus through the Gospel.

The word of the Lord. **Thanks be to God.**

GOSPEL ACCLAMATION *(See Matthew 2.2)*

Alleluia. Alleluia. We observed his star at its rising, and have come to pay homage to the Lord. **Alleluia.**

GOSPEL *(Matthew 2.1-12)*

The Lord be with you. **And with your spirit.** A reading from the holy Gospel according to Matthew. **Glory to you, O Lord.**

In the time of King Herod, after Jesus was born in Bethlehem of Judea, wise men from the East came to Jerusalem, asking, "Where is the child who has been born king of the Jews? For we observed his star at its rising, and have come to pay him homage."

When King Herod heard this, he was frightened, and all Jerusalem with him; and calling together all the chief priests and scribes of the people, he inquired of them where the Messiah was to be born. They told him, "In Bethlehem of Judea; for so it has been written by the Prophet: 'And you, Bethlehem, in the land of Judah, are by no means least among the rulers of Judah; for from you shall come a ruler who is to shepherd my people Israel.'"

Then Herod secretly called for the wise men and learned from them the exact time when the star had appeared. Then he sent them to Bethlehem, saying, "Go and search diligently for the child; and when you have found him, bring me word so that I may also go and pay him homage."

When they had heard the king, they set out; and there, ahead of them, went the star that they had seen at its rising, until it stopped over the place where the child was. When they saw that the star had stopped, they were overwhelmed with joy.

On entering the house, they saw the child with Mary his mother; and they knelt down and paid him homage. Then, opening their treasure chests, they offered him gifts of gold, frankincense, and myrrh.

And having been warned in a dream not to return to Herod, they left for their own country by another road.

The Gospel of the Lord. **Praise to you, Lord Jesus Christ.**

PROFESSION OF FAITH *(p. 11)*

PRAYER OF THE FAITHFUL

The following intentions are suggestions only. There are more suggestions at www.livingwithchrist.ca

℟. **Lord, hear our prayer.**

For Church leaders who strive to bring God's love, light and truth to all, we pray to the Lord: ℟.

For a world where peace and justice reign for all persons, we pray to the Lord: ℟.

For the millions who are kept in the darkness of poverty and injustice, we pray to the Lord: ℟.

For this congregation gathered here, committed to manifesting God's loving presence to the world, we pray to the Lord: ℟.

PREPARATION OF THE GIFTS *(p. 14)*

PRAYER OVER THE OFFERINGS

Look with favour, Lord, we pray, on these gifts of your Church, in which are offered now not gold or frankincense or myrrh, but he who by them is proclaimed, sacrificed and received, Jesus Christ. Who lives and reigns for ever and ever. **Amen.**

PREFACE *(Epiphany, p. 18)*

COMMUNION ANTIPHON *(Cf. Matthew 2.2)*
We have seen his star in the East, and have come with gifts to adore the Lord.

PRAYER AFTER COMMUNION
Go before us with heavenly light, O Lord, always and everywhere, that we may perceive with clear sight and revere with true affection the mystery in which you have willed us to participate. Through Christ our Lord. **Amen.**

SOLEMN BLESSING – EPIPHANY *(Optional)*
Bow down for the blessing.

May God, who has called you out of darkness into his wonderful light, pour out in kindness his blessing upon you and make your hearts firm in faith, hope and charity. **Amen.**

And since in all confidence you follow Christ, who today appeared in the world as a light shining in darkness, may God make you, too, a light for your brothers and sisters. **Amen.**

And so when your pilgrimage is ended, may you come to him whom the Magi sought as they followed the star and whom they found with great joy, the Light from Light, who is Christ the Lord. **Amen.**

And may the blessing of almighty God, the Father, and the Son, and the Holy Spirit, come down on you and remain with you for ever. **Amen.**

DISMISSAL *(p. 70)*

January 10

For the past seven weeks, from the First Sunday of Advent up to today's Feast of the Baptism of the Lord, the seasonal readings have brought us into the life of Jesus in ways that are very familiar to us.

Christ first directs our eyes and our minds to the end times and his return in glory. Then we begin to meet the well-known heralds of God's love, starting with that shaggy desert-dweller, John the Baptist. We witness the dialogue between the young Virgin Mary and her aging cousin Elizabeth. And at Christmas, we meet the honourable and good man, Joseph, as well as the sleepless shepherds, the singing angels and the innkeeper.

Weekly, the life of Jesus unrolls quickly in front of us, from birth through childhood to manhood, bringing us to the River Jordan for his baptism by John. Here, Luke the Evangelist gives us a tangible experience of the Holy Trinity, with the Spirit descending upon the newly baptized Jesus and the voice of the Father being heard.

These wonderful images enrich and empower us as we gather in eucharistic communion with our sisters and brothers in Jesus Christ. We are today's heralds of the Good News of God's love, and our mission is to share the joy of life with the Lord.

Marilyn Sweet, Falmouth, NS

ENTRANCE ANTIPHON *(Cf. Matthew 3.16-17)*
After the Lord was baptized, the heavens were opened, and the Spirit descended upon him like a dove, and the voice of the Father thundered: This is my beloved Son, with whom I am well pleased.

INTRODUCTORY RITES *(p. 5)*

COLLECT
Almighty ever-living God, who, when Christ had been baptized in the River Jordan and as the Holy Spirit descended upon him, solemnly declared him your beloved Son, grant that your children by adoption, reborn of water and the Holy Spirit, may always be well pleasing to you. Through our Lord Jesus Christ, your Son, who lives and reigns with you in the unity of the Holy Spirit, one God, for ever and ever. **Amen.**

or

O God, whose Only Begotten Son has appeared in our very flesh, grant, we pray, that we may be inwardly transformed through him whom we recognize as outwardly like ourselves. Who lives and reigns with you in the unity of the Holy Spirit, one God, for ever and ever. **Amen.**

These readings may be used in Year C. Alternate readings can be found on p. 145.

FIRST READING *(Isaiah 40.1-5, 9-11)*
Comfort, O comfort my people,
says your God.
Speak tenderly to Jerusalem,

and cry to her
that she has served her term,
that her penalty is paid,
that she has received from the Lord's hand
double for all her sins.

A voice cries out:
"In the wilderness prepare the way of the Lord,
make straight in the desert a highway for our God.
Every valley shall be lifted up,
and every mountain and hill be made low;
the uneven ground shall become level,
and the rough places a plain.
Then the glory of the Lord shall be revealed,
and all people shall see it together,
for the mouth of the Lord has spoken."

Get you up to a high mountain,
O Zion, herald of good tidings;
lift up your voice with strength,
O Jerusalem, herald of good tidings,
lift it up, do not fear;
say to the cities of Judah,
"Here is your God!"

See, the Lord God comes with might,
and his arm rules for him;
his reward is with him,
and his recompense before him.
He will feed his flock like a shepherd;
he will gather the lambs in his arms,
and carry them in his bosom,
and gently lead the mother sheep.

The word of the Lord. **Thanks be to God.**

RESPONSORIAL PSALM *(Psalm 104)*

℟. **O bless the Lord, my soul!**

O Lord my God, you are · **very** great.
You are clothed with honour and · **majesty,**
wrapped in light as · **with** a garment.
You stretch out the heavens · **like_a** tent. ℟.

You set the beams of your dwelling place
on · **the** waters,
you make the clouds your chariot,
you ride on the wings of the · **wind,**
you make the · **winds** your messengers,
fire and flame · **your** ministers. ℟.

O Lord, how manifold are · **your** works!
In wisdom you have made them all;
the earth is full of your · **creatures.**
Yonder is the sea, · **great** and wide,
creeping things innumerable are there,
living things both small · **and** great. ℟.

Living things all look · **to** you
to give them their food in due · **season;**
when you give to them, they · **gather** it up;
when you open your hand, they are filled
with · **good** things. ℟.

When you take away · **their** breath,
they die and return to their · **dust.**
When you send forth your spirit,
they · **are** cre-ated;
and you renew the face of · **the** earth. R.

To hear the Sunday Psalms, go to www.livingwithchrist.ca and select the psalm button at the bottom of the home page.

SECOND READING *(Titus 2.11-14; 3.4-7)*

Beloved: The grace of God has appeared, bringing salvation to all, training us to renounce impiety and worldly passions, and in the present age to live lives that are self-controlled, upright, and godly, while we wait for the blessed hope and the manifestation of the glory of our great God and Saviour, Jesus Christ.

He it is who gave himself for us that he might redeem us from all iniquity and purify for himself a people of his own who are zealous for good deeds.

For when the goodness and loving kindness of God our Saviour appeared, he saved us, not because of any works of righteousness that we had done, but according to his mercy, through the water of rebirth and renewal by the Holy Spirit. This Spirit he poured out on us richly through Jesus Christ our Saviour, so that, having been justified by his grace, we might become heirs according to the hope of eternal life.

The word of the Lord. **Thanks be to God.**

GOSPEL ACCLAMATION *(See Luke 3.16)*
Alleluia. Alleluia. John said: One more powerful than I is coming; he will baptize you with the Holy Spirit and fire. **Alleluia.**

GOSPEL *(Luke 3.15-16, 21-22)*
The Lord be with you. **And with your spirit.**
A reading from the holy Gospel according to Luke. **Glory to you, O Lord.**

As the people were filled with expectation, and all were questioning in their hearts concerning John, whether he might be the Messiah, John answered all of them by saying, "I baptize you with water; but one who is more powerful than I is coming; I am not worthy to untie the thong of his sandals. He will baptize you with the Holy Spirit and fire."

Now when all the people were baptized, and when Jesus also had been baptized and was praying, the heaven was opened, and the Holy Spirit descended upon him in bodily form like a dove. And a voice came from heaven, "You are my Son, the Beloved; with you I am well pleased."

The Gospel of the Lord. **Praise to you, Lord Jesus Christ.**

Mass resumes on p. 148.

Alternate readings:

FIRST READING *(Isaiah 42.1-4, 6-7)*
Thus says the Lord:
"Here is my servant, whom I uphold,
my chosen, in whom my soul delights;
I have put my spirit upon him;

he will bring forth justice to the nations.
He will not cry or lift up his voice,
or make it heard in the street;
a bruised reed he will not break,
and a dimly burning wick he will not quench;
he will faithfully bring forth justice.
He will not grow faint or be crushed
until he has established justice in the earth;
and the coastlands wait for his teaching.

"I am the Lord, I have called you in righteousness,
I have taken you by the hand and kept you;
I have given you as a covenant to the people,
a light to the nations,
to open the eyes that are blind,
to bring out the prisoners from the dungeon,
from the prison those who sit in darkness."

The word of the Lord. **Thanks be to God.**

RESPONSORIAL PSALM *(Psalm 29)*

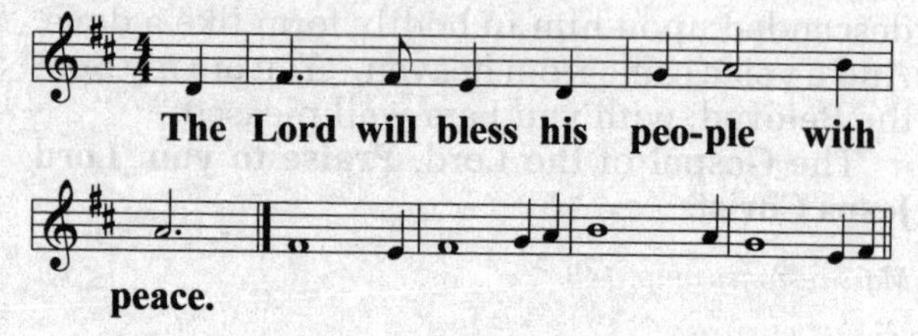

℟. **The Lord will bless his people with peace.**

Ascribe to the Lord, O heavenly · **beings,**
ascribe to the Lord glory · **and** strength.
Ascribe to the Lord the glory of his · **name;**
worship the Lord in · **holy** splendour. ℟.

The voice of the Lord is over the · **waters;**
the Lord, over · **mighty** waters.
The voice of the Lord is · **powerful;**
the voice of the Lord is · **full_of** majesty. ℟.

The God of glory · **thunders,**
and in his temple all · **say,** "Glory!"
The Lord sits enthroned over the · **flood;**
the Lord sits enthroned as king · **for**-ever. ℟.

To hear the Sunday Psalms, go to www.livingwithchrist.ca and select the psalm button at the bottom of the home page.

SECOND READING *(Acts 10.34-38)*

Peter began to speak:

"I truly understand that God shows no partiality, but in every nation anyone who fears him and does what is right is acceptable to him. You know the message he sent to the people of Israel, preaching peace by Jesus Christ — he is Lord of all. That message spread throughout Judea, beginning in Galilee after the baptism that John announced: how God anointed Jesus of Nazareth with the Holy Spirit and with power; how he went about doing good and healing all who were oppressed by the devil, for God was with him."

The word of the Lord. **Thanks be to God.**

GOSPEL ACCLAMATION *(See Mark 9.7)*

Alleluia. Alleluia. The heavens were opened and the Father's voice was heard: this is my Son, the beloved; listen to him! **Alleluia.**

GOSPEL *(Matthew 3.13-17)*
The Lord be with you. **And with your spirit.** A reading from the holy Gospel according to Matthew. **Glory to you, O Lord.**

Jesus came from Galilee to John at the Jordan, to be baptized by him. John would have prevented him, saying, "I need to be baptized by you, and do you come to me?" But Jesus answered him, "Let it be so for now; for it is proper for us in this way to fulfill all righteousness." Then John consented.

And when Jesus had been baptized, just as he came up from the water, suddenly the heavens were opened to him and he saw the Spirit of God descending like a dove and alighting on him. And a voice from heaven said, "This is my Son, the Beloved, with whom I am well pleased."

The Gospel of the Lord. **Praise to you, Lord Jesus Christ.**

PROFESSION OF FAITH *(p. 11)*

PRAYER OF THE FAITHFUL

The following intentions are suggestions only. There are more suggestions at www.livingwithchrist.ca

℟. **Lord, hear our prayer.**

For the Church, the People of God, a voice crying out for peace, we pray to the Lord: ℟.

For wise political leaders who seek to govern in peace and justice, we pray to the Lord: ℟.

For people who yearn for meaning and guidance in their daily struggle for survival, we pray to the Lord: ℟.

For this community of faith, called to constant faithfulness, we pray to the Lord: R.

PREPARATION OF THE GIFTS *(p. 14)*

PRAYER OVER THE OFFERINGS
Accept, O Lord, the offerings we have brought to honour the revealing of your beloved Son, so that the oblation of your faithful may be transformed into the sacrifice of him who willed in his compassion to wash away the sins of the world. Who lives and reigns for ever and ever. **Amen.**

PREFACE *(Baptism, p. 18)*

COMMUNION ANTIPHON *(John 1.32, 34)*
Behold the One of whom John said: I have seen and testified that this is the Son of God.

PRAYER AFTER COMMUNION
Nourished with these sacred gifts, we humbly entreat your mercy, O Lord, that, faithfully listening to your Only Begotten Son, we may be your children in name and in truth. Through Christ our Lord. **Amen.**

BLESSING AND DISMISSAL *(p. 70)*

January 17

World Day for Migrants and Refugees

Whenever we hear a passage from the Gospels, we can ask ourselves: what aspect of God does Jesus present to us? Today, Jesus reveals himself to be One who enters wholeheartedly into human celebrations, hesitates to interfere in the lives of others, yields to his mother's initiative, and exceeds all expectations.

This wedding party takes place in the middle of the week, "on the third day." This means that, in order to be present and join in the festivities, Jesus had to take time away from his usual routine. The God revealed by Jesus, then, breaks into the "ordinary" with extraordinary actions and surprises.

When the wine runs out, Jesus does not immediately rush into action. He waits until he is prompted and invited — in this case, by his mother. He acts in community and for the community.

Jesus responds to his mother's insistent action. He does turn the water into wine to save the couple from embarrassment and to keep the party going! Thus, Jesus reveals a God intimately concerned with our lives, loving and solicitous.

The wine that Jesus provides is better than the wine chosen by the couple. God as revealed by Jesus does infinitely more than we can ask or imagine. Our God is a God of plenty — plenty of love, compassion and redemption. Always.

Anne Walsh, St. John's, NL

ENTRANCE ANTIPHON *(Psalm 65.4)*
All the earth shall bow down before you, O God, and shall sing to you, shall sing to your name, O Most High!

INTRODUCTORY RITES *(p. 5)*

COLLECT
Almighty ever-living God, who govern all things, both in heaven and on earth, mercifully hear the pleading of your people and bestow your peace on our times. Through our Lord Jesus Christ, your Son, who lives and reigns with you in the unity of the Holy Spirit, one God, for ever and ever. **Amen.**

FIRST READING *(Isaiah 62.1-5)*
For Zion's sake I will not keep silent, and for Jerusalem's sake I will not rest, until her vindication shines out like the dawn, and her salvation like a burning torch.

The nations shall see your vindication, and all the kings your glory; and you shall be called by a new name that the mouth of the Lord will give. You shall be a crown of beauty in the hand of the Lord, and a royal diadem in the hand of your God.

You shall no more be termed Forsaken, and your land shall no more be termed Desolate; but you shall be called My Delight Is in Her, and your land Married; for the Lord delights in you, and your land shall be married. For as a young man marries a young woman, so shall your builder marry you, and as the bridegroom rejoices over the bride, so shall your God rejoice over you.

The word of the Lord. **Thanks be to God.**

RESPONSORIAL PSALM *(Psalm 96)*

De-clare the mar-vel-lous works of the

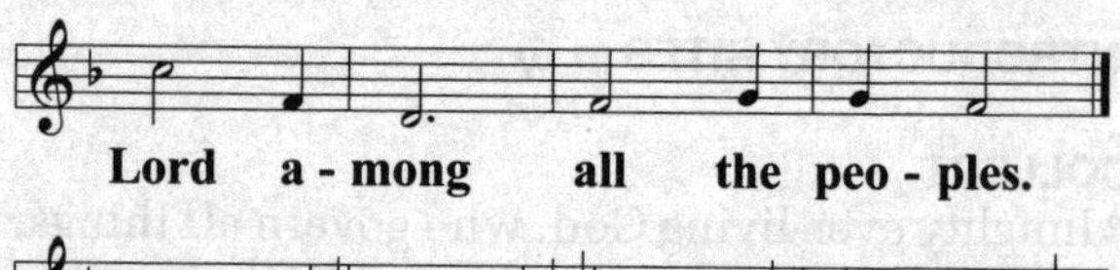

℟. **Declare the marvellous works of the Lord among all the peoples.**

O sing to the Lord · **a** new song;
sing to the Lord, · **all** the earth.
Sing to the Lord, · **bless** his name;
tell of his salvation from · **day** to day. ℟.

Declare his glory a·-**mong** the nations,
his marvellous works among · **all** the peoples.
For great is the Lord, and greatly · **to** be praised;
he is to be revered a·-**bove** all gods. ℟.

Ascribe to the Lord, O families · **of** the peoples,
ascribe to the Lord · **glory** and strength.
Ascribe to the Lord the glory · **due** his name;
bring an offering, and come · **into** his courts. ℟.

Worship the Lord in · **ho-**ly splendour;
tremble before him, · **all** the earth.
Say among the nations, "The · **Lord** is king!
He will judge the · **peoples** with equity." ℟.

SECOND READING *(1 Corinthians 12.4-11)*
Brothers and sisters: There are varieties of gifts, but the same Spirit; and there are varieties of services, but the same Lord; and there are varieties of activities, but it is the same God who activates all of them in everyone.

To each is given the manifestation of the Spirit for the common good. To one is given through the Spirit the utterance of wisdom, and to another the utterance of knowledge according to the same Spirit, to another faith by the same Spirit, to another gifts of healing by the one Spirit, to another the working of miracles, to another prophecy, to another the discernment of spirits, to another various kinds of tongues, to another the interpretation of tongues.

All these are activated by one and the same Spirit, who allots to each one individually just as the Spirit chooses.

The word of the Lord. **Thanks be to God.**

GOSPEL ACCLAMATION *(2 Thessalonians 2.14)*
Alleluia. Alleluia. God has called us through the good news, that we may obtain the glory of our Lord Jesus Christ. **Alleluia.**

GOSPEL *(John 2.1-12)*
The Lord be with you. **And with your spirit.**
A reading from the holy Gospel according to John.
Glory to you, O Lord.

On the third day there was a wedding in Cana of Galilee, and the mother of Jesus was there. Jesus and his disciples had also been invited to the wedding.

When the wine gave out, the mother of Jesus said to him, "They have no wine." And Jesus said to her, "Woman, what concern is that to you and to me? My hour has not yet come." His mother said to the servants, "Do whatever he tells you."

Now standing there were six stone water jars for the Jewish rites of purification, each holding about a hundred litres. Jesus said to the servants, "Fill the jars with water." And they filled them up to the brim. He said to them, "Now draw some out, and take it to the chief steward." So they took it.

When the steward tasted the water that had become wine, and did not know where it came from (though the servants who had drawn the water knew), the steward called the bridegroom and said to him, "Everyone serves the good wine first, and then the inferior wine after the guests have become drunk. But you have kept the good wine until now."

Jesus did this, the first of his signs, in Cana of Galilee, and revealed his glory; and his disciples believed in him. After this he went down to Capernaum with his mother, his brothers, and his disciples; and they remained there a few days.

The Gospel of the Lord. **Praise to you, Lord Jesus Christ.**

PROFESSION OF FAITH *(p. 11)*

PRAYER OF THE FAITHFUL

The following intentions are suggestions only. There are more suggestions at www.livingwithchrist.ca

℟. **Lord, hear our prayer.**

For the Church, working for unity and understanding among peoples, we pray to the Lord: ℟.

For new beginnings, which will foster peace among the nations, we pray to the Lord: ℟.

For married persons, experiencing the joys and challenges of sharing life, we pray to the Lord: ℟.

For all couples preparing for marriage, we pray to the Lord: ℟.

PREPARATION OF THE GIFTS *(p. 14)*

PRAYER OVER THE OFFERINGS

Grant us, O Lord, we pray, that we may participate worthily in these mysteries, for whenever the memorial of this sacrifice is celebrated the work of our redemption is accomplished. Through Christ our Lord. **Amen.**

PREFACE *(Sundays in Ordinary Time, p. 28)*

COMMUNION ANTIPHON *(Cf. Psalm 22.5)*

You have prepared a table before me, and how precious is the chalice that quenches my thirst.

or (1 John 4.16)

We have come to know and to believe in the love that God has for us.

PRAYER AFTER COMMUNION

Pour on us, O Lord, the Spirit of your love, and in your kindness make those you have nourished by this one heavenly Bread one in mind and heart. Through Christ our Lord. **Amen.**

BLESSING AND DISMISSAL *(p. 70)*

January 24

Week of Prayer for Christian Unity
"Called to proclaim the mighty deeds of the Lord."

Robbie Waisman, a Holocaust survivor, stood before students at our Catholic high school. As one of the small number of Jewish children who survived World War II in Nazi-occupied Europe, he felt obligated to share his story. In a clear, calm voice he told those assembled what he, as a teenager, had been forced to endure, of his liberation from the Buchenwald concentration camp, and of the painful realization that, of his family, only he and his sister survived.

In today's first reading Ezra, the priest, reads the Law to the people, survivors of the Babylonian exile and the destruction of the First Temple. God's words offer hope and healing to a broken people in a devastated land. Joy springs from the words and strengthens them.

Hope sustained Robbie Waisman in his darkest hours. This hope motivates him now in a world still torn by racial, religious and ethnic prejudices. He called upon his young listeners to build a world of peace and justice.

Paul tells us that all of us have a place and a role to play through our baptism in the church community, the body of Christ. Whether as teacher, prophet or other essential roles, we must live the vision Jesus proclaimed so long ago in Nazareth that will "bring good news to the poor" and "let the oppressed go free."

Michael Dougherty, Whitehouse, YT

ENTRANCE ANTIPHON *(Cf. Psalm 95.1, 6)*
O sing a new song to the Lord; sing to the Lord, all the earth. In his presence are majesty and splendour, strength and honour in his holy place.

INTRODUCTORY RITES *(p. 5)*

COLLECT
Almighty ever-living God, direct our actions according to your good pleasure, that in the name of your beloved Son we may abound in good works. Through our Lord Jesus Christ, your Son, who lives and reigns with you in the unity of the Holy Spirit, one God, for ever and ever. **Amen.**

FIRST READING *(Nehemiah 8.2-4a, 5-6, 8-10)*
The priest Ezra brought the Law before the assembly, both men and women and all who could hear with understanding. This was on the first day of the seventh month. He read from it facing the square before the Water Gate from early morning until midday, in the presence of the men and the women and those who could understand; and the ears of all the people were attentive to the book of the Law. The scribe Ezra stood on a wooden platform that had been made for the purpose.

And Ezra opened the book in the sight of all the people, for he was standing above all the people; and when he opened it, all the people stood up. Then Ezra blessed the Lord, the great God, and all the people answered, "Amen, Amen," lifting up their hands. Then they bowed their heads and worshipped the Lord with their faces to the ground.

So the Levites read from the book, from the Law of God, with interpretation. They gave the sense, so that the people understood the reading. And Nehemiah, who was the governor, and Ezra the priest and scribe, and the Levites who taught the people said to all the people, "This day is holy to the Lord your God; do not mourn or weep." For all the people wept when they heard the words of the Law.

Then Ezra said to them, "Go your way, eat the fat and drink sweet wine and send portions of them to those for whom nothing is prepared, for this day is holy to our Lord; and do not be grieved, for the joy of the Lord is your strength."

The word of the Lord. **Thanks be to God.**

RESPONSORIAL PSALM *(Psalm 19)*

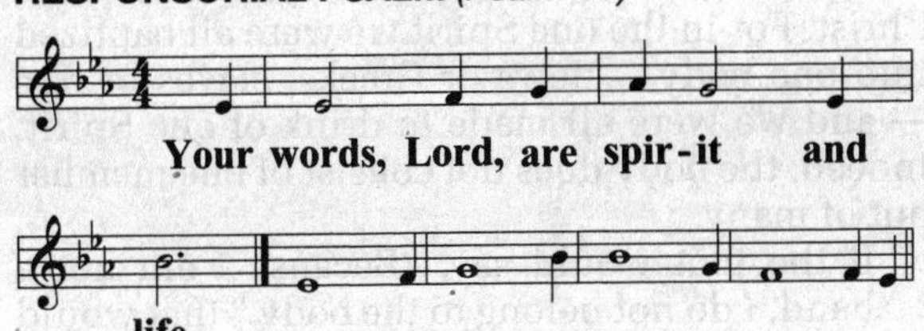

℟. **Your words, Lord, are spirit and life.**

The law of the Lord is · **perfect,**
reviving the · **soul;**
the decrees of the Lord are · **sure,**
making wise · **the** simple. ℟.

The precepts of the Lord are · **right,**
rejoicing the · **heart;**
the commandment of the Lord is · **clear,**
enlightening · **the** eyes. ℟.

The fear of the Lord is · **pure,**
enduring for·-**ever;**
the ordinances of the Lord are · **true**
and righteous · **alto**-gether. ℟.

Let the words of my · **mouth**
and the meditation of my · **heart**
be acceptable to · **you,**
O Lord, my rock and · **my_re**-deemer. ℟.

SECOND READING *(1 Corinthians 12.12-30)*

For the shorter version, omit the indented parts.

Brothers and sisters: Just as the body is one and has many members, and all the members of the body, though many, are one body, so it is with Christ. For in the one Spirit we were all baptized into one body — Jews or Greeks, slaves or free — and we were all made to drink of one Spirit. Indeed, the body does not consist of one member but of many.

If the foot would say, "Because I am not a hand, I do not belong to the body," that would not make it any less a part of the body. And if the ear would say, "Because I am not an eye, I do not belong to the body," that would not make it any less a part of the body. If the whole body were an eye, where would the hearing be? If the whole body were hearing, where would the sense of smell be?

But as it is, God arranged the members in the body, each one of them, as he chose. If all were a single member, where would the body be? As it is, there are many members, yet one body. The eye cannot say to the hand, "I have no need of you," nor again the head to the feet, "I have no need of you." On the contrary, the members of the body that seem to be weaker are indispensable, and those members of the body that we think less honourable we clothe with greater honour, and our less respectable members are treated with greater respect; whereas our more respectable members do not need this.

But God has so arranged the body, giving the greater honour to the inferior member, that there may be no dissension within the body, but the members may have the same care for one another. If one member suffers, all suffer together with it; if one member is honoured, all rejoice together with it.

Now you are the body of Christ and individually members of it.

And God has appointed in the Church first Apostles, second Prophets, third Teachers; then deeds of power, then gifts of healing, forms of assistance, forms of leadership, various kinds of tongues.

Are all Apostles? Are all Prophets? Are all Teachers? Do all work miracles? Do all possess gifts of healing? Do all speak in tongues? Do all interpret?

The word of the Lord. **Thanks be to God.**

GOSPEL ACCLAMATION *(Luke 4.18-19)*

Alleluia. Alleluia. The Lord sent me to bring good news to the poor, to proclaim release to the captives. **Alleluia.**

GOSPEL *(Luke 1.1-4; 4.14-21)*
The Lord be with you. **And with your spirit.** A reading from the holy Gospel according to Luke. **Glory to you, O Lord.**

Since many have undertaken to set down an orderly account of the events that have been fulfilled among us, just as they were handed on to us by those who from the beginning were eyewitnesses and servants of the word, I too decided, after investigating everything carewfully from the very first, to write an orderly account for you, most excellent Theophilus, so that you may know the truth concerning the things about which you have been instructed.

Jesus, filled with the power of the Spirit, returned to Galilee, and a report about him spread through all the surrounding country. He began to teach in their synagogues and was praised by everyone. When he came to Nazareth, where he had been brought up, he went to the synagogue on the Sabbath day, as was his custom.

He stood up to read, and the scroll of the Prophet Isaiah was given to him. He unrolled the scroll and found the place where it was written: "The Spirit of the Lord is upon me, because he has anointed me to bring good news to the poor. He has sent me to proclaim release to the captives and recovery of sight to the blind, to let the oppressed go free, to proclaim the year of the Lord's favour."

And he rolled up the scroll, gave it back to the attendant, and sat down. The eyes of all in the synagogue were fixed on him.

Then he began to say to them, "Today this Scripture has been fulfilled in your hearing."

The Gospel of the Lord. **Praise to you, Lord Jesus Christ.**

PROFESSION OF FAITH *(p. 11)*

PRAYER OF THE FAITHFUL

The following intentions are suggestions only. There are more suggestions at www.livingwithchrist.ca

℟. **Lord, hear our prayer.**

For the Church, a sign of God's continuing presence among us, we pray to the Lord: ℟.

For leaders, building societies of justice, peace and mutual respect, we pray to the Lord: ℟.

For the weaker members of society and for those who defend their human dignity, we pray to the Lord: ℟.

For our communities, growing in peace and love through the Eucharist, we pray to the Lord: ℟.

PREPARATION OF THE GIFTS *(p. 14)*

PRAYER OVER THE OFFERINGS

Accept our offerings, O Lord, we pray, and in sanctifying them grant that they may profit us for salvation. Through Christ our Lord. **Amen.**

PREFACE *(Sundays in Ordinary Time, p. 28)*

COMMUNION ANTIPHON *(Cf. Psalm 33.6)*
Look toward the Lord and be radiant; let your faces not be abashed.

or (John 8.12)
I am the light of the world, says the Lord; whoever follows me will not walk in darkness, but will have the light of life.

PRAYER AFTER COMMUNION
Grant, we pray, almighty God, that, receiving the grace by which you bring us to new life, we may always glory in your gift. Through Christ our Lord. **Amen.**

BLESSING AND DISMISSAL *(p. 70)*

January 31

How could a synagogue assembly begin so well and end so disastrously? One might have thought that when Jesus announced the fulfillment of the Scriptures, those gathered would rejoice. Indeed, the Nazarenes were pleased with what Jesus had to say, happy that one of their own had done so well for himself, until Jesus made it clear that his mission, divine as it was, could not be contained by the smallness and insular character of the Nazarenes' vision. God's love was without limit.

In his teaching that Sabbath Day, Jesus revealed that the Nazarenes did not know their Scriptures as well as they thought they did. Quoting stories of the prophets Elijah and Elisha, he demonstrated that God's saving will had always extended beyond Israel to all nations. This scandalized the Nazarenes' religious sensibilities and enraged them. No longer able to recognize in Jesus a prophet-figure suited to their taste, they made miracle-working impossible.

The treatment of Jesus in today's gospel positions him in a long line of prophets appointed to proclaim a divine message to their great detriment. The readings prepare us for Jesus' approaching passion and death, and for our own trials as Christ's prophetic witnesses. Yet, they also calmly assure us that those whose concern is primarily the other rather than themselves will have God's protection and the enduring gift of an authentic life.

Christine Mader, Waverley, NS

ENTRANCE ANTIPHON *(Psalm 105.47)*
Save us, O Lord our God! And gather us from the nations, to give thanks to your holy name, and make it our glory to praise you.

INTRODUCTORY RITES *(p. 5)*

COLLECT
Grant us, Lord our God, that we may honour you with all our mind, and love everyone in truth of heart. Through our Lord Jesus Christ, your Son, who lives and reigns with you in the unity of the Holy Spirit, one God, for ever and ever. **Amen.**

FIRST READING *(Jeremiah 1.4-5, 17-19)*
The word of the Lord came to me saying, "Before I formed you in the womb I knew you, and before you were born I consecrated you; I appointed you a Prophet to the nations.

"Therefore, gird up your loins; stand up and tell the people everything that I command you. Do not break down before them, or I will break you before them. And I for my part have made you today a fortified city, an iron pillar, and a bronze wall, against the whole land — against the kings of Judah, its princes, its priests, and the people of the land.

"They will fight against you; but they shall not prevail against you, for I am with you, says the Lord, to deliver you."

The word of the Lord. **Thanks be to God.**

RESPONSORIAL PSALM *(Psalm 71)*

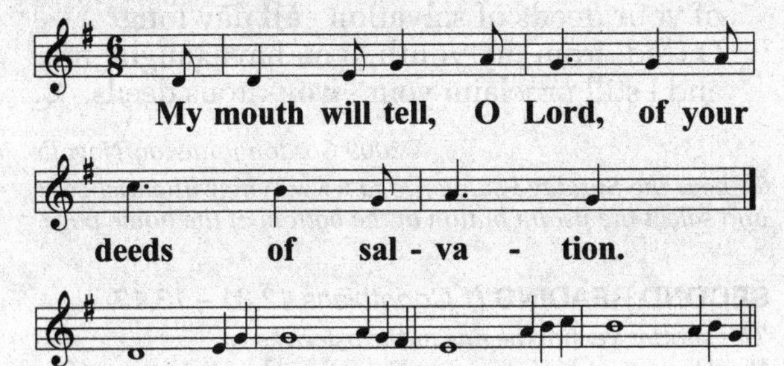

℟. **My mouth will tell, O Lord,**
of your deeds of salvation.

In you, O Lord, I · **take** refuge;
let me never be · **put** to shame.
In your righteousness de-·**liver_me**
and rescue_me;
incline your ear to · **me** and save_me. ℟.

Be to me a rock · **of** refuge,
a strong · **fortress,** to save_me,
for you are my rock · **and** my fortress.
Rescue me, O my God, from
the · **hand_of** the wicked. ℟.

For you, O Lord, are · **my** hope,
my trust, O Lord, · **from** my youth.
Upon you I have leaned · **from** my birth;
from my mother's womb you have · **been**
my strength. ℟.

My mouth will tell of your right·-**eous** acts,
of your deeds of salvation · **all** day long.
O God, from my youth · **you** have taught_me,
and I still proclaim your · **won**-drous deeds. ℟.

To hear the Sunday Psalms, go to www.livingwithchrist.ca and select the psalm button at the bottom of the home page.

SECOND READING *(1 Corinthians 12.31 – 13.13)*

The shorter version begins at the asterisks.

Brothers and sisters, strive for the greater gifts. And I will show you a still more excellent way.

If I speak in the tongues of human beings and of Angels, but do not have love, I am a noisy gong or a clanging cymbal. If I have prophetic powers, and understand all mysteries and all knowledge, and if I have all faith, so as to remove mountains, but do not have love, I am nothing. If I give away all my possessions, and if I hand over my body so that I may boast, but do not have love, I gain nothing.

* * *

Love is patient; love is kind; love is not envious or boastful or arrogant or rude. It does not insist on its own way; it is not irritable or resentful; it does not rejoice in wrongdoing, but rejoices in the truth. It bears all things, believes all things, hopes all things, endures all things. Love never ends.

But as for prophecies, they will come to an end; as for tongues, they will cease; as for knowledge, it will come to an end.

For we know only in part, and we prophesy only in part; but when the complete comes, the partial will come to an end.

When I was a child, I spoke like a child, I thought like a child, I reasoned like a child; when I became a man, I put an end to childish ways.

For now we see in a mirror, dimly, but then we will see face to face. Now I know only in part; then I will know fully, even as I have been fully known.

Now faith, hope, and love abide, these three; and the greatest of these is love.

The word of the Lord. **Thanks be to God.**

GOSPEL ACCLAMATION *(Luke 4.18-19)*

Alleluia. Alleluia. The Lord sent me to bring good news to the poor, to proclaim release to the captives. **Alleluia.**

GOSPEL *(Luke 4.21-30)*

The Lord be with you. **And with your spirit.**
A reading from the holy Gospel according to Luke. **Glory to you, O Lord.**

Jesus, filled with the power of the Spirit, came to Nazareth, where he had been brought up. He went to the synagogue on the Sabbath day, as was his custom, and read from the Prophet Isaiah. The eyes of all were fixed on him. Then he began to say to them, "Today this Scripture has been fulfilled in your hearing." All spoke well of him and were amazed at the gracious words that came from his mouth. They said, "Is not this Joseph's son?"

Jesus said to them, "Doubtless you will quote to me this proverb, 'Doctor, cure yourself!' And you will say, 'Do here also in your hometown the things that we have heard you did at Capernaum.'"

And he said, "Truly I tell you, no Prophet is accepted in his hometown. But the truth is, there were many widows in Israel in the time of Elijah, when the heaven was shut up three years and six months, and there was a severe famine over all the land; yet Elijah was sent to none of them except to a widow at Zarephath in Sidon. There were also many lepers in Israel in the time of the Prophet Elisha, and none of them was cleansed except Naaman the Syrian."

When they heard this, all in the synagogue were filled with rage. They got up, drove Jesus out of the town, and led him to the brow of the hill on which their town was built, so that they might hurl him off the cliff. But Jesus passed through the midst of them and went on his way.

The Gospel of the Lord. **Praise to you, Lord Jesus Christ.**

PROFESSION OF FAITH *(p. 11)*

PRAYER OF THE FAITHFUL

The following intentions are suggestions only. There are more suggestions at www.livingwithchrist.ca

℟. **Lord, hear our prayer.**

For Christians everywhere, called as Christ's Body to witness to the Good News, we pray to the Lord: ℟.

For nations of the world striving together to build a better life for all humanity, we pray to the Lord: ℟.

For those who suffer and struggle for meaning and purpose in life, we pray to the Lord: ℟.

For our community, whose journey is illuminated by the gifts of Scripture and the Holy Spirit, we pray to the Lord: ℟.

PREPARATION OF THE GIFTS *(p. 14)*

PRAYER OVER THE OFFERINGS
O Lord, we bring to your altar these offerings of our service: be pleased to receive them, we pray, and transform them into the Sacrament of our redemption. Through Christ our Lord. **Amen.**

PREFACE *(Sundays in Ordinary Time, p. 28)*

COMMUNION ANTIPHON *(Cf. Psalm 30.17-18)*
Let your face shine on your servant. Save me in your merciful love. O Lord, let me never be put to shame, for I call on you.

or (Matthew 5.3-4)

Blessed are the poor in spirit, for theirs is the Kingdom of Heaven. Blessed are the meek, for they shall possess the land.

PRAYER AFTER COMMUNION
Nourished by these redeeming gifts, we pray, O Lord, that through this help to eternal salvation true faith may ever increase. Through Christ our Lord. **Amen.**

BLESSING AND DISMISSAL *(p. 70)*

February Saints' Days

The following saints are traditionally remembered in February in Canada.

3	Saint Blaise Saint Ansgar
5	Saint Agatha
6	Saint Paul Miki and Companions
8	Saint Jerome Emiliani Saint Josephine Bakhita
10	Saint Scholastica
11	Our Lady of Lourdes
14	Saints Cyril and Methodius
17	The Seven Holy Founders of the Servite Order
21	Saint Peter Damian
23	Saint Polycarp

February 7

The greatest miracle of today's gospel reading may not have been that so many fish were caught, filling two boats. Rather, the most astounding miracle could have been that fishermen actually obeyed a carpenter's advice on how and where to do their job!

Many of us are unwilling to listen, much less respond, to the challenge of God's word in our lives. We may feel unworthy. (Could God *really* be that interested in me?) Certainly we can feel fear at what God's radical message challenges us to do. (Does God *really* expect me to love my neighbour as myself by visiting the prisoner, clothing the homeless, feeding the hungry?)

Yet here we are asked to consider the example of those who are renowned for giving their entire lives to God: people like Isaiah, Paul and Simon Peter. Surely they also felt trepidation at hearing God's call, felt themselves unworthy of the challenge put before them, and incapable of such faithfulness. Yet, they "put out into the deep" — and it changed their lives forever.

What is it that prevents us from "leaving everything" and following Jesus today? How are we being called, in the everyday events of our own lives? How can God's gift of faith, already present in our hearts, be encouraged to grow and bear fruit in all we do?

Joe Gunn, Ottawa, ON

ENTRANCE ANTIPHON *(Psalm 94.6-7)*
O come, let us worship God and bow low before the God who made us, for he is the Lord our God.

INTRODUCTORY RITES *(p. 5)*

COLLECT
Keep your family safe, O Lord, with unfailing care, that, relying solely on the hope of heavenly grace, they may be defended always by your protection. Through our Lord Jesus Christ, your Son, who lives and reigns with you in the unity of the Holy Spirit, one God, for ever and ever. **Amen.**

FIRST READING *(Isaiah 6.1-2a, 3-8)*
In the year that King Uzziah died, I saw the Lord sitting on a throne, high and lofty; and the hem of his robe filled the temple. Seraphs were in attendance above him; each had six wings. And one called to another and said: "Holy, holy, holy is the Lord of hosts; the whole earth is full of his glory." The pivots on the thresholds shook at the voices of those who called, and the house filled with smoke.

And I said: "Woe is me! I am lost, for I am a man of unclean lips, and I live among a people of unclean lips; yet my eyes have seen the King, the Lord of hosts!"

Then one of the seraphs flew to me, holding a live coal that had been taken from the altar with a pair of tongs. The seraph touched my mouth with it and said: "Now that this has touched your lips, your guilt has departed and your sin is blotted out."

Then I heard the voice of the Lord saying, "Whom shall I send, and who will go for us?" And I said, "Here am I; send me!"

The word of the Lord. **Thanks be to God.**

RESPONSORIAL PSALM *(Psalm 138)*

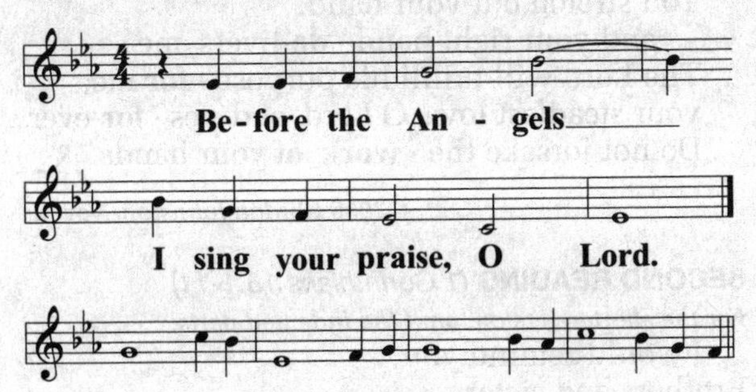

℟. **Before the Angels I sing your praise, O Lord.**

I give you thanks, O Lord,
with my · **whole** heart;
before the Angels I sing · **your** praise;
I bow down toward your holy temple,
and give thanks to · **your** name
for your steadfast · **love_and** your
faithfulness. ℟.

For you have exalted · **your** name
and your word a·-**bove** everything.
On the day I called, · **you** answered_me,
you increased my · **strength** of soul. ℟.

All the kings of the earth shall praise you,
  · **O** Lord,
for they have heard the words of · **your** mouth.
They shall sing of the ways of · **the** Lord,
for great is the · **glory** of_the Lord. ℟.

You stretch out your hand,
  and your right hand · **de**-livers_me.
The Lord will fulfill his purpose · **for** me;
your steadfast love, O Lord, endures · **for**-ever.
Do not forsake the · **work_of** your hands. ℟.

SECOND READING *(1 Corinthians 15.1-11)*

For the shorter version, omit the indented parts.

I would remind you,

Brothers and sisters,

of the good news that I proclaimed to you, which you in turn received, in which also you stand. This is the good news through which also you are being saved, if you hold firmly to the message that I proclaimed to you — unless you have come to believe in vain. For

I handed on to you as of first importance what I in turn had received: that Christ died for our sins in accordance with the Scriptures, and that he was buried, and that he was raised on the third day in accordance with the Scriptures, and that he appeared to Cephas, then to the twelve.

Then he appeared to more than five hundred of the brothers and sisters at one time, most of whom are still alive, though some have died. Then he appeared to James, then to all the Apostles. Last of all, as to one untimely born, he appeared also to me.

For I am the least of the Apostles, unfit to be called an Apostle, because I persecuted the Church of God. But by the grace of God I am what I am, and his grace toward me has not been in vain. On the contrary, I worked harder than any of the Apostles — though it was not I, but the grace of God that is with me.

Whether then it was I or they, so we proclaim and so you have come to believe.

The word of the Lord. **Thanks be to God.**

GOSPEL ACCLAMATION *(Matthew 4.19)*

Alleluia. Alleluia. Come follow me, says the Lord, and I will make you fishers of people. **Alleluia.**

GOSPEL *(Luke 5.1-11)*

The Lord be with you. **And with your spirit.** A reading from the holy Gospel according to Luke. **Glory to you, O Lord.**

While Jesus was standing beside the lake of Gennesaret, and the crowd was pressing in on him to hear the word of God, he saw two boats there at the shore of the lake; the fishermen had gone out of them and were washing their nets.

Jesus got into one of the boats, the one belonging to Simon, and asked him to put out a little way from the shore. Then he sat down and taught the crowds from the boat. When he had finished speaking, he said to Simon, "Put out into the deep water and let down your nets for a catch." Simon answered, "Master, we have worked all night long but have caught nothing. Yet if you say so, I will let down the nets." When they had done this, they caught so many fish that their nets were beginning to break. So they signalled their partners in the other boat to come and help them. And they came and filled both boats, so that they began to sink.

But when Simon Peter saw it, he fell down at Jesus' knees, saying, "Go away from me, Lord, for I am a sinful man!"

For Simon Peter and all who were with him were amazed at the catch of fish that they had taken; and so also were James and John, sons of Zebedee, who were partners with Simon. Then Jesus said to Simon, "Do not be afraid; from now on you will be catching people."

When they had brought their boats to shore, they left everything and followed Jesus.

The Gospel of the Lord. **Praise to you, Lord Jesus Christ.**

PROFESSION OF FAITH *(p. 11)*

PRAYER OF THE FAITHFUL

The following intentions are suggestions only. There are more suggestions at www.livingwithchrist.ca

℟. **Lord, hear our prayer.**

For the Church, witnessing to the life-giving Spirit of Christ in our society, we pray to the Lord: ℟.

For wisdom and integrity for leaders throughout the world, we pray to the Lord: ℟.

For those who live in hope of the spiritual blessings promised by God, we pray to the Lord: ℟.

For the grace to be open to all that God has in store for us, we pray to the Lord: ℟.

PREPARATION OF THE GIFTS *(p. 14)*

PRAYER OVER THE OFFERINGS
O Lord our God, who once established these created things to sustain us in our frailty, grant, we pray, that they may become for us now the Sacrament of eternal life. Through Christ our Lord. **Amen.**

PREFACE *(Sundays in Ordinary Time, p. 28)*

COMMUNION ANTIPHON *(Cf. Psalm 106.8-9)*
Let them thank the Lord for his mercy, his wonders for the children of men, for he satisfies the thirsty soul, and the hungry he fills with good things.

or (Matthew 5.5-6)

Blessed are those who mourn, for they shall be consoled. Blessed are those who hunger and thirst for righteousness, for they shall have their fill.

PRAYER AFTER COMMUNION
O God, who have willed that we be partakers in the one Bread and the one Chalice, grant us, we pray, so to live that, made one in Christ, we may joyfully bear fruit for the salvation of the world. Through Christ our Lord. **Amen.**

BLESSING AND DISMISSAL *(p. 70)*

February 10

Today, as we begin the season of Lent, the gospel reading gives us some tips on the *do's* and *don'ts* of our traditional Lenten practices.

In the gospel, Jesus contrasts the proud behaviour of the hypocrites with the attitude of humility that characterizes a true disciple. The hypocrites love to make a show of their spiritual practices; in contrast, Jesus instructs his disciples to do good quietly, to pray privately, and to fast with a sense of dignified joy.

The hypocrites' showy displays of piety neither please nor fool God. There is a similar message in the reading from the prophet Joel. The contrite heart pleases God more than the outward signs of fasting: "rend your hearts and not your clothing," says the Lord.

When our hearts are properly disposed, our Lenten observances help us to refocus our attention on God, to restore our relationship with God, and to recommit our lives to God. Prayer opens our hearts and minds to God. Acts of self-denial help us to detach from the things that distract us from God. Acts of charity express our participation with Jesus in proclaiming the kingdom of God.

During our celebration of the liturgy today, let us receive the ashes with joy, ever mindful, as Saint Paul writes to the Corinthians, that the time of salvation is now!

Louise McEwan, Trail, BC

ENTRANCE ANTIPHON *(Wisdom 11.24, 25, 27)*
You are merciful to all, O Lord, and despise nothing that you have made. You overlook people's sins, to bring them to repentance, and you spare them, for you are the Lord our God.

GREETING *(p. 5)*
The Penitential Act *and the* Glory to God *are omitted today.*

COLLECT
Grant, O Lord, that we may begin with holy fasting this campaign of Christian service, so that, as we take up battle against spiritual evils, we may be armed with weapons of self-restraint. Through our Lord Jesus Christ, your Son, who lives and reigns with you in the unity of the Holy Spirit, one God, for ever and ever. **Amen.**

FIRST READING *(Joel 2.12-18)*
Even now, says the Lord, return to me with all your heart, with fasting, with weeping, and with mourning; rend your hearts and not your clothing.

Return to the Lord, your God, for he is gracious and merciful, slow to anger, and abounding in steadfast love, and relents from punishing.

Who knows whether the Lord will not turn and relent, and leave a blessing behind him: a grain offering and a drink offering to be presented to the Lord, your God?

Blow the trumpet in Zion; sanctify a fast; call a solemn assembly; gather the people. Sanctify the congregation; assemble the aged; gather the children, even infants at the breast. Let the bridegroom leave his room, and the bride her canopy.

Between the vestibule and the altar let the priests, the ministers of the Lord, weep. Let them say, “Spare your people, O Lord, and do not make your heritage a mockery, a byword among the nations. Why should it be said among the peoples, ‘Where is their God?’”

Then the Lord became jealous for his land, and had pity on his people.

The word of the Lord. **Thanks be to God.**

RESPONSORIAL PSALM *(Psalm 51)*

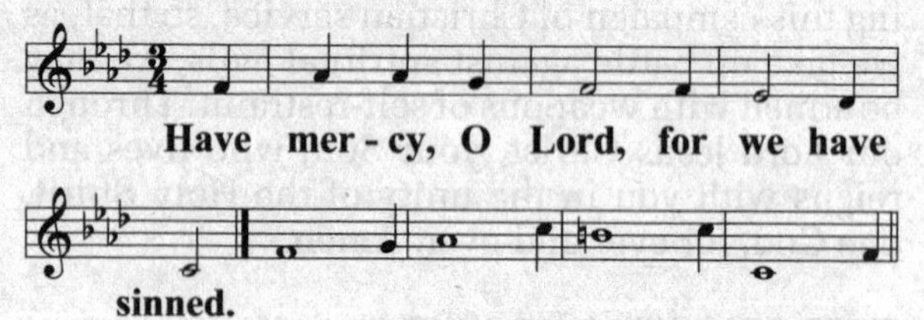

℟. **Have mercy, O Lord, for we have sinned.**

Have mercy on me, O God, according
to your steadfast · **love;**
according to your abundant mercy blot out
my trans·**-gressions.**
Wash me thoroughly from my in·**-iquity,**
and cleanse me from my · **sin.** ℟.

For I know my trans·**-gressions,**
and my sin is ever be·**-fore_me.**
Against you, you alone, have I · **sinned,**
and done what is evil in your · **sight.** ℟.

Create in me a clean heart, O · **God,**
and put a new and right spirit with·-**in_me.**
Do not cast me away from your · **presence,**
and do not take your holy spirit from · **me.** ℟.

Restore to me the joy of your sal·-**vation,**
and sustain in me a willing · **spirit.**
O Lord, open my · **lips,**
and my mouth will declare your · **praise.** ℟.

To hear the Sunday Psalms, go to www.livingwithchrist.ca and select the psalm button at the bottom of the home page.

SECOND READING *(2 Corinthians 5.20 – 6.2)*

Brothers and sisters: We are ambassadors for Christ, since God is making his appeal through us; we entreat you on behalf of Christ, be reconciled to God. For our sake God made Christ to be sin who knew no sin, so that in Christ we might become the righteousness of God. As we work together with him, we urge you also not to accept the grace of God in vain. For the Lord says, "At an acceptable time I have listened to you, and on a day of salvation I have helped you." See, now is the acceptable time; see, now is the day of salvation!

The word of the Lord. **Thanks be to God.**

GOSPEL ACCLAMATION *(Psalm 95.7-8)*

Glory and praise to you, Lord Jesus Christ! Today, do not harden your hearts, but listen to the voice of the Lord. **Glory and praise to you, Lord Jesus Christ!**

GOSPEL *(Matthew 6.1-6, 16-18)*
The Lord be with you. **And with your spirit.** A reading from the holy Gospel according to Matthew. **Glory to you, O Lord.**

Jesus said to the disciples: "Beware of practising your piety before people in order to be seen by them; for then you have no reward from your Father in heaven.

"So whenever you give alms, do not sound a trumpet before you, as the hypocrites do in the synagogues and in the streets, so that they may be praised by others. Truly I tell you, they have received their reward. But when you give alms, do not let your left hand know what your right hand is doing, so that your alms may be done in secret; and your Father who sees in secret will reward you.

"And whenever you pray, do not be like the hypocrites; for they love to stand and pray in the synagogues and at the street corners, so that they may be seen by others. Truly I tell you, they have received their reward. But whenever you pray, go into your room and shut the door and pray to your Father who is in secret; and your Father who sees in secret will reward you.

"And whenever you fast, do not look dismal, like the hypocrites, for they disfigure their faces so as to show others that they are fasting. Truly I tell you, they have received their reward. But when you fast, put oil on your head and wash your face, so that your fasting may be seen not by others but by your Father who is in secret; and your Father who sees in secret will reward you."

The Gospel of the Lord. **Praise to you, Lord Jesus Christ.**

BLESSING AND DISTRIBUTION OF ASHES

Dear brothers and sisters, let us humbly ask God our Father that he be pleased to bless with the abundance of his grace these ashes, which we will put on our heads in penitence. *(Pause)*

1 O God, who are moved by acts of humility and respond with forgiveness to works of penance, lend your merciful ear to our prayers and in your kindness pour out the grace of your blessing on your servants who are marked with these ashes, that, as they follow the Lenten observances, they may be worthy to come with minds made pure to celebrate the Paschal Mystery of your Son. Through Christ our Lord. **Amen.**

2 O God, who desire not the death of sinners, but their conversion, mercifully hear our prayers and in your kindness be pleased to bless these ashes, which we intend to receive upon our heads, that we, who acknowledge we are but ashes and shall return to dust, may, through a steadfast observance of Lent, gain pardon for sins and newness of life after the likeness of your Risen Son. Who lives and reigns for ever and ever. **Amen.**

While the faithful come forward to receive ashes, an appropriate song may be sung.

1 Repent, and believe in the Gospel.

2 Remember that you are dust, and to dust you shall return.

PRAYER OF THE FAITHFUL

The following intentions are suggestions only. More suggestions are available at www.livingwithchrist.ca

℟. **Lord, hear our prayer.**

For all Christians, as we enter this special season of Lent, we pray to the Lord: ℟.

For the nations of the world seeking truth and peace, we pray to the Lord: ℟.

For people everywhere who struggle to meet their basic needs, we pray to the Lord: ℟.

For this parish community as we begin our Lenten journey together, we pray to the Lord: ℟.

* *Ash Wednesday Service: When ashes are blessed outside Mass, the ceremony concludes with the* Prayer over the People *and the* Blessing *(p. 187).*

PREPARATION OF THE GIFTS *(p. 14)*

PRAYER OVER THE OFFERINGS

As we solemnly offer the annual sacrifice for the beginning of Lent, we entreat you, O Lord, that, through works of penance and charity, we may turn away from harmful pleasures and, cleansed from our sins, may become worthy to celebrate devoutly the Passion of your Son. Who lives and reigns for ever and ever. **Amen.**

PREFACE *(Lent III-IV, p. 20)*

COMMUNION ANTIPHON *(Cf. Psalm 1.2-3)*
He who ponders the law of the Lord day and night will yield fruit in due season.

PRAYER AFTER COMMUNION
May the Sacrament we have received sustain us, O Lord, that our Lenten fast may be pleasing to you and be for us a healing remedy. Through Christ our Lord. **Amen.**

PRAYER OVER THE PEOPLE
Pour out a spirit of compunction, O God, on those who bow before your majesty, and by your mercy may they merit the rewards you promise to those who do penance. Through Christ our Lord. **Amen.**

BLESSING AND DISMISSAL *(p. 70)*

February 14

When Jesus heads out into the wilderness, he is accompanied by the Holy Spirit, the source and author of mission. Here, Jesus is challenged to make choices about his identity and how he would live his mission.

Each test the devil poses begins, "If you are the Son of God." Citing scripture, Jesus responds, "It is written." Jesus is tested to see if he is totally committed to God's mission for him; tested to believe that he can serve God without suffering; tested about his attitude toward power and wealth. In summary, Jesus claims the primacy of God and of God's reign.

The first reading from Deuteronomy reveals the liberating love of God in history, while Saint Paul reminds us that, for us as disciples, "the word of faith that we proclaim" comes from the heart of God and must find a home in our hearts.

From my time in Peru, I can still hear the reflections of the native theologian Gustavo Gutiérrez, who would remind us that we go to the word of God to read it and it reads us; we go to it with our questions and it in turn questions us; we go to it as the revealed word of God and it reveals us to ourselves. Such is the power of the Word of God. May God's Word and God's Spirit renew our discipleship during Lent.

Fr. Jack Lynch, SFM, Scarborough, ON

Parishes engaged in the Rite of Christian Initiation of Adults (RCIA) *may celebrate the* Rite of Election *today.*

ENTRANCE ANTIPHON *(Cf. Psalm 90.15-16)*

When he calls on me, I will answer him; I will deliver him and give him glory, I will grant him length of days.

Rite of Election (Cf. Ps 104.3-4):

Let the hearts that seek the Lord rejoice; turn to the Lord and his strength; constantly seek his face.

INTRODUCTORY RITES *(p. 5)*

COLLECT

Grant, almighty God, through the yearly observances of holy Lent, that we may grow in understanding of the riches hidden in Christ and by worthy conduct pursue their effects. Through our Lord Jesus Christ, your Son, who lives and reigns with you in the unity of the Holy Spirit, one God, for ever and ever. **Amen.**

Rite of Election:

O God, who though you are ever the cause of the salvation of the human race now gladden your people with grace in still greater measure, look mercifully, we pray, upon your chosen ones, that your compassionate and protecting help may defend both those yet to be born anew and those already reborn. Through our Lord Jesus Christ, your Son, who lives and reigns with you in the unity of the Holy Spirit, one God, for ever and ever. **Amen.**

FIRST READING *(Deuteronomy 26.4-10)*
Moses spoke to the people, saying: "When the priest takes the basket from your hand and sets it down before the altar of the Lord your God, you shall make this response before the Lord your God:

"'A wandering Aramean was my father; he went down into Egypt and lived there as an alien, few in number, and there he became a great nation, mighty and populous. When the Egyptians treated us harshly and afflicted us, by imposing hard labour on us, we cried to the Lord, the God of our fathers; the Lord heard our voice and saw our affliction, our toil, and our oppression.

"'The Lord brought us out of Egypt with a mighty hand and an outstretched arm, with a terrifying display of power, and with signs and wonders; and he brought us into this place and gave us this land, a land flowing with milk and honey. So now I bring the first of the fruit of the ground that you, O Lord, have given me.'"

And Moses continued, "You shall set it down before the Lord your God and bow down before the Lord your God."

The word of the Lord. **Thanks be to God.**

RESPONSORIAL PSALM *(Psalm 91)*

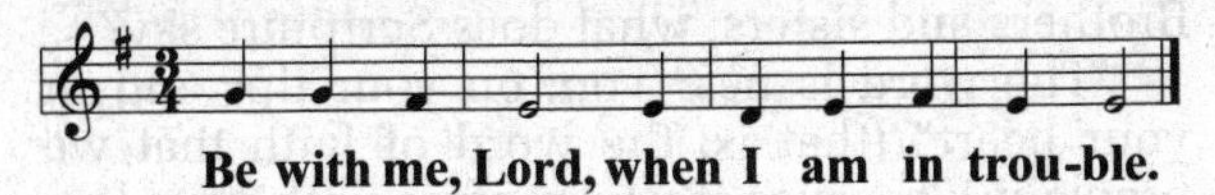

℟. **Be with me, Lord, when I am in trouble.**

You who live in the shelter of the Most · **High,**
who abide in the shadow of the · **Al**-mighty,
will say to the Lord, "My refuge
and my · **fortress;**
my God, in whom · **I** trust." ℟.

No evil shall be·-**fall_you**,
no scourge come near · **your** tent.
For he will command his Angels
con·-**cerning_you**
to guard you in all · **your** ways. ℟.

On their hands they will bear you · **up,**
so that you will not dash your foot
against · **a** stone.
You will tread on the lion and the · **adder,**
the young lion and the serpent you will
trample · **under** foot. ℟.

The one who loves me, I will de·-**liver;**
I will protect the one who knows · **my** name.
When he calls to me, I will · **answer_him**;
I will be with him in trouble, I will rescue
him· **and** honour_him. ℟.

SECOND READING *(Romans 10.8-13)*
Brothers and sisters, what does Scripture say?

"The word is near you, on your lips and in your heart" (that is, the word of faith that we proclaim); because if you confess with your lips that Jesus is Lord and believe in your heart that God raised him from the dead, you will be saved.

For one believes with the heart and so is justified, and one confesses with the mouth and so is saved.

The Scripture says, "No one who believes in him will be put to shame." For there is no distinction between Jew and Greek; the same Lord is Lord of all and is generous to all who call on him. For, "Everyone who calls on the name of the Lord shall be saved."

The word of the Lord. **Thanks be to God.**

GOSPEL ACCLAMATION *(Matthew 4.4)*
Glory and praise to you, Lord Jesus Christ! Man does not live by bread alone, but by every word that comes from the mouth of God. **Glory and praise to you, Lord Jesus Christ!**

GOSPEL *(Luke 4.1-13)*
The Lord be with you. **And with your spirit.** A reading from the holy Gospel according to Luke. **Glory to you, O Lord.**

Jesus, full of the Holy Spirit, returned from the Jordan and was led by the Spirit in the wilderness, where for forty days he was tempted by the devil. He ate nothing at all during those days, and when they were over, he was famished.

The devil said to him, "If you are the Son of God, command this stone to become a loaf of bread." Jesus answered him, "It is written, 'Man does not live by bread alone.'"

Then the devil led him up and showed him in an instant all the kingdoms of the world. And the devil said to him, "To you I will give their glory and all this authority; for it has been given over to me, and I give it to anyone I please. If you, then, will worship me, it will all be yours." Jesus answered him, "It is written, 'Worship the Lord your God, and serve only him.'"

Then the devil took him to Jerusalem, and placed him on the pinnacle of the temple, saying to him, "If you are the Son of God, throw yourself down from here, for it is written, 'He will command his Angels concerning you, to protect you,' and 'On their hands they will bear you up, so that you will not dash your foot against a stone.'" Jesus answered him, "It is said, 'Do not put the Lord your God to the test.'"

When the devil had finished every test, he departed from him until an opportune time.

The Gospel of the Lord. **Praise to you, Lord Jesus Christ.**

For parishes engaged in the RCIA, the Rite of Election *takes place now.*

PROFESSION OF FAITH *(p. 11)*

PRAYER OF THE FAITHFUL

The following intentions are suggestions only. More suggestions are available at www.livingwithchrist.ca

℟. **Lord, hear our prayer.**

For Church leaders, shining the light of the gospel on the challenges of today, we pray to the Lord: ℟.

For world leaders, called to foster God's reign on earth, we pray to the Lord: ℟.

For those who live in fear or loneliness, and for those who are called to respond to them, we pray to the Lord: ℟.

For our community, ever seeking to be true followers of Jesus, we pray to the Lord: ℟.

PREPARATION OF THE GIFTS *(p. 14)*

PRAYER OVER THE OFFERINGS

Give us the right dispositions, O Lord, we pray, to make these offerings, for with them we celebrate the beginning of this venerable and sacred time. Through Christ our Lord. **Amen.**

Rite of Election:

Almighty ever-living God, who restore us by the Sacrament of Baptism to eternal life as we confess your name, receive, we beseech you, the offerings and prayers of your servants and command that those who hope in you may have their desires fulfilled and their sins cancelled out. Through Christ our Lord. **Amen.**

PREFACE *(1st Sunday of Lent, p. 20)*

COMMUNION ANTIPHON *(Matthew 4.4)*
One does not live by bread alone, but by every word that comes forth from the mouth of God.
or (Cf. Psalm 90.4)
The Lord will conceal you with his pinions, and under his wings you will trust.
Rite of Election (Ephesians 1.7):
In Christ, we have redemption by his Blood and forgiveness of our sins, in accord with the riches of his grace.

PRAYER AFTER COMMUNION
Renewed now with heavenly bread, by which faith is nourished, hope increased, and charity strengthened, we pray, O Lord, that we may learn to hunger for Christ, the true and living Bread, and strive to live by every word which proceeds from your mouth. Through Christ our Lord. **Amen.**
Rite of Election:
May this Sacrament we have received purify us, we pray, O Lord, and grant your servants freedom from all blame, that those bound by a guilty conscience may glory in the fullness of heavenly remedy. Through Christ our Lord. **Amen.**

PRAYER OVER THE PEOPLE
May bountiful blessing, O Lord, we pray, come down upon your people, that hope may grow in tribulation, virtue be strengthened in temptation, and eternal redemption be assured. Through Christ our Lord. **Amen.**

BLESSING AND DISMISSAL *(p. 70)*

February 21

Today's gospel story is astounding! Jesus took three disciples with him to a mountaintop to pray. Before their very eyes, his appearance was gloriously transformed. Two prophets from long ago then appeared and spoke with Jesus about his imminent death. Can we even *begin* to imagine the emotions that surface in the three as they witness the unfolding scene? No strangers to Jesus' miracles, even they must have agreed that this moment surpassed anything that they had ever seen!

Although filled with a desire to sleep, "they stayed awake" and beheld the ultimate splendour of Jesus. They heard the voice of his father proclaim, "This is my Son, my Chosen; listen to Him!" What was their inner response? Fear? Awe and wonder? A deepened awareness of the identity of Jesus? A new sense of mission?

As followers of Jesus, we, too, must "stay awake" to recognize his presence in the myriad situations of our lives. We don't hear God's voice coming from a cloud, but when we listen, we hear his voice in the silence of our hearts. God also speaks to us through contemporary prophets who guide us on our spiritual journey.

At the moment of the Transfiguration, Peter and his companions beheld the face of Jesus. Our hearts longingly cry out, "Your face, O Lord, do I seek."

Barbara d'Artois, Pierrefonds, QC

ENTRANCE ANTIPHON *(Cf. Psalm 26.8-9)*
Of you my heart has spoken: Seek his face. It is your face, O Lord, that I seek; hide not your face from me.
or (Cf. Psalm 24.6, 2, 22)
Remember your compassion, O Lord, and your merciful love, for they are from of old. Let not our enemies exult over us. Redeem us, O God of Israel, from all our distress.

INTRODUCTORY RITES *(p. 5)*

COLLECT
O God, who have commanded us to listen to your beloved Son, be pleased, we pray, to nourish us inwardly by your word, that, with spiritual sight made pure, we may rejoice to behold your glory. Through our Lord Jesus Christ, your Son, who lives and reigns with you in the unity of the Holy Spirit, one God, for ever and ever. **Amen.**

FIRST READING *(Genesis 15.5-12, 17-18)*
The Lord said to Abram: "Look toward heaven and count the stars, if you are able to count them." Then he said to him, "So shall your descendants be." And he believed the Lord; and the Lord reckoned it to him as righteousness.

Then the Lord said to Abram, "I am the Lord who brought you from Ur of the Chaldeans, to give you this land to possess." But Abram said, "O Lord God, how am I to know that I shall possess it?"

The Lord said to him, "Bring me a heifer three years old, a female goat three years old, a ram three years old, a turtledove, and a young pigeon." Abram brought the Lord all these and cut them in two, laying each half over against the other; but he did not cut the birds in two. And when birds of prey came down on the carcasses, Abram drove them away.

As the sun was going down, a deep sleep fell upon Abram, and a deep and terrifying darkness descended upon him. When the sun had gone down and it was dark, a smoking fire pot and a flaming torch passed between these pieces.

On that day the Lord made a covenant with Abram, saying, "To your descendants I give this land, from the river of Egypt to the great river, the river Euphrates."

The word of the Lord. **Thanks be to God.**

RESPONSORIAL PSALM *(Psalm 27)*

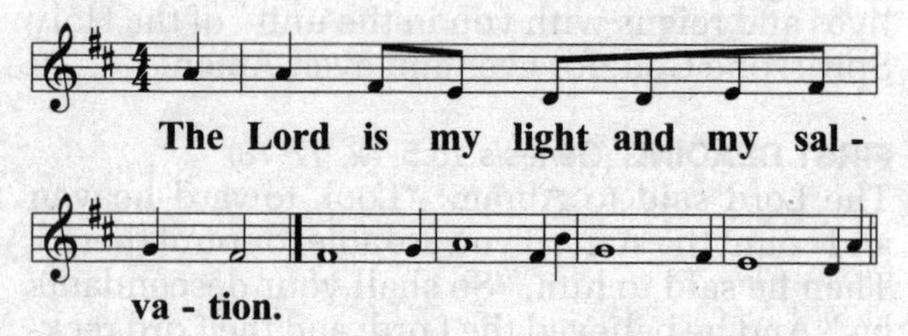

℟. **The Lord is my light and my salvation.**

The Lord is my light and my sal·-**vation;**
whom shall · **I** fear?
The Lord is the stronghold of my · **life;**
of whom shall I be · **a**-fraid? ℟.

Hear, O Lord, when I cry a·-**loud,**
be gracious to me · **and** answer_me!
"Come," my heart says, "seek his · **face!"**
Your face, Lord, do · **I** seek. ℟.

Do not hide your face from · **me.**
Do not turn your servant away · **in** anger,
you who have been my · **help.**
Do not cast me off, do not forsake me,
O God of my · **sal**-vation! ℟.

I believe that I shall see the goodness
of the · **Lord**
in the land of · **the** living.
Wait for the Lord; be · **strong,**
and let your heart take courage;
wait · **for_the** Lord! ℟.

To hear the Sunday Psalms, go to www.livingwithchrist.ca and select the psalm button at the bottom of the home page.

SECOND READING *(Philippians 3.17 – 4.1)*

The shorter version begins at the asterisks.

Brothers and sisters, join in imitating me, and observe those who live according to the example you have in us. For many live as enemies of the Cross of Christ; I have often told you of them, and now I tell you even with tears. Their end is destruction; their god is the belly; and their glory is in their shame; their minds are set on earthly things.

* * *

But our citizenship is in heaven, and it is from there that we are expecting a Saviour, the Lord Jesus Christ. He will transform the body of our humiliation that it may be conformed to the body of his glory, by the power that also enables him to make all things subject to himself.

Therefore, my brothers and sisters, whom I love and long for, my joy and crown, stand firm, my beloved, in the Lord in this way.

The word of the Lord. **Thanks be to God.**

GOSPEL ACCLAMATION *(Luke 9.35)*

Glory and praise to you, Lord Jesus Christ! From the bright cloud the Father's voice is heard: This is my Son, the Beloved; listen to him. **Glory and praise to you, Lord Jesus Christ!**

GOSPEL *(Luke 9.28b-36)*

The Lord be with you. **And with your spirit.** A reading from the holy Gospel according to Luke. **Glory to you, O Lord.**

Jesus took with him Peter and John and James, and went up on the mountain to pray. And while he was praying, the appearance of his face changed, and his clothes became dazzling white.

Suddenly they saw two men, Moses and Elijah, talking to Jesus. They appeared in glory and were speaking of his exodus, which he was about to accomplish at Jerusalem.

Now Peter and his companions were weighed down with sleep; but since they had stayed awake, they saw his glory and the two men who stood with him.

Just as they were leaving him, Peter said to Jesus, "Master, it is good for us to be here; let us make three dwellings, one for you, one for Moses, and one for Elijah," but Peter did not know what he said.

While he was saying this, a cloud came and overshadowed them; and they were terrified as they entered the cloud. Then from the cloud came a voice that said, "This is my Son, my Chosen; listen to him!" When the voice had spoken, Jesus was found alone.

And the disciples kept silent and in those days told no one any of the things they had seen.

The Gospel of the Lord. **Praise to you, Lord Jesus Christ.**

PROFESSION OF FAITH *(p. 11)*

PRAYER OF THE FAITHFUL

The following intentions are suggestions only. More suggestions are available at www.livingwithchrist.ca

℟. **Lord, hear our prayer.**

For the Church, sacrament of God's grace in the world, we pray to the Lord: ℟.

For leaders of government who long for justice for their people, we pray to the Lord: ℟.

For those who despair of receiving God's mercy and forgiveness, we pray to the Lord: ℟.

For our community, coming together to love one another, we pray to the Lord: ℟.

PREPARATION OF THE GIFTS *(p. 14)*

PRAYER OVER THE OFFERINGS

May this sacrifice, O Lord, we pray, cleanse us of our faults and sanctify your faithful in body and mind for the celebration of the paschal festivities. Through Christ our Lord. **Amen.**

PREFACE *(2nd Sunday of Lent, p. 21)*

COMMUNION ANTIPHON *(Matthew 17.5)*

This is my beloved Son, with whom I am well pleased; listen to him.

PRAYER AFTER COMMUNION

As we receive these glorious mysteries, we make thanksgiving to you, O Lord, for allowing us while still on earth to be partakers even now of the things of heaven. Through Christ our Lord. **Amen.**

PRAYER OVER THE PEOPLE

Bless your faithful, we pray, O Lord, with a blessing that endures for ever, and keep them faithful to the Gospel of your Only Begotten Son, so that they may always desire and at last attain that glory whose beauty he showed in his own Body, to the amazement of his Apostles. Through Christ our Lord. **Amen.**

BLESSING AND DISMISSAL *(p. 70)*

February 28

Time is an artificial measure established by humans to mark change. We mark the passing of time with birthdays and anniversaries; some we want to remember, others we would like to forget.

For God, there is no time. Today's reading from Isaiah reminds us that God's thoughts are not our thoughts, and God's ways are not our ways. Human understanding is limited. In the psalm, we are told that God's love is "better than life." Pope Francis teaches us that "God never tires of loving us but we tire of loving God."

God gives us the time we need to repent and return to a relationship with him, just as the gardener in today's gospel is given the time he needs to help the fig tree produce fruit. One more year in the mind of God is not the same as one more year in our limited way of thinking about time. Of course, we ought not to presume upon God's goodness, and Saint Paul does tell us that those who put Christ to the test "are struck down." Today, as we gather around the table of the Lord, we have one more time to turn to God, to refresh and renew ourselves so that we may produce good fruit and go forth to help others do the same.

Anthony Chezzi, Sudbury, ON

Parishes engaged in the Rite of Christian Initiation of Adults (RCIA) *may celebrate the* 1st Scrutiny *today (p. 210).*

ENTRANCE ANTIPHON *(Cf. Psalm 24.15-16)*
My eyes are always on the Lord, for he rescues my feet from the snare. Turn to me and have mercy on me, for I am alone and poor.
or (Cf. Ezekiel 36.23-26)
When I prove my holiness among you, I will gather you from all the foreign lands; and I will pour clean water upon you and cleanse you from all your impurities, and I will give you a new spirit, says the Lord.

INTRODUCTORY RITES *(p. 5)*

COLLECT
O God, author of every mercy and of all goodness, who in fasting, prayer and almsgiving have shown us a remedy for sin, look graciously on this confession of our lowliness, that we, who are bowed down by our conscience, may always be lifted up by your mercy. Through our Lord Jesus Christ, your Son, who lives and reigns with you in the unity of the Holy Spirit, one God, for ever and ever. **Amen.**

FIRST READING *(Exodus 3.1-8a, 13-15)*
Moses was keeping the flock of his father-in-law Jethro, the priest of Midian; he led his flock beyond the wilderness, and came to Horeb, the mountain of God. There the Angel of the Lord appeared to him in a flame of fire out of a bush; Moses looked, and the bush was blazing, yet it was not consumed.

Then Moses said, "I must turn aside and look at this great sight, and see why the bush is not burned up."

When the Lord saw that Moses had turned aside to see, God called to him out of the bush, "Moses, Moses!" And Moses said, "Here I am." Then God said, "Come no closer! Remove the sandals from your feet, for the place on which you are standing is holy ground."

God said further, "I am the God of your fathers, the God of Abraham, the God of Isaac, and the God of Jacob." And Moses hid his face, for he was afraid to look at God.

Then the Lord said, "I have observed the misery of my people who are in Egypt; I have heard their cry on account of their taskmasters. Indeed, I know their sufferings, and I have come down to deliver them from the Egyptians, and to bring them up out of that land to a good and broad land, a land flowing with milk and honey."

But Moses said to God, "If I come to the children of Israel and say to them, 'The God of your fathers has sent me to you,' and they ask me, 'What is his name?' what shall I say to them?"

God said to Moses, "I AM WHO I AM." He said further, "Thus you shall say to the children of Israel, 'I AM has sent me to you.'"

God also said to Moses, "Thus you shall say to the children of Israel, 'The Lord, the God of your fathers, the God of Abraham, the God of Isaac, and the God of Jacob, has sent me to you.' This is my name forever, and this my memorial for all generations."

The word of the Lord. **Thanks be to God.**

RESPONSORIAL PSALM *(Psalm 103)*

℟. **The Lord is merciful and gracious.**

Bless the Lord, O my · **soul,**
and all that is within me, bless his · **holy** name.
Bless the Lord, O my · **soul,**
and do not forget all · **his** benefits. ℟.

It is the Lord who forgives all your in·-**iquity,**
who heals all your · **dis**-eases,
who redeems your life from the · **Pit,**
who crowns you with steadfast love
· **and** mercy. ℟.

The Lord works vindi·-**cation**
and justice for all who are · **op**-pressed.
He made known his ways to · **Moses,**
his acts to the people · **of** Israel. ℟.

The Lord is merciful and · **gracious,**
slow to anger and abounding in
stead·-**fast** love.
For as the heavens are high above the · **earth,**
so great is his steadfast love toward those
· **who** fear_him. ℟.

To hear the Sunday Psalms, go to www.livingwithchrist.ca and select the psalm button at the bottom of the home page.

SECOND READING *(1 Corinthians 10.1-6, 10-12)*
I do not want you to be unaware, brothers and sisters, that our ancestors were all under the cloud; all passed through the sea; all were baptized into Moses in the cloud and in the sea; all ate the same spiritual food, and all drank the same spiritual drink. For they drank from the spiritual rock that followed them, and the rock was Christ. Nevertheless, God was not pleased with most of them, and they were struck down in the wilderness.

Now these things occurred as examples for us, so that we might not desire evil as they did. And do not complain as some of them did, and were destroyed by the destroyer. These things happened to them to serve as an example, and they were written down to instruct us, on whom the ends of the ages have come. So if you think you are standing, watch out that you do not fall.

The word of the Lord. **Thanks be to God.**

GOSPEL ACCLAMATION *(Matthew 4.17)*
Glory and praise to you, Lord Jesus Christ! Repent, says the Lord; the kingdom of heaven is at hand. **Glory and praise to you, Lord Jesus Christ!**

GOSPEL *(Luke 13.1-9)*
The Lord be with you. **And with your spirit.** A reading from the holy Gospel according to Luke. **Glory to you, O Lord.**

Jesus was teaching the crowds; some of those present told Jesus about the Galileans whose blood Pilate had mingled with their sacrifices.

Jesus asked them, "Do you think that because these Galileans suffered in this way they were worse sinners than all other Galileans? No, I tell you; but unless you repent, you will all perish as they did. Or those eighteen who were killed when the tower of Siloam fell on them — do you think that they were worse offenders than all the others living in Jerusalem? No, I tell you; but unless you repent, you will all perish just as they did."

Then Jesus told this parable: "A man had a fig tree planted in his vineyard; and he came looking for fruit on it and found none. So he said to the gardener, 'See here! For three years I have come looking for fruit on this fig tree, and still I find none. Cut it down! Why should it be wasting the soil?'

"The gardener replied, 'Sir, let it alone for one more year, until I dig around it and put manure on it. If it bears fruit next year, well and good; but if not, you can cut it down.'"

The Gospel of the Lord. **Praise to you, Lord Jesus Christ.**

PROFESSION OF FAITH *(p. 11)*

PRAYER OF THE FAITHFUL

The following intentions are suggestions only. More suggestions are available at www.livingwithchrist.ca

℟. **Lord, hear our prayer.**

For the Church, called to be an agent of transformation, we pray to the Lord: ℟.

For healing in all the shattered places on this earth, we pray to the Lord: ℟.

For all who feel lost and abandoned, we pray to the Lord: ℟.

For the grace, as individuals and as Church, to be faithful in our witness, we pray to the Lord: R.

PREPARATION OF THE GIFTS *(p. 14)*

PRAYER OVER THE OFFERINGS
Be pleased, O Lord, with these sacrificial offerings, and grant that we who beseech pardon for our own sins may take care to forgive our neighbour. Through Christ our Lord. **Amen.**

PREFACE *(Lent I-II, p. 19)*

COMMUNION ANTIPHON *(Cf. Psalm 83.4-5)*
The sparrow finds a home, and the swallow a nest for her young: by your altars, O Lord of hosts, my King and my God. Blessed are they who dwell in your house, for ever singing your praise.

PRAYER AFTER COMMUNION
As we receive the pledge of things yet hidden in heaven and are nourished while still on earth with the Bread that comes from on high, we humbly entreat you, O Lord, that what is being brought about in us in mystery may come to true completion. Through Christ our Lord. **Amen.**

PRAYER OVER THE PEOPLE
Direct, O Lord, we pray, the hearts of your faithful, and in your kindness grant your servants this grace: that, abiding in the love of you and their neighbour, they may fulfill the whole of your commands. Through Christ our Lord. **Amen.**

BLESSING AND DISMISSAL *(p. 70)*

CHRISTIAN INITIATION: 1ST SCRUTINY

ENTRANCE ANTIPHON *(Ezekiel 36.23-26)*
When I prove my holiness among you, I will gather you from all the foreign lands and I will pour clean water upon you and cleanse you from all your impurities, and I will give you a new spirit, says the Lord.
or (Cf. Isaiah 55.1)
Come to the waters, you who are thirsty, says the Lord; you who have no money, come and drink joyfully.

INTRODUCTORY RITES *(p. 5)*

COLLECT
Grant, we pray, O Lord, that these chosen ones may come worthily and wisely to the confession of your praise, so that in accordance with that first dignity which they lost by original sin they may be fashioned anew through your glory. Through our Lord Jesus Christ, your Son, who lives and reigns with you in the unity of the Holy Spirit, one God, for ever and ever. **Amen.**

FIRST READING *(Exodus 17.3-7)*
In the wilderness the people thirsted for water; and the people complained against Moses and said, "Why did you bring us out of Egypt, to kill us and our children and livestock with thirst?" So Moses cried out to the Lord, "What shall I do with this people? They are almost ready to stone me."
The Lord said to Moses, "Go on ahead of the people, and take some of the elders of Israel with you;

take in your hand the staff with which you struck the Nile, and go. I will be standing there in front of you on the rock at Horeb. Strike the rock, and water will come out of it, so that the people may drink." Moses did so, in the sight of the elders of Israel.

He called the place Massah and Meribah, because the children of Israel quarrelled and tested the Lord, saying, "Is the Lord among us or not?"

The word of the Lord. **Thanks be to God.**

RESPONSORIAL PSALM *(Psalm 95)*

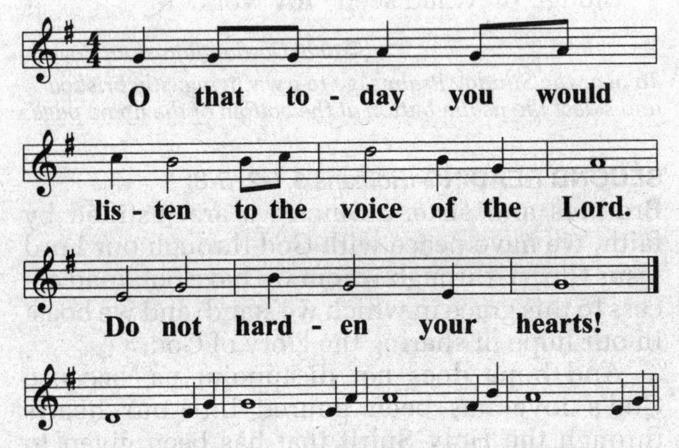

℟. **O that today you would listen to the voice of the Lord. Do not harden your hearts!**

O come, let us sing to · **the** Lord;
let us make a joyful noise to the rock
of our · **sal**-vation!
Let us come into his presence with
· **thanks**-giving;
let us make a joyful noise to him with songs
· **of** praise! ℟.

O come, let us worship and · **bow** down,
let us kneel before the Lord, · **our** Maker!
For he is our God, and we are the people
  of · **his** pasture,
and the sheep of · **his** hand. ℟.

O that today you would listen to · **his** voice!
Do not harden your hearts, as at Meribah, as on
  the day at Massah in · **the** wilderness,
when your ancestors tested me, and put me
  to · **the** proof,
though they had seen · **my** work. ℟.

To hear the Sunday Psalms, go to www.livingwithchrist.ca and select the psalm button at the bottom of the home page.

SECOND READING *(Romans 5.1-2, 5-8)*

Brothers and sisters: Since we are justified by faith, we have peace with God through our Lord Jesus Christ, through whom we have obtained access to this grace in which we stand; and we boast in our hope of sharing the glory of God.

And hope does not disappoint us, because God's love has been poured into our hearts through the Holy Spirit that has been given to us. For while we were still weak, at the right time Christ died for the ungodly. Indeed, rarely will anyone die for a righteous person — though perhaps for a good person someone might actually dare to die. But God proves his love for us in that while we still were sinners Christ died for us.

The word of the Lord. **Thanks be to God.**

GOSPEL ACCLAMATION *(John 4.42, 15)*
Glory and praise to you, Lord Jesus Christ! Lord, you are truly the Saviour of the world; give me living water, that I may never be thirsty. **Glory and praise to you, Lord Jesus Christ!**

GOSPEL *(John 4.5-42)*
For the shorter reading, omit the indented parts.
The Lord be with you. **And with your spirit.**
A reading from the holy Gospel according to John.
Glory to you, O Lord.

Jesus came to a Samaritan city called Sychar, near the plot of ground that Jacob had given to his son Joseph. Jacob's well was there, and Jesus, tired out by his journey, was sitting by the well. It was about noon.

A Samaritan woman came to draw water, and Jesus said to her, "Give me a drink." (His disciples had gone to the city to buy food.)

The Samaritan woman said to him, "How is it that you, a Jew, ask a drink of me, a woman of Samaria?" (Jews do not share things in common with Samaritans.) Jesus answered her, "If you knew the gift of God, and who it is that is saying to you, 'Give me a drink,' you would have asked him, and he would have given you living water."

The woman said to him, "Sir, you have no bucket, and the well is deep. Where do you get that living water? Are you greater than our father Jacob, who gave us the well, and with his children and his flocks drank from it?" Jesus said to her, "Everyone who drinks of this water will be thirsty again, but the one who drinks of the water that I will give will never be thirsty. The water that I will give him will become in him a spring of water gushing up to eternal life." The woman said to him, "Sir, give me this water, so that I may never be thirsty or have to keep coming here to draw water."

Jesus said to her, "Go, call your husband, and come back." The woman answered him, "I have no husband." Jesus said to her, "You are right in saying, 'I have no husband'; for you have had five husbands, and the one you have now is not your husband. What you have said is true!" The woman said to him, "Sir,

"I see that you are a Prophet. Our ancestors worshipped on this mountain, but you say that the place where people must worship is in Jerusalem."

Jesus said to her, "Woman, believe me, the hour is coming when you will worship the Father neither on this mountain nor in Jerusalem. You worship what you do not know; we worship what we know, for salvation is from the Jews. But the hour is coming, and is now here, when the true worshippers will worship the Father in spirit and truth, for the Father seeks such as these to worship him. God is spirit, and those who worship him must worship in spirit and truth."

The woman said to him, "I know that the Messiah is coming" (who is called the Christ). "When he comes, he will proclaim all things to us." Jesus said to her, "I am he, the one who is speaking to you."

Just then his disciples came. They were astonished that he was speaking with a woman, but no one said, "What do you want?" or, "Why are you speaking with her?" Then the woman left her water jar and went back to the city. She said to the people, "Come and see a man who told me everything I have ever done! He cannot be the Messiah, can he?" They left the city and were on their way to him. Meanwhile the disciples were urging him, "Rabbi, eat something." But he said to them, "I have food to eat that you do not know about." So the disciples said to one another, "Surely no one has brought him something to eat?"

Jesus said to them, "My food is to do the will of him who sent me and to complete his work. Do you not say, 'Four months more, then comes the harvest'? But I tell you, look around you, and see how the fields are ripe for harvesting. The reaper is already receiving wages and is gathering fruit for eternal life, so that sower and reaper may rejoice together. For here the saying holds true, 'One sows and another reaps.' I sent you to reap that for which you did not labour. Others have laboured, and you have entered into their labour."

Many Samaritans from that city believed in Jesus. because of the woman's testimony, "He told me everything I have ever done."

So when they [the Samaritans] came to him, they asked him to stay with them; and he stayed there two days. And many more believed because of his word. They said to the woman, "It is no longer because of what you said that we believe, for we have heard for ourselves, and we know that this is truly the Saviour of the world."

The Gospel of the Lord. **Praise to you, Lord Jesus Christ.**

PROFESSION OF FAITH *(p. 11)*

PRAYER OF THE FAITHFUL *(p. 208)*

PREPARATION OF THE GIFTS *(p. 14)*

PRAYER OVER THE OFFERINGS
May your merciful grace prepare your servants, O Lord, for the worthy celebration of these mysteries and lead them to it by a devout way of life. Through Christ our Lord. **Amen.**

PREFACE *(3rd Sunday of Lent, p. 21)*

COMMUNION ANTIPHON *(Cf. John 4.14)*
For anyone who drinks it, says the Lord, the water I shall give will become in him a spring welling up to eternal life.

PRAYER AFTER COMMUNION
Give help, O Lord, we pray, by the grace of your redemption and be pleased to protect and prepare those you are to initiate through the Sacraments of eternal life. Through Christ our Lord. **Amen.**

PRAYER OVER THE PEOPLE
Direct, O Lord, we pray, the hearts of your faithful, and in your kindness grant your servants this grace: that, abiding in the love of you and their neighbour, they may fulfill the whole of your commands. Through Christ our Lord. **Amen.**

BLESSING AND DISMISSAL *(p. 70)*

March Saints' Days

The following saints are traditionally remembered in March in Canada.

4	Saint Casimir
7	Saints Perpetua and Felicity
8	Saint John of God
9	Saint Frances of Rome
17	Saint Patrick
18	Saint Cyril of Jerusalem
19	Saint Joseph, Principal Patron of Canada
23	Saint Turibius of Mogrovejo

March 6

The younger son in today's parable experienced twists and turns on life's journey, before he "came to himself." We all need to "come to ourselves" — to know who we really are. Our good and loving God created us to be people of love and goodness. We've been given gifts and talents, for our good and the good of others. We've been created with great dignity and great responsibility.

Often, we forget that. We get lost, go astray: we make the wrong choices, take the wrong path. We need to "come to ourselves" — to remember who we are. Scripture, prayer, Reconciliation, Eucharist: they help us find our way.

Maybe our getting lost or forgetting who we are is not as extreme as with the younger son, but it still happens. It happened to the older son. He, too, needed to come to himself. His father had to remind him: "Son, you are always with me, and all that is mine is yours." We need to hear that, too. We need to know that God created us in love and calls us into relationship. When we lose track of that, we don't live as we should: we aren't being the people God meant us to be. We all need to be reminded of who we really are, so we can live from that fullness.

Dinah Simmons, Halifax, NS

Parishes engaged in the Rite of Christian Initiation of Adults (RCIA) *may celebrate the* 2nd Scrutiny *today* *(p. 225).*

ENTRANCE ANTIPHON *(Cf. Isaiah 66.10-11)*
Rejoice, Jerusalem, and all who love her. Be joyful, all who were in mourning; exult and be satisfied at her consoling breast.

INTRODUCTORY RITES *(p. 5)*

COLLECT
O God, who through your Word reconcile the human race to yourself in a wonderful way, grant, we pray, that with prompt devotion and eager faith the Christian people may hasten toward the solemn celebrations to come. Through our Lord Jesus Christ, your Son, who lives and reigns with you in the unity of the Holy Spirit, one God, for ever and ever. **Amen.**

FIRST READING *(Joshua 5.9a, 10-12)*
The Lord said to Joshua, "Today I have rolled away from you the disgrace of Egypt."

While the children of Israel were camped in Gilgal they kept the Passover in the evening on the fourteenth day of the month in the plains of Jericho.

On the day after the Passover, on that very day, they ate the produce of the land, unleavened cakes and parched grain. The manna ceased on the day they ate the produce of the land, and the children of Israel no longer had manna; they ate the crops of the land of Canaan that year.

The word of the Lord. **Thanks be to God.**

RESPONSORIAL PSALM *(Psalm 34)*

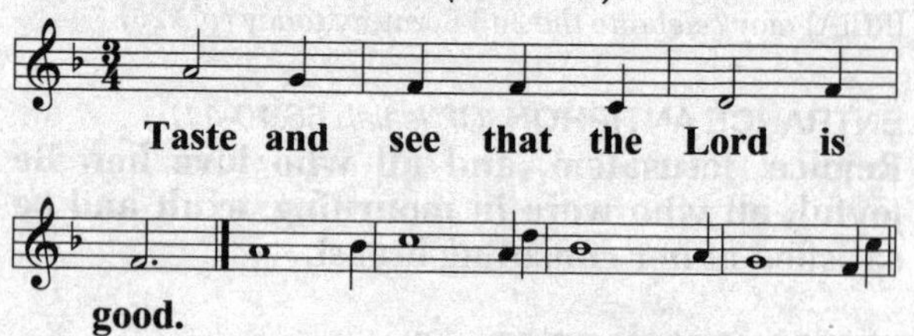

℟. **Taste and see that the Lord is good.**

I will bless the Lord at all · **times;**
his praise shall continually be in · **my** mouth.
My soul makes its boast in the · **Lord;**
let the humble hear and · **be** glad. ℟.

O magnify the Lord with · **me,**
and let us exalt his name · **to**-gether.
I sought the Lord, and he · **answered_me,**
and delivered me from all · **my** fears. ℟.

Look to him, and be · **radiant;**
so your faces shall never · **be_a**-shamed.
The poor one called, and the Lord · **heard,**
and saved that person from ev·-**ery** trouble. ℟.

SECOND READING *(2 Corinthians 5.17-21)*

Brothers and sisters: If anyone is in Christ, there is a new creation: everything old has passed away; see, everything has become new! All this is from God, who reconciled us to himself through Christ, and has given us the ministry of reconciliation; that is, in Christ, God was reconciling the world to himself, not counting their trespasses against them, and entrusting the message of reconciliation to us.

So we are ambassadors for Christ, since God is making his appeal through us; we entreat you on behalf of Christ, be reconciled to God. For our sake God made Christ to be sin who knew no sin, so that in Christ we might become the righteousness of God.

The word of the Lord. **Thanks be to God.**

GOSPEL ACCLAMATION *(Luke 15.18)*

Glory and praise to you, Lord Jesus Christ! I will get up and go to my father and say to him: Father, I have sinned against heaven and before you. **Glory and praise to you, Lord Jesus Christ!**

GOSPEL *(Luke 15.1-3, 11-32)*

The Lord be with you. **And with your spirit.** A reading from the holy Gospel according to Luke. **Glory to you, O Lord.**

All the tax collectors and sinners were coming near to listen to Jesus. And the Pharisees and the scribes were grumbling and saying, "This fellow welcomes sinners and eats with them."

So he told them a parable: "There was a man who had two sons. The younger of them said to his father, 'Father, give me the share of the property that will belong to me.' So the father divided his property between them. A few days later the younger son gathered all he had and travelled to a distant country, and there he squandered his property in dissolute living.

"When he had spent everything, a severe famine took place throughout that country, and he began to be in need. So he went and hired himself out to one of the citizens of that country, who sent him to his fields to feed the pigs. The young man would gladly have filled himself with the pods that the pigs were eating; and no one gave him anything.

"But when he came to himself he said, 'How many of my father's hired hands have bread enough and to spare, but here I am dying of hunger! I will get up and go to my father, and I will say to him, "Father, I have sinned against heaven and before you; I am no longer worthy to be called your son; treat me like one of your hired hands."'

"So he set off and went to his father. But while he was still far off, his father saw him and was filled with compassion; he ran and put his arms around him and kissed him.

"Then the son said to him, 'Father, I have sinned against heaven and before you; I am no longer worthy to be called your son.' But the father said to his slaves, 'Quickly, bring out a robe — the best one — and put it on him; put a ring on his finger and sandals on his feet. And get the fatted calf and kill it, and let us eat and celebrate; for this son of mine was dead and is alive again; he was lost and is found!' And they began to celebrate.

"Now his elder son was in the field; and when he came and approached the house, he heard music and dancing. He called one of the slaves and asked what was going on. The slave replied, 'Your brother has come, and your father has killed the fatted calf, because he has got him back safe and sound.'

"Then the elder son became angry and refused to go in. His father came out and began to plead with him. But he answered his father, 'Listen! For all these years I have been working like a slave for you, and I have never disobeyed your command; yet you have never given me even a young goat so that I might celebrate with my friends. But when this son of yours came back, who has devoured your property with prostitutes, you killed the fatted calf for him!'

"Then the father said to him, 'Son, you are always with me, and all that is mine is yours. But we had to celebrate and rejoice, because this brother of yours was dead and has come to life; he was lost and has been found.'"

The Gospel of the Lord. **Praise to you, Lord Jesus Christ.**

PROFESSION OF FAITH *(p. 11)*

PRAYER OF THE FAITHFUL

The following intentions are suggestions only. There are more suggestions at www.livingwithchrist.ca

℟. **Lord, hear our prayer.**

For the Church, calling us to live out our gospel values, we pray to the Lord: ℟.

For all nations to be more attentive to the needy, the oppressed and the displaced, we pray to the Lord: ℟.

For a deeper awareness of the voice of God in our everyday experience, we pray to the Lord: ℟.

For God's People gathered here today, open to ongoing conversion and transformation, we pray to the Lord: ℟.

PREPARATION OF THE GIFTS *(p. 14)*

PRAYER OVER THE OFFERINGS
We place before you with joy these offerings, which bring eternal remedy, O Lord, praying that we may both faithfully revere them and present them to you, as is fitting, for the salvation of all the world. Through Christ our Lord. **Amen.**

PREFACE *(Lent I-II, p. 19)*

COMMUNION ANTIPHON *(Luke 15.32)*
You must rejoice, my son, for your brother was dead and has come to life; he was lost and is found.

PRAYER AFTER COMMUNION
O God, who enlighten everyone who comes into this world, illuminate our hearts, we pray, with the splendour of your grace, that we may always ponder what is worthy and pleasing to your majesty and love you in all sincerity. Through Christ our Lord. **Amen.**

PRAYER OVER THE PEOPLE
Look upon those who call to you, O Lord, and sustain the weak; give life by your unfailing light to those who walk in the shadow of death, and bring those rescued by your mercy from every evil to reach the highest good. Through Christ our Lord. **Amen.**

BLESSING AND DISMISSAL *(p. 70)*

CHRISTIAN INITIATION: 2ND SCRUTINY

ENTRANCE ANTIPHON *(Cf. Psalm 24.15-16)*
My eyes are always on the Lord, for he rescues my feet from the snare. Turn to me and have mercy on me, for I am alone and poor.

INTRODUCTORY RITES *(p. 5)*

COLLECT
Almighty ever-living God, give to your Church an increase in spiritual joy, so that those once born of earth may be reborn as citizens of heaven. Through our Lord Jesus Christ, your Son, who lives and reigns with you in the unity of the Holy Spirit, one God, for ever and ever. **Amen.**

FIRST READING *(1 Samuel 16.1, 6-7, 10-13)*
The Lord said to Samuel, "Fill your horn with oil and set out; I will send you to Jesse of Bethlehem, for I have provided for myself a king among his sons."

When the sons of Jesse came, Samuel looked on Eliab and thought, "Surely the Lord's anointed is now before the Lord." But the Lord said to Samuel, "Do not look on his appearance or on the height of his stature, because I have rejected him; for the Lord does not see as the human sees; the human looks on the outward appearance, but the Lord looks on the heart."

Jesse made seven of his sons pass before Samuel, and Samuel said to Jesse, "The Lord has not chosen any of these." Samuel said to Jesse, "Are all your sons here?" And he said, "There remains yet the youngest, but he is keeping the sheep." And Samuel said to Jesse, "Send and bring him; for we will not sit down until he comes here." Jesse sent and brought David in. Now he was ruddy, and had beautiful eyes, and was handsome. The Lord said, "Rise and anoint him; for this is the one."

Then Samuel took the horn of oil, and anointed him in the presence of his brothers; and the spirit of the Lord came mightily upon David from that day forward.

The word of the Lord. **Thanks be to God.**

RESPONSORIAL PSALM *(Psalm 23)*

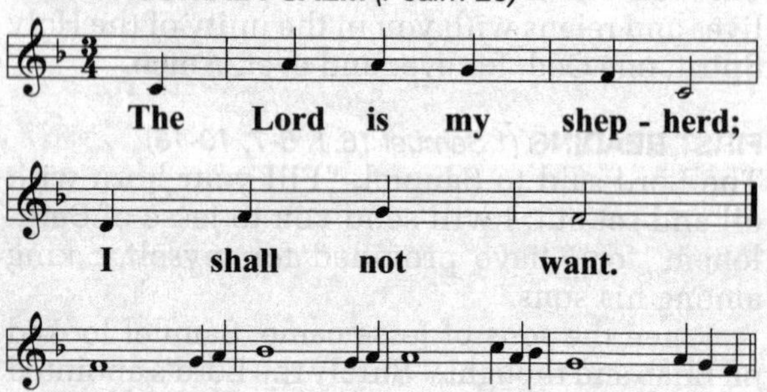

℟. **The Lord is my shepherd; I shall not want.**

The Lord is my shepherd, I shall · **not** want.
He makes me lie down in · **green** pastures;
he leads me be-·**side** still waters;
he re-·**stores** my soul. ℟.

He leads me in right paths for his · **name's** sake.
Even though I walk through the darkest valley,
I fear · **no** evil;
for · **you** are with_me;
your rod and your · **staff** — they
comfort_me. ℟.

You prepare a table · **be**-fore_me
in the presence · **of_my** enemies;
you anoint my · **head** with oil;
my · **cup** over-flows. ℟.

Surely goodness and mercy · **shall** follow_me
all the days of · **my** life,
and I shall dwell in the · **house_of** the Lord
my · **whole** life long. ℟.

To hear the Sunday Psalms, go to www.livingwithchrist.ca and select the psalm button at the bottom of the home page.

SECOND READING *(Ephesians 5.8-14)*

Brothers and sisters: Once you were darkness, but now in the Lord you are light. Live as children of light — for the fruit of the light is found in all that is good and right and true.

Try to find out what is pleasing to the Lord. Take no part in the unfruitful works of darkness, but instead expose them. For it is shameful even to mention what such people do secretly; but everything exposed by the light becomes visible, for everything that becomes visible is light. Therefore it is said, "Sleeper, awake! Rise from the dead, and Christ will shine on you."

The word of the Lord. **Thanks be to God.**

GOSPEL ACCLAMATION *(John 8.12)*
Glory and praise to you, Lord Jesus Christ! I am the light of the world, says the Lord; whoever follows me will have the light of life. **Glory and praise to you, Lord Jesus Christ!**

GOSPEL *(John 9.1-41)*
For the shorter version, omit the indented parts.
The Lord be with you. **And with your spirit.**
A reading from the holy Gospel according to John.
Glory to you, O Lord.

As Jesus walked along, he saw a man blind from birth.

> His disciples asked him, "Rabbi, who sinned, this man or his parents, that he was born blind?"
>
> Jesus answered, "Neither this man nor his parents sinned; he was born blind so that God's works might be revealed in him. We must work the works of him who sent me while it is day; night is coming when no one can work. As long as I am in the world, I am the light of the world." When he had said this,

He spat on the ground and made mud with the saliva and spread the mud on the man's eyes, saying to him, "Go, wash in the pool of Siloam" (which means Sent).

Then the man who was blind went and washed, and came back able to see. The neighbours and those who had seen him before as a beggar began to ask, "Is this not the man who used to sit and beg?" Some were saying, "It is he." Others were saying, "No, but it is someone like him." He kept saying, "I am the man."

But they kept asking him, "Then how were your eyes opened?" He answered, "The man called Jesus made mud, spread it on my eyes, and said to me, 'Go to Siloam and wash.' Then I went and washed and received my sight." They said to him, "Where is he?" He said, "I do not know."

They brought to the Pharisees the man who had formerly been blind. Now it was a Sabbath day when Jesus made the mud and opened his eyes. Then the Pharisees also began to ask him how he had received his sight. He said to them, "He put mud on my eyes. Then I washed, and now I see." Some of the Pharisees said, "This man is not from God, for he does not observe the Sabbath." But others said, "How can a man who is a sinner perform such signs?" And they were divided. So they said again to the blind man, "What do you say about him? It was your eyes he opened." He said, "He is a Prophet."

They did not believe that he had been blind and had received his sight until they called the parents of the man who had received his sight and asked them, "Is this your son, who you say was born blind? How then does he now see?" His parents answered, "We know that this is our son, and that he was born blind; but we do not know how it is that now he sees, nor do we know who opened his eyes. Ask him; he is of age. He will speak for himself." His parents said this because they were afraid of the Jewish authorities, who had already agreed that anyone who confessed Jesus to be the Messiah would be put out of the synagogue. Therefore his parents said, "He is of age; ask him."

So for the second time they called the man who had been blind, and they said to him, "Give glory to God! We know that this man is a sinner." He answered, "I do not know whether he is a sinner. One thing I do know, that though I was blind, now I see." They said to him, "What did he do to you? How did he open your eyes?" He answered them, "I have told you already, and you would not listen. Why do you want to hear it again? Do you also want to become his disciples?" Then they reviled him, saying, "You are his disciple, but we are disciples of Moses. We know that God has spoken to Moses, but as for this man, we do not know where he comes from."

The man answered, "Here is an astonishing thing! You do not know where he comes from, and yet he opened my eyes. We know that God does not listen to sinners, but he does listen to one who worships him and obeys his will. Never since the world began has it been heard that anyone opened the eyes of a person born blind. If this man were not from God, he could do nothing."

They answered him, "You were born entirely in sins, and are you trying to teach us?" And they drove him out.

Jesus heard that they had driven him out, and when he found him, he said, "Do you believe in the Son of Man?" He answered, "And who is he, sir? Tell me, so that I may believe in him." Jesus said to him, "You have seen him, and the one speaking with you is he." He said, "Lord, I believe." And he worshipped him.

Jesus said, "I came into this world for judgment so that those who do not see may see, and those who do see may become blind." Some of the Pharisees near him heard this and said to him, "Surely we are not blind, are we?" Jesus said to them, "If you were blind, you would have no sin. But now that you say, 'We see,' your sin remains."

The Gospel of the Lord. **Praise to you, Lord Jesus Christ.**

PROFESSION OF FAITH *(p. 11)*

PRAYER OF THE FAITHFUL *(p. 223)*

PREPARATION OF THE GIFTS *(p. 14)*

PRAYER OVER THE OFFERINGS

We place before you with joy these offerings, which bring eternal remedy, O Lord, praying that we may both faithfully revere them and present them to you, as is fitting, for those who seek salvation. Through Christ our Lord. **Amen.**

PREFACE *(4th Sunday of Lent, p. 22)*

COMMUNION ANTIPHON *(Cf. John 9.11, 38)*

The Lord anointed my eyes; I went, I washed, I saw and I believed in God.

PRAYER AFTER COMMUNION

Sustain your family always in your kindness, O Lord, we pray, correct them, set them in order, graciously protect them under your rule, and in your unfailing goodness direct them along the way of salvation. Through Christ our Lord. **Amen.**

PRAYER OVER THE PEOPLE

Look upon those who call to you, O Lord, and sustain the weak; give life by your unfailing light to those who walk in the shadow of death, and bring those rescued by your mercy from every evil to reach the highest good. Through Christ our Lord. **Amen.**

BLESSING AND DISMISSAL *(p. 70)*

March 13

The foundation of Jesus' ministry is expressed in his statement to the crowd — and to us. "Let anyone among you who is without sin be the first to throw a stone at her." Jesus knows, as surely as we do when we are humble and honest with ourselves, that all of us have acted badly in our relationships — with others and with creation — and will do so again. However, we can fall into the trap of continually assessing how badly we have acted and then comparing ourselves to others. This comparison inevitably leads either to self-congratulation and harsh judgment of others or to self-loathing and being victimized ourselves.

Neither leads us to becoming a more compassionate person, and compassion is what we are called to. When compassion replaces judgment and self-loathing, we are no longer as concerned with fairness. We are freed up to attend to the true purpose of the spiritual life: to contemplate and appreciate the beautiful mystery of simply being alive.

Rather than looking at one another and judging ourselves, we will become a community standing in awe before the majesty and mystery of life. The spiritual life is not about rules and consequences or excluding those who are different than ourselves; the spiritual life can be found in divesting ourselves of whatever prevents us from appreciating creation in all its splendour and diversity.

Joe Vorstermans, Richmond Hill, ON

National Collection for Development and Peace

Parishes engaged in the Rite of Christian Initiation of Adults (RCIA) *may celebrate the* 3rd Scrutiny *today (p. 240).*

ENTRANCE ANTIPHON *(Cf. Psalm 42.1-2)*
Give me justice, O God, and plead my cause against a nation that is faithless. From the deceitful and cunning rescue me, for you, O God, are my strength.

INTRODUCTORY RITES *(p. 5)*

COLLECT
By your help, we beseech you, Lord our God, may we walk eagerly in that same charity with which, out of love for the world, your Son handed himself over to death. Through our Lord Jesus Christ, your Son, who lives and reigns with you in the unity of the Holy Spirit, one God, for ever and ever. **Amen.**

FIRST READING *(Isaiah 43.16-21)*
Thus says the Lord,
who makes a way in the sea,
a path in the mighty waters,
who brings out chariot and horse, army
and warrior;
they lie down, they cannot rise,
they are extinguished, quenched like a wick:
"Do not remember the former things,
or consider the things of old.
I am about to do a new thing;
now it springs forth, do you not perceive it?
I will make a way in the wilderness
and rivers in the desert.

The wild animals will honour me,
the jackals and the ostriches;
for I give water in the wilderness, rivers
in the desert,
to give drink to my chosen people,
the people whom I formed for myself
so that they might declare my praise."

The word of the Lord. **Thanks be to God.**

RESPONSORIAL PSALM *(Psalm 126)*

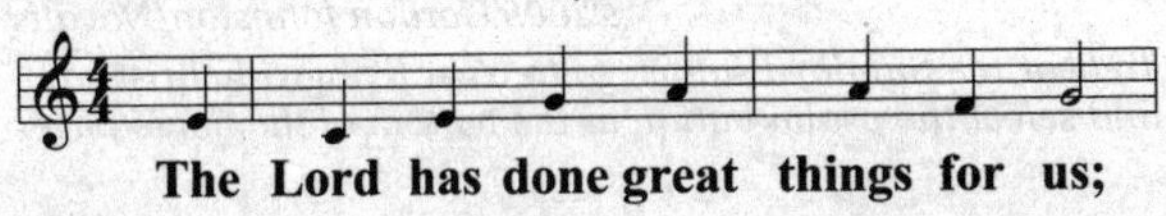

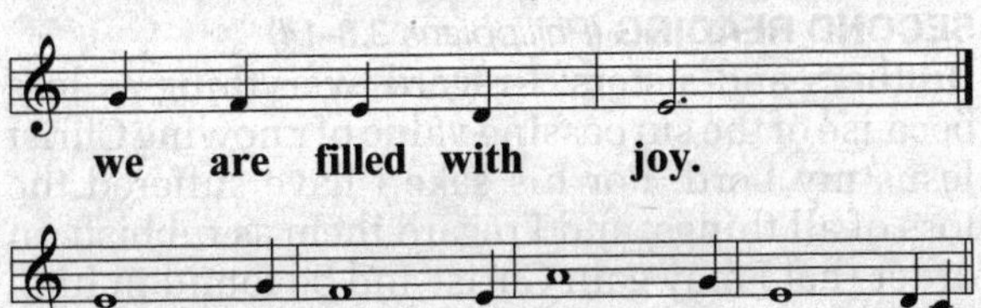

℟. **The Lord has done great things for us;
we are filled with joy.**

When the Lord restored the fortunes of · **Zion,**
we were like those who · **dream.**
Then our mouth was filled with · **laughter,**
and our tongue with shouts · **of** joy. ℟.

Then it was said among the · **nations,**
"The Lord has done great things for · **them.**"
The Lord has done great things for · **us,**
and we · **re**-joiced. ℟.

Restore our fortunes, O · **Lord,**
like the watercourses in the desert
of the · **Negev.**
May those who sow in · **tears**
reap with shouts · **of** joy. ℟.

Those who go out · **weeping,**
bearing the seed for · **sowing,**
shall come home with shouts of · **joy,**
carrying · **their** sheaves. ℟.

To hear the Sunday Psalms, go to www.livingwithchrist.ca and select the psalm button at the bottom of the home page.

SECOND READING *(Philippians 3.8-14)*

Brothers and sisters: I regard everything as loss because of the surpassing value of knowing Christ Jesus my Lord. For his sake I have suffered the loss of all things, and I regard them as rubbish, in order that I may gain Christ and be found in him, not having a righteousness of my own that comes from the law, but one that comes through faith in Christ, the righteousness from God based on faith.

I want to know Christ and the power of his resurrection and the sharing of his sufferings by becoming like him in his death, if somehow I may attain the resurrection from the dead.

Not that I have already obtained this or have already reached the goal; but I press on to make it my own, because Christ Jesus has made me his own.

Brothers and sisters, I do not consider that I have made it my own; but this one thing I do: forgetting what lies behind and straining forward to what lies ahead, I press on toward the goal for the prize of the heavenly call of God in Christ Jesus.

The word of the Lord. **Thanks be to God.**

GOSPEL ACCLAMATION *(Joel 2.12-13)*

Glory and praise to you, Lord Jesus Christ! Return to me with all your heart, says the Lord, for I am gracious and merciful. **Glory and praise to you, Lord Jesus Christ!**

GOSPEL *(John 8.1-11)*

The Lord be with you. **And with your spirit.**
A reading from the holy Gospel according to John.
Glory to you, O Lord.

Jesus went to the Mount of Olives. Early in the morning he came again to the temple. All the people came to him and he sat down and began to teach them.

The scribes and the Pharisees brought a woman who had been caught in adultery; and making her stand before the people, they said to Jesus, "Teacher, this woman was caught in the very act of committing adultery. In the law, Moses commanded us to stone such women. Now what do you say?" They said this to test Jesus, so that they might have some charge to bring against him.

Jesus bent down and wrote with his finger on the ground. When the scribes and Pharisees kept on questioning him, Jesus straightened up and said to them, "Let anyone among you who is without sin be the first to throw a stone at her." And once again Jesus bent down and wrote on the ground.

When the scribes and Pharisees heard what Jesus had said, they went away, one by one, beginning with the elders; and Jesus was left alone with the woman standing before him.

Jesus straightened up and said to her, "Woman, where are they? Has no one condemned you?" She said, "No one, sir." And Jesus said, "Neither do I condemn you. Go your way, and from now on do not sin again."

The Gospel of the Lord. **Praise to you, Lord Jesus Christ.**

PROFESSION OF FAITH *(p. 11)*

PRAYER OF THE FAITHFUL

The following intentions are suggestions only. There are more suggestions at www.livingwithchrist.ca

℟. **Lord, hear our prayer.**

For the Church, called to transformation and renewal at this time of Lent, we pray to the Lord: ℟.

For those marginalized or discriminated against because they are different, we pray to the Lord: ℟.

For our brothers and sisters in need of justice and love, we pray to the Lord: ℟.

For God's love, mercy and forgiveness upon all those preparing to be received, baptized or confirmed at Easter, we pray to the Lord: ℟.

PREPARATION OF THE GIFTS *(p. 14)*

PRAYER OVER THE OFFERINGS
Hear us, almighty God, and, having instilled in your servants the teachings of the Christian faith, graciously purify them by the working of this sacrifice. Through Christ our Lord. **Amen.**

PREFACE *(Lent I-II, p. 19)*

COMMUNION ANTIPHON *(John 8.10-11)*
Has no one condemned you, woman? No one, Lord. Neither shall I condemn you. From now on, sin no more.

PRAYER AFTER COMMUNION
We pray, almighty God, that we may always be counted among the members of Christ, in whose Body and Blood we have communion. Who lives and reigns for ever and ever. **Amen.**

PRAYER OVER THE PEOPLE
Bless, O Lord, your people, who long for the gift of your mercy, and grant that what, at your prompting, they desire they may receive by your generous gift. Through Christ our Lord. **Amen.**

BLESSING AND DISMISSAL *(p. 70)*

CHRISTIAN INITIATION: 3RD SCRUTINY

ENTRANCE ANTIPHON *(Cf. Psalm 17.5-7)*
The waves of death rose about me; the pains of the netherworld surrounded me. In my anguish I called to the Lord; and from his holy temple he heard my voice.

COLLECT
Grant, O Lord, to these chosen ones that, instructed in the holy mysteries, they may receive new life at the font of Baptism and be numbered among the members of your Church. Through our Lord Jesus Christ, your Son, who lives and reigns with you in the unity of the Holy Spirit, one God, for ever and ever. **Amen.**

FIRST READING *(Ezekiel 37.12-14)*
Thus says the Lord God: "I am going to open your graves, and bring you up from your graves, O my people; and I will bring you back to the land of Israel. And you shall know that I am the Lord, when I open your graves, and bring you up from your graves, O my people.

"I will put my spirit within you, and you shall live, and I will place you on your own soil; then you shall know that I, the Lord, have spoken and will act," says the Lord.

The word of the Lord. **Thanks be to God.**

RESPONSORIAL PSALM *(Psalm 130)*

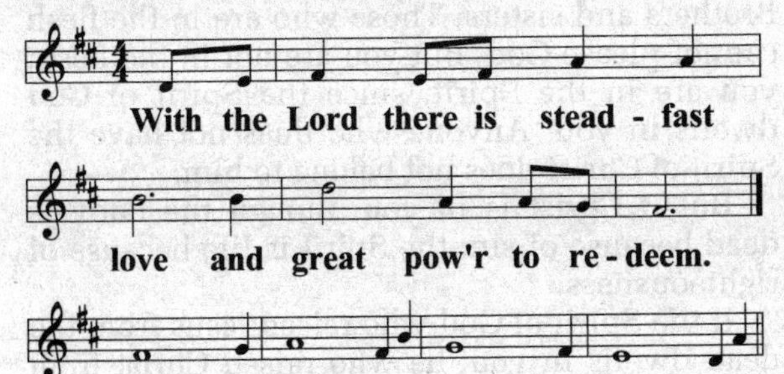

℟. **With the Lord there is steadfast love and great power to redeem.**

Out of the depths I cry to you, O · **Lord.**
Lord, hear · **my** voice!
Let your ears be at·-**tentive**
to the voice of my sup·-**pli**-cations! ℟.

If you, O Lord, should mark in·-**iquities,**
Lord, who · **could** stand?
But there is forgiveness with · **you,**
so that you may be · **re**-vered. ℟.

I wait for the · **Lord,**
my soul waits, and in his word · **I** hope;
my soul waits for the · **Lord**
more than watchmen for · **the** morning. ℟.

For with the Lord there is steadfast · **love,**
and with him is great power to · **re**-deem.
It is he who will redeem · **Israel**
from all its · **in**-iquities. ℟.

SECOND READING *(Romans 8.8-11)*
Brothers and sisters: Those who are in the flesh cannot please God. But you are not in the flesh; you are in the Spirit, since the Spirit of God dwells in you. Anyone who does not have the Spirit of Christ does not belong to him.

But if Christ is in you, though the body is dead because of sin, the Spirit is life because of righteousness.

If the Spirit of God who raised Jesus from the dead dwells in you, he who raised Christ from the dead will give life to your mortal bodies also through his Spirit that dwells in you.

The word of the Lord. **Thanks be to God.**

GOSPEL ACCLAMATION *(John 11.25, 26)*
Glory and praise to you, Lord Jesus Christ! I am the resurrection and the life, says the Lord; whoever believes in me will never die. **Glory and praise to you, Lord Jesus Christ!**

GOSPEL *(John 11.1-45)*
For the shorter version, omit the indented parts.
The Lord be with you. **And with your spirit.**
A reading from the holy Gospel according to John.
Glory to you, O Lord.

Now a certain man, Lazarus, was ill. He was from Bethany, the village of Mary and her sister Martha. Mary was the one who anointed the Lord with perfume and wiped his feet with her hair; her brother Lazarus was ill. So

The sisters [of Lazarus] sent a message to Jesus, "Lord, he whom you love is ill." But when Jesus heard this, he said, "This illness does not lead to death; rather it is for God's glory, so that the Son of God may be glorified through it." Accordingly, though Jesus loved Martha and her sister and Lazarus, after having heard that Lazarus was ill, he stayed two days longer in the place where he was. Then after this he said to the disciples, "Let us go to Judea again."

The disciples said to him, "Rabbi, the people there were just now trying to stone you, and are you going there again?" Jesus answered, "Are there not twelve hours of daylight? Those who walk during the day do not stumble, because they see the light of this world. But those who walk at night stumble, because the light is not in them."

After saying this, he told them, "Our friend Lazarus has fallen asleep, but I am going there to awaken him." The disciples said to him, "Lord, if he has fallen asleep, he will be all right." Jesus, however, had been speaking about his death, but they thought that he was referring merely to sleep. Then Jesus told them plainly, "Lazarus is dead. For your sake I am glad I was not there, so that you may believe. But let us go to him." Thomas, who was called the Twin, said to his fellow disciples, "Let us also go, that we may die with him."

When Jesus arrived, he found that Lazarus had already been in the tomb four days.

Now Bethany was near Jerusalem, some two miles away, and many Jews had come to Martha and Mary to console them about their brother.

When Martha heard that Jesus was coming, she went and met him, while Mary stayed at home. Martha said to Jesus, "Lord, if you had been here, my brother would not have died. But even now I know that God will give you whatever you ask of him." Jesus said to her, "Your brother will rise again." Martha said to him, "I know that he will rise again in the resurrection on the last day." Jesus said to her, "I am the resurrection and the life. Whoever believes in me, even though they die, will live, and everyone who lives and believes in me will never die. Do you believe this?" She said to him, "Yes, Lord, I believe that you are the Christ, the Son of God, the one coming into the world."

When she had said this, she went back and called her sister Mary, and told her privately, "The Teacher is here and is calling for you." And when Mary heard it, she got up quickly and went to him. Now Jesus had not yet come to the village, but was still at the place where Martha had met him. The Jews who were with her in the house, consoling her, saw Mary get up quickly and go out. They followed her because they thought that she was going to the tomb to weep there.

When Mary came where Jesus was and saw him, she knelt at his feet and said to him, "Lord, if you had been here, my brother would not have died." When Jesus saw her weeping, and the Jews who came with her also weeping, he

[Jesus] was greatly disturbed in spirit and deeply moved. He said, "Where have you laid him?" They said to him, "Lord, come and see." Jesus began to weep. So the Jews said, "See how he loved him!" But some of them said, "Could not he who opened the eyes of the blind man have kept this man from dying?"

Then Jesus, again greatly disturbed, came to the tomb. It was a cave, and a stone was lying against it. Jesus said, "Take away the stone." Martha, the sister of the dead man, said to him, "Lord, already there is a stench because he has been dead four days." Jesus said to her, "Did I not tell you that if you believed, you would see the glory of God?" So they took away the stone. And Jesus looked upward and said, "Father, I thank you for having heard me. I knew that you always hear me, but I have said this for the sake of the crowd standing here, so that they may believe that you sent me."

When he had said this, he cried with a loud voice, "Lazarus, come out!" The dead man came out, his hands and feet bound with strips of cloth, and his face wrapped in a cloth. Jesus said to them, "Unbind him, and let him go."

Many of the Jews therefore, who had come with Mary and had seen what Jesus did, believed in him.

The Gospel of the Lord. **Praise to you, Lord Jesus Christ.**

PROFESSION OF FAITH *(p. 11)*

PRAYER OF THE FAITHFUL *(p. 238)*

PREPARATION OF THE GIFTS *(p. 14)*

PRAYER OVER THE OFFERINGS
Hear us, almighty God, and, having instilled in your servants the first fruits of the Christian faith, graciously purify them by the working of this sacrifice. Through Christ our Lord. **Amen.**

PREFACE *(5th Sunday of Lent, p. 22)*

COMMUNION ANTIPHON *(Cf. John 11.26)*
Everyone who lives and believes in me will not die for ever, says the Lord.

PRAYER AFTER COMMUNION
May your people be at one, O Lord, we pray, and in wholehearted submission to you may they obtain this grace: that, safe from all distress, they may readily live out their joy at being saved and remember in loving prayer those to be reborn. Through Christ our Lord. **Amen.**

PRAYER OVER THE PEOPLE
Bless, O Lord, your people, who long for the gift of your mercy, and grant that what, at your prompting, they desire they may receive by your generous gift. Through Christ our Lord. **Amen.**

BLESSING AND DISMISSAL *(p. 70)*

March 20

World Day of Youth

It is tempting to approach today's readings with "theological eyes" — to focus on Jesus' suffering as affirming the fullness of his humanity, on suffering as potentially graced and transformative, or to reflect on Eucharist and resurrection as an ever-present witness to Jesus' gift of self. Yet today's scripture draws our attention to the stark reality of suffering: to its difficulties, its cost.

We all know suffering. It is hard. It is painful: physically, emotionally, spiritually. Suffering is often lonely, a place of fear, isolation and vulnerability. Sometimes it takes all we have to endure, to get through it. Sometimes it seems unfair, unjust, more than we can or should have to bear. It is this *experience* of suffering we are invited to reflect upon during Holy Week.

In Luke's gospel we encounter a Jesus who chooses a painful journey. Because we know suffering, we are able to walk with him, to be one with him. As we enter his passion, our relationship with Jesus deepens. In wonder and gratitude we recognize anew that God too knows our darkness, our suffering. No one is ever alone, even there.

Jesus' passion invites our *com*-passion: our loving presence to his suffering. And Jesus' passion, Luke tells us, makes way for the coming of the kingdom of God. Let us witness to the divine presence in our world through our compassion.

Ella Allen, Fredericton, NB

Commemoration of the Lord's Entrance into Jerusalem

FIRST FORM: The Procession

INTRODUCTION

The people, carrying palm branches, gather in a suitable place distinct from the church to which the procession will move. The assembly may sing Hosanna! *or another suitable hymn.*

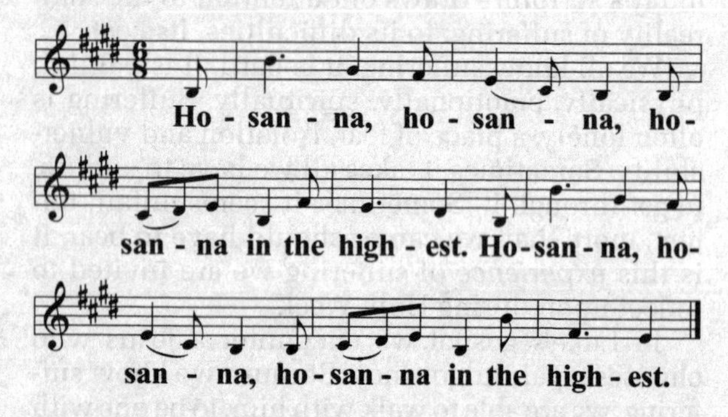

GREETING *(p. 5)*

Dear brothers and sisters, since the beginning of Lent until now we have prepared our hearts by penance and charitable works. Today we gather together to herald with the whole Church the beginning of the celebration of our Lord's Paschal Mystery, that is to say, of his Passion and Resurrection. For it was to accomplish this mystery that he entered his own city of Jerusalem. Therefore, with all faith and devotion, let us commemorate the Lord's entry into the city for our salvation, following in his footsteps, so that, being made by his grace partakers of the Cross, we may have a share also in his Resurrection and in his life.

Let us pray.

1 Almighty ever-living God, sanctify these branches with your blessing, that we, who follow Christ the King in exultation, may reach the eternal Jerusalem through him. Who lives and reigns for ever and ever. **Amen.**

2 Increase the faith of those who place their hope in you, O God, and graciously hear the prayers of those who call on you, that we, who today hold high these branches to hail Christ in his triumph, may bear fruit for you by good works accomplished in him. Who lives and reigns for ever and ever. **Amen.**

GOSPEL *(Luke 19.28-40)*

The Lord be with you. **And with your spirit.** A reading from the holy Gospel according to Luke. **Glory to you, O Lord.**

Jesus went on ahead, going up to Jerusalem. When he had come near Bethphage and Bethany, at the place called the Mount of Olives, he sent two of the disciples, saying, "Go into the village ahead of you, and as you enter it you will find tied there a colt that has never been ridden. Untie it and bring it here. If anyone asks you, 'Why are you untying it?' just say this, 'The Lord needs it.'"

So those who were sent departed and found it as Jesus had told them. As they were untying the colt, its owners asked them, "Why are you untying the colt?" They said, "The Lord needs it."

Then they brought the colt to Jesus; and after throwing their cloaks on the colt, they set Jesus on it.

As he rode along, people kept spreading their cloaks on the road. As he was now approaching the path down from the Mount of Olives, the whole multitude of the disciples began to praise God joyfully, and with a loud voice, for all the deeds of power that they had seen, saying, "Blessed is the king who comes in the name of the Lord! Peace in heaven, and glory in the highest heaven!"

Some of the Pharisees in the crowd said to him, "Teacher, order your disciples to stop."

Jesus answered, "I tell you, if these were silent, the stones would shout out."

The Gospel of the Lord. **Praise to you, Lord Jesus Christ.**

PROCESSION

1 Dear brothers and sisters, like the crowds who acclaimed Jesus in Jerusalem, let us go forth in peace.

2 Let us go forth in peace. **In the name of Christ. Amen.**

All process to the church singing a hymn in honour of Christ the King. Mass continues with the Collect *(p. 252).*

SECOND FORM: The Solemn Entrance

The blessing of branches and proclamation of the Gospel take place, as above, but in the church. After the Gospel, the priest moves solemnly through the church to the sanctuary, while all sing. Mass continues with the Collect *(p. 252).*

THIRD FORM: The Simple Entrance

The people gather in the church as usual. While the priest goes to the altar, the following Entrance Antiphon *or a suitable hymn is sung.*

ENTRANCE ANTIPHON

(Cf. John 12.1, 12-13; Psalm 23.9-10)

Six days before the Passover, when the Lord came into the city of Jerusalem, the children ran to meet him; in their hands they carried palm branches and with a loud voice cried out:

**Hosanna in the highest!
Blessed are you, who have come
in your abundant mercy!**

**O gates, lift high your heads;
grow higher, ancient doors.
Let him enter, the king of glory!
Who is this king of glory?
He, the Lord of hosts, he is the king of glory.
Hosanna in the highest!
Blessed are you, who have come
in your abundant mercy!**

INTRODUCTORY RITES *(p. 5)*

COLLECT

Almighty ever-living God, who as an example of humility for the human race to follow caused our Saviour to take flesh and submit to the Cross, graciously grant that we may heed his lesson of patient suffering and so merit a share in his Resurrection. Who lives and reigns with you in the unity of the Holy Spirit, one God, for ever and ever. **Amen.**

FIRST READING *(Isaiah 50.4-7)*

The servant of the Lord said: "The Lord God has given me the tongue of a teacher, that I may know how to sustain the weary with a word. Morning by morning he wakens — wakens my ear to listen as those who are taught. The Lord God has opened my ear, and I was not rebellious, I did not turn backward.

"I gave my back to those who struck me, and my cheeks to those who pulled out the beard; I did not hide my face from insult and spitting.

"The Lord God helps me; therefore I have not been disgraced; therefore I have set my face like flint, and I know that I shall not be put to shame."

The word of the Lord. **Thanks be to God.**

RESPONSORIAL PSALM *(Psalm 22)*

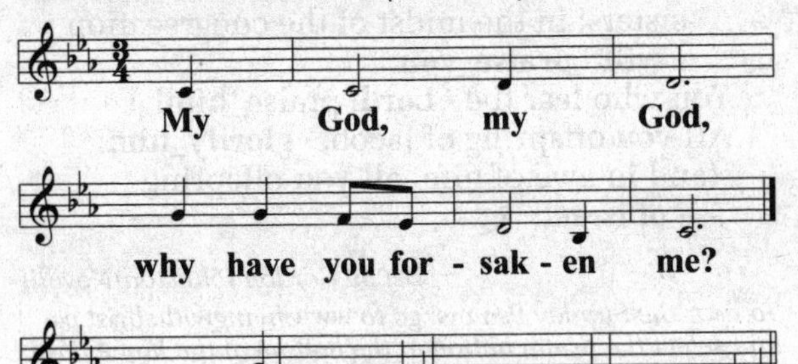

℟. My God, my God, why have you forsaken me?

All who see me · **mock_at_me;**
they make mouths at me,
they shake · **their** heads;
"Commit your cause to the Lord;
let him de·-**liver;**
let him rescue the one in whom
he · **de**-lights!" ℟.

For dogs are all a·-**round_me;**
a company of evildoers · **en**-circles_me.
My hands and feet have · **shrivelled;**
I can count all · **my** bones. ℟.

They divide my clothes a·-**mong_themselves,**
and for my clothing they · **cast** lots.
But you, O Lord, do not be far a·-**way!**
O my help, come quickly · **to_my** aid! ℟.

I will tell of your name to my brothers and
sisters; in the midst of the congregation
I will · **praise_you:**
You who fear the · **Lord,** praise_him!
All you offspring of Jacob, · **glorify_him;**
stand in awe of him, all you offspring
· **of** Israel! ℟.

To hear the Sunday Psalms, go to www.livingwithchrist.ca and select the psalm button at the bottom of the home page.

SECOND READING *(Philippians 2.6-11)*
Christ Jesus, though he was in the form of God, did not regard equality with God as something to be exploited, but emptied himself, taking the form of a slave, being born in human likeness. And being found in human form, he humbled himself and became obedient to the point of death — even death on a cross.

Therefore God highly exalted him and gave him the name that is above every name, so that at the name of Jesus every knee should bend, in heaven and on earth and under the earth, and every tongue should confess that Jesus Christ is Lord, to the glory of God the Father.

The word of the Lord. **Thanks be to God.**

GOSPEL ACCLAMATION *(Philippians 2.8-9)*
Glory and praise to you, Lord Jesus Christ! Christ became obedient for us to death, even death on a Cross. Therefore God exalted him and gave him the name above every name. **Glory and praise to you, Lord Jesus Christ!**

GOSPEL *(Luke 22.14 – 23.56)*

Several readers may proclaim the passion narrative today. N indicates the narrator, J the words of Jesus, and S the words of other speakers.

N The Passion of our Lord Jesus Christ according to Luke.

When the hour came, Jesus took his place at the table, and the Apostles with him. He said to them,

J **I have eagerly desired to eat this Passover with you before I suffer; for I tell you, I will not eat it until it is fulfilled in the kingdom of God.**

N Then he took a cup, and after giving thanks he said,

J **Take this and divide it among yourselves; for I tell you that from now on I will not drink of the fruit of the vine until the kingdom of God comes.**

N Then Jesus took a loaf of bread, and when he had given thanks, he broke it and gave it to them, saying,

J **This is my Body, which is given for you. Do this in remembrance of me.**

N And he did the same with the cup after supper, saying,

J **This cup that is poured out for you is the new covenant in my Blood. But see, the one who betrays me is with me, and his hand is on the table. For the Son of Man is going as it has been determined, but woe to that one by whom he is betrayed!**

N Then they began to ask one another, which one of them it could be who would do this.

A dispute also arose among them as to which one of them was to be regarded as the greatest. But Jesus said to them,

J **The kings of the Gentiles lord it over them; and those in authority over them are called benefactors.**

But not so with you; rather the greatest among you must become like the youngest, and the leader like one who serves. For who is greater, the one who is at the table or the one who serves? Is it not the one at the table? But I am among you as one who serves.

You are those who have stood by me in my trials; and I confer on you, just as my Father has conferred on me, a kingdom, so that you may eat and drink at my table in my kingdom, and you will sit on thrones judging the twelve tribes of Israel.

Simon, Simon, listen! Satan has demanded to sift all of you like wheat, but I have prayed for you that your own faith may not fail; and you, when once you have turned back, strengthen your brothers.

N And Peter said to Jesus,

S ***Lord, I am ready to go with you to prison and to death!***

J **I tell you, Peter, the cock will not crow this day, until you have denied three times that you know me.**

N Then Jesus said to the Apostles,

J **When I sent you out without a purse, bag, or sandals, did you lack anything?**

S ***No, not a thing.***

J **But now, the one who has a purse must take it, and likewise a bag. And the one who has no sword must sell his cloak and buy one. For I tell you, this Scripture must be fulfilled in me, "And he was counted among the lawless"; and indeed what is written about me is being fulfilled.**

S ***Lord, look, here are two swords.***

J **It is enough.**

At this point all may join in singing an appropriate acclamation.

Text: Didier Rimaud, © *CNPL.* **Music:** Jacques Berthier
Source: © *Éditions Musicales Studio SM,* 060794-2

N Jesus came out and went, as was his custom, to the Mount of Olives; and the disciples followed him. When he reached the place, he said to his disciples,

J **Pray that you may not come into the time of temptation.**

N Then Jesus withdrew from them about a stone's throw, knelt down, and prayed,

J **Father, if you are willing, remove this cup from me; yet, not my will but yours be done.**

N Then an Angel from heaven appeared to Jesus and gave him strength. In his anguish he prayed more earnestly, and his sweat became like great drops of blood falling down on the ground.

When Jesus got up from prayer, he came to the disciples and found them sleeping because of grief, and he said to them,

J **Why are you sleeping? Get up and pray that you may not come into the time of temptation.**

N While Jesus was still speaking, suddenly a crowd came, and the one called Judas, one of the twelve, was leading them. He approached Jesus to kiss him; but Jesus said to him,

J **Judas, is it with a kiss that you are betraying the Son of Man?**

N When those who were around Jesus saw what was coming, they asked,

S ***Lord, should we strike with the sword?***

N Then one of the disciples struck the slave of the high priest and cut off his right ear. But Jesus said,

J **No more of this!**

N And Jesus touched the slave's ear and healed him. Then Jesus said to the chief priests, the officers of the temple police, and the elders who had come for him,

J **Have you come out with swords and clubs as if I were a bandit? When I was with you day after day in the temple, you did not lay hands on me. But this is your hour, and the power of darkness!**

N Then they seized Jesus and led him away, bringing him into the high priest's house. But Peter was following at a distance. When they had kindled a fire in the middle of the courtyard and sat down together, Peter sat among them. Then a servant girl, seeing him in the firelight, stared at him and said,

S ***This man also was with him.***

N But Peter denied it, saying,

S ***Woman, I do not know him.***

N A little later someone else, on seeing him, said,

S ***You also are one of them.***

N But Peter said,

S ***Man, I am not!***

N Then about an hour later still another kept insisting,

S ***Surely this man also was with him; for he is a Galilean.***

N But Peter said,

S ***Man, I do not know what you are talking about!***

N At that moment, while he was still speaking, the cock crowed. The Lord turned and looked at Peter. Then Peter remembered the word of the Lord, how he had said to him, "Before the cock crows today, you will deny me three times." And Peter went out and wept bitterly.

Now the men who were holding Jesus began to mock him and beat him; they also blindfolded him and kept asking him,

S ***Prophesy! Who is it that struck you?***

N They kept heaping many other insults on him.

When day came, the assembly of the elders of the people, both chief priests and scribes, gathered together, and they brought Jesus to their council. They said,

S ***If you are the Christ, tell us.***

J **If I tell you, you will not believe; and if I question you, you will not answer. But from now on the Son of Man will be seated at the right hand of the power of God.**

N All of them asked,

S ***Are you, then, the Son of God?***

J **You say that I am.**

S ***What further testimony do we need? We have heard it ourselves from his own lips!***

At this point all may join in singing an appropriate acclamation.

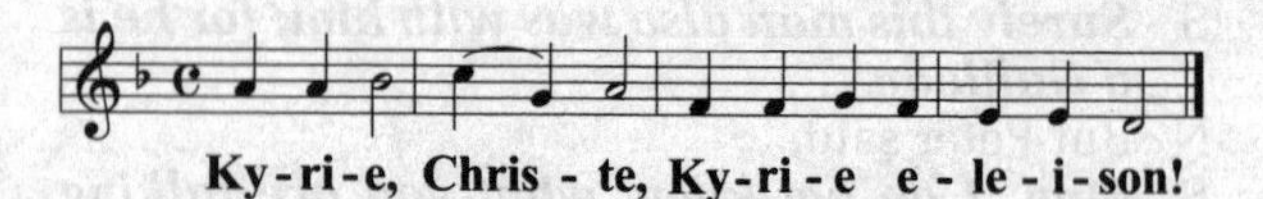

Text: Didier Rimaud, © *CNPL.* **Music:** Jacques Berthier
Source: © *Éditions Musicales Studio SM,* 060794-2

N Then the assembly rose as a body and brought Jesus before Pilate. They began to accuse him, saying,

S ***We found this man perverting our nation, forbidding us to pay taxes to the emperor, and saying that he himself is the Christ, a king.***

N Then Pilate asked Jesus,

S ***Are you the king of the Jews?***

J **You say so.**

N Then Pilate said to the chief priests and the crowds,

S ***I find no basis for an accusation against this man.***

N But they were insistent and said,

S ***He stirs up the people by teaching throughout all Judea, from Galilee where he began even to this place.***

N When Pilate heard this, he asked whether the man was a Galilean. And when he learned that he was under Herod's jurisdiction, he sent him off to Herod, who was himself in Jerusalem at that time.

When Herod saw Jesus, he was very glad, for he had been wanting to see him for a long time, because he had heard about him and was hoping to see Jesus perform some sign.

Herod questioned him at some length, but Jesus gave him no answer. The chief priests and the scribes stood by, vehemently accusing him.

Even Herod with his soldiers treated him with contempt and mocked him; then he put an elegant robe on him, and sent him back to Pilate. That same day Herod and Pilate became friends with each other; before this they had been enemies.

Pilate then called together the chief priests, the leaders, and the people, and said to them,

S ***You brought me this man as one who was perverting the people; and here I have examined him in your presence and have not found this man guilty of any of your charges against him. Neither has Herod, for he sent him back to us. Indeed, he has done nothing to deserve death. I will therefore have him flogged and release him.***

N Now Pilate was obliged to release someone for them at the festival. Then they all shouted out together,

S ***Away with this fellow! Release Barabbas for us.***

N This was a man who had been put in prison for an insurrection that had taken place in the city, and for murder.

Pilate, wanting to release Jesus, addressed them again; but they kept shouting,

S ***Crucify, crucify him!***

N A third time Pilate said to them,

S ***Why, what evil has he done? I have found in him no ground for the sentence of death; I will therefore have him flogged and then release him.***

N But they kept urgently demanding with loud shouts that he should be crucified; and their voices prevailed. So Pilate gave his verdict that their demand should be granted. He released the man they asked for, the one who had been put in prison for insurrection and murder, and he handed Jesus over as they wished.

As they led Jesus away, they seized a man, Simon of Cyrene, who was coming from the country, and they laid the Cross on him, and made him carry it behind Jesus.

A great number of the people followed him, and among them were women who were beating their breasts and wailing for him. But Jesus turned to them and said,

J **Daughters of Jerusalem, do not weep for me, but weep for yourselves and for your chil-**

dren. For the days are surely coming when they will say, "Blessed are the barren, and the wombs that never bore, and the breasts that never nursed." Then they will begin to say to the mountains, "Fall on us," and to the hills, "Cover us." For if they do this when the wood is green, what will happen when it is dry?

At this point all may join in singing an appropriate acclamation.

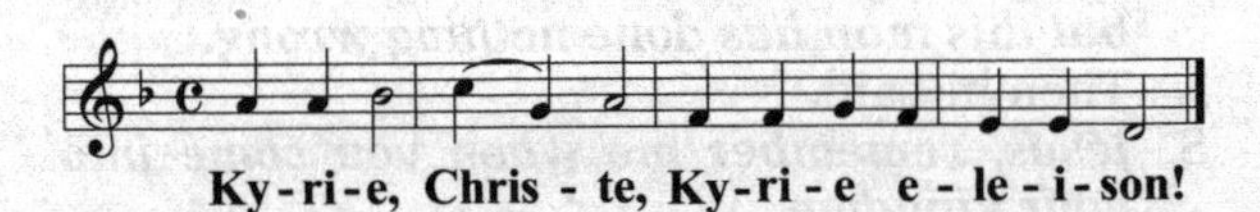

Text: Didier Rimaud, © *CNPL.* **Music:** Jacques Berthier
Source: © *Éditions Musicales Studio SM,* 060794-2

N Two others also, who were criminals, were led away to be put to death with Jesus. When they came to the place that is called The Skull, they crucified Jesus there with the criminals, one on his right and one on his left. Then Jesus said,

J **Father, forgive them; for they do not know what they are doing.**

N And they cast lots to divide his clothing. And the people stood by, watching; but the leaders scoffed at him, saying,

S ***He saved others; let him save himself if he is the Christ of God, his chosen one!***

N The soldiers also mocked Jesus, coming up and offering him sour wine, and saying,

S ***If you are the King of the Jews, save yourself!***

N There was also an inscription over him, "This is the King of the Jews."

One of the criminals who were hanged there kept deriding him and saying,

S ***Are you not the Christ? Save yourself and us!***

N But the other criminal rebuked the first, saying,

S ***Do you not fear God, since you are under the same sentence of condemnation? And we indeed have been condemned justly, for we are getting what we deserve for our deeds, but this man has done nothing wrong.***

N Then he said,

S ***Jesus, remember me when you come into your kingdom.***

J **Truly I tell you, today you will be with me in Paradise.**

N It was now about noon, and darkness came over the whole land until three in the afternoon, while the sun's light failed; and the curtain of the temple was torn in two. Then Jesus, crying with a loud voice, said,

J **Father, into your hands I commend my spirit.**

N Having said this, he breathed his last.

Here all kneel and pause for a short time.

N When the centurion saw what had taken place, he praised God and said,

S ***Certainly this man was innocent.***

N And when all the crowds who had gathered there for this spectacle saw what had taken place, they returned home, beating their breasts.

But all his acquaintances, including the women who had followed him from Galilee, stood at a distance, watching these things.

Now there was a good and righteous man named Joseph, who, though a member of the council, had not agreed to their plan and action. He came from the Jewish town of Arimathea, and he was waiting expectantly for the kingdom of God. This man went to Pilate and asked for the body of Jesus. Then he took it down, wrapped it in a linen cloth, and laid it in a rock-hewn tomb where no one had ever been laid.

It was the day of Preparation, and the Sabbath was beginning. The women who had come with Jesus from Galilee followed, and they saw the tomb and how his body was laid. Then they returned, and prepared spices and ointments. On the Sabbath these women rested according to the commandment.

The readers return to their places in silence.

PROFESSION OF FAITH *(p. 11)*

PRAYER OF THE FAITHFUL

The following intentions are suggestions only. There are more suggestions at www.livingwithchrist.ca

℟. **Lord, hear our prayer.**

For the Church, sign of hope and peace throughout the world, we pray to the Lord: ℟.

For world leaders who will govern with integrity, compassion and justice, we pray to the Lord: ℟.

For the suffering and the dying, we pray to the Lord: ℟.

For youth workers and counsellors, offering hope and life-affirming options to young people, we pray to the Lord: R.

PREPARATION OF THE GIFTS *(p. 14)*

PRAYER OVER THE OFFERINGS
Through the Passion of your Only Begotten Son, O Lord, may our reconciliation with you be near at hand, so that, though we do not merit it by our own deeds, yet by this sacrifice made once for all, we may feel already the effects of your mercy. Through Christ our Lord. **Amen.**

PREFACE *(Passion Sunday, p. 22)*

COMMUNION ANTIPHON *(Matthew 26.42)*
Father, if this chalice cannot pass without my drinking it, your will be done.

PRAYER AFTER COMMUNION
Nourished with these sacred gifts, we humbly beseech you, O Lord, that, just as through the death of your Son you have brought us to hope for what we believe, so by his Resurrection you may lead us to where you call. Through Christ our Lord. **Amen.**

PRAYER OVER THE PEOPLE
Look, we pray, O Lord, on this your family, for whom our Lord Jesus Christ did not hesitate to be delivered into the hands of the wicked and submit to the agony of the Cross. Who lives and reigns for ever and ever. **Amen.**

SOLEMN BLESSING – PASSION OF THE LORD

(Optional)

Bow down for the blessing.

May God, the Father of mercies, who has given you an example of love in the Passion of his Only Begotten Son, grant that, by serving God and your neighbour, you may lay hold of the wondrous gift of his blessing. **Amen.**

So that you may receive the reward of everlasting life from him, through whose earthly Death you believe that you escape eternal death. **Amen.**

And by following the example of his self-abasement, may you possess a share in his Resurrection. **Amen.**

And may the blessing of almighty God, the Father, and the Son, and the Holy Spirit, come down on you and remain with you for ever. **Amen.**

DISMISSAL *(p. 70)*

March 24

Mass of the Lord's Supper

We are near the end of our long Lenten journey, this solemn and sombre time of the Christian year. But before reaching the great joy of Easter, we still have to walk the painful path of the betrayal, suffering and harrowing death of Jesus. Holy Week marks the steps on that final journey.

Tonight, though, there is some respite on this terrible path. At the brink of the moment of betrayal, love is revealed. As John says, "Having loved his own who were in the world, he loved them to the end."

Jesus' friends and followers, weary, dusty, confused by what had taken place earlier in the week, were no doubt happy to have time together to share this meal. But first, expressing his love and tenderness, their leader, their teacher, their inspiration, carefully cleans and dries each one's feet.

It is an act of extraordinary intimacy. Warm water, a clean towel, but most of all the touch of love wipe away grime, soften hardened calluses, cleanse blisters, and invigorate tired and worn-out muscles.

Jesus' example of love is also a challenge: you must do this for each other, he tells them. And their challenge is also our challenge. Jesus is telling us that with hands of love extended to each other, we too must be ready to wash away life's sorrow, pain and weariness.

Patrick Gallagher, Toronto, ON

ENTRANCE ANTIPHON *(Cf. Galatians 6.14)*
We should glory in the Cross of our Lord Jesus Christ, in whom is our salvation, life and resurrection, through whom we are saved and delivered.

INTRODUCTORY RITES *(p. 5)*

COLLECT
O God, who have called us to participate in this most sacred Supper, in which your Only Begotten Son, when about to hand himself over to death, entrusted to the Church a sacrifice new for all eternity, the banquet of his love, grant, we pray, that we may draw from so great a mystery, the fullness of charity and of life. Through our Lord Jesus Christ, your Son, who lives and reigns with you in the unity of the Holy Spirit, one God, for ever and ever. **Amen.**

FIRST READING *(Exodus 12.1-8, 11-14)*
The Lord said to Moses and Aaron in the land of Egypt: This month shall mark for you the beginning of months; it shall be the first month of the year for you. Tell the whole congregation of Israel that on the tenth of this month they are to take a lamb for each family, a lamb for each household. If a household is too small for a whole lamb, it shall join its closest neighbour in obtaining one; the lamb shall be divided in proportion to the number of people who eat of it.

Your lamb shall be without blemish, a year-old male; you may take it from the sheep or from the goats. You shall keep it until the fourteenth day of this month; then the whole assembled congregation of Israel shall slaughter it at twilight. They shall take some of the blood and put it on the two doorposts and the lintel of the houses in which they eat it. They shall eat the lamb that same night; they shall eat it roasted over the fire with unleavened bread and bitter herbs.

This is how you shall eat it: your loins girded, your sandals on your feet, and your staff in your hand; and you shall eat it hurriedly. It is the Passover of the Lord. For I will pass through the land of Egypt that night, and I will strike down every firstborn in the land of Egypt, both human beings and animals; on all the gods of Egypt I will execute judgments: I am the Lord.

The blood shall be a sign for you on the houses where you live: when I see the blood, I will pass over you, and no plague shall destroy you when I strike the land of Egypt.

This day shall be a day of remembrance for you. You shall celebrate it as a festival to the Lord; throughout your generations you shall observe it as a perpetual ordinance.

The word of the Lord. **Thanks be to God.**

RESPONSORIAL PSALM *(Psalm 116)*

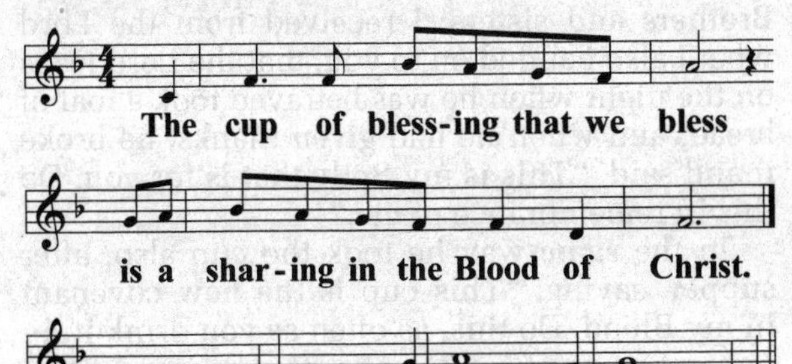

℟. **The cup of blessing that we bless**
is a sharing in the Blood of Christ.

What shall I return to the · **Lord**
for all his bounty to · **me?**
I will lift up the cup of sal·**-vation**
and call on the name · **of_the** Lord. ℟.

Precious in the sight of the · **Lord**
is the death of his · **faithful_ones.**
I am your servant, the son
of your · **serving_girl.**
You have loosed · **my** bonds. ℟.

I will offer to you a thanksgiving · **sacrifice**
and call on the name of the · **Lord.**
I will pay my vows to the · **Lord**
in the presence of all · **his** people. ℟.

To hear the Sunday Psalms, go to www.livingwithchrist.ca and select the psalm button at the bottom of the home page.

SECOND READING *(1 Corinthians 11.23-26)*
Brothers and sisters: I received from the Lord what I also handed on to you, that the Lord Jesus on the night when he was betrayed took a loaf of bread, and when he had given thanks, he broke it and said, "This is my Body that is for you. Do this in remembrance of me."

In the same way he took the cup also, after supper, saying, "This cup is the new covenant in my Blood. Do this, as often as you drink it, in remembrance of me." For as often as you eat this bread and drink the cup, you proclaim the Lord's death until he comes.

The word of the Lord. **Thanks be to God.**

GOSPEL ACCLAMATION *(John 13.34)*
Glory and praise to you, Lord Jesus Christ! I give you a new commandment: love one another as I have loved you. **Glory and praise to you, Lord Jesus Christ!**

GOSPEL *(John 13.1-15)*
The Lord be with you. **And with your spirit.**
A reading from the holy Gospel according to John.
Glory to you, O Lord.

Before the festival of the Passover, Jesus knew that his hour had come to depart from this world and go to the Father. Having loved his own who were in the world, he loved them to the end.

The devil had already put it into the heart of Judas, son of Simon Iscariot, to betray him. And during supper Jesus, knowing that the Father had given all things into his hands, and that he had come from God and was going to God, got up from the table, took off his outer robe, and tied a towel around himself. Then he poured water into a basin and began to wash the disciples' feet and to wipe them with the towel that was tied around him.

He came to Simon Peter, who said to him, "Lord, are you going to wash my feet?" Jesus answered, "You do not know now what I am doing, but later you will understand." Peter said to him, "You will never wash my feet." Jesus answered, "Unless I wash you, you have no share with me." Simon Peter said to him, "Lord, not my feet only but also my hands and my head!" Jesus said to him, "One who has bathed does not need to wash, except for the feet, but is entirely clean. And you are clean, though not all of you." For he knew who was to betray him; for this reason he said, "Not all of you are clean."

After he had washed their feet, put on his robe, and returned to the table, Jesus said to them, "Do you know what I have done to you? You call me Teacher and Lord — and you are right, for that is what I am. So if I, your Lord and Teacher, have washed your feet, you also ought to wash one another's feet. For I have set you an example, that you also should do as I have done to you."

The Gospel of the Lord. **Praise to you, Lord Jesus Christ.**

The Profession of Faith *is omitted.*

THE WASHING OF FEET *(Optional)*

During the washing of feet, an appropriate song may be sung.

PRAYER OF THE FAITHFUL

The following intentions are suggestions only. There are more suggestions at www.livingwithchrist.ca

℟. **Lord, hear our prayer.**

For the Church, active witness to repentance and conversion, we pray to the Lord: ℟.

For leaders of nations, called to care for the weak as well as the strong, we pray to the Lord: ℟.

For the healing and restoration of all of us gathered to celebrate this Eucharist, we pray to the Lord: ℟.

For our community, called to love and forgive one another, we pray to the Lord: ℟.

PREPARATION OF THE GIFTS *(p. 14)*

PRAYER OVER THE OFFERINGS

Grant us, O Lord, we pray, that we may participate worthily in these mysteries, for whenever the memorial of this sacrifice is celebrated, the work of our redemption is accomplished. Through Christ our Lord. **Amen.**

PREFACE *(Holy Eucharist I, p. 27)*

COMMUNION ANTIPHON *(1 Corinthians 11.24-25)*

This is the Body that will be given up for you; this is the Chalice of the new covenant in my Blood, says the Lord; do this, whenever you receive it, in memory of me.

PRAYER AFTER COMMUNION

Grant, almighty God, that, just as we are renewed by the Supper of your Son in this present age, so we may enjoy his banquet for all eternity. Who lives and reigns for ever and ever. **Amen.**

The Blessing and Dismissal *are omitted tonight.*

TRANSFER OF THE HOLY EUCHARIST

The Blessed Sacrament is carried through the church to the place of repose. During the procession, the hymn Pange Lingua *(p. 276, stanzas 1-4) or another eucharistic song is sung. At the place of repose, the presider incenses the Blessed Sacrament, while* Tantum ergo Sacramentum (Pange Lingua, *stanzas 5-6) or another eucharistic song is sung. The tabernacle of repose is then closed.*

After a period of silent adoration, the priests and ministers of the altar retire. The faithful are encouraged to continue adoration before the Blessed Sacrament for a suitable period of time. There should be no solemn adoration after midnight.

HAIL OUR SAVIOUR'S GLORIOUS BODY

(Pange Lingua)

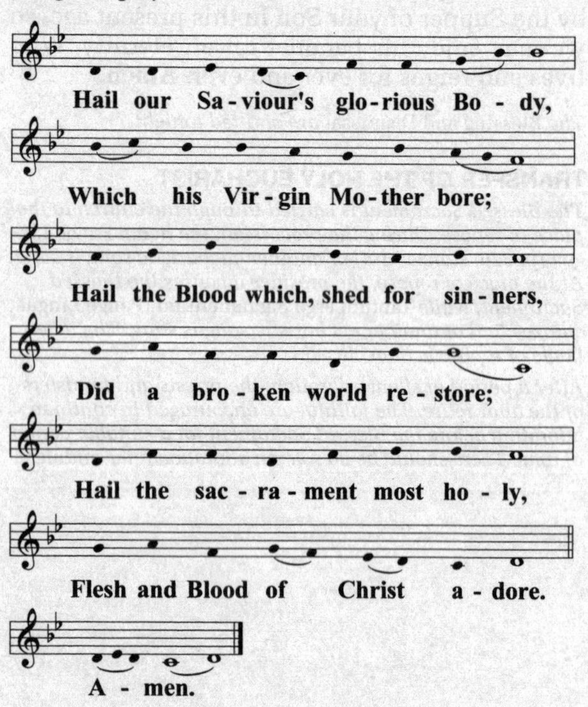

2. To the Virgin, for our healing,
His own Son the Father sends;
From the Father's love proceeding
Sower, seed and word descends;
Wondrous life of Word incarnate
With his greatest wonder ends.

3. On that paschal evening see him
   With the chosen twelve recline,
   To the old law still obedient
   In its feast of love divine;
   Love divine, the new law giving,
   Gives himself as Bread and Wine.

4. By his word the Word almighty
   Makes of bread his flesh indeed;
   Wine becomes his very life-blood;
   Faith God's living Word must heed!
   Faith alone may safely guide us
   Where the senses cannot lead!

At the incensing of the Blessed Sacrament:

5. Come, adore this wondrous presence;
   Bow to Christ, the source of grace!
   Here is kept the ancient promise
   Of God's earthly dwelling place!
   Sight is blind before God's glory,
   Faith alone may see God's face.

6. Glory be to God the Father,
   Praise to his co-equal Son,
   Adoration to the Spirit,
   Bond of love in God-head one!
   Blest be God by all creation
   Joyously while ages run! Amen.

Text: *Pange Lingua,* Thomas Aquinas, 1227-74; tr. James Quinn, SJ (1919-2010). Used by permission of Oregon Catholic Press. **Tune:** PANGE LINGUA, 87.87.87. **Music:** CBW II 583; CBW III 381

March 25

Celebration of the Passion of the Lord

Good Friday. It seems almost contradictory to call it 'good.' We come together to listen to the description of a man humiliated, rejected and tortured. Thirty-nine lashes tore his skin. Thorns pushed deep into his scalp. Forced to carry the final instrument of his death before spikes were driven through his hands and feet, he was then left to die. How do we celebrate this image, make it the emblem of our faith?

The final hours of excruciating pain Jesus endured reflect a God who can sympathize with our weaknesses and our pain because he experienced their enormous weight himself. He faced the pain of loneliness, abandonment, fear and abject heartbreak. Through the long walk to Golgotha, we join with Jesus in this mutual understanding.

Good Friday is not for us to suffer as Jesus does, nor to carry the guilt of our sins like weights around our necks. Instead we are invited, like the three Marys, to the foot of the cross to worship and to witness life-giving water pour from Jesus' pierced side. We are invited to experience God's ultimate expression of love and commitment to us. So let us gather in appreciation and hope of what we know will come in three days. It is, after all, *good* Friday.

Saskia Sivananthan, Surrey, BC

National Collection for the Church in the Holy Land

PRAYER

1 Remember your mercies, O Lord, and with your eternal protection sanctify your servants, for whom Christ your Son, by the shedding of his Blood, established the Paschal Mystery. Who lives and reigns for ever and ever. **Amen.**

2 O God, who by the Passion of Christ your Son, our Lord, abolished the death inherited from ancient sin by every succeeding generation, grant that just as, being conformed to him, we have borne by the law of nature the image of the man of earth, so by the sanctification of grace we may bear the image of the Man of heaven. Through Christ our Lord. **Amen.**

LITURGY OF THE WORD

FIRST READING *(Isaiah 52.13 – 53.12)*

See, my servant shall prosper; he shall be exalted and lifted up, and shall be very high.

Just as there were many who were astonished at him — so marred was his appearance, beyond human semblance, and his form beyond that of the sons of man — so he shall startle many nations; kings shall shut their mouths because of him; for that which had not been told them they shall see, and that which they had not heard they shall contemplate. Who has believed what we have heard? And to whom has the arm of the Lord been revealed?

For he grew up before the Lord like a young plant, and like a root out of dry ground; he had no form or majesty that we should look at him, nothing in his appearance that we should desire him. He was despised and rejected by men; a man of suffering and acquainted with infirmity; and as one from whom others hide their faces he was despised, and we held him of no account.

Surely he has borne our infirmities and carried our diseases; yet we accounted him stricken, struck down by God, and afflicted. But he was wounded for our transgressions, crushed for our iniquities; upon him was the punishment that made us whole, and by his bruises we are healed.

All we like sheep have gone astray; each has turned to their own way and the Lord has laid on him the iniquity of us all.

He was oppressed, and he was afflicted, yet he did not open his mouth; like a lamb that is led to the slaughter, and like a sheep that before its shearers is silent, so he did not open his mouth.

By a perversion of justice he was taken away. Who could have imagined his future? For he was cut off from the land of the living, stricken for the transgression of my people. They made his grave with the wicked and his tomb with the rich, although he had done no violence, and there was no deceit in his mouth.

Yet it was the will of the Lord to crush him with pain. When you make his life an offering for sin, he shall see his offspring, and shall prolong his days; through him the will of the Lord shall prosper. Out of his anguish he shall see light; he shall find satisfaction through his knowledge. The righteous one, my servant, shall make many righteous, and he shall bear their iniquities.

Therefore I will allot him a portion with the great, and he shall divide the spoil with the strong; because he poured out himself to death, and was numbered with the transgressors; yet he bore the sin of many, and made intercession for the transgressors.

The word of the Lord. **Thanks be to God.**

RESPONSORIAL PSALM *(Psalm 31)*

℟. **Father, into your hands I commend my spirit.**

In you, O Lord, I seek refuge;
  do not let me ever be put · **to** shame;
in your righteousness · **de**-liver_me.
Into your hand I commit · **my** spirit;
you have redeemed me,
  O Lord, · **faith**-ful God. ℟.

I am the scorn of all my adversaries,
  a horror to my neighbours,
  an object of dread to my · **ac**-quaintances.
Those who see me in the · **street** flee_from_me.
I have passed out of mind like one
  who · **is** dead;
I have become like a · **bro**-ken vessel. ℟.

But I trust in you, · **O** Lord;
I say, "You are · **my** God."
My times are in · **your** hand;
deliver me from the hand
of my · **enemies** and persecutors. ℟.

Let your face shine upon · **your** servant;
save me in your stead·-**fast** love.
Be strong, and let your heart · **take** courage,
all you who wait · **for** the Lord. ℟.

To hear the Sunday Psalms, go to www.livingwithchrist.ca and select the psalm button at the bottom of the home page.

SECOND READING *(Hebrews 4.14-16; 5.7-9)*

Brothers and sisters: Since we have a great high priest who has passed through the heavens, Jesus, the Son of God, let us hold fast to our confession. For we do not have a high priest who is unable to sympathize with our weaknesses, but we have one who in every respect has been tested as we are, yet without sin. Let us therefore approach the throne of grace with boldness, so that we may receive mercy and find grace to help in time of need.

In the days of his flesh, Jesus offered up prayers and supplications, with loud cries and tears, to the one who was able to save him from death, and he was heard because of his reverent submission. Although he was a Son, he learned obedience through what he suffered; and having been made perfect, he became the source of eternal salvation for all who obey him.

The word of the Lord. **Thanks be to God.**

GOSPEL ACCLAMATION *(Philippians 2.8-9)*
Glory and praise to you, Lord Jesus Christ! Christ became obedient for us to death, even death on a Cross. Therefore God exalted him and gave him the name above every name. **Glory and praise to you, Lord Jesus Christ!**

GOSPEL *(John 18.1 – 19.42)*
Several readers may proclaim the passion narrative today. N indicates the narrator, J the words of Jesus, and S the words of other speakers.

N The Passion of our Lord Jesus Christ according to John.

After they had eaten the supper, Jesus went out with his disciples across the Kidron valley to a place where there was a garden, which he and his disciples entered. Now Judas, who betrayed him, also knew the place, because Jesus often met there with his disciples. So Judas brought a detachment of soldiers together with police from the chief priests and the Pharisees, and they came there with lanterns and torches and weapons.

Then Jesus, knowing all that was to happen to him, came forward and asked them,

J **Whom are you looking for?**

N They answered,

S ***Jesus of Nazareth.***

J **I am he.**

N Judas, who betrayed him, was standing with them. When Jesus said to them, "I am he," they stepped back and fell to the ground. Again he asked them,

J **Whom are you looking for?**

S ***Jesus of Nazareth.***

J **I told you that I am he. So if you are looking for me, let these men go.**

N This was to fulfill the word that he had spoken, "I did not lose a single one of those whom you gave me."

Then Simon Peter, who had a sword, drew it, struck the high priest's slave, and cut off his right ear. The slave's name was Malchus. Jesus said to Peter,

J **Put your sword back into its sheath. Am I not to drink the cup that the Father has given me?**

N So the soldiers, their officer, and the Jewish police arrested Jesus and bound him. First they took him to Annas, who was the father-in-law of Caiaphas, the high priest that year. Caiaphas was the one who had advised the Jews that it was better to have one person die for the people.

Simon Peter and another disciple followed Jesus. Since that disciple was known to the high priest, he went with Jesus into the court-yard of the high priest, but Peter was standing outside at the gate. So the other disciple, who was known to the high priest, went out, spoke to the woman who guarded the gate, and brought Peter in. The woman said to Peter,

S ***You are not also one of this man's disciples, are you?***

N Peter said,

S ***I am not.***

N Now the slaves and the police had made a charcoal fire because it was cold, and they were standing around it and warming themselves. Peter also was standing with them and warming himself.

Then the high priest questioned Jesus about his disciples and about his teaching. Jesus answered,

J **I have spoken openly to the world; I have always taught in synagogues and in the temple, where all the Jews come together. I have said nothing in secret. Why do you ask me? Ask those who heard what I said to them; they know what I said.**

N When he had said this, one of the police standing nearby struck Jesus on the face, saying,

S ***Is that how you answer the high priest?***

J **If I have spoken wrongly, testify to the wrong. But if I have spoken rightly, why do you strike me?**

N Then Annas sent him bound to Caiaphas the high priest.

Now Simon Peter was standing and warming himself. They asked him,

S ***You are not also one of his disciples, are you?***

N He denied it and said,

S ***I am not.***

N One of the slaves of the high priest, a relative of the man whose ear Peter had cut off, asked,

S ***Did I not see you in the garden with him?***

N Again Peter denied it, and at that moment the cock crowed.

At this point all may join in singing an appropriate acclamation.

Text: Didier Rimaud, © *CNPL.* **Music:** Jacques Berthier
Source: © *Éditions Musicales Studio SM,* 060794-2

N Then they took Jesus from Caiaphas to Pilate's headquarters. It was early in the morning. They themselves did not enter the headquarters, so as to avoid ritual defilement and to be able to eat the Passover. So Pilate went out to them and said,

S ***What accusation do you bring against this man?***

N They answered,

S ***If this man were not a criminal, we would not have handed him over to you.***

N Pilate said to them,

S ***Take him yourselves and judge him according to your law.***

N They replied,

S ***We are not permitted to put anyone to death.***

N This was to fulfill what Jesus had said when he indicated the kind of death he was to die. Then Pilate entered the headquarters again, summoned Jesus, and asked him,

S ***Are you the King of the Jews?***

J **Do you ask this on your own, or did others tell you about me?**

S ***I am not a Jew, am I? Your own nation and the chief priests have handed you over to me. What have you done?***

J **My kingdom is not from this world. If my kingdom were from this world, my followers**

would be fighting to keep me from being handed over to the Jews. But as it is, my kingdom is not from here.

S ***So you are a king?***

J You say that I am a king. For this I was born, and for this I came into the world, to testify to the truth. Everyone who belongs to the truth listens to my voice.

S ***What is truth?***

N After he had said this, Pilate went out to the Jews again and told them,

S ***I find no case against him. But you have a custom that I release someone for you at the Passover. Do you want me to release for you the King of the Jews?***

N They shouted in reply,

S ***Not this man, but Barabbas!***

N Now Barabbas was a bandit. Then Pilate took Jesus and had him flogged. And the soldiers wove a crown of thorns and put it on his head, and they dressed him in a purple robe. They kept coming up to him, saying,

S ***"Hail, King of the Jews!"***

N and they struck him on the face. Pilate went out again and said to them,

S ***Look, I am bringing him out to you to let you know that I find no case against him.***

N So Jesus came out, wearing the crown of thorns and the purple robe. Pilate said to them,

S ***Here is the man!***

N When the chief priests and the police saw him, they shouted,

S ***Crucify him! Crucify him!***

N Pilate said to them,

S ***Take him yourselves and crucify him; I find no case against him.***
N They answered him,
S ***We have a law, and according to that law he ought to die because he has claimed to be the Son of God.***
N Now when Pilate heard this, he was more afraid than ever. He entered his headquarters again and asked Jesus,
S ***Where are you from?***
N But Jesus gave him no answer. Pilate therefore said to him,
S ***Do you refuse to speak to me? Do you not know that I have power to release you, and power to crucify you?***
J **You would have no power over me unless it had been given you from above; therefore the one who handed me over to you is guilty of a greater sin.**
N From then on Pilate tried to release him, but the Jews cried out,
S ***If you release this man, you are no friend of the emperor. Everyone who claims to be a king sets himself against the emperor.***
N When Pilate heard these words, he brought Jesus outside and sat on the judge's bench at a place called "The Stone Pavement," or in Hebrew "Gabbatha."

Now it was the day of Preparation for the Passover; and it was about noon. Pilate said to the Jews,

S ***Here is your King!***
N They cried out,

S ***Away with him! Away with him! Crucify him!***
N Pilate asked them,
S ***Shall I crucify your King?***
N The chief priests answered,
S ***We have no king but the emperor.***

At this point all may join in singing an appropriate acclamation.

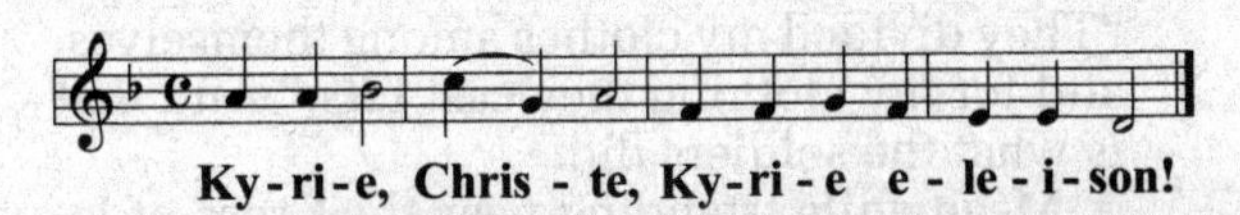

Text: *Didier Rimaud, © CNPL.* **Music:** *Jacques Berthier*
Source: *© Éditions Musicales Studio SM, 060794-2*

N Then Pilate handed Jesus over to them to be crucified. So they took Jesus; and carrying the Cross by himself, he went out to what is called The Place of the Skull, which in Hebrew is called Golgotha. There they crucified him, and with him two others, one on either side, with Jesus between them.

Pilate also had an inscription written and put on the Cross. It read, "Jesus of Nazareth, the King of the Jews." Many of the people read this inscription, because the place where Jesus was crucified was near the city; and it was written in Hebrew, in Latin, and in Greek. Then the chief priests of the Jews said to Pilate,
S ***Do not write, "The King of the Jews," but, "This man said, I am King of the Jews."***
N Pilate answered,
S ***What I have written I have written.***

N When the soldiers had crucified Jesus, they took his clothes and divided them into four parts, one for each soldier. They also took his tunic; now the tunic was seamless, woven in one piece from the top. So they said to one another,

S ***Let us not tear it, but cast lots for it to see who will get it.***

N This was to fulfill what the Scripture says, "They divided my clothes among themselves, and for my clothing they cast lots." And that is what the soldiers did.

Meanwhile, standing near the Cross of Jesus were his mother, and his mother's sister, Mary the wife of Clopas, and Mary Magdalene. When Jesus saw his mother and the disciple whom he loved standing beside her, he said to his mother,

J **Woman, here is your son.**

N Then he said to the disciple,

J **Here is your mother.**

N And from that hour the disciple took her into his own home.

After this, when Jesus knew that all was now finished, in order to fulfill the Scripture, he said,

J **I am thirsty.**

N A jar full of sour wine was standing there. So they put a sponge full of the wine on a branch of hyssop and held it to his mouth.

When Jesus had received the wine, he said,

J **It is finished.**

N Then he bowed his head and gave up his spirit.

Here all kneel and pause for a short time.

N Since it was the day of Preparation, the Jews did not want the bodies left on the cross during the Sabbath, especially because that Sabbath was a day of great Solemnity. So they asked Pilate to have the legs of the crucified men broken and the bodies removed.

Then the soldiers came and broke the legs of the first and of the other who had been crucified with him. But when they came to Jesus and saw that he was already dead, they did not break his legs. Instead, one of the soldiers pierced his side with a spear, and at once blood and water came out.

(He who saw this has testified so that you also may believe. His testimony is true, and he knows that he tells the truth.) These things occurred so that the Scripture might be fulfilled, "None of his bones shall be broken." And again another passage of Scripture says, "They will look on the one whom they have pierced."

After these things, Joseph of Arimathea, who was a disciple of Jesus, though a secret one because of his fear of the Jews, asked Pilate to let him take away the body of Jesus. Pilate gave him permission; so he came and removed his body.

Nicodemus, who had at first come to Jesus by night, also came, bringing a mixture of myrrh and aloes, weighing about a hundredweight. They took the body of Jesus and wrapped it with the spices in linen cloths, according to the burial custom of the Jews. Now there was a garden in the place where he was crucified, and in the garden there was a new tomb in which no one had ever been laid. And so, because it was the Jewish day of Preparation, and the tomb was nearby, they laid Jesus there.

The readers return to their places in silence.

THE SOLEMN INTERCESSIONS

For Holy Church

Let us pray, dearly beloved, for the holy Church of God, that our God and Lord be pleased to give her peace, to guard her and to unite her throughout the whole world and grant that, leading our life in tranquillity and quiet, we may glorify God the Father almighty. *(Pause)*

Almighty ever-living God, who in Christ revealed your glory to all the nations, watch over the works of your mercy, that your Church, spread throughout all the world, may persevere with steadfast faith in confessing your name. Through Christ our Lord. **Amen.**

For the Pope

Let us pray also for our most Holy Father Pope N., that our God and Lord, who chose him for the Order of Bishops, may keep him safe and unharmed for the Lord's holy Church, to govern the holy People of God. *(Pause)*

Almighty ever-living God, by whose decree all things are founded, look with favour on our prayers and in your kindness protect the Pope chosen for us, that, under him, the Christian people, governed by you their maker, may grow in merit by reason of their faith. Through Christ our Lord. **Amen.**

For all orders and degrees of the faithful
Let us pray also for our Bishop N., for all Bishops, Priests, and Deacons of the Church and for the whole of the faithful people. *(Pause)*

Almighty ever-living God, by whose Spirit the whole body of the Church is sanctified and governed, hear our humble prayer for your ministers, that, by the gift of your grace, all may serve you faithfully. Through Christ our Lord. **Amen.**

For catechumens
Let us pray also for (our) catechumens, that our God and Lord may open wide the ears of their inmost hearts and unlock the gates of his mercy, that, having received forgiveness of all their sins through the waters of rebirth, they, too, may be one with Christ Jesus our Lord. *(Pause)*

Almighty ever-living God, who make your Church ever fruitful with new offspring, increase the faith and understanding of (our) catechumens, that, reborn in the font of Baptism, they may be added to the number of your adopted children. Through Christ our Lord. **Amen.**

For the unity of Christians
Let us pray also for all our brothers and sisters who believe in Christ, that our God and Lord may be pleased, as they live the truth, to gather them together and keep them in his one Church. *(Pause)*

Almighty ever-living God, who gather what is scattered and keep together what you have gathered, look kindly on the flock of your Son, that those whom one Baptism has consecrated may be joined together by integrity of faith and united in the bond of charity. Through Christ our Lord. **Amen.**

For the Jewish people
Let us pray also for the Jewish people, to whom the Lord our God spoke first, that he may grant them to advance in love of his name and in faithfulness to his covenant. *(Pause)*

Almighty ever-living God, who bestowed your promises on Abraham and his descendants, graciously hear the prayers of your Church, that the people you first made your own may attain the fullness of redemption. Through Christ our Lord. **Amen.**

For those who do not believe in Christ
Let us pray also for those who do not believe in Christ, that, enlightened by the Holy Spirit, they, too, may enter on the way of salvation. *(Pause)*

Almighty ever-living God, grant to those who do not confess Christ that, by walking before you with a sincere heart, they may find the truth and that we ourselves, being constant in mutual love and striving to understand more fully the mystery of your life, may be made more perfect witnesses to your love in the world. Through Christ our Lord. **Amen.**

For those who do not believe in God
Let us pray also for those who do not acknowledge God, that, following what is right in sincerity of heart, they may find the way to God himself. *(Pause)*

Almighty ever-living God, who created all people to seek you always by desiring you and, by finding you, come to rest, grant, we pray, that, despite every harmful obstacle, all may recognize the signs of your fatherly love and the witness of the good works done by those who believe in you, and so in gladness confess you, the one true God and Father of our human race. Through Christ our Lord. **Amen.**

For those in public office
Let us pray also for those in public office, that our God and Lord may direct their minds and hearts according to his will for the true peace and freedom of all. *(Pause)*

Almighty ever-living God, in whose hand lies every human heart and the rights of peoples, look with favour, we pray, on those who govern with authority over us, that throughout the whole world, the prosperity of peoples, the assurance of peace, and freedom of religion may through your gift be made secure. Through Christ our Lord. **Amen.**

For those in tribulation
Let us pray, dearly beloved, to God the Father almighty, that he may cleanse the world of all errors, banish disease, drive out hunger, unlock prisons, loosen fetters, granting to travellers safety, to pilgrims return, health to the sick, and salvation to the dying. *(Pause)*

Almighty ever-living God, comfort of mourners, strength of all who toil, may the prayers of those who cry out in any tribulation come before you, that all may rejoice, because in their hour of need your mercy was at hand. Through Christ our Lord. **Amen.**

ADORATION OF THE HOLY CROSS

Three times the priest or deacon invites the assembly to proclaim its faith:

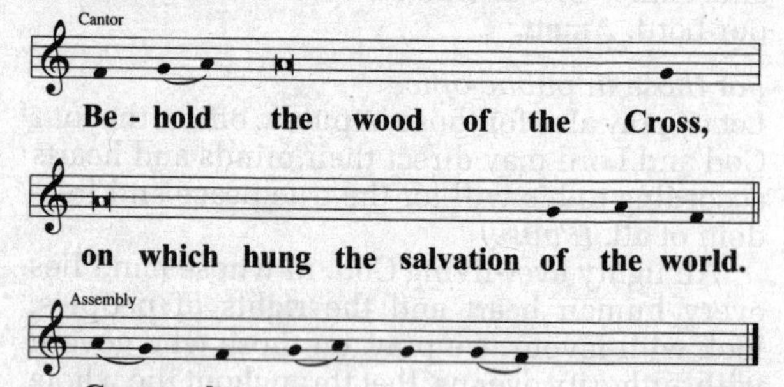

Behold the wood of the Cross, on which hung the salvation of the world. **Come, let us adore.**

After each response all adore the Cross briefly in silence. After the third response, the Cross and the candles are placed at the entrance to the sanctuary and the people approach, moving as in procession, to adore the Cross. They may make a simple genuflection or perform some other appropriate sign of reverence according to local custom.

During the adoration, suitable songs may be sung. All who have already adored the Cross remain seated. Where large numbers of people make individual adoration difficult, the priest may raise the Cross briefly for all to adore in silence.

HOLY COMMUNION

LORD'S PRAYER *(p. 68)*

PRAYER AFTER COMMUNION

Almighty ever-living God, who have restored us to life by the blessed Death and Resurrection of your Christ, preserve in us the work of your mercy, that, by partaking of this mystery, we may have a life unceasingly devoted to you. Through Christ our Lord. **Amen.**

PRAYER OVER THE PEOPLE AND DISMISSAL

Bow down for the blessing.

May abundant blessing, O Lord, we pray, descend upon your people, who have honoured the Death of your Son in the hope of their resurrection: may pardon come, comfort be given, holy faith increase, and everlasting redemption be made secure. Through Christ our Lord. **Amen.**

All genuflect to the Cross, then depart in silence.

March 26

Resurrection of the Lord

If it sounds too good to be true, it probably is.

That concept must have been rolling around in the minds of the women who loved Jesus as they trudged with broken hearts toward his tomb. These women had put all of their confidence, hope and faith in Jesus, only to see him unjustly and brutally crucified. All seemed to be lost for the grief-stricken women, who pushed to the backs of their minds the words that Jesus had told them much earlier about being handed over to sinners, being killed and rising again on the third day.

Then, they arrived at the tomb and found it empty. Their grief and emptiness must have descended to a new low as they pondered the final indignity of having the body removed by God knows who. Suddenly, the men in dazzling clothes appeared and queried them about looking for the living among the dead. Recalling what Jesus had said about his resurrection, the overwhelmed women still thought it might be too good to be true.

We all approach the tomb with some apprehension and doubt. But unlike the host of wordly promises that really are too good to be true, the word of Jesus this Easter — that he conquers sin and death and offers everlasting life — is just too true not to be good.

Frank Campbell, Enfield, NS

SOLEMN BEGINNING OF THE VIGIL *(Lucernarium)*

GREETING

The priest and the ministers, one of whom carries the unlit paschal candle, approach the fire.

In the name of the Father, and of the Son, and of the Holy Spirit. **Amen.**

1 The grace of our Lord Jesus Christ, and the love of God, and the communion of the Holy Spirit be with you all.

2 Grace to you and peace from God our Father and the Lord Jesus Christ.

3 The Lord be with you.

And with your spirit.

BLESSING OF THE FIRE

Dear brothers and sisters, on this most sacred night, in which our Lord Jesus Christ passed over from death to life, the Church calls upon her sons and daughters, scattered throughout the world, to come together to watch and pray. If we keep the memorial of the Lord's paschal solemnity in this way, listening to his word and celebrating his mysteries, then we shall have the sure hope of sharing his triumph over death and living with him in God.

Let us pray. O God, who through your Son bestowed upon the faithful the fire of your glory, sanctify this new fire, we pray, and grant that, by these paschal celebrations, we may be so inflamed with heavenly desires, that with minds made pure we may attain festivities of unending splendour. Through Christ our Lord. **Amen.**

PREPARATION AND LIGHTING OF THE CANDLE

The priest cuts a cross in the paschal candle and traces the Greek letters alpha (A) and omega (Ω) and the numerals 2016, saying:

Christ yesterday and today, the Beginning and the End, the Alpha and the Omega. All time belongs to him, and all the ages. To him be glory and power, through every age and for ever. Amen.

When the marks have been made, the priest may insert five grains of incense into the candle in the form of a cross, saying:

By his holy and glorious wounds, may Christ our Lord guard us and protect us. Amen.

The priest lights the paschal candle from the new fire, saying:

May the light of Christ rising in glory dispel the darkness of our hearts and minds.

PROCESSION WITH THE PASCHAL CANDLE

The deacon or another suitable minister holds the paschal candle and, three times during the procession to the altar, lifts it high and sings.

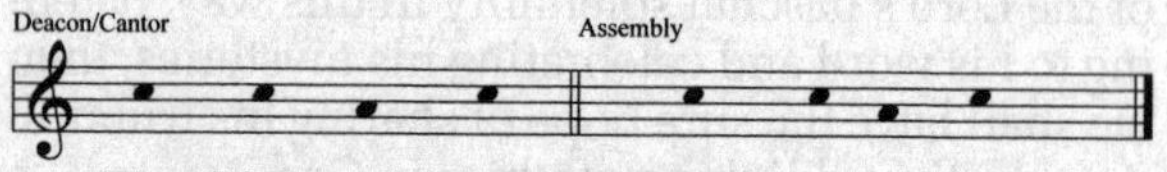

The Light of Christ. **Thanks be to God.**

After the first response, the priest lights his candle from the paschal candle.

After the second response, all the people light their candles from the flame of the paschal candle.

After the third response, all the lights in the church are lit, except for the altar candles.

EASTER PROCLAMATION *(EXSULTET)*

For the shorter version, omit the indented parts.

Exult, let them exult, the hosts of heaven,
exult, let Angel ministers of God exult,
let the trumpet of salvation
sound aloud our mighty King's triumph!
Be glad, let earth be glad, as glory floods her,
ablaze with light from her eternal King,
let all corners of the earth be glad,
knowing an end to gloom and darkness.
Rejoice, let Mother Church also rejoice,
arrayed with the lightning of his glory,
let this holy building shake with joy,
filled with the mighty voices of the peoples.

> (Therefore, dearest friends,
> standing in the awesome glory of this holy light,
> invoke with me, I ask you,
> the mercy of God almighty,
> that he, who has been pleased to number me,
> though unworthy, among the Levites,
> may pour into me his light unshadowed,
> that I may sing this candle's perfect praises.)

(The Lord be with you. **And with your spirit.**)
Lift up your hearts. **We lift them up to the Lord.**
Let us give thanks to the Lord our God. **It is right and just.**

It is truly right and just,
with ardent love of mind and heart
and with devoted service of our voice,
to acclaim our God invisible, the almighty Father,
and Jesus Christ, our Lord, his Son, his Only Begotten.
Who for our sake paid Adam's debt to the eternal Father,

and, pouring out his own dear Blood,
wiped clean the record of our ancient sinfulness.

These, then, are the feasts of Passover,
in which is slain the Lamb, the one true Lamb,
whose Blood anoints the doorposts of believers.

This is the night
when once you led our forebears, Israel's children,
from slavery in Egypt
and made them pass dry-shod through the Red Sea.

This is the night
that with a pillar of fire
banished the darkness of sin.

This is the night
that even now, throughout the world,
sets Christian believers apart from worldly vices
and from the gloom of sin,
leading them to grace
and joining them to his holy ones.

This is the night
when Christ broke the prison-bars of death
and rose victorious from the underworld.

Our birth would have been no gain,
had we not been redeemed.

O wonder of your humble care for us!
O love, O charity beyond all telling,
to ransom a slave you gave away your Son!
O truly necessary sin of Adam,
destroyed completely by the Death of Christ!
O happy fault
that earned so great, so glorious a Redeemer!

longer version:

O truly blessed night,
worthy alone to know
the time and hour
when Christ rose from
the underworld!

This is the night of
which it is written:
The night shall be as
bright as day, dazzling
is the night for me,
and full of gladness.

The sanctifying
power of this night
dispels wickedness,
washes faults away,
restores innocence
to the fallen, and joy
to mourners, drives
out hatred, fosters
concord, and brings
down the mighty.

On this, your night of
grace, O holy Father,
accept this candle, a
solemn offering, the
work of bees and of
your servants' hands,
an evening sacrifice of
praise, this gift from
your most holy Church.

shorter version:

The sanctifying
power of this night
dispels wickedness,
washes faults away,
restores innocence
to the fallen, and
joy to mourners.

O truly blessed night,
when things of heaven
are wed to those of
earth and divine to
the human.

On this, your night of
grace, O holy Father,
accept this candle, a
solemn offering, the
work of bees and of
your servants' hands,
an evening sacrifice of
praise, this gift from
your most holy Church.

But now we know the praises of this pillar, which glowing fire ignites for God's honour, a fire into many flames divided, yet never dimmed by sharing of its light, for it is fed by melting wax, drawn out by mother bees to build a torch so precious.

O truly blessed night, when things of heaven are wed to those of earth, and divine to the human.

Therefore, O Lord,
we pray you that this candle,
hallowed to the honour of your name,
may persevere undimmed,
to overcome the darkness of this night.
Receive it as a pleasing fragrance,
and let it mingle with the lights of heaven.
May this flame be found still burning
by the Morning Star:
the one Morning Star who never sets,
Christ your Son,
who, coming back from death's domain,
has shed his peaceful light on humanity,
and lives and reigns for ever and ever.
Amen.

LITURGY OF THE WORD

Dear brothers and sisters, now that we have begun our solemn Vigil, let us listen with quiet hearts to the Word of God. Let us meditate on how God in times past saved his people and in these, the last days, has sent us his Son as our Redeemer. Let us pray that our God may complete this paschal work of salvation by the fullness of redemption.

FIRST READING *(Genesis 1.1 – 2.2)*

For the shorter version, omit the indented parts.

In the beginning when God created the heavens and the earth,

> the earth was a formless void and darkness covered the face of the deep, while the spirit of God swept over the face of the waters. Then God said, "Let there be light"; and there was light. And God saw that the light was good; and God separated the light from the darkness. God called the light "Day," and the darkness he called "Night." And there was evening and there was morning, the first day.
>
> And God said, "Let there be a dome in the midst of the waters, and let it separate the waters from the waters." So God made the dome and separated the waters that were under the dome from the waters that were above the dome. And it was so. God called the dome "Sky." And there was evening and there was morning, the second day.
>
> And God said, "Let the waters under the sky be gathered together into one place, and let the dry land appear." And it was so. God

called the dry land "Earth," and the waters that were gathered together he called "Seas." And God saw that it was good.

Then God said, "Let the earth put forth vegetation: plants yielding seed, and fruit trees of every kind on earth that bear fruit with the seed in it." And it was so. The earth brought forth vegetation: plants yielding seed of every kind, and trees of every kind bearing fruit with the seed in it. And God saw that it was good. And there was evening and there was morning, the third day.

And God said, "Let there be lights in the dome of the sky to separate the day from the night; and let them be for signs and for seasons and for days and years, and let them be lights in the dome of the sky to give light upon the earth." And it was so.

God made the two great lights — the greater light to rule the day and the lesser light to rule the night — and the stars. God set them in the dome of the sky to give light upon the earth, to rule over the day and over the night, and to separate the light from the darkness. And God saw that it was good. And there was evening and there was morning, the fourth day.

And God said, "Let the waters bring forth swarms of living creatures, and let birds fly above the earth across the dome of the sky." So God created the great sea monsters and every living creature that moves, of every kind, with which the waters swarm, and every winged bird of every kind. And God saw that it was good. God blessed them, saying, "Be fruitful and multiply and fill the waters in the seas, and let birds multiply on the earth." And there was evening and there was morning, the fifth day.

And God said, "Let the earth bring forth living creatures of every kind: cattle and creeping things and wild animals of the earth of every kind." And it was so. God made the wild animals of the earth of every kind, and the cattle of every kind, and everything that creeps upon the ground of every kind. And God saw that it was good. Then

God said, "Let us make man in our image, according to our likeness; and let them have dominion over the fish of the sea, and over the birds of the air, and over the cattle, and over all the wild animals of the earth, and over every creeping thing that creeps upon the earth." So God created man in his image, in the image of God he created him; male and female he created them.

God blessed them, and God said to them, "Be fruitful and multiply, and fill the earth and subdue it; and have dominion over the fish of the sea and over the birds of the air and over every living thing that moves upon the earth."

God said, "See, I have given you every plant yielding seed that is upon the face of all the earth, and every tree with seed in its fruit; you shall have them for food. And to every beast of the earth, and to every bird of the air, and to everything that creeps on the earth, everything that has the breath of life, I have given every green plant for food." And it was so.

God saw everything that he had made, and indeed, it was very good. And there was evening and there was morning, the sixth day.

Thus the heavens and the earth were finished, and all their multitude. And on the seventh day God finished the work that he had done, and he rested on the seventh day from all the work that he had done.

The word of the Lord. **Thanks be to God.**

An alternate psalm follows.

RESPONSORIAL PSALM *(Psalm 104)*

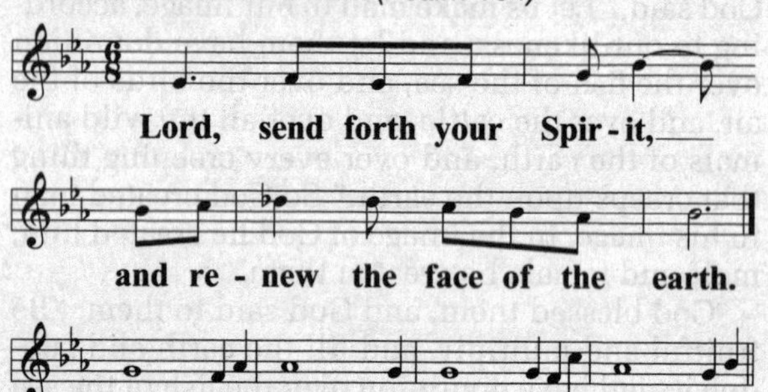

℟. **Lord, send forth your Spirit,**
and renew the face of the earth.

Bless the Lord, O · **my** soul.
O Lord my God, you are very · **great.**
You are clothed with · **honour** and majesty,
wrapped in light as with · **a** garment. ℟.

You set the earth on its · **foun-**dations,
so that it shall never be · **shaken.**
You cover it with the deep as · **with** a garment;
the waters stood above · **the** mountains. ℟.

You make springs gush forth in · **the** valleys;
they flow between the · **hills.**
By the streams the birds of the air
have their · **ha-**bi-tation;
they sing among · **the** branches. ℟.

From your lofty abode
you water · **the** mountains;
the earth is satisfied with the fruit
of your · **work.**
You cause the grass to · **grow_for** the cattle,
and plants for people to use,
to bring forth food from · **the** earth. ℟.

O Lord, how manifold are · **your** works!
In wisdom you have made them · **all;**
the earth is · **full_of** your creatures.
Bless the Lord, O · **my** soul. ℟.

or

RESPONSORIAL PSALM *(Psalm 33)*

℟. **The earth is full of the steadfast love of the Lord.**

The word of the Lord · **is** upright,
and all his work is done · **in** faithfulness.
He loves righteousness · **and** justice;
the earth is full of the steadfast love
of · **the** Lord. ℟.

By the word of the Lord
the heavens · **were** made,
and all their host by the breath of · **his** mouth.
He gathered the waters of the sea
as in · **a** bottle;
he put the deeps · **in** storehouses. ℟.

Blessed is the nation whose God is · **the** Lord,
the people whom he has chosen
as · **his** heritage.
The Lord looks down · **from** heaven;
he sees all · **human** beings. ℟.

Our soul waits for · **the** Lord;
he is our help · **and** shield.
Let your steadfast love, O Lord, be · **up-**on_us,
even as we hope · **in** you. ℟.

To hear the Sunday Psalms, go to www.livingwithchrist.ca and select the psalm button at the bottom of the home page.

PRAYER

Let us pray. *(Pause)*

1 Almighty ever-living God, who are wonderful in the ordering of all your works, may those you have redeemed understand that there exists nothing more marvellous than the world's creation in the beginning except that, at the end of the ages, Christ our Passover has been sacrificed. Who lives and reigns for ever and ever. **Amen.**

2 O God, who wonderfully created human nature and still more wonderfully redeemed it, grant us, we pray, to set our minds against the enticements of sin, that we may merit to attain eternal joys. Through Christ our Lord. **Amen.**

SECOND READING *(Genesis 22.1-18)*

For the shorter version, omit the indented parts.

God tested Abraham. He said to him, "Abraham!" And Abraham said, "Here I am." God said, "Take your son, your only son Isaac, whom you love, and go to the land of Moriah, and offer him there as a burnt offering on one of the mountains that I shall show you."

So Abraham rose early in the morning, saddled his donkey, and took two of his young men with him, and his son Isaac; he cut the wood for the burnt offering, and set out and went to the place in the distance that God had shown him.

On the third day Abraham looked up and saw the place far away. Then Abraham said to his young men, "Stay here with the donkey; the boy and I will go over there; we will worship, and then we will come back to you." Abraham took the wood of the burnt offering and laid it on his son Isaac, and he himself carried the fire and the knife. So the two of them walked on together.

Isaac said to his father Abraham, "Father!" And Abraham said, "Here I am, my son." Isaac said, "The fire and the wood are here, but where is the lamb for a burnt offering?" Abraham said, "God himself will provide the lamb for a burnt offering, my son." So the two of them walked on together.

When Abraham and Isaac came to the place that God had shown him, Abraham built an altar there and laid the wood in order. He bound his son Isaac, and laid him on the altar, on top of the wood. Then Abraham reached out his hand and took the knife to kill his son.

But the Angel of the Lord called to him from heaven, and said, "Abraham, Abraham!" And he said, "Here I am." The Angel said, "Do not lay your hand on the boy or do anything to him; for now I know that you fear God, since you have not withheld your son, your only son, from me." And

Abraham looked up and saw a ram, caught in a thicket by its horns. Abraham went and took the ram and offered it up as a burnt offering instead of his son.

So Abraham called that place "The Lord will provide"; as it is said to this day, "On the mount of the Lord it shall be provided."

The Angel of the Lord called to Abraham a second time from heaven, and said, "By myself I have sworn, says the Lord: Because you have done this, and have not withheld your son, your only son, I will indeed bless you, and I will make your offspring as numerous as the stars of heaven and as the sand that is on the seashore. And your offspring shall possess the gate of their enemies, and by your offspring shall all the nations of the earth gain blessing for themselves, because you have obeyed my voice."

The word of the Lord. **Thanks be to God.**

RESPONSORIAL PSALM *(Psalm 16)*

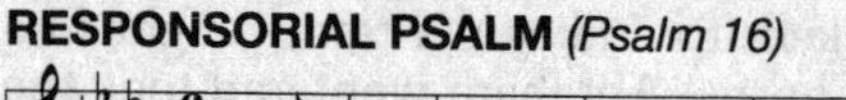

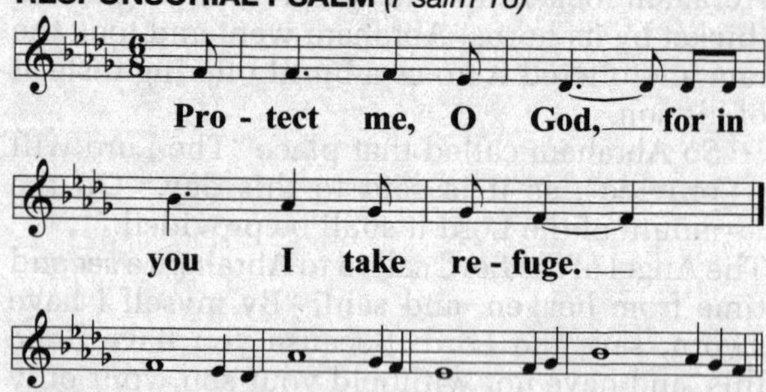

℟. **Protect me, O God, for in you I take refuge.**

The Lord is my chosen portion · **and_my** cup;
you hold · **my** lot.
I keep the Lord always · **be-**fore_me;
because he is at my right hand,
  I shall · **not** be moved. ℟.

Therefore my heart is glad,
  and my soul · **re-**joices;
my body also rests · **se-**cure.
For you do not give me up · **to** Sheol,
or let your faithful one · **see** the Pit. ℟.

You show me the path · **of** life.
In your presence there is fullness · **of** joy;
in your right hand · **are** pleasures
for·-**ev**-er-more. ℟.

PRAYER

Let us pray. *(Pause)* O God, supreme Father of the faithful, who increase the children of your promise by pouring out the grace of adoption throughout the whole world and who through the Paschal Mystery make your servant Abraham father of nations, as once you swore, grant, we pray, that your peoples may enter worthily into the grace to which you call them. Through Christ our Lord. **Amen.**

THIRD READING *(Exodus 14.15-31; 15.20, 1)*
The Lord said to Moses, "Why do you cry out to me? Tell the children of Israel to go forward. But you, lift up your staff, and stretch out your hand over the sea and divide it, that the children of Israel may go into the sea on dry ground. Then I will harden the hearts of the Egyptians so that they will go in after them; and so I will gain glory for myself over Pharaoh and all his army, his chariots, and his chariot drivers. And the Egyptians shall know that I am the Lord, when I have gained glory for myself over Pharaoh, his chariots, and his chariot drivers."

The Angel of God who was going before the Israelite army moved and went behind them; and the pillar of cloud moved from in front of them and took its place behind them. It came between the army of Egypt and the army of Israel. And so the cloud was there with the darkness, and it lit up the night; one did not come near the other all night. Then Moses stretched out his hand over the sea. The Lord drove the sea back by a strong east wind all night, and turned the sea into dry land; and the waters were divided. The children of Israel went into the sea on dry ground, the waters forming a wall for them on their right and on their left.

The Egyptians pursued, and went into the sea after them, all of Pharaoh's horses, chariots, and chariot drivers. At the morning watch, the Lord in the pillar of fire and cloud looked down upon the Egyptian army, and threw the Egyptian army into panic. He clogged their chariot wheels so that they turned with difficulty. The Egyptians said, "Let us flee from the children of Israel, for the Lord is fighting for them against Egypt."

Then the Lord said to Moses, "Stretch out your hand over the sea, so that the water may come back upon the Egyptians, upon their chariots and chariot drivers." So Moses stretched out his hand over the sea, and at dawn the sea returned to its normal depth. As the Egyptians fled before it, the Lord tossed the Egyptians into the sea. The waters returned and covered the chariots and the chariot drivers, the entire army of Pharaoh that had followed them into the sea; not one of them remained.

But the children of Israel walked on dry ground through the sea, the waters forming a wall for them on their right and on their left. Thus the Lord saved Israel that day from the Egyptians; and Israel saw the Egyptians dead on the seashore. Israel saw the great work that the Lord did against the Egyptians. So the people feared the Lord and believed in the Lord and in his servant Moses.

The Prophet Miriam, Aaron's sister, took a tambourine in her hand; and all the women went out after her with tambourines and with dancing. Moses and the children of Israel sang this song to the Lord:

RESPONSORIAL PSALM *(Exodus 15)*

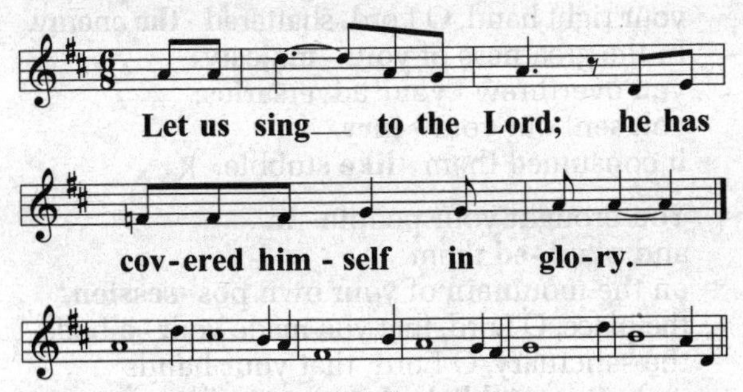

℟. **Let us sing to the Lord;**
he has covered himself in glory.

I will sing to the Lord,
for he has triumphed · **gloriously;**
horse and rider he has thrown into · **the** sea.
The Lord is my strength and my · **might,**
and he has become my · **sal-**vation;
this is my God, and I will · **praise_him,**
my father's God, and I will · **ex-**alt_him. ℟.

The Lord is a · **warrior;**
the Lord is · **his** name.
Pharaoh's chariots and his army
he cast into the · **sea;**
his picked officers were sunk in the · **Red** Sea.
The floods · **covered_them;**
they went down into the depths
· **like_a** stone. ℟.

Your right hand, O Lord, glorious in · **power;**
your right hand, O Lord, shattered · **the** enemy.
In the greatness of your · **majesty**
you overthrew · **your** adversaries;
you sent out your · **fury,**
it consumed them · **like** stubble. ℟.

You brought your people · **in**
and plant·-**ed** them
on the mountain of your own pos·-**session,**
the place, O Lord, that you made your · **a**-bode,
the sanctuary, O Lord, that your hands
have es·-**tablished.**
The Lord will reign forever · **and** ever. ℟.

PRAYER

Let us pray. *(Pause)*

1 O God, whose ancient wonders remain undimmed in splendour even in our day, for what you once bestowed on a single people, freeing them from Pharaoh's persecution by the power of your right hand, now you bring about as the salvation of the nations through the waters of rebirth, grant, we pray, that the whole world may become children of Abraham and inherit the dignity of Israel's birthright. Through Christ our Lord. **Amen.**

2 O God, who by the light of the New Testament have unlocked the meaning of wonders worked in former times, so that the Red Sea prefigures the sacred font and the nation delivered from slavery foreshadows the Christian people, grant, we pray, that all nations,

obtaining the privilege of Israel by merit of faith, may be reborn by partaking of your Spirit. Through Christ our Lord. **Amen.**

FOURTH READING *(Isaiah 54.5-14)*

Thus says the Lord, the God of hosts. Your Maker is your husband, the Lord of hosts is his name; the Holy One of Israel is your Redeemer, the God of the whole earth he is called. For the Lord has called you like a wife forsaken and grieved in spirit, like the wife of a man's youth when she is cast off, says your God.

For a brief moment I abandoned you, but with great compassion I will gather you. In overflowing wrath for a moment I hid my face from you, but with everlasting love I will have compassion on you, says the Lord, your Redeemer.

This is like the days of Noah to me: Just as I swore that the waters of Noah would never again go over the earth, so I have sworn that I will not be angry with you and will not rebuke you. For the mountains may depart and the hills be removed, but my steadfast love shall not depart from you, and my covenant of peace shall not be removed, says the Lord, who has compassion on you.

O afflicted one, storm-tossed, and not comforted, I am about to set your stones in antimony, and lay your foundations with sapphires. I will make your pinnacles of rubies, your gates of jewels, and all your walls of precious stones.

All your children shall be taught by the Lord, and great shall be the prosperity of your children. In righteousness you shall be established; you

shall be far from oppression, for you shall not fear;
and from terror, for it shall not come near you.
The word of the Lord. **Thanks be to God.**

RESPONSORIAL PSALM *(Psalm 30)*

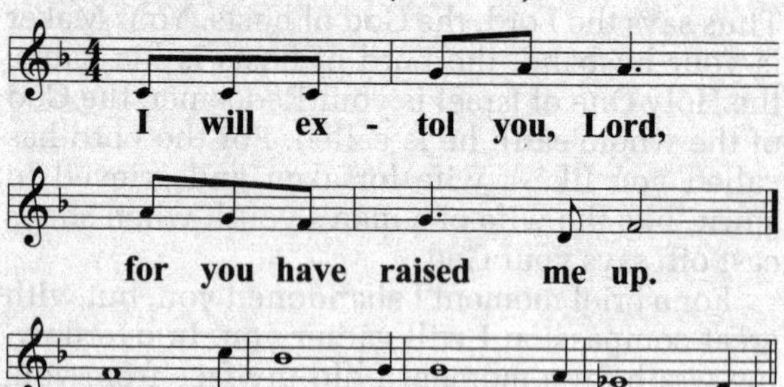

℟. **I will extol you, Lord,
for you have raised me up.**

I will extol you, O Lord, for you have
drawn me · **up,**
and did not let my foes rejoice · **over_me.**
O Lord, you brought up my soul from · **Sheol,**
restored me to life from among those gone
down · **to_the** Pit. ℟.

Sing praises to the Lord,
O you his · **faithful_ones,**
and give thanks to his holy · **name.**
For his anger is but for a moment;
his favour is for a · **lifetime.**
Weeping may linger for the night,
but joy comes · **with_the** morning. ℟.

Hear, O Lord, and be gracious to · **me!**
O Lord, be my · **helper!**
You have turned my mourning into · **dancing.**
O Lord my God, I will give thanks
to you · **for-**ever. ℟.

PRAYER

Let us pray. *(Pause)* Almighty ever-living God, surpass, for the honour of your name, what you pledged to the Patriarchs by reason of their faith, and through sacred adoption increase the children of your promise, so that what the Saints of old never doubted would come to pass your Church may now see in great part fulfilled. Through Christ our Lord. **Amen.**

FIFTH READING *(Isaiah 55.1-11)*

Thus says the Lord: "Everyone who thirsts, come to the waters; and you that have no money, come, buy and eat! Come, buy wine and milk without money and without price. Why do you spend your money for that which is not bread, and your labour for that which does not satisfy? Listen carefully to me, and eat what is good, and delight yourselves in rich food. Incline your ear, and come to me; listen, so that you may live. I will make with you an everlasting covenant, my steadfast, sure love for David.

"See, I made him a witness to the peoples, a leader and commander for the peoples. See, you shall call nations that you do not know, and nations that do not know you shall run to you, because of the Lord your God, the Holy One of Israel, for he has glorified you.

"Seek the Lord while he may be found, call upon him while he is near; let the wicked person forsake their way, and the unrighteous person their thoughts; let that person return to the Lord that he may have mercy on them, and to our God, for he will abundantly pardon.

"For my thoughts are not your thoughts, nor are your ways my ways, says the Lord. For as the heavens are higher than the earth, so are my ways higher than your ways and my thoughts than your thoughts. For as the rain and the snow come down from heaven, and do not return there until they have watered the earth, making it bring forth and sprout, giving seed to the sower and bread to the one who eats, so shall my word be that goes out from my mouth; it shall not return to me empty, but it shall accomplish that which I purpose, and succeed in the thing for which I sent it."

The word of the Lord. **Thanks be to God.**

RESPONSORIAL PSALM *(Isaiah 12)*

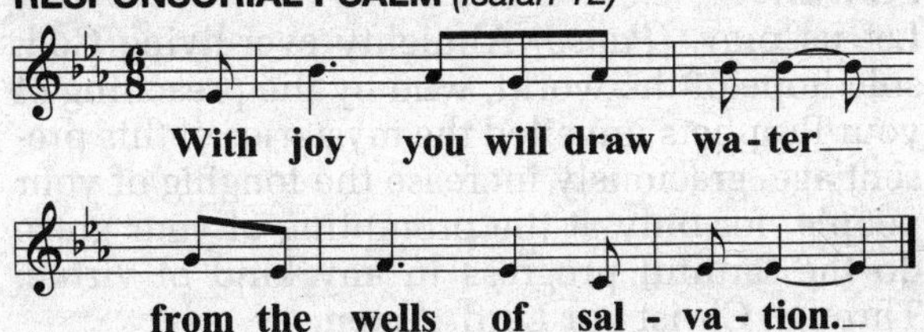

R. **With joy you will draw water**
from the wells of salvation.

Surely God is my salvation;
 I will trust, and will not · **be** a-fraid,
for the Lord God is my strength and my might;
 he has be·**-come_my** sal-vation.
With joy · **you_will** draw water
from the wells · **of** sal-vation. R.

Give thanks · **to** the Lord,
call · **on** his name;
make known his deeds a·**-mong** the nations;
proclaim that his · **name_is** ex-alted. R.

Sing praises to the Lord,
 for he · **has** done gloriously;
let this be known in · **all** the earth.
Shout aloud and sing for joy, O · **roy-**al Zion,
for great in your midst
 is the Holy · **One** of Israel. R.

To hear the Sunday Psalms, go to www.livingwithchrist.ca and select the psalm button at the bottom of the home page.

PRAYER
Let us pray. *(Pause)* Almighty ever-living God, sole hope of the world, who by the preaching of your Prophets unveiled the mysteries of this present age, graciously increase the longing of your people, for only at the prompting of your grace do the faithful progress in any kind of virtue. Through Christ our Lord. **Amen.**

SIXTH READING *(Baruch 3.9-15, 32 – 4.4)*
Hear the commandments of life, O Israel; give ear, and learn wisdom! Why is it, O Israel, why is it that you are in the land of your enemies, that you are growing old in a foreign country, that you are defiled with the dead, that you are counted among those in Hades? You have forsaken the fountain of wisdom. If you had walked in the way of God, you would be living in peace forever.

Learn where there is wisdom, where there is strength, where there is understanding, so that you may at the same time discern where there is length of days, and life, where there is light for the eyes, and peace. Who has found her place? And who has entered her storehouses?

But the one who knows all things knows her, he found her by his understanding. The one who prepared the earth for all time filled it with four-footed creatures; the one who sends forth the light, and it goes; he called it, and it obeyed him, trembling; the stars shone in their watches, and were glad; he called them, and they said, "Here we are!" They shone with gladness for him who made them.

This is our God; no other can be compared to him. He found the whole way to knowledge, and gave her to his servant Jacob and to Israel, whom he loved. Afterward she appeared on earth and lived with humanity. She is the book of the commandments of God, the law that endures forever. All who hold her fast will live, and those who forsake her will die. Turn, O Jacob, and take her; walk toward the shining of her light. Do not give your glory to another, or your advantages to an alien people.

Happy are we, O Israel, for we know what is pleasing to God.

The word of the Lord. **Thanks be to God.**

RESPONSORIAL PSALM *(Psalm 19)*

℟. **Lord, you have the words of eternal life.**

The law of the Lord is · **perfect,**
reviving the · **soul;**
the decrees of the Lord are · **sure,**
making · **wise** the simple. ℟.

The precepts of the Lord are · **right,**
rejoicing the · **heart;**
the commandment of the Lord is · **clear,**
en·-**lightening** the eyes. ℟.

The fear of the Lord is · **pure,**
enduring for·-**ever;**
the ordinances of the Lord are · **true**
and righteous · **al**-to-gether. ℟.

More to be desired are they than · **gold,**
even much fine · **gold;**
sweeter also than · **honey,**
and drippings · **of** the honeycomb. ℟.

PRAYER

Let us pray. *(Pause)* O God, who constantly increase your Church by your call to the nations, graciously grant to those you wash clean in the waters of Baptism the assurance of your unfailing protection. Through Christ our Lord. **Amen.**

SEVENTH READING *(Ezekiel 36.16-17a, 18-28)*

The word of the Lord came to me: Son of man, when the house of Israel lived on their own soil, they defiled it with their ways and their deeds; their conduct in my sight was unclean. So I poured out my wrath upon them for the blood that they had shed upon the land, and for the idols with which they had defiled it. I scattered them among the nations, and they were dispersed through the countries; in accordance with their conduct and their deeds I judged them.

But when they came to the nations, wherever they came, they profaned my holy name, in that it was said of them, "These are the people of the Lord, and yet they had to go out of his land."

But I had concern for my holy name, which the house of Israel had profaned among the nations to which they came. Therefore say to the house of Israel, Thus says the Lord God: It is not for your sake, O house of Israel, that I am about to act, but for the sake of my holy name, which you have profaned among the nations to which you came.

I will sanctify my great name, which has been profaned among the nations, and which you have profaned among them; and the nations shall know that I am the Lord, says the Lord God, when through you I display my holiness before their eyes.

I will take you from the nations, and gather you from all the countries, and bring you into your own land.

I will sprinkle clean water upon you, and you shall be clean from all your uncleanness, and from all your idols I will cleanse you.

A new heart I will give you, and a new spirit I will put within you; and I will remove from your body the heart of stone and give you a heart of flesh. I will put my spirit within you, and make you follow my statutes and be careful to observe my ordinances. Then you shall live in the land that I gave to your ancestors; and you shall be my people, and I will be your God.

The word of the Lord. **Thanks be to God.**

An alternate psalm follows. When baptism is celebrated, sing Isaiah 12 (p. 323).

RESPONSORIAL PSALM *(Psalm 42; 43)*

℞. **As a deer longs for flowing streams,**
my soul longs for you, O God.

My soul thirsts for · **God,**
for the living · **God.**
When shall I · **come**
and behold the face · **of** God? ℞.

I went with the · **throng,**
and led them in procession
to the house of · **God,**
with glad shouts and songs of · **thanksgiving,**
a multitude · **keeping** festival. ℞.

O send out your light and your · **truth;**
let them · **lead_me;**
let them bring me to your holy · **mountain**
and to · **your** dwelling. ℞.

Then I will go to the altar of · **God,**
to God my exceeding · **joy;**
and I will praise you with the · **harp,**
O God, · **my** God. ℞.

or

RESPONSORIAL PSALM *(Psalm 51)*

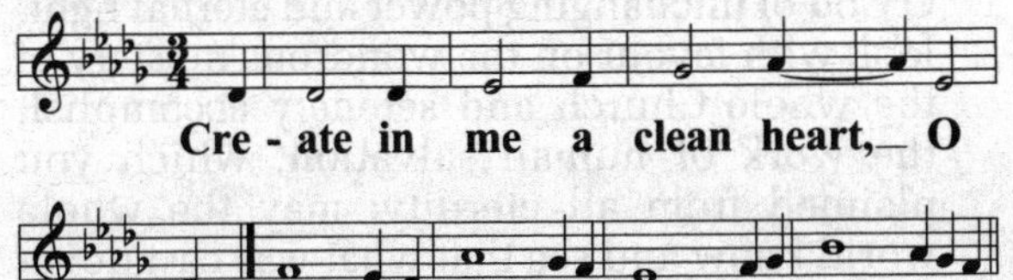

℟. **Create in me a clean heart, O God.**

Create in me a clean heart, · **O** God,
and put a new and right spirit · **with-**in_me.
Do not cast me away from · **your** presence,
and do not take your holy · **spirit** from me. ℟.

Restore to me the joy of your · **sal-**vation,
and sustain in me a will·**-ing** spirit.
Then I will teach transgressors · **your** ways,
and sinners will re·**-turn** to you. ℟.

For you have no delight · **in** sacrifice;
if I were to give a burnt offering,
  you would not · **be** pleased.
The sacrifice acceptable to God
  is a bro·**-ken** spirit;
a broken and contrite heart, O God,
  you will · **not** de-spise. ℟.

PRAYER

Let us pray. *(Pause)*

1 O God of unchanging power and eternal light, look with favour on the wondrous mystery of the whole Church and serenely accomplish the work of human salvation, which you planned from all eternity; may the whole world know and see that what was cast down is raised up, what had become old is made new, and all things are restored to integrity through Christ, just as by him they came into being. Who lives and reigns for ever and ever. **Amen**.

2 O God, who by the pages of both Testaments instruct and prepare us to celebrate the Paschal Mystery, grant that we may comprehend your mercy, so that the gifts we receive from you this night may confirm our hope of the gifts to come. Through Christ our Lord. **Amen.**

GLORY TO GOD *(p. 10)*

COLLECT

Let us pray. O God, who make this most sacred night radiant with the glory of the Lord's Resurrection, stir up in your Church a spirit of adoption, so that, renewed in body and mind, we may render you undivided service. Through our Lord Jesus Christ, your Son, who lives and reigns with you in the unity of the Holy Spirit, one God, for ever and ever. **Amen.**

EPISTLE *(Romans 6.3-11)*

Brothers and sisters: Do you not know that all of us who have been baptized into Christ Jesus were baptized into his death? Therefore we have been buried with him by baptism into death, so that, just as Christ was raised from the dead by the glory of the Father, so we too might walk in newness of life. For if we have been united with him in a death like his, we will certainly be united with him in a resurrection like his.

We know that our old self was crucified with him so that the body of sin might be destroyed, and we might no longer be enslaved to sin. For whoever has died is freed from sin. But if we have died with Christ, we believe that we will also live with him.

We know that Christ, being raised from the dead, will never die again; death no longer has dominion over him. The death he died, he died to sin, once for all; but the life he lives, he lives to God. So you also must consider yourselves dead to sin and alive to God in Christ Jesus.

The word of the Lord. **Thanks be to God.**

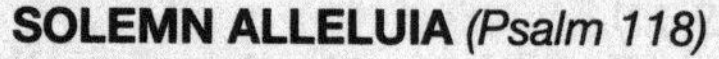

SOLEMN ALLELUIA *(Psalm 118)*

℟. **Alleluia! Alleluia! Alleluia!**

O give thanks to the Lord, for · **he** is good;
his steadfast love en·-**dures** for-ever.
Let Is·-**rael** say,
"His steadfast love en·-**dures** for-ever." ℟.

"The right hand of the Lord · **is** ex-alted;
the right hand of the · **Lord** does valiantly."
I shall not die, but · **I_shall** live,
and recount the · **deeds_of** the Lord. ℟.

The stone that the · **builders** re-jected
has become · **the** chief cornerstone.
This is the · **Lord's** doing;
it is marvellous · **in** our eyes. ℟.

GOSPEL *(Luke 24.1-12)*

The Lord be with you. **And with your spirit.** A reading from the holy Gospel according to Luke. **Glory to you, O Lord.**

On the first day of the week, at early dawn, the women who had accompanied Jesus from Galilee came to the tomb, taking the spices that they had prepared. They found the stone rolled away from the tomb, but when they went in, they did not find the body.

While they were perplexed about this, suddenly two men in dazzling clothes stood beside them. The women were terrified and bowed their faces to the ground, but the men said to them, “Why do you look for the living among the dead? He is not here, but has risen. Remember how he told you, while he was still in Galilee, that the Son of Man must be handed over to sinners, and be crucified, and on the third day rise again.”

Then the women remembered Jesus’ words, and returning from the tomb, they told all this to the eleven and to all the rest. Now it was Mary Magdalene, Joanna, Mary the mother of James, and the other women with them who told this to the Apostles.

These words seemed to the Apostles an idle tale, and they did not believe the women. But Peter got up and ran to the tomb; stooping and looking in, he saw the linen cloths by themselves; then he went home, amazed at what had happened.

The Gospel of the Lord. **Praise to you, Lord Jesus Christ.**

BAPTISMAL LITURGY

This celebration combines text from The Roman Missal *(2011) and the* Rite of Christian Initiation of Adults *(1987), where appropriate.*

INTRODUCTION

1 *If there are candidates for baptism:*

Dearly beloved, with one heart and one soul, let us by our prayers come to the aid of these our brothers and sisters in their blessed hope, so that, as they approach the font of rebirth, the almighty Father may bestow on them all his merciful help.

2 *If there are no candidates for baptism:*

Dearly beloved, let us humbly invoke upon this font the grace of God the almighty Father, that those who from it are born anew may be numbered among the children of adoption in Christ.

3 *If there are no candidates for baptism and the font is not to be blessed, proceed to the Blessing of Water, p. 342.*

LITANY OF THE SAINTS

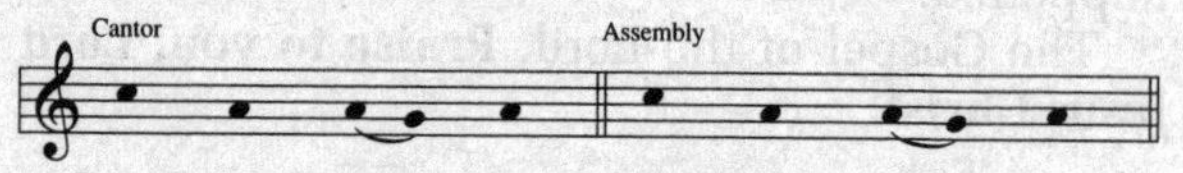

Lord, have mer - cy. Lord, have mer - cy.

Lord, have mercy. **Lord, have mercy.**
Christ, have mercy. **Christ, have mercy.**
Lord, have mercy. **Lord, have mercy.**

Holy Mary, Mother of God, **pray for us.**
Saint Michael,
Holy Angels of God,
Saint John the Baptist,
Saint Joseph,
Saint Peter and Saint Paul,
Saint Andrew,
Saint John,
Saint Mary Magdalene,
Saint Stephen,
Saint Ignatius of Antioch,
Saint Lawrence,
Saint Perpetua and Saint Felicity,
Saint Agnes,
Saint Gregory,
Saint Augustine,
Saint Athanasius,
Saint Basil,
Saint Martin,
Saint Benedict,
Saint Francis and Saint Dominic,
Saint Francis Xavier,
Saint John Vianney,
Saint Catherine of Siena,
Saint Teresa of Jesus,
(other saints)
All holy men and women, Saints of God,

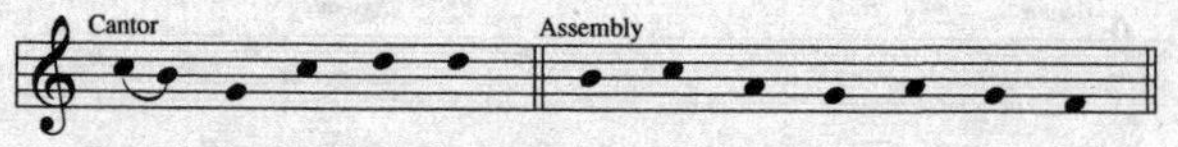

Lord, be merciful, **Lord, deliver us, we pray.**
From all evil,
From every sin,
From everlasting death,
By your Incarnation,
By your Death and Resurrection,
By the outpouring of the Holy Spirit,

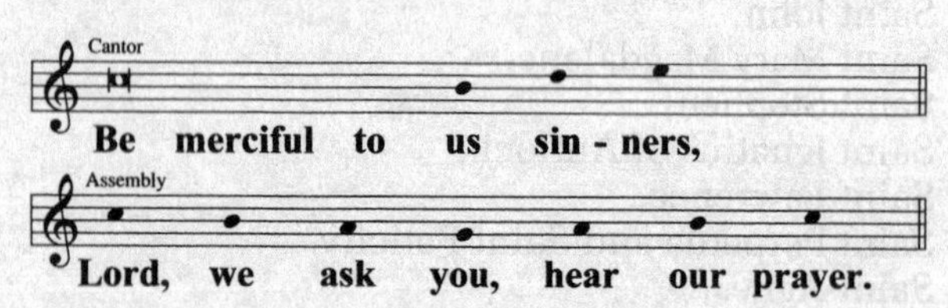

Be merciful to us sinners, **Lord, we ask you, hear our prayer.**

1 *If there are candidates for baptism:*
Bring these chosen ones to new birth through the grace of Baptism, **Lord, we ask you, hear our prayer.**

2 *If there are no candidates for baptism:*
Make this font holy by your grace for the new birth of your children, **Lord, we ask you, hear our prayer.**

Jesus, Son of the living God, **Lord, we ask you, hear our prayer.**

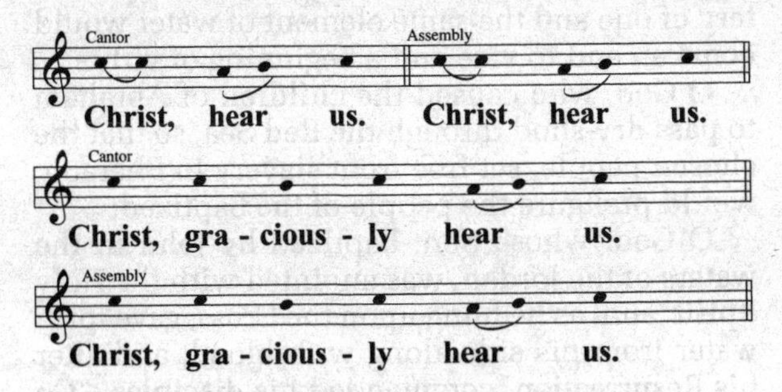

Christ, hear us. **Christ, hear us.**
Christ, graciously hear us. **Christ, graciously hear us.**

If there are candidates for baptism, the priest prays:
Almighty ever-living God, be present by the mysteries of your great love and send forth the spirit of adoption to create the new peoples brought to birth for you in the font of Baptism, so that what is to be carried out by our humble service may be brought to fulfillment by your mighty power. Through Christ our Lord. **Amen.**

BLESSING OF BAPTISMAL WATER

O God, who by invisible power accomplish a wondrous effect through sacramental signs and who in many ways have prepared water, your creation, to show forth the grace of Baptism;

O God, whose Spirit in the first moments of the world's creation hovered over the waters, so that the very substance of water would even then take to itself the power to sanctify;

O God, who by the outpouring of the flood foreshadowed regeneration, so that from the mystery of one and the same element of water would come an end to vice and a beginning of virtue;

O God, who caused the children of Abraham to pass dry-shod through the Red Sea, so that the chosen people, set free from slavery to Pharaoh, would prefigure the people of the baptized;

O God, whose Son, baptized by John in the waters of the Jordan, was anointed with the Holy Spirit, and, as he hung upon the Cross, gave forth water from his side along with blood, and after his Resurrection, commanded his disciples: "Go forth, teach all nations, baptizing them in the name of the Father and of the Son and of the Holy Spirit," look now, we pray, upon the face of your Church and graciously unseal for her the fountain of Baptism.

May this water receive by the Holy Spirit the grace of your Only Begotten Son, so that human nature, created in your image and washed clean through the Sacrament of Baptism from all the squalor of the life of old, may be found worthy to rise to the life of newborn children through water and the Holy Spirit.

May the power of the Holy Spirit, O Lord, we pray, come down through your Son into the fullness of this font, so that all who have been buried with Christ by Baptism into death may rise again to life with him. Who lives and reigns with you in the unity of the Holy Spirit, one God, for ever and ever. **Amen.**

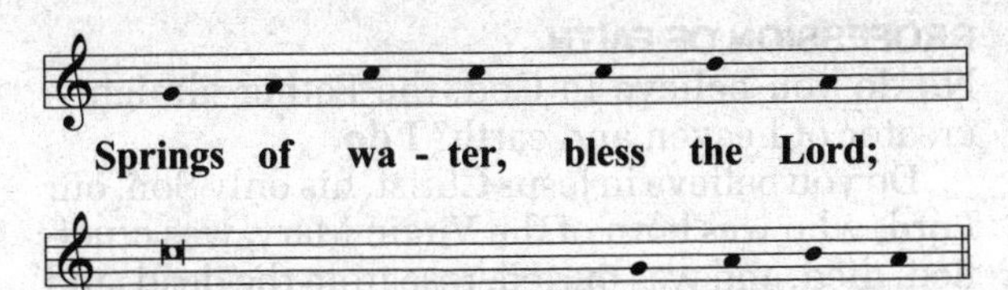

Springs of water, bless the Lord;
praise and exalt him above all for ever.

RENUNCIATION OF SIN

Using one of the following formularies, the priest questions all the candidates together or individually.

1 Do you reject sin so as to live in the freedom of God's children? **I do.**
Do you reject the glamour of evil, and refuse to be mastered by sin? **I do.**
Do you reject Satan, father of sin and prince of darkness? **I do.**

2 Do you reject Satan, and all his works, and all his empty promises? **I do.**

3 Do you reject Satan? **I do.**
And all his works? **I do.**
And all his empty promises? **I do.**

Adult candidates may now be anointed with the Oil of Catechumens.

We anoint you with the oil of salvation in the name of Christ our Saviour. May he strengthen you with his power. **Amen.**

PROFESSION OF FAITH

N., do you believe in God, the Father almighty, creator of heaven and earth? **I do.**

Do you believe in Jesus Christ, his only Son, our Lord, who was born of the Virgin Mary, was crucified, died, and was buried, rose from the dead, and is now seated at the right hand of the Father? **I do.**

Do you believe in the Holy Spirit, the holy catholic Church, the communion of saints, the forgiveness of sins, the resurrection of the body, and the life everlasting? **I do.**

BAPTISM

The priest baptizes each candidate either by immersion or by the pouring of water.

N., I baptize you in the name of the Father, and of the Son, and of the Holy Spirit.

ANOINTING AFTER BAPTISM

Any newly baptized infants are anointed now with chrism.

The God of power and Father of our Lord Jesus Christ has freed you from sin and brought you to new life through water and the Holy Spirit.

He now anoints you with the chrism of salvation, so that, united with his people, you may remain for ever a member of Christ who is Priest, Prophet, and King. **Amen.**

CLOTHING WITH A BAPTISMAL GARMENT

All the newly baptized receive a white garment.

N. and N., you have become a new creation and have clothed yourselves in Christ. Receive this baptismal garment and bring it unstained to the judgment seat of our Lord Jesus Christ, so that you may have everlasting life. **Amen.**

PRESENTATION OF A LIGHTED CANDLE

Godparents, please come forward to give to the newly baptized the light of Christ.

A godparent of each of the newly baptized lights a candle from the paschal candle and presents it to the newly baptized.

You have been enlightened by Christ. Walk always as children of the light and keep the flame of faith alive in your hearts. When the Lord comes, may you go out to meet him with all the saints in the heavenly kingdom. **Amen.**

CONFIRMATION OF ADULTS

The newly baptized adults with their godparents stand before the priest.

My dear candidates for confirmation, by your baptism you have been born again in Christ and you have become members of Christ and of his priestly people. Now you are to share in the outpouring of the Holy Spirit among us, the Spirit sent by the Lord upon his apostles at Pentecost and given by them and their successors to the baptized.

The promised strength of the Holy Spirit, which you are to receive, will make you more like Christ and help you to be witnesses to his suffering, death, and resurrection. It will strengthen you to be active members of the Church and to build up the Body of Christ in faith and love.

My dear friends, let us pray to God our Father, that he will pour out the Holy Spirit on these candidates for confirmation to strengthen them with his gifts and anoint them to be more like Christ, the Son of God.

LAYING ON OF HANDS

All-powerful God, Father of our Lord Jesus Christ, by water and the Holy Spirit you freed your sons and daughters from sin and gave them new life.

Send your Holy Spirit upon them to be their helper and guide.

Give them the spirit of wisdom and understanding, the spirit of right judgment and courage, the spirit of knowledge and reverence. Fill them with the spirit of wonder and awe in your presence. We ask this through Christ our Lord. **Amen.**

ANOINTING WITH CHRISM

During the conferral of the sacrament an appropriate song may be sung.

N., be sealed with the Gift of the Holy Spirit. **Amen.**
Peace be with you. **And with your spirit.**

BLESSING OF WATER

(when no one is to be baptized)

Dear brothers and sisters, let us humbly beseech the Lord our God to bless this water he has created, which will be sprinkled upon us as a memorial of our Baptism. May he graciously renew us, that we may remain faithful to the Spirit whom we have received. *(Pause)*

Lord our God, in your mercy be present to your people who keep vigil on this most sacred night, and, for us who recall the wondrous work of our creation and the still greater work of our redemption, graciously bless this water. For you created water to make the fields fruitful and to refresh and cleanse our bodies. You also made water the instrument of your mercy: for through water you freed your people from slavery and quenched their thirst in the desert; through water the Prophets proclaimed the new covenant you were to enter upon with the human race; and last of all, through water, which Christ made holy in the Jordan, you have renewed our corrupted nature in the bath of regeneration.

Therefore, may this water be for us a memorial of the Baptism we have received, and grant that we may share in the gladness of our brothers and sisters, who at Easter have received their Baptism. Through Christ our Lord. **Amen.**

RENEWAL OF BAPTISMAL PROMISES

While holding lit candles, the entire community renews its baptismal promises, if it has not already done so.

Dear brothers and sisters, through the Paschal Mystery we have been buried with Christ in Baptism, so that we may walk with him in newness of life. And so, now that our Lenten observance is concluded, let us renew the promises of Holy Baptism, by which we once renounced Satan and his works and promised to serve God in the holy Catholic Church.

And so I ask you:

1 Do you renounce Satan? **I do.**
And all his works? **I do.**
And all his empty show? **I do.**

2 Do you renounce sin, so as to live in the freedom of the children of God? **I do.**

Do you renounce the lure of evil, so that sin may have no mastery over you? **I do.**
Do you renounce Satan, the author and prince of sin? **I do.**

3 Do you reject sin so as to live in the freedom of God's children? **I do.**
Do you reject the glamour of evil, and refuse to be mastered by sin? **I do.**
Do you reject Satan, father of sin and prince of darkness? **I do.**

The community professes its faith:

Do you believe in God, the Father almighty, Creator of heaven and earth? **I do.**

Do you believe in Jesus Christ, his only Son, our Lord, who was born of the Virgin Mary, suffered death and was buried, rose again from the dead and is seated at the right hand of the Father? **I do.**

Do you believe in the Holy Spirit, the holy catholic Church, the communion of saints, the forgiveness of sins, the resurrection of the body, and life everlasting? **I do.**

And may almighty God, the Father of our Lord Jesus Christ, who has given us new birth by water and the Holy Spirit and bestowed on us forgiveness of our sins, keep us by his grace, in Christ Jesus our Lord, for eternal life. **Amen.**

The priest sprinkles the people with blessed water, while an appropriate song is sung.

PRAYER OF THE FAITHFUL

The following intentions are suggestions only. There are more suggestions at www.livingwithchrist.ca

℟. **Lord, hear our prayer.**

For the Church, a sign of God's covenant with the world, we pray to the Lord: ℟.

For people everywhere in need of repentance, forgiveness and compassion, we pray to the Lord: ℟.

For those in our own community who yearn for the Spirit of peace, we pray to the Lord: ℟.

For the new members of our community who have received the sacraments this Easter, we pray to the Lord: ℟.

LITURGY OF THE EUCHARIST

PREPARATION OF THE GIFTS *(p. 14)*

PRAYER OVER THE OFFERINGS

Accept, we ask, O Lord, the prayers of your people with the sacrificial offerings, that what has begun in the paschal mysteries may, by the working of your power, bring us to the healing of eternity. Through Christ our Lord. **Amen.**

PREFACE *(Easter I, p. 23)*

COMMUNION ANTIPHON *(1 Corinthians 5.7-8)*

Christ our Passover has been sacrificed; therefore let us keep the feast with the unleavened bread of purity and truth, alleluia.

PRAYER AFTER COMMUNION

Pour out on us, O Lord, the Spirit of your love, and in your kindness make those you have nourished by this paschal Sacrament one in mind and heart. Through Christ our Lord. **Amen.**

SOLEMN BLESSING – EASTER

Bow down for the blessing.

May almighty God bless you through today's Easter Solemnity and, in his compassion, defend you from every assault of sin. **Amen.**

And may he, who restores you to eternal life in the Resurrection of his Only Begotten, endow you with the prize of immortality. **Amen.**

Now that the days of the Lord's Passion have drawn to a close, may you who celebrate the gladness of the Paschal Feast come with Christ's help, and exulting in spirit, to those feasts that are celebrated in eternal joy. **Amen.**

And may the blessing of almighty God, the Father, and the Son, and the Holy Spirit, come down on you and remain with you for ever. **Amen.**

DISMISSAL

1 Go forth, the Mass is ended, alleluia, alleluia!
2 Go in peace, alleluia, alleluia!

℟. **Thanks be to God, alleluia, alleluia!**

March 27

Resurrection of the Lord

People may say to others, sometimes unkindly, "Get a life!" But there may be truth for us in this advice. We can feel weary, trapped in a rut. Easter joy and the compassionate presence of the resurrected Jesus can seem far away.

For Christians, "getting a life" means finding our meaning and centre in God's great love and peace, and then acting from the wisdom and generosity of spirit that come of this communion. It was in their deep desolation that Jesus appeared to his friends. God is with us always, but when we lack hope and things seem at their worst, we may not best be able to perceive God's presence. However, we need to choose to find moments of quiet attentiveness. It was Mary who stayed in the garden and who met the "gardener" Jesus.

To help us understand the profound significance of Easter, today's liturgy associates Jesus with the paschal lamb sacrificed at Passover. The lamb enabled the Hebrews to flee slavery. Jewish people retell this ancient event annually, reminding themselves that it is as if each of them also journeys from slavery into freedom. Besides pointing to how deeply our Christian faith is rooted in Judaism, the image of the paschal lamb reminds us that we too can choose to leave our slavery. Let us give thanks!

Beth Porter, Richmond Hill, ON

ENTRANCE ANTIPHON *(Cf. Psalm 138.18, 5-6)*
I have risen, and I am with you still, alleluia. You have laid your hand upon me, alleluia. Too wonderful for me, this knowledge, alleluia, alleluia.
or (Luke 24.34; cf. Revelation 1.6)
The Lord is truly risen, alleluia. To him be glory and power for all the ages of eternity, alleluia, alleluia.

INTRODUCTORY RITES *(p. 5)*

COLLECT
O God, who on this day, through your Only Begotten Son, have conquered death and unlocked for us the path to eternity, grant, we pray, that we who keep the solemnity of the Lord's Resurrection may, through the renewal brought by your Spirit, rise up in the light of life. Through our Lord Jesus Christ, your Son, who lives and reigns with you in the unity of the Holy Spirit, one God, for ever and ever. **Amen.**

FIRST READING *(Acts 10.34a, 37-43)*
Peter began to speak: "You know the message that spread throughout Judea, beginning in Galilee after the baptism that John announced: how God anointed Jesus of Nazareth with the Holy Spirit and with power; how he went about doing good and healing all who were oppressed by the devil, for God was with him.

"We are witnesses to all that he did both in Judea and in Jerusalem. They put him to death by hanging him on a tree; but God raised him on the third day and allowed him to appear, not to all the people but to us who were chosen by God as witnesses, and who ate and drank with him after he rose from the dead.

"He commanded us to preach to the people and to testify that he is the one ordained by God as judge of the living and the dead. All the Prophets testify about him that everyone who believes in him receives forgiveness of sins through his name."

The word of the Lord. **Thanks be to God.**

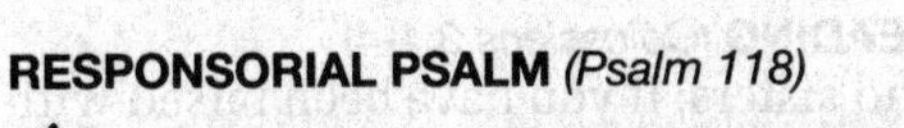

RESPONSORIAL PSALM *(Psalm 118)*

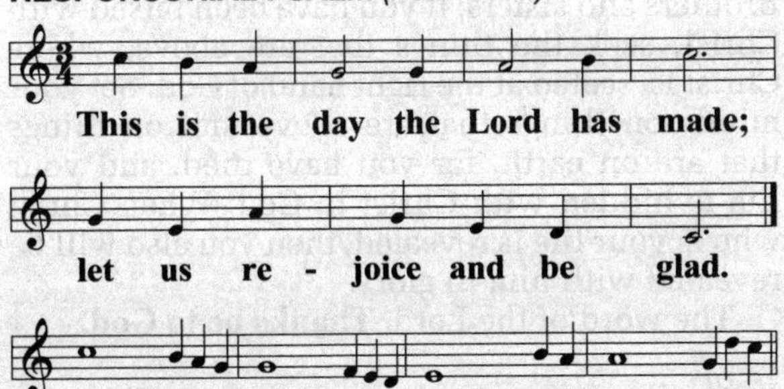

℞. **This is the day the Lord has made;**
let us rejoice and be glad.
or **Alleluia! Alleluia! Alleluia!**

O give thanks to the Lord, for · **he** is good;
his steadfast love en·-**dures** for-ever.
Let Is·-**rael** say,
"His steadfast love en·-**dures** for-ever." ℞.

"The right hand of the Lord · **is** ex-alted;
the right hand of the · **Lord** does valiantly."
I shall not die, but · **I_shall** live,
and recount the · **deeds_of** the Lord. ℞.

The stone that the · **builders** re-jected
has become · **the** chief cornerstone.
This is the · **Lord's** doing;
it is marvellous · **in** our eyes. R.

To hear the Sunday Psalms, go to www.livingwithchrist.ca and select the psalm button at the bottom of the home page.

An alternate reading follows.

SECOND READING *(Colossians 3.1-4)*
Brothers and sisters: If you have been raised with Christ, seek the things that are above, where Christ is, seated at the right hand of God. Set your minds on things that are above, not on things that are on earth, for you have died, and your life is hidden with Christ in God. When Christ who is your life is revealed, then you also will be revealed with him in glory.

The word of the Lord. **Thanks be to God.**

or

SECOND READING *(1 Corinthians 5.6b-8)*
Do you not know that a little yeast leavens the whole batch of dough? Clean out the old yeast so that you may be a new batch, as you really are unleavened. For our paschal lamb, Christ, has been sacrificed. Therefore, let us celebrate the festival, not with the old yeast, the yeast of malice and evil, but with the unleavened bread of sincerity and truth.

The word of the Lord. **Thanks be to God.**

EASTER SEQUENCE

On this day the following sequence is sung. It may also be used during the Easter Octave.

1. Christians, praise the paschal victim!
   Offer thankful sacrifice!
2. Christ the Lamb has saved the sheep,
   Christ the just one paid the price,
   Reconciling sinners to the Father.
3. Death and life fought bitterly
   For this wondrous victory;
   The Lord of life who died reigns glorified!
4. "O Mary, come and say
   what you saw at break of day."
5. "The empty tomb of my living Lord!
   I saw Christ Jesus risen and adored!
6. "Bright Angels testified,
   Shroud and grave clothes side by side!
7. "Yes, Christ my hope rose gloriously.
   He goes before you into Galilee."
8. Share the Good News, sing joyfully:
   His death is victory!
   Lord Jesus, Victor King, show us mercy.

Text: *Victimae Paschali Laudes;* tr. © 1983 *Peter J. Scagnelli.*
Tune: VICTIMAE PASCHALI LAUDES. **Music:** *CBW III* 690

GOSPEL ACCLAMATION *(1 Corinthians 5.7-8)*

Alleluia. Alleluia. Christ, our Paschal Lamb, has been sacrificed; let us feast with joy in the Lord. **Alleluia.**

The Gospel from the Easter Vigil *(p. 332)* *may be read instead. For an afternoon or evening Mass,* *see p. 353.*

GOSPEL *(John 20.1-18)*

The shorter version ends at the asterisks.

The Lord be with you. **And with your spirit.**
A reading from the holy Gospel according to John.
Glory to you, O Lord.

Early on the first day of the week, while it was still dark, Mary Magdalene came to the tomb and saw that the stone had been removed from the tomb. So she ran and went to Simon Peter and the other disciple, the one whom Jesus loved, and said to them, "They have taken the Lord out of the tomb, and we do not know where they have laid him."

Then Peter and the other disciple set out and went toward the tomb. The two were running together, but the other disciple outran Peter and reached the tomb first. He bent down to look in and saw the linen wrappings lying there, but he did not go in.

Then Simon Peter came, following him, and went into the tomb. He saw the linen wrappings lying there, and the cloth that had been on Jesus' head, not lying with the linen wrappings but rolled up in a place by itself. Then the other disciple, who reached the tomb first, also went in, and he saw and believed; for as yet they did not understand the Scripture, that he must rise from the dead.

***

Then the disciples returned to their homes. But Mary Magdalene stood weeping outside the tomb. As she wept, she bent over to look into the tomb; and she saw two Angels in white, sitting where the body of Jesus had been lying, one at the head and the other at the feet. They said to her, "Woman, why are you weeping?" She said to them, "They have taken away my Lord, and I do not know where they have laid him."

When she had said this, she turned around and saw Jesus standing there, but she did not know that it was Jesus. Jesus said to her, "Woman, why are you weeping? Whom are you looking for?" Supposing him to be the gardener, she said to him, "Sir, if you have carried him away, tell me where you have laid him, and I will take him away."

Jesus said to her, "Mary!" She turned and said to him in Hebrew, "Rabbouni!" which means Teacher. Jesus said to her, "Do not hold on to me, because I have not yet ascended to the Father. But go to my brothers and say to them, 'I am ascending to my Father and your Father, to my God and your God.'"

Mary Magdalene went and announced to the disciples, "I have seen the Lord," and she told them that he had said these things to her.

The Gospel of the Lord. **Praise to you, Lord Jesus Christ.**

Alternate Gospel for an afternoon or evening Mass:

GOSPEL *(Luke 24.13-35)*
The Lord be with you. **And with your spirit.** A reading from the holy Gospel according to Luke. **Glory to you, O Lord.**

On the first day of the week, two of the disciples were going to a village called Emmaus, about eleven kilometres from Jerusalem, and talking with each other about all these things that had happened. While they were talking and discussing, Jesus himself came near and went with them, but their eyes were kept from recognizing him.

And he said to them, "What are you discussing with each other while you walk along?" They stood still, looking sad. Then one of them, whose name was Cleopas, answered him, "Are you the only stranger in Jerusalem who does not know the things that have taken place there in these days?"

He asked them, "What things?" They replied, "The things about Jesus of Nazareth, who was a Prophet mighty in deed and word before God and all the people, and how our chief priests and leaders handed him over to be condemned to death and crucified him. But we had hoped that he was the one to redeem Israel. Yes, and besides all this, it is now the third day since these things took place. Moreover, some women of our group astounded us. They were at the tomb early this morning, and when they did not find his body there, they came back and told us that they had indeed seen a vision of Angels who said that he was alive. Some of those who were with us went to the tomb and found it just as the women had said; but they did not see him."

Then he said to them, "Oh, how foolish you are, and how slow of heart to believe all that the Prophets have declared! Was it not necessary that the Christ should suffer these things and then enter into his glory?"

Then beginning with Moses and all the Prophets, he interpreted to them the things about himself in all the Scriptures. As they came near the village to which they were going, he walked ahead as if he were going on. But they urged him strongly, saying, "Stay with us, because it is almost evening and the day is now nearly over." So he went in to stay with them.

When he was at the table with them, he took bread, blessed and broke it, and gave it to them. Then their eyes were opened, and they recognized him; and he vanished from their sight.

They said to each other, "Were not our hearts burning within us while he was talking to us on the road, while he was opening the Scriptures to us?"

That same hour they got up and returned to Jerusalem; and they found the eleven and their companions gathered together. These were saying, "The Lord has risen indeed, and he has appeared to Simon!"

Then they told what had happened on the road, and how he had been made known to them in the breaking of the bread.

The Gospel of the Lord. **Praise to you, Lord Jesus Christ.**

RENEWAL OF BAPTISMAL PROMISES *(p. 343)*

PRAYER OF THE FAITHFUL

The following intentions are suggestions only. There are more suggestions at www.livingwithchrist.ca

℟. **Lord, hear our prayer.**

For the Church, open to receive the gift of the resurrection, we pray to the Lord: ℟.

For world leaders who will govern with integrity, compassion and justice, we pray to the Lord: ℟.

For the lonely, the sick and the broken-hearted, we pray to the Lord: R.

For the Spirit of Easter hope and faith in our eucharistic community, we pray to the Lord: R.

PREPARATION OF THE GIFTS *(p. 14)*

PRAYER OVER THE OFFERINGS
Exultant with paschal gladness, O Lord, we offer the sacrifice by which your Church is wondrously reborn and nourished. Through Christ our Lord. **Amen.**

PREFACE *(Easter I, p. 23)*

COMMUNION ANTIPHON *(1 Corinthians 5.7-8)*
Christ our Passover has been sacrificed, alleluia; therefore let us keep the feast with the unleavened bread of purity and truth, alleluia, alleluia.

PRAYER AFTER COMMUNION
Look upon your Church, O God, with unfailing love and favour, so that, renewed by the paschal mysteries, she may come to the glory of the resurrection. Through Christ our Lord. **Amen.**

SOLEMN BLESSING *(Optional)*
AND DISMISSAL *(p. 346)*

April Saints' Days

The following saints are traditionally remembered in April in Canada.

2	Saint Francis of Paola
4	Saint Isidore
5	Saint Vincent Ferrer
7	Saint John Baptist de la Salle
11	Saint Stanislaus
13	Saint Martin I
17	Saint Kateri Tekakwitha
18	Blessed Marie-Anne Blondin
21	Saint Anselm
23	Saint George
	Saint Adalbert
24	Saint Fidelis of Sigmaringen
25	Saint Mark
26	Our Lady of Good Counsel
28	Saint Peter Chanel
	Saint Louis Grignion de Montfort
29	Saint Catherine of Siena
30	Saint Pius V
	Saint Marie of the Incarnation

April 3

Divine Mercy Sunday

A novelist I admire was interviewed shortly before her death. She had been ill for some time, and spoke plainly about what she expected to happen when she died. She said something like this: "I believe that death is the end. We live, we die, and that's all."

I felt saddened by her words. I wanted to think of ways to convince her otherwise, to give her and everyone who shares that view some proof that they will rise again and live in the fullness of life with God forever.

Nearly 2,000 years after Jesus' death and resurrection, we are far removed in time from the disciples, who saw with their own eyes, and from "doubting" Thomas, who could even touch the wounds in Christ's hands and side. But we can still rely on these disciples' testimony, which has been handed down from one person to another over the centuries — authentic and trustworthy.

When our faith seems shaky, we need only look to those who went before us and those around us whose faith is unwavering. They can support us and bolster us. As our faith grows stronger, we become anchors for others who may be drifting. The scriptures, too, are a great source of hope and faith for us today, for we are not the first to doubt, to question. Signs and wonders are all around us, if we have eyes to see and ears to hear!

Anne Louise Mahoney, Ottawa, ON

ENTRANCE ANTIPHON *(1 Peter 2.2)*
Like newborn infants, you must long for the pure, spiritual milk, that in him you may grow to salvation, alleluia.

or (4 Esdras 2.36-37)
Receive the joy of your glory, giving thanks to God, who has called you into the heavenly kingdom, alleluia.

INTRODUCTORY RITES *(p. 5)*

COLLECT
God of everlasting mercy, who in the very recurrence of the paschal feast kindle the faith of the people you have made your own, increase, we pray, the grace you have bestowed, that all may grasp and rightly understand in what font they have been washed, by whose Spirit they have been reborn, by whose Blood they have been redeemed. Through our Lord Jesus Christ, your Son, who lives and reigns with you in the unity of the Holy Spirit, one God, for ever and ever. **Amen.**

FIRST READING *(Acts 5.12-16)*
Many signs and wonders were done among the people through the Apostles. And the believers were all together in Solomon's Portico. None of the rest dared to join them, but the people held them in high esteem.

Yet more than ever believers were added to the Lord, great numbers of both men and women, so that they even carried out the sick into the streets, and laid them on cots and mats, in order that Peter's shadow might fall on some of them as he came by.

A great number of people would also gather from the towns around Jerusalem, bringing the sick and those tormented by unclean spirits, and they were all cured.

The word of the Lord. **Thanks be to God.**

RESPONSORIAL PSALM *(Psalm 118)*

℞. **Give thanks to the Lord, for he is good;**
his steadfast love endures forever.
or **Alleluia!**

Let Israel · **say,**
"His steadfast love endures for-·**ever.**"
Let the house of Aaron · **say,**
"His steadfast love endures for-·**ever.**"
Let those who fear the Lord · **say,**
"His steadfast love endures for-·**ever.**" ℞.

The stone that the builders re-·**jected**
has become the chief · **cornerstone.**
This is the Lord's · **doing;**
it is marvellous in our · **eyes.**
This is the day that the Lord has · **made;**
let us rejoice and be glad in · **it.** ℞.

Save us, we beseech you, O · **Lord!**
O Lord, we beseech you, give us suc·-**cess!**
Blessed is the one who comes in the name
of the · **Lord.**
We bless you from the house of the · **Lord.**
The Lord is · **God,**
and he has given us · **light.** ℟.

To hear the Sunday Psalms, go to www.livingwithchrist.ca and select the psalm button at the bottom of the home page.

SECOND READING *(Revelation 1.9-11a, 12-13, 17-19)*
I, John, your brother who share with you in Jesus the persecution and the kingdom and the patient endurance, was on the island called Patmos because of the word of God and the testimony of Jesus. I was in the spirit on the Lord's day, and I heard behind me a loud voice like a trumpet saying, "Write in a book what you see and send it to the seven Churches."

Then I turned to see whose voice it was that spoke to me, and on turning I saw seven golden lampstands, and in the midst of the lampstands I saw one like the Son of Man, clothed with a long robe and with a golden sash across his chest.

When I saw him, I fell at his feet as though dead. But he placed his right hand on me, saying, "Do not be afraid; I am the first and the last, and the living one. I was dead, but see, I am alive forever and ever; and I have the keys of Death and of Hades. Now write what you have seen, what is, and what is to take place after this."

The word of the Lord. **Thanks be to God.**

GOSPEL ACCLAMATION *(See John 20.29)*
Alleluia. Alleluia. You believed, Thomas, because you have seen me; blessed are those who have not seen, and yet believe. **Alleluia.**

GOSPEL *(John 20.19-31)*
The Lord be with you. **And with your spirit.**
A reading from the holy Gospel according to John.
Glory to you, O Lord.

It was evening on the day Jesus rose from the dead, the first day of the week, and the doors of the house where the disciples had met were locked for fear of the Jews. Jesus came and stood among them and said, "Peace be with you." After he said this, he showed them his hands and his side. Then the disciples rejoiced when they saw the Lord. Jesus said to them again, "Peace be with you. As the Father has sent me, so I send you."

When he had said this, he breathed on them and said to them, "Receive the Holy Spirit. If you forgive the sins of any, they are forgiven them; if you retain the sins of any, they are retained."

But Thomas, who was called the Twin, one of the twelve, was not with them when Jesus came. So the other disciples told him, "We have seen the Lord." But he said to them, "Unless I see the mark of the nails in his hands, and put my finger in the mark of the nails and my hand in his side, I will not believe."

After eight days his disciples were again in the house, and Thomas was with them. Although the doors were shut, Jesus came and stood among them and said, "Peace be with you." Then he said to Thomas, "Put your finger here and see my hands. Reach out your hand and put it in my side. Do not doubt but believe." Thomas answered him, "My Lord and my God!"

Jesus said to him, "Have you believed because you have seen me? Blessed are those who have not seen and yet have come to believe."

Now Jesus did many other signs in the presence of his disciples, which are not written in this book. But these are written so that you may come to believe that Jesus is the Christ, the Son of God, and that through believing you may have life in his name.

The Gospel of the Lord. **Praise to you, Lord Jesus Christ.**

PROFESSION OF FAITH *(p. 11)*

PRAYER OF THE FAITHFUL

The following intentions are suggestions only. There are more suggestions at www.livingwithchrist.ca

℟. **Lord, hear our prayer.**

For all Christian people gathered today in the Spirit of the Risen Christ, we pray to the Lord: ℟.

For the Spirit of peace and true forgiveness throughout the world, we pray to the Lord: ℟.

For those facing changes in their lives and for those who journey with them, we pray to the Lord: ℟.

For continued growth in faith for the recently baptized, received and confirmed, we pray to the Lord: ℟.

PREPARATION OF THE GIFTS *(p. 14)*

PRAYER OVER THE OFFERINGS
Accept, O Lord, we pray, the oblations of your people (and of those you have brought to new birth), that, renewed by confession of your name and by Baptism, they may attain unending happiness. Through Christ our Lord. **Amen.**

PREFACE *(Easter I, p. 23)*

COMMUNION ANTIPHON *(Cf. John 20.27)*
Bring your hand and feel the place of the nails, and do not be unbelieving but believing, alleluia.

PRAYER AFTER COMMUNION
Grant, we pray, almighty God, that our reception of this paschal Sacrament may have a continuing effect in our minds and hearts. Through Christ our Lord. **Amen.**

SOLEMN BLESSING — EASTER TIME *(Optional)*
Bow down for the blessing.

May God, who by the Resurrection of his Only Begotten Son was pleased to confer on you the gift of redemption and of adoption, give you gladness by his blessing. **Amen.**

May he, by whose redeeming work you have received the gift of everlasting freedom, make you heirs to an eternal inheritance. **Amen.**

And may you, who have already risen with Christ in Baptism through faith, by living in a right manner on this earth, be united with him in the homeland of heaven. **Amen.**

And may the blessing of almighty God, the Father, and the Son, and the Holy Spirit, come down on you and remain with you for ever. **Amen.**

DISMISSAL

1 Go forth, the Mass is ended, alleluia, alleluia!
2 Go in peace, alleluia, alleluia!

℟. **Thanks be to God, alleluia, alleluia!**

April 10

Nothing good ever seems to happen at night in the Gospel of John, and today's reading is no exception. On this Third Sunday of Easter, fish can only be caught — and truth can only emerge — at daybreak or, in this case, when Jesus shows up on the shore and starts a charcoal fire to cook the fish.

After slinking back to their old workplace, stripping off and heaving the boat into the water, the apostles were astounded when Jesus showed up for breakfast. I wonder what Peter thought when he saw Jesus on the shore — in his surprise he put his clothes back on before he jumped into the water!

Read this story carefully: Peter and Jesus seem to have some time alone before the others join them. I wonder what they spoke of. How did Peter feel, facing Jesus again after having denied him a few nights previous? During this third visit, Jesus asks Peter three times "Do you love me?" and Peter answers three times. Is the number three used just to even out the score from Peter's denial at that other charcoal fire, under the cover of darkness? Or perhaps, during that Easter season and this one, Jesus means to call Peter and all of us into a trinitarian perfection of that love.

Maureen Wicken, Vancouver, BC

ENTRANCE ANTIPHON *(Cf. Psalm 65.1-2)*
Cry out with joy to God, all the earth; O sing to the glory of his name. O render him glorious praise, alleluia.

INTRODUCTORY RITES *(p. 5)*

COLLECT
May your people exult for ever, O God, in renewed youthfulness of spirit, so that, rejoicing now in the restored glory of our adoption, we may look forward in confident hope to the rejoicing of the day of resurrection. Through our Lord Jesus Christ, your Son, who lives and reigns with you in the unity of the Holy Spirit, one God, for ever and ever. **Amen.**

FIRST READING *(Acts 5.28-32, 40b-41)*
In those days: The high priest questioned the Apostles, saying, "We gave you strict orders not to teach in this name, yet here you have filled Jerusalem with your teaching and you are determined to bring this man's blood on us."

But Peter and the Apostles answered, "We must obey God rather than human beings. The God of our ancestors raised up Jesus, whom you had killed by hanging him on a tree. God exalted him at his right hand as Leader and Saviour that he might give repentance to Israel and forgiveness of sins. And we are witnesses to these things, and so is the Holy Spirit whom God has given to those who obey him."

Then the council ordered the Apostles not to speak in the name of Jesus, and let them go. As they left the council, they rejoiced that they were considered worthy to suffer dishonour for the sake of the name.

The word of the Lord. **Thanks be to God.**

RESPONSORIAL PSALM *(Psalm 30)*

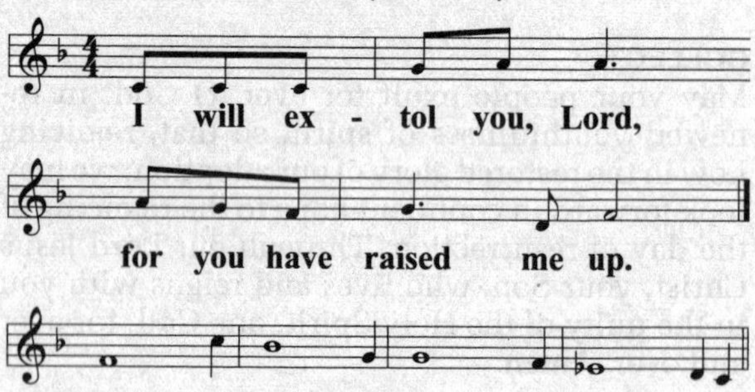

℟. **I will extol you, Lord,**
for you have raised me up.
or **Alleluia!**

I will extol you, O Lord, for you have
 drawn me · **up,**
and did not let my foes rejoice · **over_me.**
O Lord, you brought up my soul from · **Sheol,**
restored me to life from among those gone
 down · **to_the** Pit. ℟.

Sing praises to the Lord, O you
 his · **faithful_ones,**
and give thanks to his holy · **name.**
For his anger is but for a moment; his favour
 is for a · **lifetime.**
Weeping may linger for the night, but joy
 comes · **with_the** morning. ℟.

Hear, O Lord, and be gracious to · **me!**
O Lord, be my · **helper!**
You have turned my mourning into · **dancing.**
O Lord my God, I will give thanks to you
· **for**-ever. R.

To hear the Sunday Psalms, go to www.livingwithchrist.ca and select the psalm button at the bottom of the home page.

SECOND READING *(Revelation 5.11-14)*

I, John, looked, and I heard the voice of many Angels surrounding the throne and the living creatures and the elders; they numbered myriads of myriads and thousands of thousands, singing with full voice, "Worthy is the Lamb that was slaughtered to receive power and wealth and wisdom and might and honour and glory and blessing!"

Then I heard every creature in heaven and on earth and under the earth and in the sea, and all that is in them, singing, "To the one seated on the throne and to the Lamb be blessing and honour and glory and might forever and ever!" And the four living creatures said, "Amen!" And the elders fell down and worshipped.

The word of the Lord. **Thanks be to God.**

GOSPEL ACCLAMATION

Alleluia. Alleluia. Christ is risen, the Lord of all creation; he has shown pity on all people. **Alleluia.**

GOSPEL *(John 21.1-19)*
The Lord be with you. **And with your spirit.**
A reading from the holy Gospel according to John.
Glory to you, O Lord.

Jesus showed himself again to the disciples by the Sea of Tiberias; and he showed himself in this way. Gathered there together were Simon Peter, Thomas called the Twin, Nathanael of Cana in Galilee, the sons of Zebedee, and two others of his disciples. Simon Peter said to them, "I am going fishing." They said to him, "We will go with you." They went out and got into the boat, but that night they caught nothing.

Just after daybreak, Jesus stood on the beach; but the disciples did not know that it was Jesus. Jesus said to them, "Children, you have no fish, have you?" They answered him, "No." He said to them, "Cast the net to the right side of the boat, and you will find some." So they cast it, and now they were not able to haul it in because there were so many fish.

That disciple whom Jesus loved said to Peter, "It is the Lord!" When Simon Peter heard that it was the Lord, he put on some clothes, for he was naked, and jumped into the sea. But the other disciples came in the boat, dragging the net full of fish, for they were not far from the land, only about ninety metres off.

When they had gone ashore, they saw a charcoal fire there, with fish on it, and bread. Jesus said to them, "Bring some of the fish that you have just caught." So Simon Peter went aboard and hauled the net ashore, full of large fish, a hundred fifty-three of them; and though there were so many, the net was not torn. Jesus said to them, "Come and have breakfast." Now none of the disciples dared to ask him, "Who are you?" because they knew it was the Lord. Jesus came and took the bread and gave it to them, and did the same with the fish. This was now the third time that Jesus appeared to the disciples after he was raised from the dead.

When they had finished breakfast, Jesus said to Simon Peter, "Simon son of John, do you love me more than these?" He said to him, "Yes, Lord; you know that I love you." Jesus said to him, "Feed my lambs."

A second time he said to him, "Simon son of John, do you love me?" He said to him, "Yes, Lord; you know that I love you." Jesus said to him, "Tend my sheep."

He said to him the third time, "Simon son of John, do you love me?" Peter felt hurt because he said to him the third time, "Do you love me?" And he said to him, "Lord, you know everything; you know that I love you." Jesus said to him, "Feed my sheep. Very truly, I tell you, when you were younger, you used to fasten your own belt and to go wherever you wished. But when you grow old, you will stretch out your hands, and someone else will fasten a belt around you and take you where you do not wish to go." (He said this to indicate the kind of death by which he would glorify God.)

After this he said to him, "Follow me."

The Gospel of the Lord. **Praise to you, Lord Jesus Christ.**

PROFESSION OF FAITH *(p. 11)*

PRAYER OF THE FAITHFUL

The following intentions are suggestions only. There are more suggestions at www.livingwithchrist.ca

℟. **Lord, hear our prayer.**

For the Church, working to overcome divisions between persons, races and nations, we pray to the Lord: ℟.

For leaders of nations in search of justice for the needy, we pray to the Lord: ℟.

For the Spirit of healing where there is suffering, fear or doubt, we pray to the Lord: ℟.

For us, God's people, seeking to serve despite our own needs and concerns, we pray to the Lord: ℟.

PREPARATION OF THE GIFTS *(p. 14)*

PRAYER OVER THE OFFERINGS

Receive, O Lord, we pray, these offerings of your exultant Church, and, as you have given her cause for such great gladness, grant also that the gifts we bring may bear fruit in perpetual happiness. Through Christ our Lord. **Amen.**

PREFACE *(Easter, p. 23)*

COMMUNION ANTIPHON *(Luke 24.35)*

The disciples recognized the Lord Jesus in the breaking of the bread, alleluia.

or (Cf. John 21.12-13)

Jesus said to his disciples: Come and eat. And he took bread and gave it to them, alleluia.

PRAYER AFTER COMMUNION
Look with kindness upon your people, O Lord, and grant, we pray, that those you were pleased to renew by eternal mysteries may attain in their flesh the incorruptible glory of the resurrection. Through Christ our Lord. **Amen.**

SOLEMN BLESSING *(Optional, p. 364)*

DISMISSAL *(p. 70)*

April 17

World Day of Prayer for Vocations

"Listen," says one sheep to the others, "he's calling us!" Over the clatter of many feet on the ground, above the shoulders of everyone jostling about, cutting through the noise of many voices and the din of life in motion, Jesus is also calling out to each of us to follow him.

"My sheep hear my voice. I know them, and they follow me," the Good Shepherd confidently proclaims. "I give them eternal life, and they will never perish... What my Father has given me is greater than all else, and no one can snatch it out of the Father's hand."

In today's first reading, Paul and Barnabas respond to the call of Jesus. Even though they face persecution and times are hard, when they live out their calling they are filled with joy and with the Holy Spirit. Doubtless they are numbered in the great multitude robed in white depicted by John in Revelation, a host standing in continuous Eucharist before the throne and the shepherd, who is himself the Lamb of God.

Today, as we join with the 'sheep' of all ages at the altar of the Shepherd and Lamb, Jesus the Christ, let us respond to his calling, to our vocation, with a resounding, joyful "Yes!" Like Paul and Barnabas, let us shake the dust off our feet and head out, filled with joy and the Holy Spirit.

Beverly Illauq, Kemptville, ON

ENTRANCE ANTIPHON *(Cf. Psalm 32.5-6)*
The merciful love of the Lord fills the earth; by the word of the Lord the heavens were made, alleluia.

INTRODUCTORY RITES *(p. 5)*

COLLECT
Almighty ever-living God, lead us to a share in the joys of heaven, so that the humble flock may reach where the brave Shepherd has gone before. Who lives and reigns with you in the unity of the Holy Spirit, one God, for ever and ever. **Amen.**

FIRST READING *(Acts 13.14, 43-52)*
Paul and Barnabas went on from Perga and came to Antioch in Pisidia. On the Sabbath day they went into the synagogue and sat down.

When the meeting of the synagogue broke up, many Jews and devout converts to Judaism followed Paul and Barnabas, who spoke to them and urged them to continue in the grace of God.

The next Sabbath almost the whole city gathered to hear the word of the Lord. But when the Jewish officials saw the crowds, they were filled with jealousy; and blaspheming, they contradicted what was spoken by Paul.

Then both Paul and Barnabas spoke out boldly, saying, "It was necessary that the word of God should be spoken first to you. Since you reject it and judge yourselves to be unworthy of eternal life, we are now turning to the Gentiles. For so the Lord has commanded us, saying, 'I have set you to be a light for the Gentiles, so that you may bring salvation to the ends of the earth.'" When the Gentiles heard this, they were glad and praised the word of the Lord; and as many as had been destined for eternal life became believers.

Thus the word of the Lord spread throughout the region. But the officials incited the devout women of high standing and the leading men of the city, and stirred up persecution against Paul and Barnabas, and drove them out of their region. So they shook the dust off their feet in protest against them, and went to Iconium. And the disciples were filled with joy and with the Holy Spirit.

The word of the Lord. **Thanks be to God.**

RESPONSORIAL PSALM *(Psalm 100)*

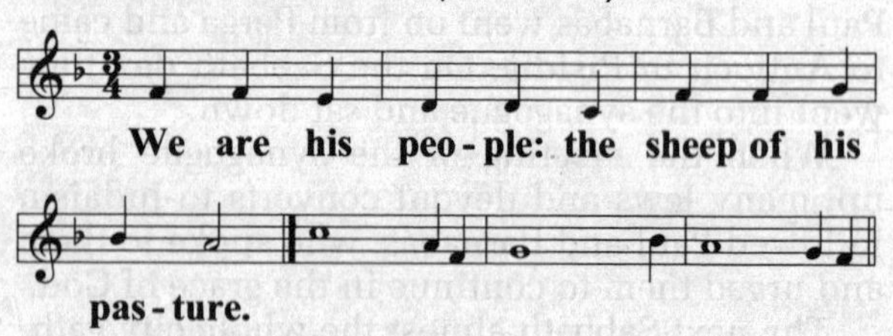

℟. **We are his people: the sheep of his pasture.**
or **Alleluia!**

Make a joyful noise to the Lord,
all · **the** earth.
Worship the Lord with · **gladness;**
come into his presence · **with** singing. ℟.

Know that the Lord · **is** God.
It is he that made us, and we are · **his;**
we are his people, and the sheep
of · **his** pasture. ℟.

For the Lord · **is** good;
his steadfast love endures for·-**ever**,
and his faithfulness to all · **gener**-ations. ℟.

©2009 Gordon Johnston/Novalis

To hear the Sunday Psalms, go to www.livingwithchrist.ca and select the psalm button at the bottom of the home page.

SECOND READING *(Revelation 7.9, 14b-17)*
After this I, John, looked, and there was a great multitude that no one could count, from every nation, from all tribes and peoples and languages, standing before the throne and before the Lamb, robed in white, with palm branches in their hands. And one of the elders then said to me, "These are they who have come out of the great ordeal; they have washed their robes and made them white in the blood of the Lamb. For this reason they are before the throne of God, and worship him day and night within his temple, and the one who is seated on the throne will shelter them. They will hunger no more, and thirst no more; the sun will not strike them, nor any scorching heat; for the Lamb at the centre of the throne will be their shepherd, and he will guide them to springs of the water of life, and God will wipe away every tear from their eyes."

The word of the Lord. **Thanks be to God.**

GOSPEL ACCLAMATION *(John 10.14)*
Alleluia. Alleluia. I am the good shepherd, says the Lord; I know my sheep, and my own know me. **Alleluia.**

GOSPEL *(John 10.27-30)*

The Lord be with you. **And with your spirit.**
A reading from the holy Gospel according to John.
Glory to you, O Lord.

Jesus said: "My sheep hear my voice. I know them, and they follow me. I give them eternal life, and they will never perish. No one will snatch them out of my hand. What my Father has given me is greater than all else, and no one can snatch it out of the Father's hand. The Father and I are one."

The Gospel of the Lord. **Praise to you, Lord Jesus Christ.**

PROFESSION OF FAITH *(p. 11)*

PRAYER OF THE FAITHFUL

The following intentions are suggestions only. There are more suggestions at www.livingwithchrist.ca

℟. **Lord, hear our prayer.**

For the Church, sent by God to shepherd his flock, we pray to the Lord: ℟.

For tolerance and peace among believers of all faiths, we pray to the Lord: ℟.

For those who suffer under the weary burden of loneliness, we pray to the Lord: ℟.

For all the members of this community, working to be faithful followers of Jesus, we pray to the Lord: ℟.

PREPARATION OF THE GIFTS *(p. 14)*

PRAYER OVER THE OFFERINGS
Grant, we pray, O Lord, that we may always find delight in these paschal mysteries, so that the renewal constantly at work within us may be the cause of our unending joy. Through Christ our Lord. **Amen.**

PREFACE *(Easter, p. 23)*

COMMUNION ANTIPHON
The Good Shepherd has risen, who laid down his life for his sheep and willingly died for his flock, alleluia.

PRAYER AFTER COMMUNION
Look upon your flock, kind Shepherd, and be pleased to settle in eternal pastures the sheep you have redeemed by the Precious Blood of your Son. Who lives and reigns for ever and ever. **Amen.**

SOLEMN BLESSING *(Optional, p. 364)*

DISMISSAL *(p. 70)*

April 24

For the past four weeks we have been basking in the glow of the Resurrection. However, the readings today convey a simple but urgent message directly related to living out one's Christian mission.

The account from Acts sounds like a travelogue instead of what it really is: a description of the birth of the early Church. The faith of the early Christians represents the miraculous movement from disbelief and confusion to faith and order, a passage to which so many of us can relate as our faith grows and matures.

How do we participate in the building of "a new heaven and a new earth" today? The gospel prepares us for this overwhelming task. There is a poignant moment when Jesus tells his disciples, "I am with you only a little longer." What a blow for his friends and family. It is easy to imagine them asking each other: How will we manage? What will we do? How can we go on?

But Jesus gives the perfect answer to all their questions — and ours: "I give you a new commandment, that you love one another." This is often much easier said than done. Yet it is precisely this love for each other which marks us not only as disciples of Christ but as ordinary people who seek to bring about the kingdom of God on earth in this day and age.

Marilyn-Ann Elphick, Toronto, ON

ENTRANCE ANTIPHON *(Cf. Psalm 97.1-2)*
O sing a new song to the Lord, for he has worked wonders; in the sight of the nations he has shown his deliverance, alleluia.

INTRODUCTORY RITES *(p. 5)*

COLLECT
Almighty ever-living God, constantly accomplish the Paschal Mystery within us, that those you were pleased to make new in Holy Baptism may, under your protective care, bear much fruit and come to the joys of life eternal. Through our Lord Jesus Christ, your Son, who lives and reigns with you in the unity of the Holy Spirit, one God, for ever and ever. **Amen.**

FIRST READING *(Acts 14.21b-27)*
Paul and Barnabas returned to Lystra, then on to Iconium and Antioch. There they strengthened the souls of the disciples and encouraged them to continue in the faith, saying, "It is through many persecutions that we must enter the kingdom of God." And after they had appointed elders for them in each Church, with prayer and fasting they entrusted them to the Lord in whom they had come to believe.

Then they passed through Pisidia and came to Pamphylia. When they had spoken the word in Perga, they went down to Attalia. From there they sailed back to Antioch, where they had been commended to the grace of God for the work that they had completed.

When they arrived, they called the Church together and related all that God had done with them, and how he had opened a door of faith for the Gentiles.

The word of the Lord. **Thanks be to God.**

RESPONSORIAL PSALM *(Psalm 145)*

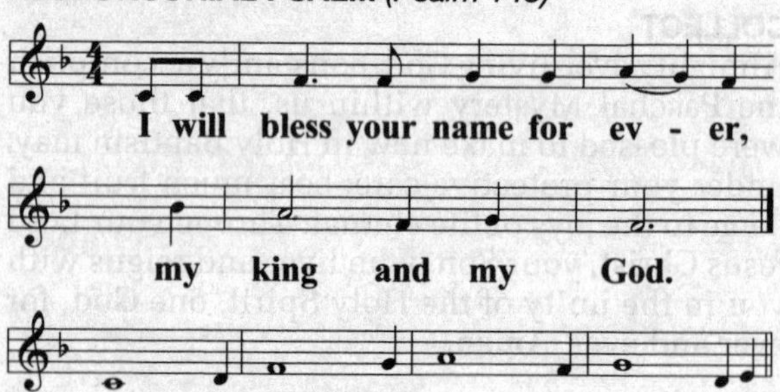

℟. **I will bless your name for ever,**
my King and my God.
or **Alleluia!**

The Lord is gracious and · **merciful,**
slow to anger and abounding in steadfast · **love.**
The Lord is good to · **all,**
and his compassion is over all that he
· **has** made. ℟.

All your works shall give thanks to you,
O · **Lord,**
and all your faithful shall · **bless_you.**
They shall speak of the glory of your · **kingdom,**
and tell of · **your** power. ℟.

To make known to human beings your
mighty · **deeds,**
and the glorious splendour of your · **kingdom.**
Your kingdom is an everlasting · **kingdom,**
and your dominion endures throughout
all · **gener**-ations. ℟.

To hear the Sunday Psalms, go to www.livingwithchrist.ca and select the psalm button at the bottom of the home page.

SECOND READING *(Revelation 21.1-5a)*

Then I, John, saw a new heaven and a new earth; for the first heaven and the first earth had passed away, and the sea was no more.

And I saw the holy city, the new Jerusalem, coming down out of heaven from God, prepared as a bride adorned for her husband.

And I heard a loud voice from the throne saying, "See, the home of God is among humans. He will dwell with them as their God; they will be his peoples, and God himself will be with them; he will wipe every tear from their eyes. Death will be no more; mourning and crying and pain will be no more, for the first things have passed away." And the one who was seated on the throne said, "See, I am making all things new."

The word of the Lord. **Thanks be to God.**

GOSPEL ACCLAMATION *(See John 13.34)*

Alleluia. Alleluia. I give you a new commandment: love one another just as I have loved you. **Alleluia.**

GOSPEL *(John 13.1, 31-33a, 34-35)*
The Lord be with you. **And with your spirit.**
A reading from the holy Gospel according to John.
Glory to you, O Lord.

Before the festival of the Passover, Jesus knew that his hour had come to depart from this world and go to the Father. Having loved his own who were in the world, he loved them to the end.

During the supper, when Judas had gone out, Jesus said, "Now the Son of Man has been glorified, and God has been glorified in him. If God has been glorified in him, God will also glorify him in himself and will glorify him at once.

"Little children, I am with you only a little longer. I give you a new commandment, that you love one another. Just as I have loved you, you also should love one another. By this everyone will know that you are my disciples, if you have love for one another."

The Gospel of the Lord. **Praise to you, Lord Jesus Christ.**

PROFESSION OF FAITH *(p. 11)*

PRAYER OF THE FAITHFUL
The following intentions are suggestions only. There are more suggestions at www.livingwithchrist.ca

℟. Lord, hear our prayer.

For the Church, witness to the saving life, death and resurrection of Jesus, we pray to the Lord: ℟.

For world leaders, entrusted with serving their people, we pray to the Lord: ℟.

For the Spirit of prophecy and healing where there is suffering and persecution, we pray to the Lord: ℟.

For Easter hope in our eucharistic community, we pray to the Lord: ℟.

PREPARATION OF THE GIFTS *(p. 14)*

PRAYER OVER THE OFFERINGS
O God, who by the wonderful exchange effected in this sacrifice have made us partakers of the one supreme Godhead, grant, we pray, that, as we have come to know your truth, we may make it ours by a worthy way of life. Through Christ our Lord. **Amen.**

PREFACE *(Easter, p. 23)*

COMMUNION ANTIPHON *(Cf. John 15.1, 5)*
I am the true vine and you are the branches, says the Lord. Whoever remains in me, and I in him, bears fruit in plenty, alleluia.

PRAYER AFTER COMMUNION
Graciously be present to your people, we pray, O Lord, and lead those you have imbued with heavenly mysteries to pass from former ways to newness of life. Through Christ our Lord. **Amen.**

SOLEMN BLESSING *(Optional, p. 364)*

DISMISSAL *(p. 70)*

May Saints' Days

The following saints are traditionally remembered in May in Canada.

1 Saint Joseph the Worker

2 Saint Athanasius

3 Saints Philip and James

4 Blessed Marie-Léonie Paradis

6 Saint François de Laval

8 Blessed Catherine of Saint Augustine

12 Saints Nereus and Achilleus
Saint Pancras

13 Our Lady of Fatima

14 Saint Matthias

18 Saint John I

20 Saint Bernardine of Siena

21 Saint Christopher Magallanes and Companions
Saint Eugène de Mazenod

22 Saint Rita of Cascia

24 Blessed Louis-Zéphirin Moreau

25 Saint Bede the Venerable
Saint Gregory VII
Saint Mary Magdalene de' Pazzi

26 Saint Philip Neri

27 Saint Augustine of Canterbury

May 1

Did you ever know a family who didn't have disagreements? Members of families often squabble over things trivial to cataclysmic. But when the disagreement passes, peace is restored and the family emerges stronger.

This is true of the Church as well, as we hear in today's readings. There were disagreements when the groups the apostles left behind wrestled with questions of how to separate cultural practices from the essentials of Scripture. There are still differences today as bishops around the globe try to reconcile Christ's teachings in a world of clashing cultures.

The apostles had no road map to the New Jerusalem — the city of peace — beautifully and mystically described in Revelation. But Jesus gave them a key to unlock the mystery: "Peace I leave with you; my peace I give to you... Do not let your hearts be troubled, and do not let them be afraid."

This is no ordinary peace. It is a peace that is alive and leavened with compassion and justice. "The Holy Spirit... will teach you everything, and remind you of all that I have said to you." The Holy Spirit is alive today, guiding the Church in the perpetual reinterpretation of the gospel. These words are as relevant today as they were at the beginning. This is the eternal peace we are promised.

Patrick M. Doyle, Carleton Place, ON

National Collection for the Pope's Pastoral Works

ENTRANCE ANTIPHON *(Cf. Isaiah 48.20)*
Proclaim a joyful sound and let it be heard; proclaim to the ends of the earth: The Lord has freed his people, alleluia.

INTRODUCTORY RITES *(p. 5)*

COLLECT
Grant, almighty God, that we may celebrate with heartfelt devotion these days of joy, which we keep in honour of the risen Lord, and that what we relive in remembrance we may always hold to in what we do. Through our Lord Jesus Christ, your Son, who lives and reigns with you in the unity of the Holy Spirit, one God, for ever and ever. **Amen.**

FIRST READING *(Acts 15.1-2, 22-29)*
Certain individuals came down from Judea and were teaching the brothers, "Unless you are circumcised according to the custom of Moses, you cannot be saved." And after Paul and Barnabas had no small dissension and debate with them, Paul and Barnabas and some of the others were appointed to go up to Jerusalem to discuss this question with the Apostles and the elders.

Then the Apostles and the elders, with the consent of the whole Church, decided to choose men from among their members and to send them to Antioch with Paul and Barnabas. They sent Judas called Barsabbas, and Silas, leaders among the brothers, with the following letter:

"The brothers, both the Apostles and the elders, to the believers of Gentile origin in Antioch and Syria and Cilicia, greetings. Since we have heard that certain persons who have gone out from us, though with no instructions from us, have said things to disturb you and have unsettled your minds, we have decided unanimously to choose representatives and send them to you, along with our beloved Barnabas and Paul, who have risked their lives for the sake of our Lord Jesus Christ. We have therefore sent Judas and Silas, who themselves will tell you the same things by word of mouth.

"For it has seemed good to the Holy Spirit and to us to impose on you no further burden than these essentials: that you abstain from what has been sacrificed to idols, and from blood and from what is strangled, and from fornication. If you keep yourselves from these, you will do well. Farewell."

The word of the Lord. **Thanks be to God.**

RESPONSORIAL PSALM *(Psalm 67)*

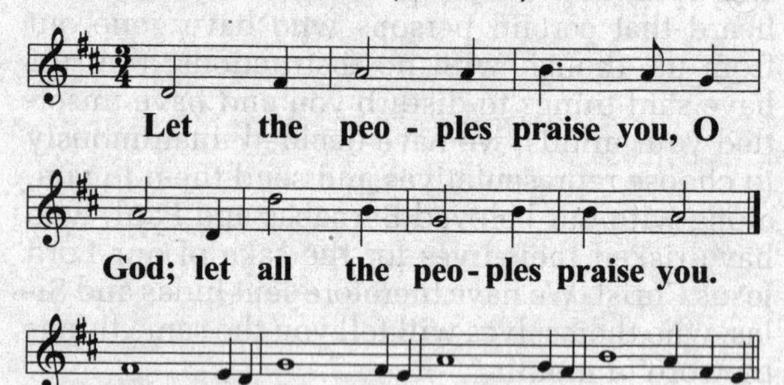

℟. **Let the peoples praise you, O God;**
let all the peoples praise you.
or **Alleluia!**

May God be gracious to us · **and** bless_us
and make his face to shine · **up**-on_us,
that your way may be known up·-**on** earth,
your saving power a·-**mong** all nations. ℟.

Let the nations be glad and sing · **for** joy,
for you judge the peoples with equity
and guide the nations · **upon** earth.
Let the peoples praise you, · **O** God;
let all the · **peo**-ples praise_you. ℟.

The earth has yielded · **its** increase;
God, our God, · **has** blessed_us.
May God continue · **to** bless_us;
let all the ends of the · **earth** re-vere_him. ℟.

To hear the Sunday Psalms, go to www.livingwithchrist.ca and select the psalm button at the bottom of the home page.

SECOND READING *(Revelation 21.10-14, 22-23)*
In the spirit the Angel carried me away to a great, high mountain and showed me the holy city Jerusalem coming down out of heaven from God. It has the glory of God and a radiance like a very rare jewel, like jasper, clear as crystal.

It has a great, high wall with twelve gates, and at the gates twelve Angels, and on the gates are inscribed the names of the twelve tribes of the children of Israel; on the east there were three gates, on the north three gates, on the south three gates, and on the west three gates. And the wall of the city has twelve foundations, and on them are the twelve names of the twelve Apostles of the Lamb.

I saw no temple in the city, for its temple is the Lord God the Almighty and the Lamb. And the city has no need of sun or moon to shine on it, for the glory of God is its light, and its lamp is the Lamb.

The word of the Lord. **Thanks be to God.**

GOSPEL ACCLAMATION *(John 14.23)*
Alleluia. Alleluia. Whoever loves me will keep my word, and my Father will love him, and we will come to him. **Alleluia.**

GOSPEL *(John 14.23-29)*
The Lord be with you. **And with your spirit.**
A reading from the holy Gospel according to John.
Glory to you, O Lord.

Jesus said to his disciples: "Whoever loves me will keep my word, and my Father will love him, and we will come to him and make our home with him. Whoever does not love me does not keep my words; and the word that you hear is not mine, but is from the Father who sent me.

"I have said these things to you while I am still with you. But the Advocate, the Holy Spirit, whom the Father will send in my name, will teach you everything, and remind you of all that I have said to you.

"Peace I leave with you; my peace I give to you. I do not give to you as the world gives. Do not let your hearts be troubled, and do not let them be afraid.

"You heard me say to you, 'I am going away, and I am coming to you.' If you loved me, you would rejoice that I am going to the Father, because the Father is greater than I. And now I have told you this before it occurs, so that when it does occur, you may believe."

The Gospel of the Lord. **Praise to you, Lord Jesus Christ.**

PROFESSION OF FAITH *(p. 11)*

PRAYER OF THE FAITHFUL

The following intentions are suggestions only. There are more suggestions at www.livingwithchrist.ca

℟. **Lord, hear our prayer.**

For all Christian people gathered today in the Spirit of the Risen Christ, we pray to the Lord: ℟.

For people who hunger and thirst for justice, we pray to the Lord: ℟.

For families responding to the call to be a community of God's love, we pray to the Lord: ℟.

For our parish community, striving to bring God's love to those with whom we live and work, we pray to the Lord: ℟.

PREPARATION OF THE GIFTS *(p. 14)*

PRAYER OVER THE OFFERINGS
May our prayers rise up to you, O Lord, together with the sacrificial offerings, so that, purified by your graciousness, we may be conformed to the mysteries of your mighty love. Through Christ our Lord. **Amen.**

PREFACE *(Easter, p. 23)*

COMMUNION ANTIPHON *(John 14.15-16)*
If you love me, keep my commandments, says the Lord, and I will ask the Father and he will send you another Paraclete, to abide with you for ever, alleluia.

PRAYER AFTER COMMUNION
Almighty ever-living God, who restore us to eternal life in the Resurrection of Christ, increase in us, we pray, the fruits of this paschal Sacrament and pour into our hearts the strength of this saving food. Through Christ our Lord. **Amen.**

SOLEMN BLESSING *(Optional, p. 364)*

DISMISSAL *(p. 70)*

May 8

World Communications Day

For many, the admonition "Go fly a kite" could be a put-down. But those who know me know I would gratefully go and joyfully fly a kite! The freedom of the wind in its tails, the connection of the string pulling on the spindle and the joy of the community of all ages and stages gathering to watch and smile... there are few joys greater. It brings a smile to my face just picturing it.

So I put myself into the readings for today. Why do I stand here, looking up at the sky? As Jesus was blessing the disciples (me) he left them (me) and was taken up into heaven. Before their very eyes, he was taken and a cloud hid him from their sight.

Maybe it is Jesus' promise of the Holy Spirit. Or could it be the community waiting together for the fullness of the time promised by Jesus. Maybe it's the freedom of the wind in my tails. All I know is I keep waiting, I keep coming back and, yes, I do clap my hands and shout out in cries of joy... "Our God is an awesome God!"

I haven't flown a kite in years. I have several in the garage and I even take them in the car periodically, but they never seem to make it out of their packaging. Maybe this year, this Sunday, this feast of the Ascension, I'll go fly a kite, joyfully!

Sr. Susan Kidd, CND, Charlottetown, PE

ENTRANCE ANTIPHON *(Acts 1.11)*
Men of Galilee, why gaze in wonder at the heavens? This Jesus whom you saw ascending into heaven will return as you saw him go, alleluia.

INTRODUCTORY RITES *(p. 5)*

COLLECT
Gladden us with holy joys, almighty God, and make us rejoice with devout thanksgiving, for the Ascension of Christ your Son is our exaltation, and, where the Head has gone before in glory, the Body is called to follow in hope. Through our Lord Jesus Christ, your Son, who lives and reigns with you in the unity of the Holy Spirit, one God, for ever and ever. **Amen.**

or

Grant, we pray, almighty God, that we, who believe that your Only Begotten Son, our Redeemer, ascended this day to the heavens, may in spirit dwell already in heavenly realms. Who lives and reigns with you in the unity of the Holy Spirit, one God, for ever and ever. **Amen.**

FIRST READING *(Acts 1.1-11)*
In the first book, Theophilus, I wrote about all that Jesus did and taught from the beginning until the day when he was taken up to heaven, after giving instructions through the Holy Spirit to the Apostles whom he had chosen. After his suffering he presented himself alive to them by many convincing proofs, appearing to them during forty days and speaking about the kingdom of God.

While staying with them, he ordered them not to leave Jerusalem, but to wait there for the promise of the Father. "This," he said, "is what you have heard from me; for John baptized with water, but you will be baptized with the Holy Spirit not many days from now."

So when they had come together, they asked him, "Lord, is this the time when you will restore the kingdom to Israel?" He replied, "It is not for you to know the times or periods that the Father has set by his own authority. But you will receive power when the Holy Spirit has come upon you; and you will be my witnesses in Jerusalem, in all Judea and Samaria, and to the ends of the earth."

When he had said this, as they were watching, he was lifted up, and a cloud took him out of their sight. While he was going and they were gazing up toward heaven, suddenly two men in white robes stood by them. They said, "Men of Galilee, why do you stand looking up toward heaven? This Jesus, who has been taken up from you into heaven, will come in the same way as you saw him go into heaven."

The word of the Lord. **Thanks be to God.**

RESPONSORIAL PSALM *(Psalm 47)*

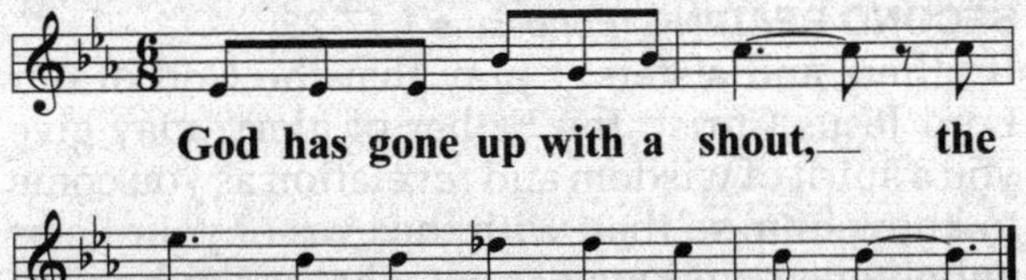

℟. **God has gone up with a shout,**
the Lord with the sound of a trumpet.
or **Alleluia!**

Clap your hands, all · **you** peoples;
shout to God with loud songs · **of** joy.
For the Lord, the Most High, · **is** awesome,
a great king over · **all** the earth. ℟.

God has gone up · **with_a** shout,
the Lord with the sound of · **a** trumpet.
Sing praises to God, · **sing** praises;
sing praises to our · **King,** sing praises. ℟.

For God is the king of all · **the** earth;
sing praises · **with_a** Psalm.
God is king over · **the** nations;
God sits on his · **ho**-ly throne. ℟.

To hear the Sunday Psalms, go to www.livingwithchrist.ca and select the psalm button at the bottom of the home page.

An alternate reading follows.

SECOND READING *(Ephesians 1.17-23)*
Brothers and sisters: I pray that the God of our Lord Jesus Christ, the Father of glory, may give you a spirit of wisdom and revelation as you come to know him, so that, with the eyes of your heart enlightened, you may know what is the hope to which he has called you, what are the riches of his glorious inheritance among the saints, and what is the immeasurable greatness of his power for us who believe, according to the working of his great power.

God put this power to work in Christ when he raised him from the dead and seated him at his right hand in the heavenly places, far above all rule and authority and power and dominion, and above every name that is named, not only in this age but also in the age to come.

And he has put all things under his feet and has made him the head over all things for the Church, which is his body, the fullness of him who fills all in all.

The word of the Lord. **Thanks be to God.**

or

SECOND READING *(Hebrews 9.24-28; 10.19-23)*
Christ did not enter a sanctuary made by human hands, a mere copy of the true one, but he entered into heaven itself, now to appear in the presence of God on our behalf. Nor was it to offer himself again and again, as the high priest enters the Holy Place year after year with blood that is not his own; for then he would have had to suffer again

and again since the foundation of the world. But as it is, he has appeared once for all at the end of the age to remove sin by the sacrifice of himself.

And just as it is appointed for human beings to die once, and after that comes the judgment, so Christ, having been offered once to bear the sins of many, will appear a second time, not to deal with sin, but to save those who are eagerly waiting for him.

Therefore, brothers and sisters, since we have confidence to enter the sanctuary by the blood of Jesus, by the new and living way that he opened for us through the curtain, that is, through his flesh, and since we have a great priest over the house of God, let us approach with a true heart in full assurance of faith, with our hearts sprinkled clean from an evil conscience and our bodies washed with pure water. Let us hold fast to the confession of our hope without wavering, for he who has promised is faithful.

The word of the Lord. **Thanks be to God.**

GOSPEL ACCLAMATION *(Matthew 28.19, 20)*

Alleluia. Alleluia. Go, make disciples of all nations; I am with you always, to the end of the age. **Alleluia.**

GOSPEL *(Luke 24.46-53)*

The Lord be with you. **And with your spirit.** A reading from the holy Gospel according to Luke. **Glory to you, O Lord.**

Jesus said to the disciples, "These are my words that I spoke to you while I was still with you — that everything written about me in the Law of Moses, the Prophets, and the Psalms must be fulfilled."

Then he opened their minds to understand the Scriptures, and he said to them, "Thus it is written, that the Christ is to suffer and to rise from the dead on the third day, and that repentance and forgiveness of sins is to be proclaimed in his name to all nations, beginning from Jerusalem. You are witnesses of these things.

"And see, I am sending upon you what my Father promised; so stay here in the city until you have been clothed with power from on high."

Then he led them out as far as Bethany, and, lifting up his hands, he blessed them. While he was blessing them, he withdrew from them and was carried up into heaven. And they worshipped him, and returned to Jerusalem with great joy; and they were continually in the temple blessing God.

The Gospel of the Lord. **Praise to you, Lord Jesus Christ.**

PROFESSION OF FAITH *(p. 11)*

PRAYER OF THE FAITHFUL

The following intentions are suggestions only. There are more suggestions at www.livingwithchrist.ca

℟. **Lord, hear our prayer.**

On this World Communications Day, for Christians at work in the media, promoting justice and peace, we pray to the Lord: ℟.

For all who experience division and conflict, especially those who suffer discrimination, we pray to the Lord: ℟.

For mothers everywhere, nurturing the next generation, and for those who share in child-rearing, we pray to the Lord: ℟.

For ourselves here today, called to follow Jesus in the service of others, we pray to the Lord: ℟.

PREPARATION OF THE GIFTS *(p. 14)*

PRAYER OVER THE OFFERINGS

We offer sacrifice now in supplication, O Lord, to honour the wondrous Ascension of your Son: grant, we pray, that through this most holy exchange we, too, may rise up to the heavenly realms. Through Christ our Lord. **Amen.**

PREFACE *(Ascension, p. 25)*

COMMUNION ANTIPHON *(Matthew 28.20)*

Behold, I am with you always, even to the end of the age, alleluia.

PRAYER AFTER COMMUNION

Almighty ever-living God, who allow those on earth to celebrate divine mysteries, grant, we pray, that Christian hope may draw us onward to where our nature is united with you. Through Christ our Lord. **Amen.**

SOLEMN BLESSING – ASCENSION *(Optional)*

Bow down for the blessing.

May almighty God bless you, for on this very day his Only Begotten Son pierced the heights of heaven and unlocked for you the way to ascend to where he is. **Amen.**

May he grant that, as Christ after his Resurrection was seen plainly by his disciples, so when he comes as Judge he may show himself merciful to you for all eternity. **Amen.**

And may you, who believe he is seated with the Father in his majesty, know with joy the fulfillment of his promise to stay with you until the end of time. **Amen.**

And may the blessing of almighty God, the Father, and the Son, and the Holy Spirit, come down on you and remain with you for ever. **Amen.**

DISMISSAL *(p. 70)*

May 15

I'm a high school teacher and a mother of teenagers. A lot of my life is spent teaching and reminding. Mainly reminding.

Today's kids don't really need us to teach facts. With a few clicks of their phone — a phone they probably know how to operate better than we do — information is, literally, at their fingertips. But that doesn't make teaching or parenting obsolete. In fact, I'd say it makes our role as mentors even more important. We help kids navigate real moments. We teach them things they won't find on the Internet, like how to be still and reflect. How to discern and grow in wisdom. We show them that, contrary to popular belief, they are not their Facebook status or their latest selfie. We remind them who they really are — children of God.

We need that reminder, too. Caught up in our worlds and worries, it's easy to forget to pray. We call it "stress" but really it's forgetfulness. We have forgotten who we are, whose we are and sadly, we have forgotten what power we have at our fingertips if we just clasp them together in prayer.

Look for the Holy Spirit's nudge. What is it urging you to do? Listen for the lesson and learn from it. For there is no better teacher or mentor than very spirit of God within.

Caroline Pignat, Kanata, ON

ENTRANCE ANTIPHON *(Wisdom 1.7)*
The Spirit of the Lord has filled the whole world and that which contains all things understands what is said, alleluia.

or (Romans 5.5; cf. 8.11)
The love of God has been poured into our hearts through the Spirit of God dwelling within us, alleluia.

INTRODUCTORY RITES *(p. 5)*

COLLECT
O God, who by the mystery of today's great feast sanctify your whole Church in every people and nation, pour out, we pray, the gifts of the Holy Spirit across the face of the earth and, with the divine grace that was at work when the Gospel was first proclaimed, fill now once more the hearts of believers. Through our Lord Jesus Christ, your Son, who lives and reigns with you in the unity of the Holy Spirit, one God, for ever and ever. **Amen.**

FIRST READING *(Acts 2.1-11)*
When the day of Pentecost had come, they were all together in one place. And suddenly from heaven there came a sound like the rush of a violent wind, and it filled the entire house where they were sitting. Divided tongues, as of fire, appeared among them, and a tongue rested on each of them. All of them were filled with the Holy Spirit and began to speak in other languages, as the Spirit gave them ability.

Now there were devout Jews from every nation under heaven living in Jerusalem. And at this sound the crowd gathered and was bewildered, because each one heard them speaking in their own language. Amazed and astonished, they asked, "Are not all these who are speaking Galileans? And how is it that we hear, each of us, in our own language? Parthians, Medes, Elamites, and residents of Mesopotamia, Judea and Cappadocia, Pontus and Asia, Phrygia and Pamphylia, Egypt and the parts of Libya belonging to Cyrene, and visitors from Rome, both Jews and converts, Cretans and Arabs — in our own languages we hear them speaking about God's deeds of power."

The word of the Lord. **Thanks be to God.**

RESPONSORIAL PSALM *(Psalm 104)*

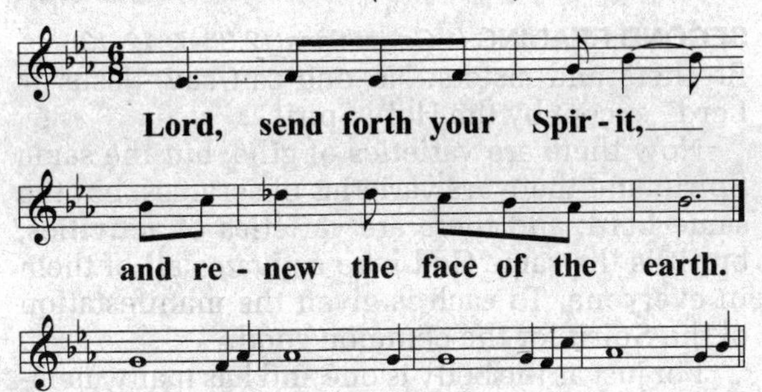

℞. **Lord, send forth your Spirit,**
and renew the face of the earth.
or **Alleluia!**

Bless the Lord, O · **my** soul.
O Lord my God, you are very · **great.**
O Lord, how manifold · **are** your works!
The earth is full of · **your** creatures. ℞.

When you take away · **their** breath,
they die and return to their · **dust.**
When you send forth your spirit, they
· **are** cre-ated;
and you renew the face of · **the** earth. ℟.

May the glory of the Lord endure · **for**-ever;
may the Lord rejoice in his · **works.**
May my meditation be · **pleasing** to him,
for I rejoice in · **the** Lord. ℟.

To hear the Sunday Psalms, go to www.livingwithchrist.ca and select the psalm button at the bottom of the home page.

An alternate reading follows.

SECOND READING *(1 Corinthians 12.3b-7, 12-13)*
Brothers and sisters: No one can say "Jesus is Lord" except by the Holy Spirit.

Now there are varieties of gifts, but the same Spirit; and there are varieties of services, but the same Lord; and there are varieties of activities, but it is the same God who activates all of them in everyone. To each is given the manifestation of the Spirit for the common good.

For just as the body is one and has many members, and all the members of the body, though many, are one body, so it is with Christ. For in the one Spirit we were all baptized into one body — Jews or Greeks, slaves or free — and we were all made to drink of one Spirit.

The word of the Lord. **Thanks be to God.**

or

SECOND READING *(Romans 8.8-17)*
Brothers and sisters: Those who are in the flesh cannot please God. But you are not in the flesh; you are in the Spirit, since the Spirit of God dwells in you. Anyone who does not have the Spirit of Christ does not belong to him.

But if Christ is in you, though the body is dead because of sin, the Spirit is life because of righteousness. If the Spirit of God who raised Jesus from the dead dwells in you, he who raised Christ from the dead will give life to your mortal bodies also through his Spirit that dwells in you.

So then, brothers and sisters, we are debtors, not to the flesh, to live according to the flesh — for if you live according to the flesh, you will die; but if by the Spirit you put to death the deeds of the body, you will live. For all who are led by the Spirit of God are sons and daughters of God. For you did not receive a spirit of slavery to fall back into fear, but you have received a spirit of adoption to sonship. When we cry, "Abba! Father!" it is that very Spirit bearing witness with our spirit that we are children of God, and if children, then heirs, heirs of God and joint heirs with Christ — if, in fact, we suffer with him so that we may also be glorified with him.

The word of the Lord. **Thanks be to God.**

SEQUENCE

3. Of consolers, wisest, best,
   And our soul's most welcome guest,
   Sweet refreshment, sweet repose.

4. In our labour rest most sweet,
   Pleasant coolness in the heat,
   Consolation in our woes.

5. Light most blessed, shine with grace
   In our heart's most secret place,
   Fill your faithful through and through.

6. Left without your presence here,
   Life itself would disappear,
   Nothing thrives apart from you!

7. Cleanse our soiled hearts of sin,
   Arid souls refresh within,
   Wounded lives to health restore.

8. Bend the stubborn heart and will,
   Melt the frozen, warm the chill,
   Guide the wayward home once more!

9. On the faithful who are true
   And profess their faith in you,
   In your sev'nfold gift descend!

10. Give us virtue's sure reward,
    Give us your salvation, Lord,
    Give us joys that never end!

Text: *Veni Sancte Spiritus;* tr. E. Caswell; adapt. © *Peter J. Scagnelli.* **Tune:** *©1995 Albert Dunn*

GOSPEL ACCLAMATION

Alleluia. Alleluia. Come, Holy Spirit, fill the hearts of your faithful and kindle in them the fire of your love. **Alleluia.**

An alternate reading follows.

GOSPEL *(John 20.19-23)*

The Lord be with you. **And with your spirit.** A reading from the holy Gospel according to John. **Glory to you, O Lord.**

It was evening on the day Jesus rose from the dead, the first day of the week, and the doors of the house where the disciples had met were locked for fear of the Jews. Jesus came and stood among them and said, "Peace be with you." After he said this, he showed them his hands and his side. Then the disciples rejoiced when they saw the Lord.

Jesus said to them again, "Peace be with you. As the Father has sent me, so I send you."

When he had said this, he breathed on them and said to them, "Receive the Holy Spirit. If you forgive the sins of any, they are forgiven them; if you retain the sins of any, they are retained."

The Gospel of the Lord. **Praise to you, Lord Jesus Christ.**

or

GOSPEL *(John 14.15-16, 23b-26)*

The Lord be with you. **And with your spirit.**
A reading from the holy Gospel according to John.
Glory to you, O Lord.

Jesus said to the disciples: "If you love me, you will keep my commandments. And I will ask the Father, and he will give you another Advocate, to be with you forever.

"Whoever loves me will keep my word, and my Father will love him, and we will come to him and make our home with him. Whoever does not love me does not keep my words; and the word that you hear is not mine, but is from the Father who sent me.

"I have said these things to you while I am still with you. But the Advocate, the Holy Spirit, whom the Father will send in my name, will teach you everything, and remind you of all that I have said to you."

The Gospel of the Lord. **Praise to you, Lord Jesus Christ.**

PROFESSION OF FAITH *(p. 11)*

PRAYER OF THE FAITHFUL

The following intentions are suggestions only. There are more suggestions at www.livingwithchrist.ca

℟. **Send forth your Spirit, O Lord.**

For the Church, calling for lasting peace among nations, we pray to the Lord: ℟.

For an outpouring of the Spirit of truth upon the world, we pray to the Lord: ℟.

For the sick and the dying, for those who are alone, and for those who find themselves strangers in a strange land, we pray to the Lord: ℟.

For our parish community, especially in our efforts to reflect God's love, we pray to the Lord: ℟.

PREPARATION OF THE GIFTS *(p. 14)*

PRAYER OVER THE OFFERINGS

Grant, we pray, O Lord, that, as promised by your Son, the Holy Spirit may reveal to us more abundantly the hidden mystery of this sacrifice and graciously lead us into all truth. Through Christ our Lord. **Amen.**

PREFACE *(Pentecost,* *p. 26)*

COMMUNION ANTIPHON *(Acts 2.4, 11)*

They were all filled with the Holy Spirit and spoke of the marvels of God, alleluia.

PRAYER AFTER COMMUNION

O God, who bestow heavenly gifts upon your Church, safeguard, we pray, the grace you have given, that the gift of the Holy Spirit poured out upon her may retain all its force and that this spiritual food may gain her abundance of eternal redemption. Through Christ our Lord. **Amen.**

SOLEMN BLESSING – THE HOLY SPIRIT *(Optional)*

Bow down for the blessing.

May God, the Father of lights, who was pleased to enlighten the disciples' minds by the outpouring of the Spirit, the Paraclete, grant you gladness by his blessing and make you always abound with the gifts of the same Spirit. **Amen.**

May the wondrous flame that appeared above the disciples powerfully cleanse your hearts from every evil and pervade them with its purifying light. **Amen.**

And may God, who has been pleased to unite many tongues in the profession of one faith, give you perseverance in that same faith and, by believing, may you journey from hope to clear vision. **Amen.**

And may the blessing of almighty God, the Father, and the Son, and the Holy Spirit, come down on you and remain with you for ever. **Amen.**

DISMISSAL

1 Go forth, the Mass is ended, alleluia, alleluia!
2 Go in peace, alleluia, alleluia!

℟. **Thanks be to God, alleluia, alleluia!**

May 22

While the mystery of God is beyond our comprehension, today's readings offer a tangible connection to God's great wisdom. We begin with a front-row seat at the creation of the universe: God, with Wisdom at his side, delighting in the work of all creation. With humble awe, we receive glory and honour beyond our understanding.

On one level, we know many things. We know we are created in the image and likeness of God, the Creator. We know God's very being walked on this earth, in the person of his son, Jesus Christ. We know that when Jesus returned home to the Father, he sent his Spirit to teach and guide us.

On another level, we cannot comprehend the "Why?" of it all. Wisely, we turn to a question we can answer: "How?" Whenever we delight in creation, we are in harmony with our Creator. We honour the Redeemer by living with faith, hope and love. Quietly attentive, we hear in our hearts the whispered wisdom of the Sanctifier.

Each time we bless ourselves with the Sign of the Cross, we are acknowledging the mystery of the threefold presence. Refreshing ourselves in Word and Sacrament, we receive the grace to live holy and sacred lives. Rejoicing, we share in God's sense of delight.

Brenda Merk Hildebrand, Campbell River, BC

ENTRANCE ANTIPHON

Blest be God the Father, and the Only Begotten Son of God, and also the Holy Spirit, for he has shown us his merciful love.

INTRODUCTORY RITES *(p. 5)*

COLLECT

God our Father, who by sending into the world the Word of truth and the Spirit of sanctification made known to the human race your wondrous mystery, grant us, we pray, that in professing the true faith, we may acknowledge the Trinity of eternal glory and adore your Unity, powerful in majesty. Through our Lord Jesus Christ, your Son, who lives and reigns with you in the unity of the Holy Spirit, one God, for ever and ever. **Amen.**

FIRST READING *(Proverbs 8.22-31)*

Thus says the Wisdom of God:
"The Lord created me at the beginning of his work,
the first of his acts of long ago.
Ages ago I was set up,
at the first, before the beginning of the earth.
When there were no depths I was brought forth,
when there were no springs abounding
with water.
Before the mountains had been shaped,
before the hills, I was brought forth —
when he had not yet made earth and fields,
or the world's first bits of soil.
When he established the heavens, I was there,
when he drew a circle on the face of the deep,
when he made firm the skies above,

when he established the fountains of the deep,
when he assigned to the sea its limit,
so that the waters might not transgress his
 command,
when he marked out the foundations
 of the earth,
then I was beside him, like a master worker;
and I was daily his delight,
rejoicing before him always,
rejoicing in his inhabited world
and delighting in the children of Adam."

The word of the Lord. **Thanks be to God.**

RESPONSORIAL PSALM *(Psalm 8)*

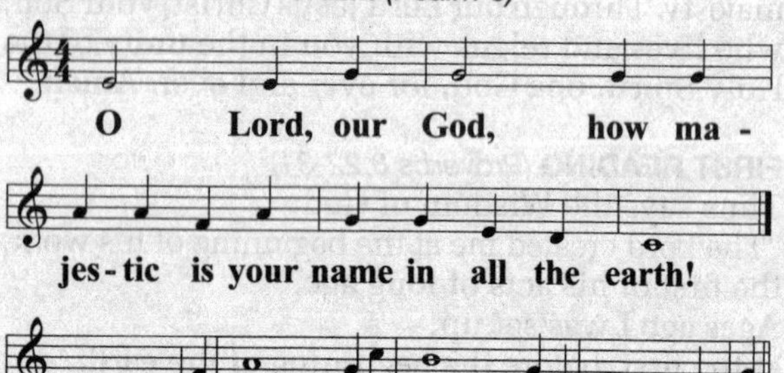

℟. **O Lord, our God, how majestic is your name in all the earth!**

When I look at your heavens, the work of
 · **your** fingers,
the moon and the stars that you have
 · **es**-tablished;
what is a man that you · **are** mindful_of_him,
or the son of man · **that** you care_for_him? ℟.

Yet you have made him a little lower
· **than_the** Angels,
and crowned him with glory · **and** honour.
You have given him dominion over the works
of · **your** hands;
you have put all things · **under** his feet. ℟.

All sheep · **and** oxen,
and also the beasts of · **the** field,
the birds of the air, and the fish of · **the** sea,
whatever passes along the · **paths_of**
the seas. ℟.

To hear the Sunday Psalms, go to www.livingwithchrist.ca and select the psalm button at the bottom of the home page.

SECOND READING *(Romans 5.1-5)*

Brothers and sisters: Since we are justified by faith, we have peace with God through our Lord Jesus Christ, through whom we have obtained access to this grace in which we stand; and we boast in our hope of sharing the glory of God.

And not only that, but we also boast in our sufferings, knowing that suffering produces endurance, and endurance produces character, and character produces hope, and hope does not disappoint us, because God's love has been poured into our hearts through the Holy Spirit that has been given to us.

The word of the Lord. **Thanks be to God.**

GOSPEL ACCLAMATION

Alleluia. Alleluia. Glory to the Father, the Son, and the Holy Spirit: to God who is, who was, and who is to come. **Alleluia.**

GOSPEL *(John 16.12-15)*

The Lord be with you. **And with your spirit.** A reading from the holy Gospel according to John. **Glory to you, O Lord.**

Jesus said to his disciples: "I still have many things to say to you, but you cannot bear them now. When the Spirit of truth comes, he will guide you into all the truth; for he will not speak on his own, but will speak whatever he hears, and he will declare to you the things that are to come. He will glorify me, because he will take what is mine and declare it to you. All that the Father has is mine. For this reason I said that he will take what is mine and declare it to you."

The Gospel of the Lord. **Praise to you, Lord Jesus Christ.**

PROFESSION OF FAITH *(p. 11)*

PRAYER OF THE FAITHFUL

The following intentions are suggestions only. There are more suggestions at www.livingwithchrist.ca

℟. **Lord, hear our prayer.**

For the People of God, striving to embody the love of the Trinity, we pray to the Lord: ℟.

For peace among all nations and for peace in human hearts, we pray to the Lord: ℟.

For growing respect among people of all races, cultures and religions, we pray to the Lord: ℟.

For the assembly gathered here and for those who cannot be here, we pray to the Lord: ℟.

PREPARATION OF THE GIFTS *(p. 14)*

PRAYER OVER THE OFFERINGS
Sanctify by the invocation of your name, we pray, O Lord our God, this oblation of our service, and by it make of us an eternal offering to you. Through Christ our Lord. **Amen.**

PREFACE *(Trinity, p. 27)*

COMMUNION ANTIPHON *(Galatians 4.6)*
Since you are children of God, God has sent into your hearts the Spirit of his Son, the Spirit who cries out: Abba, Father.

PRAYER AFTER COMMUNION
May receiving this Sacrament, O Lord our God, bring us health of body and soul, as we confess your eternal holy Trinity and undivided Unity. Through Christ our Lord. **Amen.**

BLESSING AND DISMISSAL *(p. 70)*

May 29

Today we join the crowds following Jesus. Our hearts are afire with anticipation and joy as he speaks about the kingdom of God. To hear his voice, to walk in his presence, to see him healing the sick with gentleness and compassion, touches our hearts with wonder.

Jesus receives the people and speaks to them about the kingdom of God, and he heals those who need to be cured. Above all, he feeds them, the five thousand, "with five loaves and two fish" and when the leftovers are gathered up, they fill twelve baskets. This miracle foreshadows God's great love for us and his abundance through the Eucharist.

Come to the feast with trust and hope and belief that God will always provide, and that God is present in the celebration of the Eucharist. It is here that we are fed with the body and blood of Christ and are satisfied. It is here that we come for forgiveness and it is here that we are nourished by God's everlasting love.

Today's readings centre on God's presence and intervention in the lives of people down through the ages. God continues to be with us today in and through the gift of the Eucharist. Our response is one of praise and thanksgiving to Almighty God for the gift of everlasting love, freely given to us.

Sr. Johanna d'Agostino, IBVM, Toronto, ON

ENTRANCE ANTIPHON *(Cf. Psalm 80.17)*
He fed them with the finest wheat and satisfied them with honey from the rock.

INTRODUCTORY RITES *(p. 5)*

COLLECT
O God, who in this wonderful Sacrament have left us a memorial of your Passion, grant us, we pray, so to revere the sacred mysteries of your Body and Blood that we may always experience in ourselves the fruits of your redemption. Who live and reign with God the Father in the unity of the Holy Spirit, one God, for ever and ever. **Amen.**

FIRST READING *(Genesis 14.18-20)*
In those days: After Abram's return King Melchizedek of Salem brought out bread and wine; he was priest of God Most High. He blessed Abram and said, "Blessed be Abram by God Most High, maker of heaven and earth; and blessed be God Most High, who has delivered your enemies into your hand!" And Abram gave him one tenth of everything.

The word of the Lord. **Thanks be to God.**

RESPONSORIAL PSALM *(Psalm 110)*

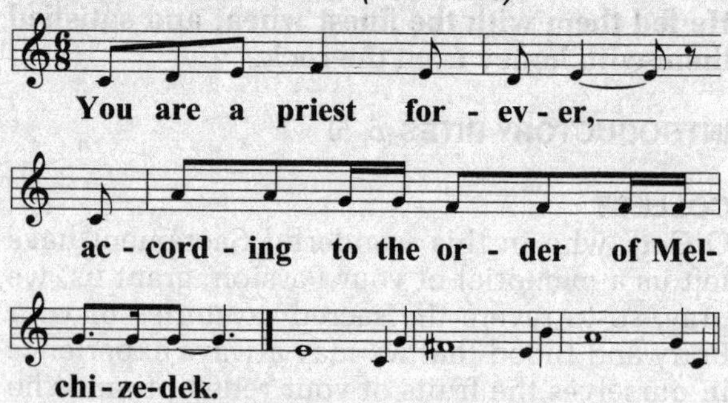

℞. **You are a priest forever,**
according to the order of Melchizedek.

The Lord says to · **my** lord,
"Sit at my · **right** hand
until I make your enemies · **your** footstool." ℞.

The Lord sends out · **from** Zion
your might·-**y** sceptre.
Rule in the midst of · **your** foes. ℞.

Your people will offer them·-**selves** willingly
on the day you lead your forces on
the · **holy** mountains.
From the womb of the morning, like dew,
your youth · **will** come_to_you. ℞.

The Lord has sworn and will not change
· **his** mind,
"You are a priest · **for**-ever
according to the order of · **Mel**-chizedek." ℞.

SECOND READING *(1 Corinthians 11.23-26)*
Brothers and sisters: I received from the Lord what I also handed on to you, that the Lord Jesus on the night when he was betrayed took a loaf of bread, and when he had given thanks, he broke it and said, "This is my Body that is for you. Do this in remembrance of me."

In the same way he took the cup also, after supper, saying, "This cup is the new covenant in my Blood. Do this, as often as you drink it, in remembrance of me."

For as often as you eat this bread and drink the cup, you proclaim the Lord's death until he comes.

The word of the Lord. **Thanks be to God.**

SEQUENCE *(Optional)*
This sequence is to be sung. The shorter version begins at the asterisks (p. 425). An earlier version of this Sequence is set to music in CBW III, 693.

1. Laud, O Sion, your salvation,
laud with hymns of exultation
Christ, your King and Shepherd true:
bring him all the praise you know,
he is more than you bestow;
never can you reach his due.

2. Wondrous theme for glad thanksgiving
is the living and life-giving
bread today before you set,
from his hands of old partaken,
as we know, by faith unshaken,
where the Twelve at supper met.

3. Full and clear ring out your chanting,
let not joy nor grace be wanting.
From your heart let praises burst.
For this day the Feast is holden,
when the institution olden
of that Supper was rehearsed.

4. Here the new law's new oblation,
by the new King's revelation,
ends the forms of ancient rite.
Now the new the old effaces,
substance now the shadow chases,
light of day dispels the night.

5. What he did at supper seated,
Christ ordained to be repeated,
his remembrance not to cease.
And his rule for guidance taking,
bread and wine we hallow, making,
thus, our sacrifice of peace.

6. This the truth each Christian learns:
bread into his own flesh Christ turns,
to his precious Blood the wine.
Sight must fail, no thought conceives,
but a steadfast faith believes,
resting on a power divine.

7. Here beneath these signs are hidden
priceless things to sense forbidden.
Signs alone, not things, we see:
blood and flesh as wine, bread broken;
yet beneath each wondrous token,
Christ entire we know to be.

8. All who of this great food partake,
they sever not the Lord, nor break:
Christ is whole to all that taste.
Be one or be a thousand fed
they eat alike that living Bread,
eat of him who cannot waste.

9. Good and guilty likewise sharing,
though their different ends preparing:
timeless death, or blessed life.
Life to these, to those damnation,
even like participation
is with unlike outcomes rife.

10. When the sacrament is broken,
doubt not, but believe as spoken,
that each severed outward token
does the very whole contain.
None that precious gift divides,
breaking but the sign betides.
Jesus still the same abides,
still unbroken he remains.

* * *

11. Hail, the food of Angels given
to the pilgrim who has striven,
to the child as bread from heaven,
food alone for spirit meant:
Now the former types fulfilling —
Isaac bound, a victim willing,
Paschal Lamb, its life-blood spilling,
manna to the ancients sent.

12. Bread yourself, good Shepherd, tend us;
Jesus, with your love befriend us.
You refresh us and defend us;

to your lasting goodness send us
that the land of life we see.
Lord, who all things both rule and know,
who on this earth such food bestow,
grant that with your saints we follow
to that banquet ever hallow,
with them heirs and guests to be.

GOSPEL ACCLAMATION *(John 6.51)*
Alleluia. Alleluia. I am the living bread of heaven, says the Lord; whoever eats of this bread will live forever. **Alleluia.**

GOSPEL *(Luke 9.11b-17)*
The Lord be with you. **And with your spirit.** A reading from the holy Gospel according to Luke. **Glory to you, O Lord.**

Jesus spoke to the crowds about the kingdom of God, and healed those who needed to be cured.

The day was drawing to a close, and the twelve came to him and said, "Send the crowd away, so that they may go into the surrounding villages and countryside, to lodge and get provisions; for we are here in a deserted place."

But Jesus said to them, "You give them something to eat." They said, "We have no more than five loaves and two fish — unless we are to go and buy food for all these people." For there were about five thousand men.

And Jesus said to his disciples, "Make the people sit down in groups of about fifty each." They did so and made them all sit down.

And taking the five loaves and the two fish, he looked up to heaven, and blessed and broke them, and gave them to the disciples to set before the crowd.

And all ate and were filled. What was left over was gathered up, twelve baskets of broken pieces.

The Gospel of the Lord. **Praise to you, Lord Jesus Christ.**

PROFESSION OF FAITH *(p. 11)*

PRAYER OF THE FAITHFUL

The following intentions are suggestions only. There are more suggestions at www.livingwithchrist.ca

℟. **Lord, hear our prayer.**

For the Church, striving to bring Good News to those who hunger for bread and for recognition of their human dignity, we pray to the Lord: ℟.

For global society, entrusted with the care of the earth and its labourers, we pray to the Lord: ℟.

For people who struggle for their daily bread, we pray to the Lord: ℟.

For our community, nourished by the Body and Blood of Christ and called by him to minister to the poor and to those who hunger, we pray to the Lord: ℟.

PREPARATION OF THE GIFTS *(p. 14)*

PRAYER OVER THE OFFERINGS

Grant your Church, O Lord, we pray, the gifts of unity and peace, whose signs are to be seen in mystery in the offerings we here present. Through Christ our Lord. **Amen.**

PREFACE *(Holy Eucharist, p. 27)*

COMMUNION ANTIPHON *(John 6.57)*

Whoever eats my flesh and drinks my blood remains in me and I in him, says the Lord.

PRAYER AFTER COMMUNION

Grant, O Lord, we pray, that we may delight for all eternity in that share in your divine life, which is foreshadowed in the present age by our reception of your precious Body and Blood. Who live and reign for ever and ever. **Amen.**

BLESSING AND DISMISSAL *(p. 70)*

June Saints' Days

The following saints are traditionally remembered in June in Canada.

1	Saint Justin
2	Saints Marcellinus and Peter
3	Saint Charles Lwanga and Companions
5	Saint Boniface
6	Saint Norbert
9	Saint Ephrem
11	Saint Barnabas
13	Saint Anthony of Padua
19	Saint Romuald
21	Saint Aloysius Gonzaga
22	Saint Paulinus of Nola Saints John Fisher and Thomas More
24	The Nativity of John the Baptist
27	Saint Cyril of Alexandria Blesseds Nykyta Budka and Vasyl Velychkowsky
28	Saint Irenaeus
29	Saints Peter and Paul
30	The First Martyrs of the Holy Roman Church

June 5

What are the stages of the spiritual journey? Today we hear that, in many ways, the journey begins with a willingness to listen. Although we *hear* many things in the course of a day, often we *listen* less frequently than we hear. Listening requires an openness and attentiveness to the source of wisdom in our lives, the voice that calls us to rise up, to be alive.

Frequently in our prayers we ask God for something specific. Yet God calls us to a more profound relationship than one between giver and recipient: God has created us for an end that surpasses all of our temporal needs. Perhaps the answer to our prayers is built into the very request we make, for within it lies a glimpse of our deeper need lying beneath the surface. We must learn to trust the unknown, as the mothers in today's readings did, so that God can answer our prayers.

On a Sunday with readings focused on mothers and their children, let us consider the hope and promise in every life. God plays a part in the hope and promise that preceded our birth; it is through God's grace that we are blessed with the gift of life each day. Let us pause and consider the wonder of this gift: a gift worthy of praise and thanksgiving.

John O'Brien, Oakville, ON

ENTRANCE ANTIPHON *(Cf. Psalm 26.1-2)*
The Lord is my light and my salvation; whom shall I fear? The Lord is the stronghold of my life; whom should I dread? When those who do evil draw near, they stumble and fall.

INTRODUCTORY RITES *(p. 5)*

COLLECT
O God, from whom all good things come, grant that we, who call on you in our need, may at your prompting discern what is right, and by your guidance do it. Through our Lord Jesus Christ, your Son, who lives and reigns with you in the unity of the Holy Spirit, one God, for ever and ever. **Amen.**

FIRST READING *(1 Kings 17.17-21a, 22-24)*
In those days, the son of the woman, the mistress of the house, became ill; his illness was so severe that there was no breath left in him.

She then said to Elijah, "What have you against me, O man of God? You have come to me to bring my sins to remembrance, and to cause the death of my son!"

But Elijah said to her, "Give me your son." He took him from her bosom, carried him up into the upper chamber where he was lodging, and laid him on his own bed. Elijah cried out to the Lord, "O Lord my God, have you brought calamity even upon the widow with whom I am staying, by killing her son?" Three times he cried out to the Lord, "O Lord my God, let this child's life come into him again."

The Lord listened to the voice of Elijah; the life of the child came into him again, and he revived.

Elijah took the child, brought him down from the upper chamber into the house, and gave him to his mother; then Elijah said, "See, your son is alive."

So the woman said to Elijah, "Now I know that you are a man of God, and that the word of the Lord in your mouth is truth."

The word of the Lord. **Thanks be to God.**

RESPONSORIAL PSALM *(Psalm 30)*

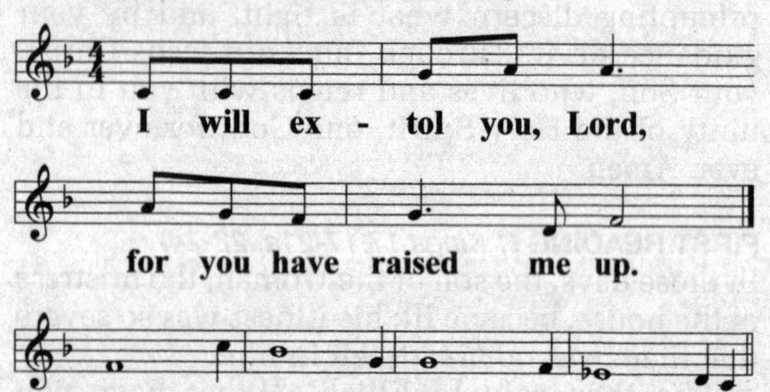

℟. **I will extol you, Lord,**
for you have raised me up.

I will extol you, O Lord, for you have
drawn me · **up,**
and did not let my foes rejoice · **over_me.**
O Lord, you brought up my soul from · **Sheol,**
restored me to life from among those gone
down · **to_the** Pit. ℟.

Sing praises to the Lord, O you
his · **faithful_ones,**
and give thanks to his holy · **name.**

For his anger is but for a moment; his favour
is for a · **lifetime.**
Weeping may linger for the night, but joy
comes · **with_the** morning. ℟.

Hear, O Lord, and be gracious to · **me!**
O Lord, be my · **helper!**
You have turned my mourning into · **dancing.**
O Lord my God, I will give thanks to you
· **for**-ever. ℟.

To hear the Sunday Psalms, go to www.livingwithchrist.ca and select the psalm button at the bottom of the home page.

SECOND READING *(Galatians 1.11-19)*

I want you to know, brothers and sisters, that the Gospel that was proclaimed by me is not of human origin; for I did not receive it from a human being, nor was I taught it, but I received it through a revelation of Jesus Christ.

You have heard, no doubt, of my earlier life in Judaism. I was violently persecuting the Church of God and was trying to destroy it. I advanced in Judaism beyond many among my people of the same age, for I was far more zealous for the traditions of my ancestors.

But when God, who had set me apart before I was born and called me through his grace, was pleased to reveal his Son to me, so that I might proclaim him among the Gentiles, I did not confer with flesh and blood, nor did I go up to Jerusalem to those who were already Apostles before me, but I went away at once into Arabia, and afterwards I returned to Damascus.

Then after three years I did go up to Jerusalem to visit Cephas and stayed with him fifteen days; but I did not see any other apostle except James the Lord's brother.

The word of the Lord. **Thanks be to God.**

GOSPEL ACCLAMATION *(Luke 7.16)*

Alleluia. Alleluia. A great Prophet has risen among us; God has looked favourably on his people. **Alleluia.**

GOSPEL *(Luke 7.11-17)*

The Lord be with you. **And with your spirit.** A reading from the holy Gospel according to Luke. **Glory to you, O Lord.**

Jesus went to a town called Nain, and his disciples and a large crowd went with him. As he approached the gate of the town, a man who had died was being carried out. He was his mother's only son, and she was a widow; and with her was a large crowd from the town.

When the Lord saw her, he had compassion for her and said to her, "Do not weep."

Then he came forward and touched the pallet, and the bearers stood still. And Jesus said, "Young man, I say to you, rise!" The dead man sat up and began to speak, and Jesus gave him to his mother.

Fear seized all of them; and they glorified God, saying, "A great Prophet has risen among us!" and "God has looked favourably on his people!" This word about Jesus spread throughout Judea and all the surrounding country.

The Gospel of the Lord. **Praise to you, Lord Jesus Christ.**

PROFESSION OF FAITH *(p. 11)*

PRAYER OF THE FAITHFUL

The following intentions are suggestions only. There are more suggestions at www.livingwithchrist.ca

℟. **Lord, hear our prayer.**

For the Church, sign of God's compassion for the world, we pray to the Lord: ℟.

For nations and peoples seeking justice and peace, we pray to the Lord: ℟.

For those who have lost loved ones, especially their own children, we pray to the Lord: ℟.

For our faith community as we strive to live with one heart, one mind and one spirit, we pray to the Lord: ℟.

PREPARATION OF THE GIFTS *(p. 14)*

PRAYER OVER THE OFFERINGS

Look kindly upon our service, O Lord, we pray, that what we offer may be an acceptable oblation to you and lead us to grow in charity. Through Christ our Lord. **Amen.**

PREFACE *(Sundays in Ordinary Time, p. 28)*

COMMUNION ANTIPHON *(Psalm 17.3)*

The Lord is my rock, my fortress, and my deliverer; my God is my saving strength.

or (1 John 4.16)

God is love, and whoever abides in love abides in God, and God in him.

PRAYER AFTER COMMUNION

May your healing work, O Lord, free us, we pray, from doing evil and lead us to what is right. Through Christ our Lord. **Amen.**

BLESSING AND DISMISSAL *(p. 70)*

June 12

We know Jesus loves us. Some readings, however, remind us of just how much.

A woman crashes a dinner party at Simon the Pharisee's home. She falls at the feet of Jesus, bathing his feet with her tears, drying them with her hair and kissing them while anointing them with precious oil. Simon seems to know she's a notorious sinner, prompting him to wonder what sort of prophet Jesus might be to associate with her. Suddenly, Jesus tells the story of the two debtors — one with a big debt, the other with a little one. The creditor forgives them both. Who will love him more? Jesus asks. Reluctantly, Simon answers. Then Jesus lets him have it. Simon invited Jesus to dinner but offered no water for his feet, no kiss, no oil. The woman, though, was lavish in her love. Jesus knew the woman's sins were many but he also knew her love was greater than her sins.

Luke then tells us of the other women who are also his disciples. While initially this may seem like a disconnect, it reminds us that Jesus' love in inclusive, welcoming all. The welcome Jesus offered women would have been countercultural — even shocking. It should prompt us today to think about to whom we offer welcome. Are we stingy and judgmental or do we give of ourselves lovingly to all we meet?

Lauretta Santarossa, Toronto, ON

ENTRANCE ANTIPHON *(Cf. Psalm 26.7, 9)*
O Lord, hear my voice, for I have called to you; be my help. Do not abandon or forsake me, O God, my Saviour!

INTRODUCTORY RITES *(p. 5)*

COLLECT
O God, strength of those who hope in you, graciously hear our pleas, and, since without you mortal frailty can do nothing, grant us always the help of your grace, that in following your commands we may please you by our resolve and our deeds. Through our Lord Jesus Christ, your Son, who lives and reigns with you in the unity of the Holy Spirit, one God, for ever and ever. **Amen.**

FIRST READING *(2 Samuel 12.7-10, 13)*
David did what displeased the Lord, and the Lord sent the Prophet Nathan to David. Nathan said to David, "Thus says the Lord, the God of Israel: I anointed you king over Israel, and I rescued you from the hand of Saul; I gave you your master's house, and your master's wives into your bosom, and gave you the house of Israel and of Judah; if that had been too little, I would have added as much more.

"Why have you despised the word of the Lord, to do what is evil in his sight? You have struck down Uriah the Hittite with the sword, and have taken his wife to be your wife, and have killed Uriah with the sword of the Ammonites.

"Now therefore the sword shall never depart from your house, for you have despised me, and have taken the wife of Uriah the Hittite to be your wife."

David said to Nathan, "I have sinned against the Lord." Nathan said to David, "Now the Lord has put away your sin; you shall not die."

The word of the Lord. **Thanks be to God.**

RESPONSORIAL PSALM *(Psalm 32)*

℟. **Lord, forgive the guilt of my sin.**

Blessed is the one whose transgression is
for··**given**,
whose sin is · **covered.**
Blessed is the one to whom the Lord imputes
no in··**iquity**,
and in whose spirit there is no de··**ceit**. ℟.

I acknowledged my sin to · **you**,
and I did not hide my in··**iquity**;
I said, "I will confess my transgressions
to the · **Lord**,"
and you forgave the guilt of my · **sin**. ℟.

1 - You are a hiding place for · **me**;
2 - you preserve me from · **trouble**;
4 - you surround me with glad cries
of de··**liverance**. ℟.

1 - Be glad in the Lord and rejoice, O · **righteous**,
4 - and shout for joy, all you upright in · **heart**. ℟.

SECOND READING *(Galatians 2.16, 19-21)*
Brothers and sisters: We know that a person is justified not by the works of the law but through faith in Jesus Christ. And we have come to believe in Christ Jesus, so that we might be justified by faith in Christ, and not by doing the works of the law, because no one will be justified by the works of the law. For through the law I died to the law, so that I might live to God.

I have been crucified with Christ; and it is no longer I who live, but it is Christ who lives in me. And the life I now live in the flesh I live by faith in the Son of God, who loved me and gave himself for me. I do not nullify the grace of God; for if justification comes through the law, then Christ died for nothing.

The word of the Lord. **Thanks be to God.**

GOSPEL ACCLAMATION *(1 John 4.10)*
Alleluia. Alleluia. God loved us and sent his Son to be the atoning sacrifice for our sins. **Alleluia.**

GOSPEL *(Luke 7.36 – 8.3)*
The Lord be with you. **And with your spirit.** A reading from the holy Gospel according to Luke. **Glory to you, O Lord.**

One of the Pharisees asked Jesus to eat with him, and he went into the Pharisee's house and took his place at the table.

A woman in the city, who was a sinner, having learned that Jesus was eating in the Pharisee's house, brought an alabaster jar of ointment. She stood behind Jesus at his feet, weeping, and began to bathe his feet with her tears and to dry them with her hair. Then she continued kissing his feet and anointing them with the ointment.

Now when the Pharisee who had invited Jesus saw it, he said to himself, "If this man were a Prophet, he would have known who and what kind of woman this is who is touching him — that she is a sinner."

Jesus spoke up and said to him, "Simon, I have something to say to you." "Teacher," he replied, "speak."

"A certain creditor had two debtors; one owed five hundred denarii, and the other fifty. When they could not pay, he cancelled the debts for both of them. Now which of them will love him more?" Simon answered, "I suppose the one for whom he cancelled the greater debt." And Jesus said to him, "You have judged rightly."

Then turning toward the woman, he said to Simon, "Do you see this woman? I entered your house; you gave me no water for my feet, but she has bathed my feet with her tears and dried them with her hair.

"You gave me no kiss, but from the time I came in she has not stopped kissing my feet. You did not anoint my head with oil, but she has anointed my feet with ointment.

"Therefore, I tell you, her sins, which were many, have been forgiven; hence she has shown great love. But the one to whom little is forgiven, loves little." Then Jesus said to her, "Your sins are forgiven."

But those who were at the table with him began to say among themselves, "Who is this who even forgives sins?" And Jesus said to the woman, "Your faith has saved you; go in peace."

Soon afterwards Jesus went on through cities and villages, proclaiming and bringing the good news of the kingdom of God. The twelve were with him, as well as some women who had been cured of evil spirits and infirmities: Mary, called Magdalene, from whom seven demons had gone out, and Joanna, the wife of Herod's steward Chuza, and Susanna, and many others, who provided for them out of their resources.

The Gospel of the Lord. **Praise to you, Lord Jesus Christ.**

PROFESSION OF FAITH *(p. 11)*

PRAYER OF THE FAITHFUL

The following intentions are suggestions only. There are more suggestions at www.livingwithchrist.ca

℟. **Lord, hear our prayer.**

For the Church, open to the Holy Spirit's presence in the world, we pray to the Lord: ℟.

For nations striving for the greater good of all people, we pray to the Lord: ℟.

For those bearing heavy crosses, seeking strength from our love and encouragement, we pray to the Lord: ℟.

For us here today, the people of God, we pray to the Lord: ℟.

PREPARATION OF THE GIFTS *(p. 14)*

PRAYER OVER THE OFFERINGS

O God, who in the offerings presented here provide for the twofold needs of human nature, nourishing us with food and renewing us with your Sacrament, grant, we pray, that the sustenance they provide may not fail us in body or in spirit. Through Christ our Lord. **Amen.**

PREFACE *(Sundays in Ordinary Time, p. 28)*

COMMUNION ANTIPHON *(Psalm 26.4)*

There is one thing I ask of the Lord, only this do I seek: to live in the house of the Lord all the days of my life.

or (John 17.11)

Holy Father, keep in your name those you have given me, that they may be one as we are one, says the Lord.

PRAYER AFTER COMMUNION

As this reception of your Holy Communion, O Lord, foreshadows the union of the faithful in you, so may it bring about unity in your Church. Through Christ our Lord. **Amen.**

BLESSING AND DISMISSAL *(p. 70)*

June 19

In today's gospel we find Jesus taking time to pray and reflect on his ministry. After performing many miracles and speaking about the kingdom in parables, Jesus takes his disciples aside and checks that they are getting the message. Who do the people say that I am? And who do you say that I am? These are loaded questions!

The disciples would be justified in being afraid and anxious when they learn what lies ahead of them — what fate awaits Jesus and what crosses they will bear. I recently learned that "Do not be afraid," which appears so often in the Gospels, can also be translated, "There is no need to be afraid." Rather than being a command, it is an affirmation that there is no reason to be afraid. As Peter acknowledges, Jesus is the Christ of God and by following him they will save their lives.

We know Jesus is with us in all of our lives: and yet we are reminded today that there are consequences to following Christ. Sometimes when we have the courage to speak up, our fears are realized and we are rejected, ignored or ridiculed; we will indeed have crosses to bear. But this is what God has called us to: our efforts to speak up in truth with God's help are not in vain. There is no need to be afraid.

Sr. Nancy Sullivan, CSJ, Hamilton, ON

ENTRANCE ANTIPHON *(Cf. Psalm 27.8-9)*
The Lord is the strength of his people, a saving refuge for the one he has anointed. Save your people, Lord, and bless your heritage, and govern them for ever.

INTRODUCTORY RITES *(p. 5)*

COLLECT
Grant, O Lord, that we may always revere and love your holy name, for you never deprive of your guidance those you set firm on the foundation of your love. Through our Lord Jesus Christ, your Son, who lives and reigns with you in the unity of the Holy Spirit, one God, for ever and ever. **Amen.**

FIRST READING *(Zechariah 12.10-11)*
The Lord says this: "I will pour out a spirit of compassion and supplication on the house of David and the inhabitants of Jerusalem, so that, when they look on the one whom they have pierced, they shall mourn for him, as one mourns for an only-begotten son, and weep bitterly over him, as one weeps over a firstborn.

"On that day the mourning in Jerusalem will be as great as the mourning for Hadad-rimmon in the plain of Megiddo."

The word of the Lord. **Thanks be to God.**

RESPONSORIAL PSALM *(Psalm 63)*

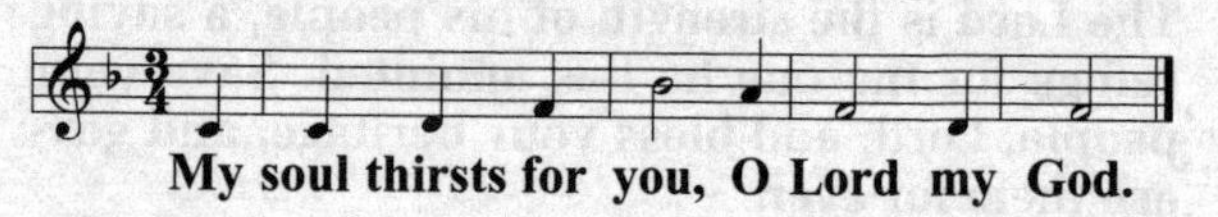

℟. **My soul thirsts for you, O Lord my God.**

O God, you are my God, I · **seek_you,**
my soul · **thirsts_for_you;**
my flesh · **faints_for_you,**
as in a dry and weary land where there
· **is** no water. ℟.

So I have looked upon you in the · **sanctuary,**
beholding your power and · **glory.**
Because your steadfast love is better than · **life,**
my · **lips** will praise_you. ℟.

So I will bless you as long as I · **live;**
I will lift up my hands and call on your · **name.**
My soul is satisfied as with a rich · **feast,**
and my mouth praises you with · **joy**-ful lips. ℟.

For you have been my · **help,**
and in the shadow of your wings I sing for · **joy.**
My soul · **clings_to_you;**
your right · **hand** up-holds_me. ℟.

To hear the Sunday Psalms, go to www.livingwithchrist.ca and select the psalm button at the bottom of the home page.

SECOND READING *(Galatians 3.26-29)*
Brothers and sisters, in Christ Jesus you are all sons and daughters of God through faith. As many of you as were baptized into Christ have clothed yourselves with Christ.

There is no longer Jew or Greek, there is no longer slave or free, there is no longer male and female; for all of you are one in Christ Jesus.

And if you belong to Christ, then you are Abraham's offspring, heirs according to the promise.

The word of the Lord. **Thanks be to God.**

GOSPEL ACCLAMATION *(John 10.27)*
Alleluia. Alleluia. My sheep hear my voice, says the Lord; I know them, and they follow me. **Alleluia.**

GOSPEL *(Luke 9.18-24)*
The Lord be with you. **And with your spirit.** A reading from the holy Gospel according to Luke. **Glory to you, O Lord.**

One day when Jesus was praying alone, with only the disciples near him, he asked them, "Who do the crowds say that I am?"

They answered, "John the Baptist; but others, Elijah; and still others, that one of the ancient Prophets has arisen." Jesus said to them, "But who do you say that I am?" Peter answered, "The Christ of God."

Jesus sternly ordered and commanded the disciples not to tell anyone, saying, "The Son of Man must undergo great suffering, and be rejected by the elders, chief priests, and scribes, and be killed, and on the third day be raised."

Then he said to them all, "If anyone wants to become my follower, let him deny himself and take up his cross daily and follow me. For whoever wants to save their life will lose it, and whoever loses their life for my sake will save it."

The Gospel of the Lord. **Praise to you, Lord Jesus Christ.**

PROFESSION OF FAITH *(p. 11)*

PRAYER OF THE FAITHFUL

The following intentions are suggestions only. There are more suggestions at www.livingwithchrist.ca

℟. **Lord, hear our prayer.**

For Church leaders attentive to those in need, we pray to the Lord: ℟.

For leaders of countries, entrusted with serving their people, we pray to the Lord: ℟.

For victims of war, political oppression and human greed, we pray to the Lord: ℟.

For all fathers today: in gratitude for their love and witness, we pray to the Lord: ℟.

For our parish members, shaping lives of service in the worship of the living God, we pray to the Lord: ℟.

PREPARATION OF THE GIFTS *(p. 14)*

PRAYER OVER THE OFFERINGS

Receive, O Lord, the sacrifice of conciliation and praise and grant that, cleansed by its action, we may make offering of a heart pleasing to you. Through Christ our Lord. **Amen.**

PREFACE *(Sundays in Ordinary Time, p. 28)*

COMMUNION ANTIPHON *(Psalm 144.15)*
The eyes of all look to you, Lord, and you give them their food in due season.
or (John 10.11, 15)
I am the Good Shepherd, and I lay down my life for my sheep, says the Lord.

PRAYER AFTER COMMUNION
Renewed and nourished by the Sacred Body and Precious Blood of your Son, we ask of your mercy, O Lord, that what we celebrate with constant devotion may be our sure pledge of redemption. Through Christ our Lord. **Amen.**

BLESSING AND DISMISSAL *(p. 70)*

June 26

Today's readings look at the nature of a calling. The first reading examines Elisha's call to serve, while Paul's Letter to the Galatians talks about the calling of all Christians to find freedom by living in the spirit. The gospel then tells us about Jesus setting his face to Jerusalem, about to begin his journey towards the end — his passion and death.

These passages underscore two important points about the nature of our summons as Christians. First, a calling involves redirection. Elisha departs from what is familiar, leaving behind his fields and family to follow God. Paul calls us away from gratifying the desires of the flesh. Finally, Jesus orients himself through unfriendly territories (Samaria and ultimately Jerusalem).

The second point is made most clearly by the rejection of Jesus by the Samaritans. Following God's path involves hardship and difficulty. Embracing God means letting go of the world. Jesus responded to rejection with love and compassion, showing us by example how to persevere in times of difficulty.

These readings point to our need for God's grace. Without grace, the entire reorientation of our lives towards God is too great a struggle. Every time we gather for the Eucharist we take in spiritual nourishment so that we too, like Elisha and Jesus, will boldly follow God's call, undeterred by those who are the hostile and unwelcoming Samaritans of our day.

Andrew Hume, Toronto, ON

ENTRANCE ANTIPHON *(Psalm 46.2)*
All peoples, clap your hands. Cry to God with shouts of joy!

INTRODUCTORY RITES *(p. 5)*

COLLECT
O God, who through the grace of adoption chose us to be children of light, grant, we pray, that we may not be wrapped in the darkness of error but always be seen to stand in the bright light of truth. Through our Lord Jesus Christ, your Son, who lives and reigns with you in the unity of the Holy Spirit, one God, for ever and ever. **Amen.**

FIRST READING *(1 Kings 19.16b, 19-21)*
The Lord spoke to the Prophet Elijah and said, "You shall anoint Elisha, son of Shaphat, as Prophet in your place."

So Elijah set out from there, and found Elisha, who was ploughing. There were twelve yoke of oxen ahead of him, and he was with the twelfth.

Elijah passed by Elisha and threw his mantle over him. Elisha left the oxen, ran after Elijah, and said, "Let me kiss my father and my mother, and then I will follow you."

Then Elijah said to him, "Go back again; for what have I done to you?" Elisha returned from following Elijah, took the yoke of oxen, and slaughtered them; using the equipment from the oxen, he boiled their flesh, and gave it to the people, and they ate. Then Elisha set out and followed Elijah, and became his servant.

The word of the Lord. **Thanks be to God.**

RESPONSORIAL PSALM *(Psalm 16)*

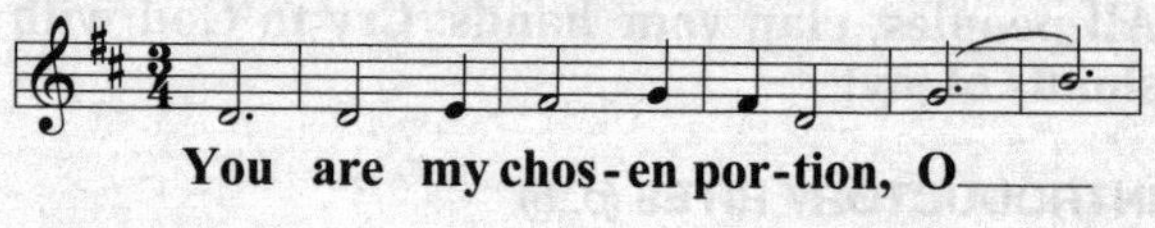

℟. **You are my chosen portion, O Lord.**

Protect me, O God, for in you I · **take** refuge.
I say to the Lord, "You are · **my** Lord;
I have no good apart · **from** you."
The Lord is my chosen portion and my cup;
you · **hold** my lot. ℟.

I bless the Lord who gives · **me** counsel;
in the night also my heart · **in**-structs_me.
I keep the Lord always · **be**-fore_me;
because he is at my right hand, I shall
· **not** be moved. ℟.

Therefore my heart is glad, and my soul
· **re**-joices;
my body also rests · **se**-cure.
For you do not give me up · **to** Sheol,
or let your faithful one · **see** the Pit. ℟.

1 - You show me the path · **of** life.
2 - In your presence there is fullness · **of** joy;
4 - in your right hand are pleasures
for·-**ev**-er-more. ℟.

To hear the Sunday Psalms, go to www.livingwithchrist.ca and select the psalm button at the bottom of the home page.

SECOND READING *(Galatians 5.1, 13-18)*
Brothers and sisters: For freedom Christ has set us free. Stand firm, therefore, and do not submit again to a yoke of slavery. For you were called to freedom, brothers and sisters; only do not use your freedom as an opportunity for self-indulgence, but through love become slaves to one another.

For the whole law is summed up in a single commandment, "You shall love your neighbour as yourself." If, however, you bite and devour one another, take care that you are not consumed by one another.

Live by the Spirit, I say, and do not gratify the desires of the flesh. For what the flesh desires is opposed to the Spirit, and what the Spirit desires is opposed to the flesh; for these are opposed to each other, to prevent you from doing what you want. But if you are led by the Spirit, you are not subject to the law.

The word of the Lord. **Thanks be to God.**

GOSPEL ACCLAMATION *(1 Samuel 3.9; John 6.69)*
Alleluia. Alleluia. Speak, O Lord, for your servant is listening; you have the words of eternal life. **Alleluia.**

GOSPEL *(Luke 9.51-62)*
The Lord be with you. **And with your spirit.**
A reading from the holy Gospel according to Luke. **Glory to you, O Lord.**

When the days drew near for him to be taken up, Jesus set his face to go to Jerusalem.

And he sent messengers ahead of him. On their way they entered a village of the Samaritans to make ready for Jesus; but the Samaritans did not receive him, because his face was set toward Jerusalem.

When his disciples James and John saw it, they said, "Lord, do you want us to command fire to come down from heaven and consume them?" But Jesus turned and rebuked them. Then they went on to another village.

As they were going along the road, someone said to him, "I will follow you wherever you go." And Jesus said to him, "Foxes have holes, and birds of the air have nests; but the Son of Man has nowhere to lay his head."

To another Jesus said, "Follow me." But he replied, "Lord, first let me go and bury my father." But Jesus said to him, "Let the dead bury their own dead; but as for you, go and proclaim the kingdom of God."

Another said, "I will follow you, Lord; but let me first say farewell to those at my home." Jesus said to him, "No one who puts a hand to the plough and looks back is fit for the kingdom of God."

The Gospel of the Lord. **Praise to you, Lord Jesus Christ.**

PROFESSION OF FAITH *(p. 11)*

PRAYER OF THE FAITHFUL

The following intentions are suggestions only. There are more suggestions at www.livingwithchrist.ca

℟. **Lord, hear our prayer.**

For the Church, called to be a prophetic voice for justice, we pray to the Lord: ℟.

For world leaders who work together for peace and reconciliation, we pray to the Lord: ℟.

For all those in our community, who are in need of food, housing, employment, or respect, we pray to the Lord: ℟.

For all of us here today, called to live our faith with humility, gentleness, and love, we pray to the Lord: ℟.

PREPARATION OF THE GIFTS *(p. 14)*

PRAYER OVER THE OFFERINGS

O God, who graciously accomplish the effects of your mysteries, grant, we pray, that the deeds by which we serve you may be worthy of these sacred gifts. Through Christ our Lord. **Amen.**

PREFACE *(Sundays in Ordinary Time, p. 28)*

COMMUNION ANTIPHON *(Cf. Psalm 102.1)*

Bless the Lord, O my soul, and all within me, his holy name.

or (John 17.20-21)

O Father, I pray for them, that they may be one in us, that the world may believe that you have sent me, says the Lord.

PRAYER AFTER COMMUNION

May this divine sacrifice we have offered and received fill us with life, O Lord, we pray, so that, bound to you in lasting charity, we may bear fruit that lasts for ever. Through Christ our Lord. **Amen.**

BLESSING AND DISMISSAL *(p. 70)*

July Saints' Days

The following saints are traditionally remembered in July in Canada.

3	Saint Thomas
4	Saint Elizabeth of Portugal
5	Saint Anthony Zaccaria
6	Saint Maria Goretti
9	Saint Augustine Zhao Rong and Companions
11	Saint Benedict
13	Saint Henry
14	Saint Camillus de Lellis
15	Saint Bonaventure
16	Our Lady of Mount Carmel
20	Saint Apollinaris
21	Saint Lawrence of Brindisi
22	Saint Mary Magdalene
23	Saint Bridget
24	Saint Sharbel Makhlūf
25	Saint James
26	Saint Anne and Saint Joachim
29	Saint Martha
30	Saint Peter Chrysologus
31	Saint Ignatius of Loyola

July 3

In Mel Gibson's much talked-about movie of a few years back, *The Passion of the Christ*, a scene that struck me as particularly poignant sees Jesus fall, be crushed by the cross and then whipped, prompting Mary to run to help him, saying "I'm here." Jesus holds Mary's face and says to her, "See, Mother, I make all things new." I feel the power of those words, especially in Mary's pain of losing her son and in Jesus' suffering.

In today's gospel, Jesus sends out the seventy, like lambs into the midst of wolves, and calls them to leave their material goods behind and bring peace everywhere they go.

Jesus' name is so powerful that even the demons submit to the seventy when they call on his name. Today, Jesus is also calling us to go out in faith and bring his peace and love to everyone we meet. He has given us authority to tread on whatever snakes and scorpions we encounter, and over all the power of the enemy, whoever they may be; nothing will hurt us. This authority should prompt us to say, as Mary does, "I'm here."

The readings in today's Mass give us much to rejoice about. How could we not boast in the cross of our Lord? Our names are written in heaven!

Sarah Du Broy, Ottawa, ON

ENTRANCE ANTIPHON *(Cf. Psalm 47.10-11)*
Your merciful love, O God, we have received in the midst of your temple. Your praise, O God, like your name, reaches the ends of the earth; your right hand is filled with saving justice.

INTRODUCTORY RITES *(p. 5)*

COLLECT
O God, who in the abasement of your Son have raised up a fallen world, fill your faithful with holy joy, for on those you have rescued from slavery to sin you bestow eternal gladness. Through our Lord Jesus Christ, your Son, who lives and reigns with you in the unity of the Holy Spirit, one God, for ever and ever. **Amen.**

FIRST READING *(Isaiah 66.10-14)*
Rejoice with Jerusalem,
and be glad for her,
all you who love her;
rejoice with her in joy,
all you who mourn over her —
that you may nurse and be satisfied
from her consoling breast;
that you may drink deeply with delight
from her glorious bosom.

For thus says the Lord:
"I will extend prosperity to her like a river,
and the wealth of the nations like
an overflowing stream;
and you shall nurse and be carried on her arm,
and dandled on her knees.

As a mother comforts her child,
so I will comfort you;
you shall be comforted in Jerusalem.
You shall see, and your heart shall rejoice;
your bodies shall flourish like the grass;
and it shall be known
that the hand of the Lord is with his servants."

The word of the Lord. **Thanks be to God.**

RESPONSORIAL PSALM *(Psalm 66)*

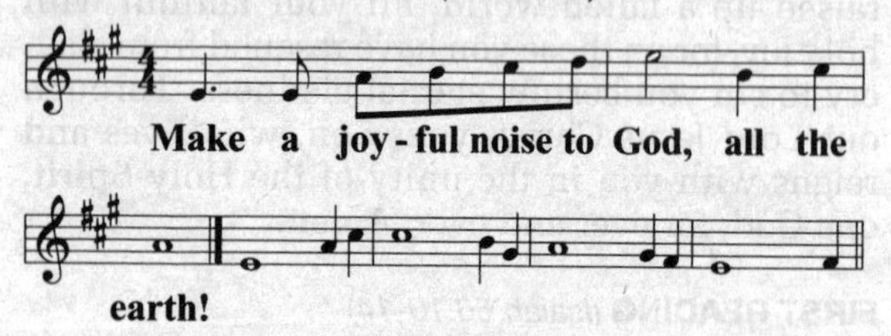

℟. **Make a joyful noise to God, all the earth!**

Make a joyful noise to God, all · **the** earth;
sing the glory · **of_his** name;
give to him · **glorious** praise.
Say to God, "How awesome are your
· **deeds!"** ℟.

"All the earth · **worships** you;
they sing praises to you, sing praises
· **to_your** name."
Come and see what God · **has** done:
he is awesome in his deeds among the
children of · **Adam.** ℟.

He turned the sea into · **dry** land;
they passed through the river · **on** foot.
There we rejoiced · **in** him,
who rules by his might for·-**ever.** R.

Come and hear, all you who · **fear** God,
and I will tell what he · **has** done_for_me.
Blessed be God, because he has not rejected
· **my** prayer
or removed his steadfast love from · **me.** R.

To hear the Sunday Psalms, go to www.livingwithchrist.ca and select the psalm button at the bottom of the home page.

SECOND READING *(Galatians 6.14-18)*

Brothers and sisters: May I never boast of anything except the Cross of our Lord Jesus Christ, by which the world has been crucified to me, and I to the world. For neither circumcision nor uncircumcision is anything; but a new creation is everything!

As for those who will follow this rule — peace be upon them, and mercy, and upon the Israel of God. From now on, let no one make trouble for me; for I carry the marks of Jesus branded on my body.

May the grace of our Lord Jesus Christ be with your spirit, brothers and sisters. Amen.

The word of the Lord. **Thanks be to God.**

GOSPEL ACCLAMATION *(Colossians 3.15, 16)*

Alleluia. Alleluia. Let the peace of Christ rule in your hearts, let the word of Christ dwell in you richly. **Alleluia.**

GOSPEL *(Luke 10.1-12, 17-20)*

The shorter version ends at the asterisks.

The Lord be with you. **And with your spirit.**
A reading from the holy Gospel according to Luke. **Glory to you, O Lord.**

The Lord appointed seventy others and sent them on ahead of him in pairs to every town and place where he himself intended to go.

He said to them, "The harvest is plentiful, but the labourers are few; therefore ask the Lord of the harvest to send out labourers into his harvest. Go on your way. See, I am sending you out like lambs into the midst of wolves. Carry no purse, no bag, no sandals; and greet no one on the road.

"Whatever house you enter, first say, 'Peace to this house!' And if someone of peace is there, your peace will rest on that person; but if not, it will return to you. Remain in the same house, eating and drinking whatever they provide, for the labourer deserves his wage. Do not move about from house to house.

"Whenever you enter a town and its people welcome you, eat what is set before you; cure the sick who are there, and say to them, 'The kingdom of God has come near to you.'

* * *

"But whenever you enter a town and they do not welcome you, go out into its streets and say, 'Even the dust of your town that clings to our feet, we wipe off in protest against you. Yet know this: the kingdom of God has come near.' I tell you, on that day it will be more tolerable for Sodom than for that town."

The seventy returned with joy, saying, “Lord, in your name even the demons submit to us!” Jesus said to them, “I watched Satan fall from heaven like a flash of lightning. See, I have given you authority to tread on snakes and scorpions, and over all the power of the enemy; and nothing will hurt you.

“Nevertheless, do not rejoice at this, that the spirits submit to you, but rejoice that your names are written in heaven.”

The Gospel of the Lord. **Praise to you, Lord Jesus Christ.**

PROFESSION OF FAITH *(p. 11)*

PRAYER OF THE FAITHFUL

The following intentions are suggestions only. There are more suggestions at www.livingwithchrist.ca

℟. **Lord, hear our prayer.**

For the Church, called to live God’s word in service to others, we pray to the Lord: ℟.

For our fragile world in need of the saving message of God’s mercy and love, we pray to the Lord: ℟.

For all individuals who labour in God’s name, we pray to the Lord: ℟.

For our parish, as we support one another in faith and service, we pray to the Lord: ℟.

PREPARATION OF THE GIFTS *(p. 14)*

PRAYER OVER THE OFFERINGS
May this oblation dedicated to your name purify us, O Lord, and day by day bring our conduct closer to the life of heaven. Through Christ our Lord. **Amen.**

PREFACE *(Sundays in Ordinary Time, p. 28)*

COMMUNION ANTIPHON *(Psalm 33.9)*
Taste and see that the Lord is good; blessed the man who seeks refuge in him.
or (Matthew 11.28)
Come to me, all who labour and are burdened, and I will refresh you, says the Lord.

PRAYER AFTER COMMUNION
Grant, we pray, O Lord, that, having been replenished by such great gifts, we may gain the prize of salvation and never cease to praise you. Through Christ our Lord. **Amen.**

BLESSING AND DISMISSAL *(p. 70)*

July 10

"Do this, and you will live." Doesn't everyone want to know the secret to eternal life? But when I read that I must love God and my neighbour, my enthusiasm dissipates. I've heard it before. I was hoping for something more.

It's as if Jesus anticipates my response, and he doesn't let me down. In the parable of the Good Samaritan, Jesus goes on to provide the example of mercy lived well. Jesus challenges us to put our time, talent and treasure at the service of our neighbour. To reach out to the homeless stranger on a downtown street, the hurting teenager next door, and the elderly relative who yearns for a visitor — or even a phone call. My spirit sags: O Lord, too often I have failed to love and show mercy.

I can sense God looking at me, still patient but a little weary, wondering why so many reminders are necessary. Before I can get too worked up over my failings, Jesus delivers the proverbial kick in the seat of the pants, saying, "Go and do likewise."

Jesus knows we remain works in progress and so he persists. He calls us to imitate him, to dig deeper, to love and show mercy to all, every day, with no time-outs. We are wise when we heed Jesus' example and his words: "Do this, and you will live."

Harry McAvoy, Oakville, ON

ENTRANCE ANTIPHON *(Cf. Psalm 16.15)*
As for me, in justice I shall behold your face; I shall be filled with the vision of your glory.

INTRODUCTORY RITES *(p. 5)*

COLLECT
O God, who show the light of your truth to those who go astray, so that they may return to the right path, give all who for the faith they profess are accounted Christians the grace to reject whatever is contrary to the name of Christ and to strive after all that does it honour. Through our Lord Jesus Christ, your Son, who lives and reigns with you in the unity of the Holy Spirit, one God, for ever and ever. **Amen.**

FIRST READING *(Deuteronomy 30.10-14)*
Moses spoke to the people, saying, "Obey the Lord your God by observing his commandments and decrees that are written in this book of the Law; turn to the Lord your God with all your heart and with all your soul.

"Surely this commandment that I am commanding you today is not too hard for you, nor is it too far away. It is not in heaven, that you should say, 'Who will go up to heaven for us, and get it for us so that we may hear it and observe it?'

"Neither is it beyond the sea, that you should say, 'Who will cross to the other side of the sea for us, and get it for us so that we may hear it and observe it?'

"No, the word is very near to you; it is in your mouth and in your heart for you to observe."

The word of the Lord. **Thanks be to God.**

An alternate psalm follows.

RESPONSORIAL PSALM *(Psalm 69)*

℟. **Seek God in your need,
and let your hearts revive.**

As for me, my prayer is to you, · **O** Lord.
At an acceptable time, O God,
in the abundance of your steadfast · **love,**
answer_me.
With your · **steadfast** help, rescue_me.
Answer me, O Lord, for your steadfast love
is good; according to your abundant mercy,
· **turn** to me. ℟.

But I am lowly and · **in** pain;
let your salvation, O God, · **pro**-tect_me.
I will praise the name of God · **with** a song;
I will magnify him · **with** thanks-giving. ℟.

1 - Let the oppressed see it and · **be** glad;
3 - you · **who** seek God,
4 - let your · **hearts** re-vive. ℟.

For God will · **save** Zion
and rebuild the cities · **of** Judah;
the children of his servants · **shall** in-herit_it,
those who love his · **name** shall live_in_it. ℟.

To hear the Sunday Psalms, go to www.livingwithchrist.ca and select the psalm button at the bottom of the home page.

or

RESPONSORIAL PSALM *(Psalm 19)*

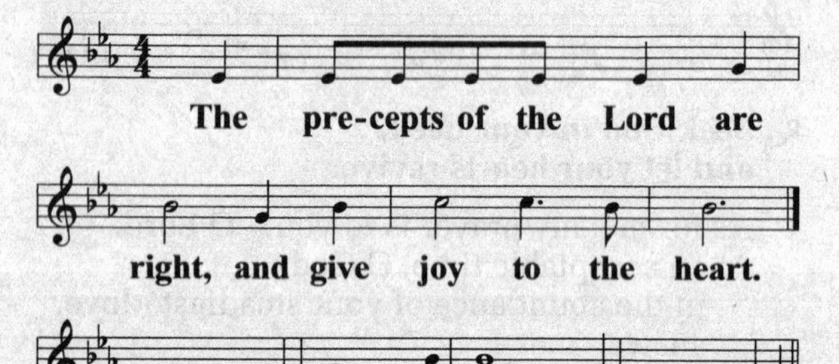

℟. **The precepts of the Lord are right,
and give joy to the heart.**

The law of the Lord is · **perfect,**
reviving the · **soul;**
the decrees of the Lord are · **sure,**
making wise · **the** simple. ℟.

The precepts of the Lord are · **right,**
rejoicing the · **heart;**
the commandment of the Lord is · **clear,**
enlightening · **the** eyes. ℟.

The fear of the Lord is · **pure,**
enduring for·-**ever;**
the ordinances of the Lord are · **true**
and righteous · **alto**-gether. ℟.

More to be desired are they than · **gold,**
even much fine · **gold;**
sweeter also than · **honey,**
and drippings · **of_the** honeycomb. ℟.

To hear the Sunday Psalms, go to www.livingwithchrist.ca and select the psalm button at the bottom of the home page.

SECOND READING *(Colossians 1.15-20)*

Christ is the image of the invisible God, the firstborn of all creation; for in him all things in heaven and on earth were created, things visible and invisible, whether thrones or dominions or rulers or powers — all things have been created through him and for him.

Christ is before all things, and in him all things hold together. He is the head of the body, the Church; he is the beginning, the firstborn from the dead, so that he might come to have first place in everything.

For in Christ all the fullness of God was pleased to dwell, and through him God was pleased to reconcile to himself all things, whether on earth or in heaven, by making peace through the blood of his Cross.

The word of the Lord. **Thanks be to God.**

GOSPEL ACCLAMATION *(John 6.63, 68)*
Alleluia. Alleluia. Your words, Lord, are spirit and life; you have the words of eternal life. **Alleluia.**

GOSPEL *(Luke 10.25-37)*
The Lord be with you. **And with your spirit.** A reading from the holy Gospel according to Luke. **Glory to you, O Lord.**

A lawyer stood up to test Jesus. "Teacher," he said, "what must I do to inherit eternal life?"

Jesus said to him, "What is written in the Law? What do you read there?" The lawyer answered, "You shall love the Lord your God with all your heart, and with all your soul, and with all your strength, and with all your mind; and your neighbour as yourself."

And Jesus said to him, "You have given the right answer; do this, and you will live." But wanting to justify himself, the lawyer asked Jesus, "And who is my neighbour?"

Jesus replied, "A man was going down from Jerusalem to Jericho, and fell into the hands of robbers, who stripped him, beat him, and went away, leaving him half dead. Now by chance a priest was going down that road; and when he saw him, he passed by on the other side. So likewise a Levite, when he came to the place and saw him, passed by on the other side.

"But a Samaritan while travelling came near him; and when he saw him, he was moved with pity. He went to him and bandaged his wounds, having poured oil and wine on them. Then he put him on his own animal, brought him to an inn, and took care of him.

"The next day the Samaritan took out two denarii, gave them to the innkeeper, and said, 'Take care of him; and when I come back, I will repay you whatever more you spend.'"

Jesus asked, "Which of these three, do you think, was a neighbour to the man who fell into the hands of the robbers?" The lawyer said, "The one who showed him mercy." Jesus said to him, "Go and do likewise."

The Gospel of the Lord. **Praise to you, Lord Jesus Christ.**

PROFESSION OF FAITH *(p. 11)*

PRAYER OF THE FAITHFUL

The following intentions are suggestions only. There are more suggestions at www.livingwithchrist.ca

℟. **Lord, hear our prayer.**

For the Church, called to be people of compassion, we pray to the Lord: ℟.

For all peoples striving for a world of peace, justice and reconciliation, we pray to the Lord: ℟.

For all who suffer because of violence and for all who need God's gentle healing, we pray to the Lord: ℟.

For this community, seeking to grow in love and support for one another, we pray to the Lord: ℟.

PREPARATION OF THE GIFTS *(p. 14)*

PRAYER OVER THE OFFERINGS
Look upon the offerings of the Church, O Lord, as she makes her prayer to you, and grant that, when consumed by those who believe, they may bring ever greater holiness. Through Christ our Lord. **Amen.**

PREFACE *(Sundays in Ordinary Time, p. 28)*

COMMUNION ANTIPHON *(Cf. Psalm 83.4-5)*
The sparrow finds a home, and the swallow a nest for her young: by your altars, O Lord of hosts, my King and my God. Blessed are they who dwell in your house, for ever singing your praise.

or (John 6.57)

Whoever eats my flesh and drinks my blood remains in me and I in him, says the Lord.

PRAYER AFTER COMMUNION
Having consumed these gifts, we pray, O Lord, that, by our participation in this mystery, its saving effects upon us may grow. Through Christ our Lord. **Amen.**

BLESSING AND DISMISSAL *(p. 70)*

July 17

In the ancient Near East, meals had greater significance than today. In our hectic modern society many families do not share a daily meal, often not even on Sunday. Even when family members are home at mealtime, they are often clustered around a television or alone in front of a computer or gaming console.

In contrast, most meals in the ancient world were communal events. Farmers and shepherds might eat alone at midday, but in the evening they joined each other or family members to share a meal, conversation and each other's company. Including strangers at meals meant welcoming them into the family circle and sharing the family's resources. Such hospitality treated the newcomer as a member of the family, even to the point of protecting her or his life from others. Abraham feeding the three men who appeared in his camp reflects the importance of such table fellowship.

So too does Martha's effort at providing hospitality to Jesus when she received him into her home. But there was another way to receive Jesus, which Mary demonstrated by sitting at his feet like a disciple to receive his teaching. In the Eucharist we are invited to combine both responses to Jesus' presence: hearing his word proclaimed in the Scriptures and sharing his food of bread and wine.

John L. McLaughlin, Toronto, ON

ENTRANCE ANTIPHON *(Psalm 53.6, 8)*
See, I have God for my help. The Lord sustains my soul. I will sacrifice to you with willing heart, and praise your name, O Lord, for it is good.

INTRODUCTORY RITES *(p. 5)*

COLLECT
Show favour, O Lord, to your servants and mercifully increase the gifts of your grace, that, made fervent in hope, faith and charity, they may be ever watchful in keeping your commands. Through our Lord Jesus Christ, your Son, who lives and reigns with you in the unity of the Holy Spirit, one God, for ever and ever. **Amen.**

FIRST READING *(Genesis 18.1-10a)*
The Lord appeared to Abraham by the oaks of Mamre, as Abraham sat at the entrance of his tent in the heat of the day. Abraham looked up and saw three men standing near him. When he saw them, he ran from the tent entrance to meet them, and bowed down to the ground.

He said, "My lord, if I find favour with you, do not pass by your servant. Let a little water be brought, and wash your feet, and rest yourselves under the tree. Let me bring a little bread, that you may refresh yourselves, and after that you may pass on — since you have come to your servant." So they said, "Do as you have said."

And Abraham hastened into the tent to Sarah, and said, "Make ready quickly three measures of choice flour, knead it, and make cakes." Abraham ran to the herd, and took a calf, tender and good, and gave it to the servant, who hastened to prepare it. Then he took curds and milk and the calf that he had prepared, and set it before them; and he stood by them under the tree while they ate.

They said to Abraham, "Where is your wife Sarah?" And he said, "There, in the tent."

Then one said, "I will surely return to you in due season, and your wife Sarah shall have a son."

The word of the Lord. **Thanks be to God.**

RESPONSORIAL PSALM *(Psalm 15)*

℟. **O Lord, who may abide in your tent?**

Whoever walks · **blamelessly,**
and does what is · **right,**
and speaks the truth from their · **heart;**
whoever does not slander · **with_their**
tongue. ℟.

Whoever does no evil to a · **friend,**
nor takes up a reproach against a · **neighbour;**
in whose eyes the wicked one is de-·**spised,**
but who honours those who fear · **the** Lord. ℟.

Whoever stands by their oath even
to their · **hurt;**
who does not lend money at · **interest,**
and does not take a bribe against the · **innocent.**
One who does these things shall never · **be**
moved. ℟.

SECOND READING *(Colossians 1.24-28)*

Brothers and sisters: I am now rejoicing in my sufferings for your sake, and in my flesh I am completing what is lacking in Christ's afflictions for the sake of his body, that is, the Church.

I became its servant according to God's commission that was given to me for you, to make the word of God fully known, the mystery that has been hidden throughout the ages and generations but has now been revealed to his saints.

To them God chose to make known how great among the Gentiles are the riches of the glory of this mystery, which is Christ in you, the hope of glory. It is Christ whom we proclaim, warning every person and teaching every person in all wisdom, so that we may present every person mature in Christ.

The word of the Lord. **Thanks be to God.**

GOSPEL ACCLAMATION *(Luke 8.15)*

Alleluia. Alleluia. Blessed are they who hold fast to God's word in an honest and good heart, and bear fruit with patient endurance. **Alleluia.**

GOSPEL *(Luke 10.38-42)*

The Lord be with you. **And with your spirit.** A reading from the holy Gospel according to Luke. **Glory to you, O Lord.**

Now as Jesus and his disciples went on their way, he entered a certain village, where a woman named Martha welcomed him into her home. She had a sister named Mary, who sat at the Lord's feet and listened to what he was saying.

But Martha was distracted by her many tasks; so she came to Jesus and asked, "Lord, do you not care that my sister has left me to do all the work by myself? Tell her then to help me."

But the Lord answered her, "Martha, Martha, you are worried and distracted by many things; there is need of only one thing. Mary has chosen the better part, which will not be taken away from her."

The Gospel of the Lord. **Praise to you, Lord Jesus Christ.**

PROFESSION OF FAITH *(p. 11)*

PRAYER OF THE FAITHFUL

The following intentions are suggestions only. There are more suggestions at www.livingwithchrist.ca

℟. **Lord, hear our prayer.**

For the Church, as we work together to proclaim the Good News, we pray to the Lord: ℟.

For leaders of nations working toward peace, we pray to the Lord: ℟.

For those who suffer worry, anxiety, distraction and depression, we pray to the Lord: ℟.

For our parish, a sign of God's presence offered today, we pray to the Lord: ℟.

PREPARATION OF THE GIFTS *(p. 14)*

PRAYER OVER THE OFFERINGS
O God, who in the one perfect sacrifice brought to completion varied offerings of the law, accept, we pray, this sacrifice from your faithful servants and make it holy, as you blessed the gifts of Abel, so that what each has offered to the honour of your majesty may benefit the salvation of all. Through Christ our Lord. **Amen.**

PREFACE *(Sundays in Ordinary Time, p. 28)*

COMMUNION ANTIPHON *(Psalm 110.4-5)*
The Lord, the gracious, the merciful, has made a memorial of his wonders; he gives food to those who fear him.

or (Revelation 3.20)

Behold, I stand at the door and knock, says the Lord. If anyone hears my voice and opens the door to me, I will enter his house and dine with him, and he with me.

PRAYER AFTER COMMUNION
Graciously be present to your people, we pray, O Lord, and lead those you have imbued with heavenly mysteries to pass from former ways to newness of life. Through Christ our Lord. **Amen.**

BLESSING AND DISMISSAL *(p. 70)*

July 24

Imagine a father and teenage son who rarely speak. They are strangers living under the same roof. For years the father has tried to restore the relationship but the son is always cold, distant and non-responsive. The sad father longs for things to be the way they used to be.

For some of us, unfortunately, our relationship with God is not so different. This is because we don't pray. Like the son, we sometimes ignore our heavenly father's calls to spend that quality time with him.

Never giving up hope, the father again asks his son if he wants to play catch. Astonishingly, the son agrees. At first it is a bit awkward, but before long they are laughing and really connecting. Afterwards, the son says, "Dad, this was so much fun. We need to do this more often." Unbeknownst to him, his father is holding back tears.

In today's gospel, Jesus invites us to connect (or reconnect) with our heavenly father through prayer. No matter how distant we have been or how far away we have turned, God will rejoice if we respond to his call to spend time with him. He knocks on the door of our hearts every day and waits. Today is the time to let him in. Today is the time to pray!

Connor Brownrigg, Ottawa, ON

ENTRANCE ANTIPHON *(Cf. Psalm 67.6-7, 36)*
God is in his holy place, God who unites those who dwell in his house; he himself gives might and strength to his people.

INTRODUCTORY RITES *(p. 5)*

COLLECT
O God, protector of those who hope in you, without whom nothing has firm foundation, nothing is holy, bestow in abundance your mercy upon us and grant that, with you as our ruler and guide, we may use the good things that pass in such a way as to hold fast even now to those that ever endure. Through our Lord Jesus Christ, your Son, who lives and reigns with you in the unity of the Holy Spirit, one God, for ever and ever. **Amen.**

FIRST READING *(Genesis 18.20-32)*
The Lord said: "How great is the outcry against Sodom and Gomorrah and how very grave their sin! I must go down and see whether they have done altogether according to the outcry that has come to me; and if not, I will know."

So the men turned from there, and went toward Sodom, while Abraham remained standing before the Lord. Then Abraham came near and said, "Will you indeed sweep away the righteous with the wicked? Suppose there are fifty righteous within the city; will you then sweep away the place and not forgive it for the fifty righteous who are in it? Far be it from you to do such a thing, to slay the righteous with the wicked, so that the righteous fare as the wicked! Far be that from you! Shall not the Judge of all the earth do what is just?" And the Lord said, "If I find at Sodom fifty righteous in the city, I will forgive the whole place for their sake."

Abraham answered, "Let me take it upon myself to speak to the Lord, I who am but dust and ashes. Suppose five of the fifty righteous are lacking? Will you destroy the whole city for lack of five?" And the Lord said, "I will not destroy it if I find forty-five there."

Again Abraham spoke to the Lord, "Suppose forty are found there." He answered, "For the sake of forty I will not do it."

Then Abraham said, "Oh do not let the Lord be angry if I speak. Suppose thirty are found there." The Lord answered, "I will not do it, if I find thirty there."

Abraham said, "Let me take it upon myself to speak to the Lord. Suppose twenty are found there." The Lord answered, "For the sake of twenty I will not destroy it."

Then Abraham said, "Oh do not let the Lord be angry if I speak just once more. Suppose ten are found there." The Lord answered, "For the sake of ten I will not destroy it."

The word of the Lord. **Thanks be to God.**

RESPONSORIAL PSALM *(Psalm 138)*

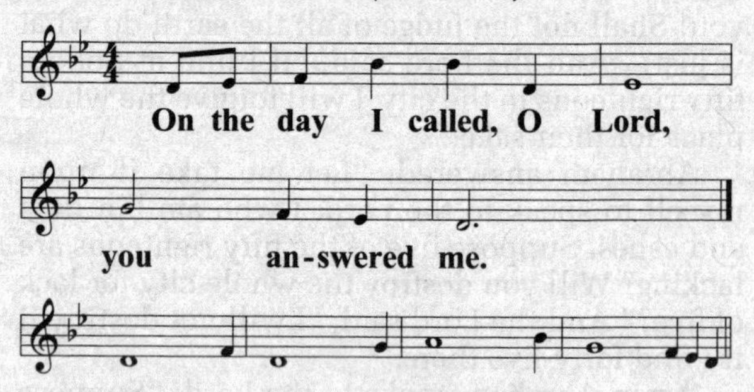

℟. **On the day I called, O Lord, you answered me.**

I give you thanks, O Lord, with my
whole · **heart;**
before the Angels I sing your · **praise;**
I bow down toward your holy temple,
and give thanks to your · **name**
for your steadfast love · **and** your faithfulness. ℟.

For you have exalted your · **name**
and your word above · **everything.**
On the day I called, you · **answered_me,**
you increased my · **strength** of soul. ℟.

For though the Lord is high, he regards
the · **lowly;**
but the haughty he perceives from far a·-**way.**
Though I walk in the midst of · **trouble,**
you preserve me against the wrath
· **of** my enemies. ℟.

You stretch out your hand and your right hand de-·**livers_me.**
The Lord will fulfill his purpose for · **me;**
your steadfast love, O Lord, endures for-·**ever.**
Do not forsake the · **work_of** your hands. ℟.

To hear the Sunday Psalms, go to www.livingwithchrist.ca and select the psalm button at the bottom of the home page.

SECOND READING *(Colossians 2.12-14)*
Brothers and sisters, When you were buried with Christ in baptism, you were also raised with him through faith in the power of God, who raised Christ from the dead.

And when you were dead in trespasses and the uncircumcision of your flesh, God made you alive together with him, when he forgave us all our trespasses, erasing the record that stood against us with its legal demands. He set this aside, nailing it to the Cross.

The word of the Lord. **Thanks be to God.**

GOSPEL ACCLAMATION *(Romans 8.15)*
Alleluia. Alleluia. You have received a Spirit of adoption, in whom we cry, Abba! Father! **Alleluia.**

GOSPEL *(Luke 11.1-13)*
The Lord be with you. **And with your spirit.** A reading from the holy Gospel according to Luke. **Glory to you, O Lord.**

Jesus was praying in a certain place, and after he had finished, one of his disciples said to him, "Lord, teach us to pray, as John taught his disciples."

He said to them, "When you pray, say: 'Father, hallowed be your name. Your kingdom come. Give us each day our daily bread. And forgive us our sins, for we ourselves forgive everyone indebted to us. And lead us not into temptation.'"

And Jesus said to the disciples, "Suppose one of you has a friend, and you go to him at midnight and say to him, 'Friend, lend me three loaves of bread; for a friend of mine has arrived, and I have nothing to set before him.' And your friend answers from within, 'Do not bother me; the door has already been locked, and my children are with me in bed; I cannot get up and give you anything.'

"I tell you, even though he will not get up and give him anything because he is his friend, at least because of his persistence he will get up and give him whatever he needs.

"So I say to you: Ask, and it will be given you; search, and you will find; knock, and the door will be opened for you. For everyone who asks receives, and everyone who searches finds, and for everyone who knocks, the door will be opened.

"Is there any father among you who, if your child asks for a fish, will give the child a snake instead of a fish? Or if the child asks for an egg, will give a scorpion?

"If you then, who are evil, know how to give good gifts to your children, how much more will the heavenly Father give the Holy Spirit to those who ask him!"

The Gospel of the Lord. **Praise to you, Lord Jesus Christ.**

PROFESSION OF FAITH *(p. 11)*

PRAYER OF THE FAITHFUL

The following intentions are suggestions only. There are more suggestions at www.livingwithchrist.ca

℟. **Lord, hear our prayer.**

For the Church, witness to God's love in the world, we pray to the Lord: ℟.

For all who work prayerfully and tirelessly for the freedom of all people, we pray to the Lord: ℟.

For people who cry out in their helplessness for assistance and compassion, we pray to the Lord: ℟.

For hearts receptive to peace and justice here in our community, we pray to the Lord: ℟.

PREPARATION OF THE GIFTS *(p. 14)*

PRAYER OVER THE OFFERINGS

Accept, O Lord, we pray, the offerings which we bring from the abundance of your gifts, that through the powerful working of your grace these most sacred mysteries may sanctify our present way of life and lead us to eternal gladness. Through Christ our Lord. **Amen.**

PREFACE *(Sundays in Ordinary Time, p. 28)*

COMMUNION ANTIPHON *(Psalm 102.2)*

Bless the Lord, O my soul, and never forget all his benefits.

or (Matthew 5.7-8)
Blessed are the merciful, for they shall receive mercy. Blessed are the clean of heart, for they shall see God.

PRAYER AFTER COMMUNION
We have consumed, O Lord, this divine Sacrament, the perpetual memorial of the Passion of your Son; grant, we pray, that this gift, which he himself gave us with love beyond all telling, may profit us for salvation. Through Christ our Lord. **Amen.**

BLESSING AND DISMISSAL *(p. 70)*

July 31

In our first reading today from the Book of Ecclesiastes, its author, Qoheleth, wrote some 2300 years ago: "All is vanity." In this book from the Hebrew Scriptures, the Teacher, as his name translates, relays to us from across the millennia the stark futility of our reality. The good suffer, heartbreaks beset us all and in the end everyone dies. This is as true of life today as then.

Still, we foolishly strive to amass personal wealth and seek to protect it from others. For example, one estimate places yearly global military expenditures at more than $1.75 trillion. This does not include all that we spend on our individual efforts to safeguard our property and persons. How much would it cost per year to adequately house, feed and educate the needy on our planet? The world's 85 richest people have as much accumulated wealth as the poorest 3.5 billion inhabitants. Where does our security truly lie? Where is justice?

The parable Jesus tells in the gospel reading today calls on us to be on guard "against all kinds of greed," striving for what matters to God, not seeking an "abundance of possessions" as our life's purpose. Meaning in our all-too-short lives comes from one source and one source alone, God. As Paul writes to the Colossians, "Christ is all and in all."

Michael Dougherty, Whitehorse, YT

ENTRANCE ANTIPHON *(Psalm 69.2, 6)*
O God, come to my assistance; O Lord, make haste to help me! You are my rescuer, my help; O Lord, do not delay.

INTRODUCTORY RITES *(p. 5)*

COLLECT
Draw near to your servants, O Lord, and answer their prayers with unceasing kindness, that, for those who glory in you as their Creator and guide, you may restore what you have created and keep safe what you have restored. Through our Lord Jesus Christ, your Son, who lives and reigns with you in the unity of the Holy Spirit, one God, for ever and ever. **Amen.**

FIRST READING *(Ecclesiastes 1.2; 2.21-23)*
Vanity of vanities, says the Teacher,
vanity of vanities! All is vanity.

Sometimes one who has toiled with wisdom
and knowledge and skill
must leave all to be enjoyed by another
who did not toil for it.
This also is vanity and a great evil.

What does a person get from all their toil
and strain,
their toil under the sun?
For their days are full of pain,
and their work is a vexation;
even at night their mind does not rest.
This also is vanity.

The word of the Lord. **Thanks be to God.**

RESPONSORIAL PSALM *(Psalm 90)*

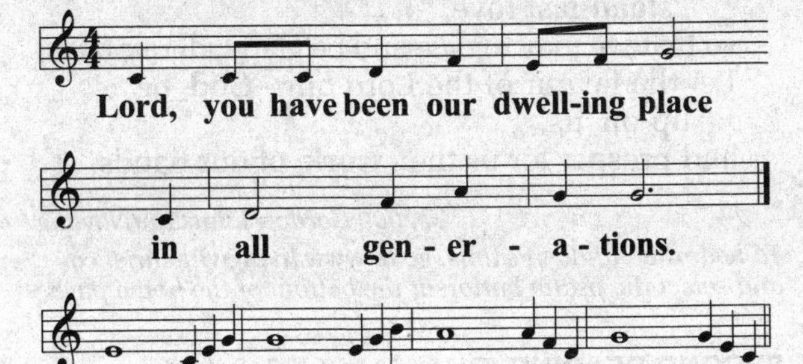

℟. **Lord, you have been our dwelling place
in all generations.**

You turn man back to · **dust**, and say,
"Turn back, you · **children** of Adam."
For a thousand years in your sight are like
yesterday when · **it** is past,
or like a watch · **in** the night. ℟.

You sweep them away; they are · **like** a dream,
like grass that is re-·**newed_in** the morning;
in the morning it flourishes and · **is** re-newed;
in the evening it · **fades** and withers. ℟.

So teach us to · **count** our days
that we may gain · **a** wise heart.
Turn, O · **Lord!** How long?
Have compassion · **on** your servants! ℟.

Satisfy us in the morning with your
· **stead**-fast love,
so that we may rejoice and be glad · **all** our days.
Let the favour of the Lord our · **God_be**
up-on_us,
and prosper for us the · **work_of** our hands. ℟.

To hear the Sunday Psalms, go to www.livingwithchrist.ca and select the psalm button at the bottom of the home page.

SECOND READING *(Colossians 3.1-5, 9-11)*

Brothers and sisters: If you have been raised with Christ, seek the things that are above, where Christ is, seated at the right hand of God.

Set your minds on things that are above, not on things that are on earth, for you have died, and your life is hidden with Christ in God. When Christ who is your life is revealed, then you also will be revealed with him in glory.

Put to death, therefore, whatever in you is earthly: fornication, impurity, passion, evil desire, and greed, which is idolatry.

Do not lie to one another, seeing that you have stripped off the old self with its practices and have clothed yourselves with the new self, which is being renewed in knowledge according to the image of its creator.

In that renewal there is no longer Greek and Jew, circumcised and uncircumcised, barbarian, Scythian, slave and free; but Christ is all and in all!

The word of the Lord. **Thanks be to God.**

GOSPEL ACCLAMATION *(Matthew 5.3)*
Alleluia. Alleluia. Blessed are the poor in spirit, for theirs is the kingdom of heaven! **Alleluia.**

GOSPEL *(Luke 12.13-21)*
The Lord be with you. **And with your spirit.** A reading from the holy Gospel according to Luke. **Glory to you, O Lord.**

Someone in the crowd said to Jesus, "Teacher, tell my brother to divide the family inheritance with me." But Jesus said to him, "Friend, who set me to be a judge or arbitrator over you?"

And Jesus said to the crowd, "Take care! Be on your guard against all kinds of greed; for one's life does not consist in the abundance of possessions."

Then Jesus told them a parable: "The land of a rich man produced abundantly. And he thought to himself, 'What should I do, for I have no place to store my crops?' Then he said, 'I will do this: I will pull down my barns and build larger ones, and there I will store all my grain and my goods. And I will say to my soul, "Soul, you have ample goods laid up for many years; relax, eat, drink, be merry."'

"But God said to him, 'You fool! This very night your life is being demanded of you. And the things you have prepared, whose will they be?' So it is with those who store up treasures for themselves but are not rich toward God."

The Gospel of the Lord. **Praise to you, Lord Jesus Christ.**

PROFESSION OF FAITH *(p. 11)*

PRAYER OF THE FAITHFUL

The following intentions are suggestions only. There are more suggestions at www.livingwithchrist.ca

℟. **Lord, hear our prayer.**

For the Church, working to overcome divisions between persons, races and nations, we pray to the Lord: ℟.

For world leaders seeking equity for all peoples, we pray to the Lord: ℟.

For those who lack the basic necessities of life, we pray to the Lord: ℟.

For us, God's People gathered here, called to journey with Christ in joy and peace, we pray to the Lord: ℟.

PREPARATION OF THE GIFTS *(p. 14)*

PRAYER OVER THE OFFERINGS

Graciously sanctify these gifts, O Lord, we pray, and, accepting the oblation of this spiritual sacrifice, make of us an eternal offering to you. Through Christ our Lord. **Amen.**

PREFACE *(Sundays in Ordinary Time, p. 28)*

COMMUNION ANTIPHON *(Wisdom 16.20)*

You have given us, O Lord, bread from heaven, endowed with all delights and sweetness in every taste.

or (John 6.35)
I am the bread of life, says the Lord; whoever comes to me will not hunger and whoever believes in me will not thirst.

PRAYER AFTER COMMUNION
Accompany with constant protection, O Lord, those you renew with these heavenly gifts and, in your never-failing care for them, make them worthy of eternal redemption. Through Christ our Lord. **Amen.**

BLESSING AND DISMISSAL *(p. 70)*

August Saints' Days

The following saints are traditionally remembered in August in Canada.

1 Saint Alphonsus Mary Ligouri

2 Saint Eusebius of Vercelli
Saint Peter Julian Eymard

4 Saint John Mary Vianney

5 Blessed Frédéric Janssoone

7 Saint Sixtus II and Companions
Saint Cajetan

8 Saint Dominic

9 Saint Teresa Benedicta of the Cross

10 Saint Lawrence

11 Saint Clare

12 Saint Jane Frances de Chantal

13 Saints Pontian and Hippolytus

14 Saint Maximilian Kolbe

16 Saint Stephen of Hungary

19 Saint John Eudes

20 Saint Bernard

21 Saint Pius X

23 Saint Rose of Lima

24 Saint Bartholomew

25 Saint Louis
Saint Joseph Calasanz

27 Saint Monica

28 Saint Augustine

August 7

For where your treasure is, there your heart will be also.

Don't treasure money: Check. I already know not to focus on wealth. I was feeling pretty pleased with myself, too, until that small voice inside asked: So what, exactly, fills your focus? What's on your mind?

If I'm honest, I'd have to say it's worry. Today, it's my job. Other times I worry about health, finances or relationships. I just have to watch the news for a world of worries. But everyone worries over things we feel are out of our control. Worry is really the fear of what *might* happen and we can imagine the worst what-ifs. We play those reels over and over, giving that fear more power, more focus, more energy. Ultimately, we make worry our treasure — like J.R.R. Tolkien's character Gollum and his ring.

I don't *treasure* my worries — that's ridiculous! Is it? Don't those worries take up our thoughts and energy? Aren't they what we talk about most and think about always? Some have even become our stories — a part of how we define ourselves. Sounds like we've made them quite 'precious.'

Fears are legitimate concerns. It's natural to worry — but it's not productive. If we focus on God, if we bring our fears to him, even the greatest worry can become a powerful prayer.

Caroline Pignat, Kanata, ON

ENTRANCE ANTIPHON *(Cf. Psalm 73.20, 19, 22, 23)*
Look to your covenant, O Lord, and forget not the life of your poor ones for ever. Arise, O God, and defend your cause, and forget not the cries of those who seek you.

INTRODUCTORY RITES *(p. 5)*

COLLECT
Almighty ever-living God, whom, taught by the Holy Spirit, we dare to call our Father, bring, we pray, to perfection in our hearts the spirit of adoption as your sons and daughters, that we may merit to enter into the inheritance which you have promised. Through our Lord Jesus Christ, your Son, who lives and reigns with you in the unity of the Holy Spirit, one God, for ever and ever. **Amen.**

FIRST READING *(Wisdom 18.6-9)*
The night of the deliverance from Egypt was made known beforehand to our ancestors, so that they might rejoice in sure knowledge of the oaths in which they trusted.

The deliverance of the righteous and the destruction of their enemies were expected by your people. For by the same means by which you punished our enemies you called us to yourself and glorified us.

For in secret the holy children of good people offered sacrifices, and with one accord agreed to the divine law, so that the saints would share alike the same things, both blessings and dangers; and already they were singing the praises of the ancestors.

The word of the Lord. **Thanks be to God.**

RESPONSORIAL PSALM *(Psalm 33)*

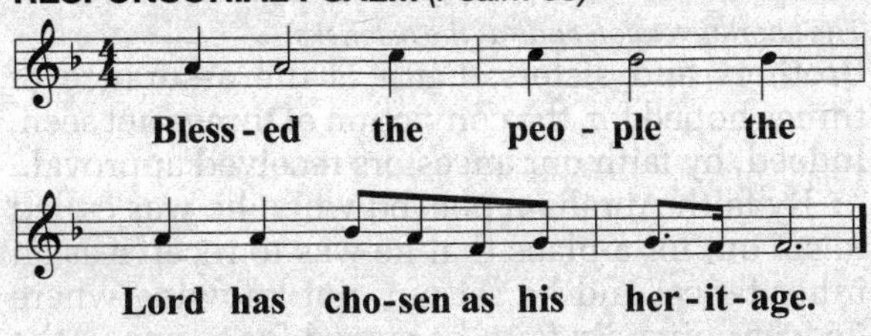

℟. **Blessed the people the Lord has chosen as his heritage.**

Rejoice in the Lord, · **O** you righteous.
Praise be·-**fits** the upright.
Blessed is the nation whose God · **is** the Lord,
the people whom he has · **chosen_as**
his heritage. ℟.

Truly the eye of the Lord is on · **those** who
fear_him,
on those who hope in his · **stead**-fast love,
to deliver their · **souls** from death,
and to keep them a·-**live** in famine. ℟.

Our soul waits · **for** the Lord;
he is our · **help** and shield.
Let your steadfast love, O Lord, · **be** up-on_us,
even as we · **hope** in you. ℟.

To hear the Sunday Psalms, go to www.livingwithchrist.ca and select the psalm button at the bottom of the home page.

SECOND READING *(Hebrews 11.1-2, 8-19)*

The shorter version ends at the asterisks.

Brothers and sisters: Faith is the assurance of things hoped for, the conviction of things not seen. Indeed, by faith our ancestors received approval.

By faith Abraham obeyed when he was called to set out for a place that he was to receive as an inheritance; and he set out, not knowing where he was going. By faith he stayed for a time in the land he had been promised, as in a foreign land, living in tents, as did Isaac and Jacob, who were heirs with him of the same promise.

For Abraham looked forward to the city that has foundations, whose architect and builder is God. By faith Sarah herself, though barren, received power to conceive, even when she was too old, because she considered him faithful who had promised.

Therefore from one person, and this one as good as dead, descendants were born, "as many as the stars of heaven and as the innumerable grains of sand by the seashore."

* * *

All of these died in faith without having received the promises, but from a distance they saw and greeted them. They confessed that they were strangers and foreigners on the earth, for people who speak in this way make it clear that they are seeking a homeland. If they had been thinking of the land that they had left behind, they would have had opportunity to return.

But as it is, they desire a better country, that is, a heavenly one. Therefore God is not ashamed to be called their God; indeed, he has prepared a city for them.

By faith Abraham, when put to the test, offered up Isaac. He who had received the promises was ready to offer up his only-begotten son, of whom he had been told, "It is through Isaac that descendants shall be named for you." Abraham considered the fact that God is able even to raise someone from the dead — and figuratively speaking, he did receive Isaac back.

The word of the Lord. **Thanks be to God.**

GOSPEL ACCLAMATION *(Matthew 24.42, 44)*

Alleluia. Alleluia. Keep awake and be ready, for you know not when the Son of Man is coming. **Alleluia.**

GOSPEL *(Luke 12.32-48)*

For the shorter version, omit the indented parts.

The Lord be with you. **And with your spirit.**
A reading from the holy Gospel according to Luke. **Glory to you, O Lord.**

> Jesus said to his disciples, "Do not be afraid, little flock, for it is your Father's good pleasure to give you the kingdom. Sell your possessions, and give alms.
>
> "Make purses for yourselves that do not wear out, an unfailing treasure in heaven, where no thief comes near and no moth destroys. For where your treasure is, there your heart will be also.

"Be dressed for action and have your lamps lit; be like those who are waiting for their master to return from the wedding banquet, so that they may open the door for him as soon as he comes and knocks. Blessed are those slaves whom the master finds alert when he comes; truly I tell you, he will fasten his belt and have them sit down to eat, and he will come and serve them. If he comes during the middle of the night, or near dawn, and finds them so, blessed are those slaves.

"But know this: if the owner of the house had known at what hour the thief was coming, he would not have let his house be broken into. You also must be ready, for the Son of Man is coming at an unexpected hour."

Peter said, "Lord, are you telling this parable for us or for everyone?" And the Lord said, "Who then is the faithful and prudent manager whom his master will put in charge of his slaves, to give them their allowance of food at the proper time? Blessed is that slave whom his master will find at work when he arrives. Truly I tell you, he will put that one in charge of all his possessions. But if that slave says to himself, 'My master is delayed in coming,' and if he begins to beat the other slaves, men and women, and to eat and drink and get drunk, the master of that slave will come on a day when he does not expect him and at an hour that he does not know, and will cut him in pieces, and put him with the unfaithful.

"That slave who knew what his master wanted, but did not prepare himself or do what was wanted, will receive a severe beating. But the one who did not know and did what deserved a beating will receive a light beating. From everyone to whom much has been given, much will be required; and from the one to whom much has been entrusted, even more will be demanded."

The Gospel of the Lord. **Praise to you, Lord Jesus Christ.**

PROFESSION OF FAITH *(p. 11)*

PRAYER OF THE FAITHFUL

The following intentions are suggestions only. There are more suggestions at www.livingwithchrist.ca

℟. **Lord, hear our prayer.**

For Church leaders, continually seeking to do God's will, we pray to the Lord: ℟.

For global peace born of justice and righteousness among nations, we pray to the Lord: ℟.

For persons experiencing changes in their lives and for those who journey with them, we pray to the Lord: ℟.

For this parish, building a community of compassion and justice, we pray to the Lord: ℟.

PREPARATION OF THE GIFTS *(p. 14)*

PRAYER OVER THE OFFERINGS

Be pleased, O Lord, to accept the offerings of your Church, for in your mercy you have given them to be offered and by your power you transform them into the mystery of our salvation. Through Christ our Lord. **Amen.**

PREFACE *(Sundays in Ordinary Time, p. 28)*

COMMUNION ANTIPHON *(Psalm 147.12, 14)*
O Jerusalem, glorify the Lord, who gives you your fill of finest wheat.
or (Cf. John 6.51)
The bread that I will give, says the Lord, is my flesh for the life of the world.

PRAYER AFTER COMMUNION
May the communion in your Sacrament that we have consumed, save us, O Lord, and confirm us in the light of your truth. Through Christ our Lord. **Amen.**

BLESSING AND DISMISSAL *(p. 70)*

August 14

Occasionally the words of Jesus seem to smack us in the face. We shake our heads and move on to something more comforting. Such are the words in today's gospel. Most of us do not want to imagine the possibility of strife and animosity in our family.

Nonetheless, Jesus knew that sometimes families are a hindrance for disciples. In his day, family was often the one structure protecting individuals — but at the cost of a patriarchal system demanding conformity and obedience to authoritarian demands.

In our day, I have seen parents oppose a possible vocation for one of their children, or react negatively when a son or daughter wishes to spend a year working for and with the poor in another country. We also know the pain of parents whose children distance themselves from the faith, despite a good education and faith-filled upbringing.

Choosing the Way of Jesus has never been easy. That is no different today. What Jesus asks of us, however, is that we focus our attention on the true kingdom, that of our Father in heaven, where all are brothers and sisters, especially those most in need. When we work to build God's kingdom, our earthly families can follow along — or go their own way. As painful as that may be for the disciple, the Way is what Jesus demands.

Fr. Mark Miller, CSsR, Toronto, ON

ENTRANCE ANTIPHON *(Psalm 83.10-11)*
Turn your eyes, O God, our shield; and look on the face of your anointed one; one day within your courts is better than a thousand elsewhere.

INTRODUCTORY RITES *(p. 5)*

COLLECT
O God, who have prepared for those who love you good things which no eye can see, fill our hearts, we pray, with the warmth of your love, so that, loving you in all things and above all things, we may attain your promises, which surpass every human desire. Through our Lord Jesus Christ, your Son, who lives and reigns with you in the unity of the Holy Spirit, one God, for ever and ever. **Amen.**

FIRST READING *(Jeremiah 38.4-6, 8-10)*
The officials said to the king, "This man ought to be put to death, because he is discouraging the soldiers who are left in this city, and all the people, by speaking such words to them. For this man is not seeking the welfare of this people, but their harm."

King Zedekiah said, "Here he is; he is in your hands; for the king is powerless against you."

So they took Jeremiah and threw him into the cistern of Malchiah, the king's son, which was in the court of the guard, letting Jeremiah down by ropes. Now there was no water in the cistern, but only mud, and Jeremiah sank in the mud.

So Ebed-melech the Ethiopian, an officer in the king's house, left the king's house and spoke to the king, "My lord king, these men have acted wickedly in all they did to the Prophet Jeremiah by throwing him into the cistern to die there of hunger, for there is no bread left in the city." Then the king commanded Ebed-melech the Ethiopian, "Take three men with you from here, and pull the Prophet Jeremiah up from the cistern before he dies."

The word of the Lord. **Thanks be to God.**

RESPONSORIAL PSALM *(Psalm 40)*

℟. **Lord, make haste to help me!**

1 - I waited patiently for the · **Lord;**
4 - he inclined to me and heard · **my** cry. ℟.

He drew me up from the desolate · **pit,**
out of the · **miry** bog,
and set my feet upon a · **rock,**
making my steps · **se**-cure. ℟.

He put a new song in my · **mouth,**
a song of praise to · **our** God.
Many will see and · **fear,**
and put their trust · **in_the** Lord. ℟.

As for me, I am poor and · **needy,**
but the Lord · **takes** thought_for_me.
You are my help and my de-·**liverer;**
do not delay, O · **my** God. ℟.

To hear the Sunday Psalms, go to www.livingwithchrist.ca and select the psalm button at the bottom of the home page.

SECOND READING *(Hebrews 12.1-4)*

Brothers and sisters: Since we are surrounded by so great a cloud of witnesses, let us also lay aside every weight and the sin that clings so closely, and let us run with perseverance the race that is set before us, looking to Jesus the pioneer and perfecter of our faith, who for the sake of the joy that was set before him endured the Cross, disregarding its shame, and has taken his seat at the right hand of the throne of God.

Consider Jesus who endured such hostility against himself from sinners, so that you may not grow weary or lose heart. In your struggle against sin you have not yet resisted to the point of shedding your blood.

The word of the Lord. **Thanks be to God.**

GOSPEL ACCLAMATION *(John 10.27)*

Alleluia. Alleluia. My sheep hear my voice, says the Lord; I know them, and they follow me. **Alleluia.**

GOSPEL *(Luke 12.49-53)*

The Lord be with you. **And with your spirit.** A reading from the holy Gospel according to Luke. **Glory to you, O Lord.**

Jesus said to his disciples: "I came to bring fire to the earth, and how I wish it were already kindled! I have a baptism with which to be baptized, and what stress I am under until it is completed!

"Do you think that I have come to bring peace to the earth? No, I tell you, but rather division! From now on five in one household will be divided, three against two and two against three; they will be divided: father against son and son against father, mother against daughter and daughter against mother, mother-in-law against her daughter-in-law and daughter-in-law against mother-in-law."

The Gospel of the Lord. **Praise to you, Lord Jesus Christ.**

PROFESSION OF FAITH *(p. 11)*

PRAYER OF THE FAITHFUL

The following intentions are suggestions only. There are more suggestions at www.livingwithchrist.ca

℟. **Lord, hear our prayer.**

For humility in leaders of the Church, we pray to the Lord: ℟.

For justice and peace in countries torn by war and poverty, we pray to the Lord: ℟.

For the hungry, we pray to the Lord: ℟.

For openness to the Holy Spirit in this community of faith, we pray to the Lord: ℟.

PREPARATION OF THE GIFTS *(p. 14)*

PRAYER OVER THE OFFERINGS
Receive our oblation, O Lord, by which is brought about a glorious exchange, that, by offering what you have given, we may merit to receive your very self. Through Christ our Lord. **Amen.**

PREFACE *(Sundays in Ordinary Time, p. 28)*

COMMUNION ANTIPHON *(Psalm 129.7)*
With the Lord there is mercy; in him is plentiful redemption.

or (John 6.51-52)

I am the living bread that came down from heaven, says the Lord. Whoever eats of this bread will live for ever.

PRAYER AFTER COMMUNION
Made partakers of Christ through these Sacraments, we humbly implore your mercy, Lord, that, conformed to his image on earth, we may merit also to be his co-heirs in heaven. Who lives and reigns for ever and ever. **Amen.**

BLESSING AND DISMISSAL *(p. 70)*

August 21

Ah, the narrow door! A procrastinator by nature, I must confess that today's gospel makes me uncomfortable. Clean up my act, I say to myself, or I'll find myself in that throng, knocking on heaven's door, at risk of joining those who are weeping and gnashing their teeth because they realize that they took for granted all the promise of the kingdom of God.

But just as I am stewing about being ready to enter heaven, I am reminded, "some are last who will be first, and some are first who will be last." With this, my earthly sense of fair play kicks in and I am, yet again, full of righteous indignation that those who seemingly haven't played by the rules are going to bypass the rest of us. So much for my preparedness for passage through that narrow door!

Today we are reminded that we cannot impose earthly rules and expectations on eternal life. God offers all of us passage to the kingdom, but we are required, as St Paul notes, to live a life of discipline — God's discipline. Being loved by God does not mean we won't face trials and pain, but out of our experiences comes the "peaceful fruit of righteousness," the very kind of sustenance that draws people to the banquet in the kingdom of God.

Catherine Mulroney, Toronto, ON

ENTRANCE ANTIPHON *(Cf. Psalm 85.1-3)*
Turn your ear, O Lord, and answer me; save the servant who trusts in you, my God. Have mercy on me, O Lord, for I cry to you all the day long.

INTRODUCTORY RITES *(p. 5)*

COLLECT
O God, who cause the minds of the faithful to unite in a single purpose, grant your people to love what you command and to desire what you promise, that, amid the uncertainties of this world, our hearts may be fixed on that place where true gladness is found. Through our Lord Jesus Christ, your Son, who lives and reigns with you in the unity of the Holy Spirit, one God, for ever and ever. **Amen.**

FIRST READING *(Isaiah 66.18-21)*
Thus says the Lord: "For I know their works and their thoughts, and I am coming to gather all nations and tongues; and they shall come and shall see my glory, and I will set a sign among them.

"From them I will send survivors to the nations, to Tarshish, Put, and Lud — which draw the bow — to Tubal and Javan, to the coastlands far away that have not heard of my fame or seen my glory; and they shall declare my glory among the nations.

"They shall bring all your kindred from all the nations as an offering to the Lord, on horses, and in chariots, and in litters, and on mules, and on dromedaries, to my holy mountain Jerusalem," says the Lord, "just as the children of Israel bring a grain offering in a clean vessel to the house of the Lord.

"And I will also take some of them as priests and as Levites," says the Lord.

The word of the Lord. **Thanks be to God.**

RESPONSORIAL PSALM *(Psalm 117)*

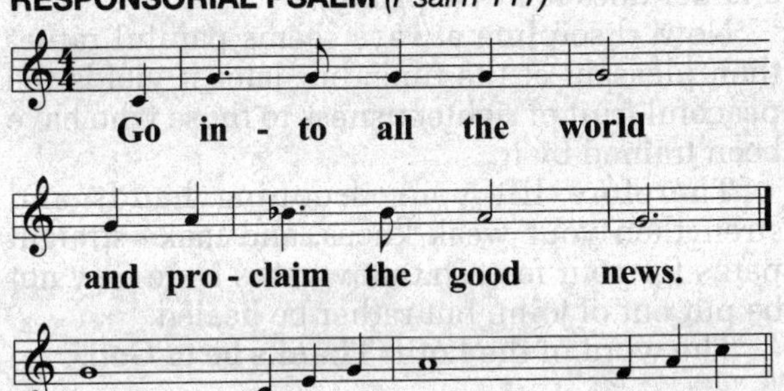

℟. **Go into all the world**
and proclaim the good news.
or **Alleluia!**

Praise the Lord, · **all** you nations!
Extol him, · **all** you peoples! ℟.

For great is his steadfast · **love** toward us,
and the faithfulness of the Lord
en-·**dures** for-ever. ℟.

To hear the Sunday Psalms, go to www.livingwithchrist.ca and select the psalm button at the bottom of the home page.

SECOND READING *(Hebrews 12.5-7, 11-13)*

Brothers and sisters: You have forgotten the exhortation that addresses you as children — "My son, do not regard lightly the discipline of the Lord, or lose heart when you are punished by him; for the Lord disciplines the one whom he loves, and chastises every son whom he accepts."

Endure trials for the sake of discipline. God is treating you as sons; for what son is there whom a father does not discipline?

Now, discipline always seems painful rather than pleasant at the time, but later it yields the peaceful fruit of righteousness to those who have been trained by it.

Therefore lift your drooping hands and strengthen your weak knees, and make straight paths for your feet, so that what is lame may not be put out of joint, but rather be healed.

The word of the Lord. **Thanks be to God.**

GOSPEL ACCLAMATION *(John 14.6)*

Alleluia. Alleluia. I am the way, the truth, and the life, says the Lord; no one comes to the Father, except through me. **Alleluia.**

GOSPEL *(Luke 13.22-30)*

The Lord be with you. **And with your spirit.** A reading from the holy Gospel according to Luke. **Glory to you, O Lord.**

Jesus went through one town and village after another, teaching as he made his way to Jerusalem. Someone asked him, "Lord, will only a few be saved?"

Jesus said to them, "Strive to enter through the narrow door; for many, I tell you, will try to enter and will not be able.

"When once the owner of the house has got up and shut the door, and you begin to stand outside and to knock at the door, saying, 'Lord, open to us,' then in reply he will say to you, 'I do not know where you come from.'

"Then you will begin to say, 'We ate and drank with you, and you taught in our streets.' But the Lord will say, 'I do not know where you come from; go away from me, all you evildoers!'

"There will be weeping and gnashing of teeth when you see Abraham and Isaac and Jacob and all the Prophets in the kingdom of God, and you yourselves thrown out. Then people will come from east and west, from north and south, and will eat in the kingdom of God. Indeed, some are last who will be first, and some are first who will be last."

The Gospel of the Lord. **Praise to you, Lord Jesus Christ.**

PROFESSION OF FAITH *(p. 11)*

PRAYER OF THE FAITHFUL

The following intentions are suggestions only. There are more suggestions at www.livingwithchrist.ca

℟. **Lord, hear our prayer.**

For the Church, working to be a sign of humble service to all, we pray to the Lord: ℟.

For world leaders who respect the law of love written in each heart, we pray to the Lord: ℟.

For people who encounter a 'narrow door' when seeking justice, fair employment or suitable healthcare, we pray to the Lord: ℟.

For this parish, building a community of compassion and justice, we pray to the Lord: ℟.

PREPARATION OF THE GIFTS *(p. 14)*

PRAYER OVER THE OFFERINGS
O Lord, who gained for yourself a people by adoption through the one sacrifice offered once for all, bestow graciously on us, we pray, the gifts of unity and peace in your Church. Through Christ our Lord. **Amen.**

PREFACE *(Sundays in Ordinary Time, p. 28)*

COMMUNION ANTIPHON *(Cf. Psalm 103.13-15)*
The earth is replete with the fruits of your work, O Lord; you bring forth bread from the earth and wine to cheer the heart.

or (Cf. John 6.54)

Whoever eats my flesh and drinks my blood has eternal life, says the Lord, and I will raise him up on the last day.

PRAYER AFTER COMMUNION
Complete within us, O Lord, we pray, the healing work of your mercy and graciously perfect and sustain us, so that in all things we may please you. Through Christ our Lord. **Amen.**

BLESSING AND DISMISSAL *(p. 70)*

August 28

Do you remember the time you volunteered at the big parish fundraiser? You threw yourself into the work, sacrificing an enormous amount of your free time, donating generously to help the parish make it a great success. At the parish thank-you dinner, you expected to be seated at the head table but weren't. You *expected* that your efforts would be recognized.

How then should we act? What should be our attitude? Today's first reading and the passage from the Gospel of Luke offer guidance. They speak of the humility we need as Christians, because, as Sirach says, it is only when we are humble that we are truly exalted. Through our humility the Lord is truly glorified.

Our humility grows from the authenticity of our love and our concern for others. Jesus says everyone who "exalts himself will be humbled, and whoever humbles himself will be exalted." Our proximity to the 'head table' in our lives is linked to our invitation to the poor *into* our lives. Pope Francis reminds us we must not place ourselves above others but step down to serve them, especially the poor and vulnerable. As he wrote on Twitter, "To live charitably means not looking out for our own interests, but carrying the burdens of the weakest and poorest among us."

Jack Panozzo, Toronto, ON

ENTRANCE ANTIPHON *(Cf. Psalm 85.3, 5)*
Have mercy on me, O Lord, for I cry to you all the day long. O Lord, you are good and forgiving, full of mercy to all who call to you.

INTRODUCTORY RITES *(p. 5)*

COLLECT
God of might, giver of every good gift, put into our hearts the love of your name, so that, by deepening our sense of reverence, you may nurture in us what is good and, by your watchful care, keep safe what you have nurtured. Through our Lord Jesus Christ, your Son, who lives and reigns with you in the unity of the Holy Spirit, one God, for ever and ever. **Amen.**

FIRST READING *(Sirach 3.17-20, 28-29)*
My child, perform your tasks with humility; then you will be loved by those whom God accepts. The greater you are, the more you must humble yourself; so you will find favour in the sight of the Lord. Many are lofty and renowned, but to the humble the Lord reveals his secrets. For great is the might of the Lord; but by the humble he is glorified.

When calamity befalls someone proud, there is no healing, for an evil plant has taken root in them.

The mind of the intelligent appreciates proverbs, and an attentive ear is the desire of the wise.

The word of the Lord. **Thanks be to God.**

RESPONSORIAL PSALM *(Psalm 68)*

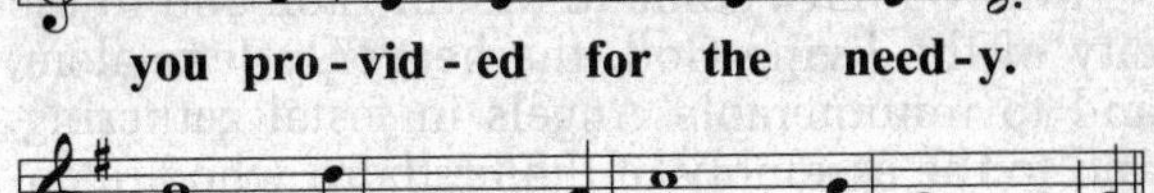

℟. **In your goodness, O God,**
you provided for the needy.

Let the righteous be joyful; let them exult
before · **God;**
let them be jubilant with · **joy.**
Sing to God, sing praises to his · **name;**
his name is the Lord, be exultant
· **be**-fore_him. ℟.

Father of orphans and protector of · **widows**
is God in his holy habi·-**tation.**
God gives the desolate a home to · **live_in;**
he leads out the prisoners · **to_pros**-perity. ℟.

Rain in abundance, O God, you showered
a·-**broad;**
you restored your heritage when it
· **languished;**
your flock found a · **dwelling_in_it;**
in your goodness, O God, you provided
· **for_the** needy. ℟.

SECOND READING *(Hebrews 12.18-19, 22-24a)*
Brothers and sisters: You have not come to something that can be touched, a blazing fire, and darkness, and gloom, and a tempest, and the sound of a trumpet, and a voice whose words made the hearers beg that not another word be spoken to them.

But you have come to Mount Zion and to the city of the living God, the heavenly Jerusalem, and to innumerable Angels in festal gathering, and to the assembly of the firstborn who are enrolled in heaven, and to God the judge of all, and to the spirits of the righteous made perfect, and to Jesus, the mediator of a new covenant.

The word of the Lord. **Thanks be to God.**

GOSPEL ACCLAMATION *(Matthew 11.29)*
Alleluia. Alleluia. Take my yoke upon you, and learn from me, for I am gentle and humble in heart. **Alleluia.**

GOSPEL *(Luke 14.1, 7-14)*
The Lord be with you. **And with your spirit.**
A reading from the holy Gospel according to Luke. **Glory to you, O Lord.**

On one occasion when Jesus was going to the house of a leader of the Pharisees to eat a meal on the Sabbath, the lawyers and Pharisees were watching him closely. When Jesus noticed how the guests chose the places of honour, he told them a parable.

"When you are invited by someone to a wedding banquet, do not sit down at the place of honour, in case someone more distinguished than you has been invited by your host; and the host who invited both of you may come and say to you, 'Give this person your place,' and then in disgrace you would start to take the lowest place.

"But when you are invited, go and sit down at the lowest place, so that when your host comes, he may say to you, 'Friend, move up higher'; then you will be honoured in the presence of all who sit at the table with you. For whoever exalts himself will be humbled, and whoever humbles himself will be exalted."

Jesus said also to the Pharisee who had invited him, "When you give a luncheon or a dinner, do not invite your friends or your brothers or sisters or your relatives or rich neighbours, in case they may invite you in return, and you would be repaid. But when you give a banquet, invite the poor, the crippled, the lame, and the blind. And you will be blessed, because they cannot repay you, for you will be repaid at the resurrection of the righteous."

The Gospel of the Lord. **Praise to you, Lord Jesus Christ.**

PROFESSION OF FAITH *(p. 11)*

PRAYER OF THE FAITHFUL

The following intentions are suggestions only. There are more suggestions at www.livingwithchrist.ca

℟. **Lord, hear our prayer.**

For the Church, working to be a sign of humble service to all, we pray to the Lord: ℟.

For world leaders, called to work for the betterment of all, we pray to the Lord: ℟.

For those who live in poverty and whose lives are not valued, we pray to the Lord: ℟.

For openness to the Holy Spirit in this community of faith, we pray to the Lord: ℟.

PREPARATION OF THE GIFTS *(p. 14)*

PRAYER OVER THE OFFERINGS

May this sacred offering, O Lord, confer on us always the blessing of salvation, that what it celebrates in mystery it may accomplish in power. Through Christ our Lord. **Amen.**

PREFACE *(Sundays in Ordinary Time, p. 28)*

COMMUNION ANTIPHON *(Psalm 30.20)*

How great is the goodness, Lord, that you keep for those who fear you.

or (Matthew 5.9-10)

Blessed are the peacemakers, for they shall be called children of God. Blessed are they who are persecuted for the sake of righteousness, for theirs is the Kingdom of Heaven.

PRAYER AFTER COMMUNION

Renewed by this bread from the heavenly table, we beseech you, Lord, that, being the food of charity, it may confirm our hearts and stir us to serve you in our neighbour. Through Christ our Lord. **Amen.**

BLESSING AND DISMISSAL *(p. 70)*

September Saints' Days

The following saints are traditionally remembered in September in Canada.

- 2 Blessed André Grasset
- 3 Saint Gregory the Great
- 4 Blessed Dina Bélanger
- 9 Saint Peter Claver
- 13 Saint John Chrysostom
- 15 Our Lady of Sorrows
- 16 Saints Cornelius and Cyprian
- 17 Saint Robert Bellarmine
- 19 Saint Januarius
- 20 Saints Andrew Kim Tae-gon, Paul Chong Ha-sang and Companions
- 21 Saint Matthew
- 23 Saint Pius of Pietrelcina
- 24 Blessed Émilie Tavernier-Gamelin
- 25 Saints Cosmas and Damian
- 26 Saints John de Brebeuf, Isaac Jogues and Companions, Secondary Patrons of Canada
- 27 Saint Vincent de Paul
- 28 Saint Wenceslaus
  Saint Lawrence Ruiz and Companions
- 29 Saints Michael, Gabriel and Raphael
- 30 Saint Jerome

September 4

Today the words of the gospel call us to look beyond our treasured possessions, obsessions and addictions for the sake of following Jesus without distraction.

"Whoever does not carry their cross and follow me cannot be my disciple," cautions Jesus. Again, he warns, "So therefore, whoever of you does not give up all their possessions cannot become my disciple."

Jesus is calling us to a deeper commitment, to look beyond people and possessions to a relationship with God. Jesus is calling us to understand the true meaning of "Come, follow me." To be a disciple of Jesus Christ is an all-consuming vocation; it is never-ending. There is no other priority that takes precedence over a decision to follow and to imitate the life of Christ.

Ironically, if we can find the courage to commit to a life of discipleship, God takes on the care of our most precious and personal needs. We are not forsaking or abandoning them — we are giving them over to the love and care of our heavenly Father. Only by letting go of our pursuit of earthly things can we find perfect joy in the love of God. Today, let us reflect on what we might let go of, in order to better follow Jesus.

Fr. Matthew Durham, CSB, Windsor, ON

ENTRANCE ANTIPHON *(Psalm 118.137, 124)*
You are just, O Lord, and your judgment is right; treat your servant in accord with your merciful love.

INTRODUCTORY RITES *(p. 5)*

COLLECT
O God, by whom we are redeemed and receive adoption, look graciously upon your beloved sons and daughters, that those who believe in Christ may receive true freedom and an everlasting inheritance. Through our Lord Jesus Christ, your Son, who lives and reigns with you in the unity of the Holy Spirit, one God, for ever and ever. **Amen.**

FIRST READING *(Wisdom 9.13-18)*

For who can learn the counsel of God?
Or who can discern what the Lord wills?
For the reasoning of mortals is worthless,
and our designs are likely to fail;
for a perishable body weighs down the soul,
and this earthly tent burdens the thoughtful mind.

We can hardly guess at what is on earth,
and what is at hand we find with labour;
but who has traced out what is in the heavens?
Who has learned your counsel,
unless you have given wisdom
and sent your holy spirit from on high?

And thus the paths of those on earth were set right,
and people were taught what pleases you,
and were saved by wisdom.

The word of the Lord. **Thanks be to God.**

RESPONSORIAL PSALM *(Psalm 90)*

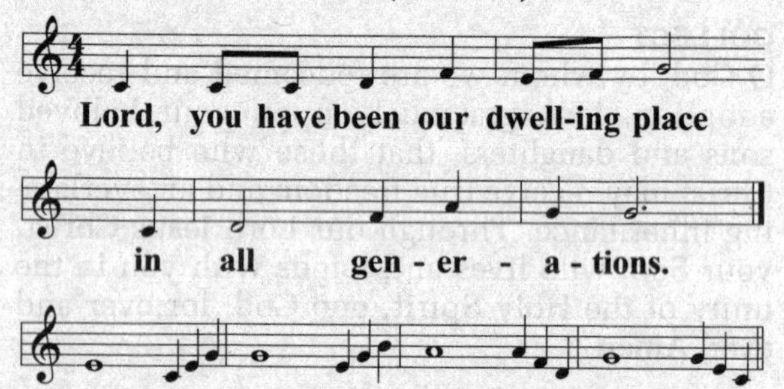

℟. **Lord, you have been our dwelling place**
in all generations.

You turn man back to · **dust,** and say,
"Turn back, you · **children** of Adam."
For a thousand years in your sight are like
yesterday when · **it** is past,
or like a watch · **in** the night. ℟.

You sweep them away; they are · **like** a dream,
like grass that is re-·**newed_in** the morning;
in the morning it flourishes and · **is** re-newed;
in the evening it · **fades** and withers. ℟.

So teach us to · **count** our days
that we may gain · **a** wise heart.
Turn, O · **Lord!** How long?
Have compassion · **on** your servants! ℟.

Satisfy us in the morning with your
· **stead**-fast love,
so that we may rejoice and be glad · **all** our days.
Let the favour of the Lord our · **God_be**
up-on_us,
and prosper for us the · **work_of** our hands. ℟.

To hear the Sunday Psalms, go to www.livingwithchrist.ca and select the psalm button at the bottom of the home page.

SECOND READING *(Philemon 9-10, 12-17)*

Beloved: I, Paul, do this as an old man, and now also as a prisoner of Christ Jesus. I am appealing to you for my child, Onesimus, whose father I have become during my imprisonment.

I am sending him, that is, my own heart, back to you. I wanted to keep him with me, so that he might be of service to me in your place during my imprisonment for the Gospel; but I preferred to do nothing without your consent, in order that your good deed might be voluntary and not something forced.

Perhaps this is the reason he was separated from you for a while, so that you might have him back forever, no longer as a slave but more than a slave, a beloved brother — especially to me but how much more to you, both in the flesh and in the Lord.

So if you consider me your partner, welcome him as you would welcome me.

The word of the Lord. **Thanks be to God.**

GOSPEL ACCLAMATION *(Psalm 119.135)*
Alleluia. Alleluia. Make your face shine upon your servant, and teach me your statutes. **Alleluia.**

GOSPEL *(Luke 14.25-33)*
The Lord be with you. **And with your spirit.**
A reading from the holy Gospel according to Luke. **Glory to you, O Lord.**

Large crowds were travelling with Jesus; and he turned and said to them, "Whoever comes to me and does not hate their father and mother, spouse and children, brothers and sisters, yes, and even their life itself, cannot be my disciple. Whoever does not carry their cross and follow me cannot be my disciple.

"For which of you, intending to build a tower, does not first sit down and estimate the cost, to see whether he has enough to complete it? Otherwise, when he has laid a foundation and is not able to finish, all who see it will begin to ridicule him, saying, 'This fellow began to build and was not able to finish.'

"Or what king, going out to wage war against another king, will not sit down first and consider whether he is able with ten thousand to oppose the one who comes against him with twenty thousand? If he cannot, then, while the other is still far away, he sends a delegation and asks for the terms of peace.

"So therefore, whoever of you does not give up all their possessions cannot be my disciple."

The Gospel of the Lord. **Praise to you, Lord Jesus Christ.**

PROFESSION OF FAITH *(p. 11)*

PRAYER OF THE FAITHFUL

The following intentions are suggestions only. There are more suggestions at www.livingwithchrist.ca

℟. **Lord, hear our prayer.**

For our Church in its mission to further the reign of God in the world, we pray to the Lord: ℟.

For wisdom and selflessness in those committed to public service, we pray to the Lord: ℟.

For strength and comfort for all who are suffering physically, spiritually or emotionally, we pray to the Lord: ℟.

For our parish community, challenged to see the face of Christ in everyone, we pray to the Lord: ℟.

PREPARATION OF THE GIFTS *(p. 14)*

PRAYER OVER THE OFFERINGS

O God, who give us the gift of true prayer and of peace, graciously grant that, through this offering, we may do fitting homage to your divine majesty and, by partaking of the sacred mystery, we may be faithfully united in mind and heart. Through Christ our Lord. **Amen.**

PREFACE *(Sundays in Ordinary Time, p. 28)*

COMMUNION ANTIPHON *(Cf. Psalm 41.2-3)*
Like the deer that yearns for running streams, so my soul is yearning for you, my God; my soul is thirsting for God, the living God.

or (John 8.12)
I am the light of the world, says the Lord; whoever follows me will not walk in darkness, but will have the light of life.

PRAYER AFTER COMMUNION
Grant that your faithful, O Lord, whom you nourish and endow with life through the food of your Word and heavenly Sacrament, may so benefit from your beloved Son's great gifts that we may merit an eternal share in his life. Who lives and reigns for ever and ever. **Amen.**

BLESSING AND DISMISSAL *(p. 70)*

September 11

It's not fair.

That's a popular refrain for children and adults alike. Youngsters with an abiding sense of entitlement don't like it when they are denied something by their parents. Adults share the same sentiment when things don't go their way. Kids who rail against dad, mom and each other soon grow into adults who castigate neighbours, bosses, spouses, co-workers and even God for what they believe is unjust treatment.

Most of us can identify with the gospel's elder son, who complains that he got the short end of the stick when the father generously welcomed back the little brother who had frittered away half the family fortune on fast and depraved living. It's little wonder we empathize with the elder brother, the reliable, hard-working and trustworthy son who feels taken for granted by a foolish father.

Fettered by human thought, we might join the steadfast elder son in thinking it unwise to traipse off in search of one lost sheep while leaving 99 more unattended in the wilderness, at the mercy of any passing predator. But for God, the shepherd and father, it's reclaiming the lost one that yields boundless joy and relief.

God's tremendous capacity for forgiveness and unconditional love eludes our narrow grasp. God's ways are not our ways, and for this let us be grateful.

Francis Campbell, Enfield, NS

ENTRANCE ANTIPHON *(Cf. Sirach 36.18)*
Give peace, O Lord, to those who wait for you, that your prophets be found true. Hear the prayers of your servant, and of your people Israel.

INTRODUCTORY RITES *(p. 5)*

COLLECT
Look upon us, O God, Creator and ruler of all things, and, that we may feel the working of your mercy, grant that we may serve you with all our heart. Through our Lord Jesus Christ, your Son, who lives and reigns with you in the unity of the Holy Spirit, one God, for ever and ever. **Amen.**

FIRST READING *(Exodus 32.7-11, 13-14)*
The Lord said to Moses, "Go down at once! Your people, whom you brought up out of the land of Egypt, have acted perversely; they have been quick to turn aside from the way that I commanded them; they have cast for themselves an image of a calf, and have worshipped it and sacrificed to it, and said, 'These are your gods, O Israel, who brought you up out of the land of Egypt!'"

The Lord said to Moses, "I have seen this people, how stiff-necked they are. Now let me alone, so that my wrath may burn hot against them and I may consume them; and of you I will make a great nation."

But Moses implored the Lord his God, and said, "O Lord, why does your wrath burn hot against your people, whom you brought out of the land of Egypt with great power and with a mighty hand? Remember Abraham, Isaac, and

Israel, your servants, how you swore to them by your own self, saying to them, 'I will multiply your descendants like the stars of heaven, and all this land that I have promised I will give to your descendants, and they shall inherit it forever.'"

And the Lord changed his mind about the disaster that he planned to bring on his people.

The word of the Lord. **Thanks be to God.**

RESPONSORIAL PSALM *(Psalm 51)*

℟. **I will get up and go to my Father.**

Have mercy on me, O God, according to
your stead·-**fast** love;
according to your abundant mercy blot out
my · **trans**-gressions.
Wash me thoroughly from my · **in**-iquity,
and cleanse me · **from** my sin. ℟.

Create in me a clean heart, · **O** God,
and put a new and right spirit · **with**-in_me.
Do not cast me away from · **your** presence,
and do not take your holy · **spirit** from me. ℟.

O Lord, open · **my** lips,
and my mouth will declare · **your** praise.
The sacrifice acceptable to God is
a · **broken** spirit;
a broken and contrite heart, O God, you will
· **not** des-pise. ℞.

To hear the Sunday Psalms, go to www.livingwithchrist.ca and select the psalm button at the bottom of the home page.

SECOND READING *(1 Timothy 1.12-17)*

Beloved: I am grateful to Christ Jesus our Lord, who has strengthened me, because he judged me faithful and appointed me to his service, even though I was formerly a blasphemer, a persecutor, and a man of violence.

But I received mercy because I had acted ignorantly in unbelief, and the grace of our Lord overflowed for me with the faith and love that are in Christ Jesus.

The saying is sure and worthy of full acceptance, that Christ Jesus came into the world to save sinners — of whom I am the foremost.

But for that very reason I received mercy, so that in me, as the foremost, Jesus Christ might display the utmost patience, making me an example to those who would come to believe in him for eternal life.

To the King of the ages, immortal, invisible, the only God, be honour and glory forever and ever. Amen.

The word of the Lord. **Thanks be to God.**

GOSPEL ACCLAMATION *(2 Corinthians 5.19)*
Alleluia. Alleluia. In Christ God was reconciling the world to himself, and entrusting the message of reconciliation to us. **Alleluia.**

GOSPEL *(Luke 15.1-32)*
The shorter version ends at the asterisks.
The Lord be with you. **And with your spirit.** A reading from the holy Gospel according to Luke. **Glory to you, O Lord.**

All the tax collectors and sinners were coming near to listen to Jesus. And the Pharisees and the scribes were grumbling and saying, "This fellow welcomes sinners and eats with them."

So he told them a parable: "Which one of you, having a hundred sheep and losing one of them, does not leave the ninety-nine in the wilderness and go after the one that is lost until he finds it? When he has found it, he lays it on his shoulders and rejoices. And when he comes home, he calls together his friends and neighbours, saying to them, 'Rejoice with me, for I have found my sheep that was lost.' Just so, I tell you, there will be more joy in heaven over one sinner who repents than over ninety-nine righteous persons who need no repentance.

"Or what woman having ten silver coins, if she loses one of them, does not light a lamp, sweep the house, and search carefully until she finds it? When she has found it, she calls together her friends and neighbours, saying, 'Rejoice with me, for I have found the coin that I had lost.' Just so, I tell you, there is joy in the presence of the Angels of God over one sinner who repents."

* * *

Then Jesus said, "There was a man who had two sons. The younger of them said to his father, 'Father, give me the share of the property that will belong to me.' So the father divided his property between them.

"A few days later the younger son gathered all he had and travelled to a distant country, and there he squandered his property in dissolute living. When he had spent everything, a severe famine took place throughout that country, and he began to be in need. So he went and hired himself out to one of the citizens of that country, who sent him to his fields to feed the pigs. The young man would gladly have filled himself with the pods that the pigs were eating; and no one gave him anything.

"But when he came to himself he said, 'How many of my father's hired hands have bread enough and to spare, but here I am dying of hunger! I will get up and go to my father, and I will say to him, "Father, I have sinned against heaven and before you; I am no longer worthy to be called your son; treat me like one of your hired hands."'

"So he set off and went to his father. But while he was still far off, his father saw him and was filled with compassion; he ran and put his arms around him and kissed him. Then the son said to him, 'Father, I have sinned against heaven and before you; I am no longer worthy to be called your son.'

"But the father said to his slaves, 'Quickly, bring out a robe — the best one — and put it on him; put a ring on his finger and sandals on his feet. And get the fatted calf and kill it, and let us eat and celebrate; for this son of mine was dead and is alive again; he was lost and is found!' And they began to celebrate.

"Now his elder son was in the field; and when he came and approached the house, he heard music and dancing. He called one of the slaves and asked what was going on. The slave replied, 'Your brother has come, and your father has killed the fatted calf, because he has got him back safe and sound.'

"Then the elder son became angry and refused to go in. His father came out and began to plead with him. But he answered his father, 'Listen! For all these years I have been working like a slave for you, and I have never disobeyed your command; yet you have never given me even a young goat so that I might celebrate with my friends. But when this son of yours came back, who has devoured your property with prostitutes, you killed the fatted calf for him!'

"Then the father said to him, 'Son, you are always with me, and all that is mine is yours. But we had to celebrate and rejoice, because this brother of yours was dead and has come to life; he was lost and has been found.'"

The Gospel of the Lord. **Praise to you, Lord Jesus Christ.**

PROFESSION OF FAITH *(p. 11)*

PRAYER OF THE FAITHFUL

The following intentions are suggestions only. There are more suggestions at www.livingwithchrist.ca

℟. **Lord, hear our prayer.**

For the Church, called to proclaim God's love not only by what we preach but by what we practise in our daily lives, we pray to the Lord: ℟.

For wealthy nations and their responsibility towards those who have less, we pray to the Lord: ℟.

For those of us who are wounded, homeless, hungry, frightened or abandoned, we pray to the Lord: ℟.

For each one of us, called to share what we have generously and joyfully, we pray to the Lord: ℟.

PREPARATION OF THE GIFTS *(p. 14)*

PRAYER OVER THE OFFERINGS

Look with favour on our supplications, O Lord, and in your kindness accept these, your servants' offerings, that what each has offered to the honour of your name may serve the salvation of all. Through Christ our Lord. **Amen.**

PREFACE *(Sundays in Ordinary Time, p. 28)*

COMMUNION ANTIPHON *(Cf. Psalm 35.8)*
How precious is your mercy, O God! The children of men seek shelter in the shadow of your wings.
or (Cf. 1 Corinthians 10.16)
The chalice of blessing that we bless is a communion in the Blood of Christ; and the bread that we break is a sharing in the Body of the Lord.

PRAYER AFTER COMMUNION
May the working of this heavenly gift, O Lord, we pray, take possession of our minds and bodies, so that its effects, and not our own desires, may always prevail in us. Through Christ our Lord. **Amen.**

BLESSING AND DISMISSAL *(p. 70)*

September 18

Today's readings bring up a difficult question: is it possible for one who enjoys a life of privilege to be a true Christian? I am reminded of the uncomfortable image of the camel trying to pass through the eye of the needle. Are good intentions enough?

Amos and Paul offer some valuable clues. The first reading sternly warns the rich and powerful against cheating and taking advantage of the poor in the pursuit of profit. The second reading reminds us that "kings and all who are in high positions" need our prayerful support in order to carry out their responsibilities to promote peace and dignity for all.

The psalm, however, draws us deeper. We are told, "The Lord raises the poor from the dust... to make them sit with princes." In other words, God erases the artificial distinction between rich and poor, between the powerful and the needy. For the Christian, there can be no "us" and "them." "There is one God," says Paul, and so we are all members of the same family, the same body. As we work to promote justice, peace and equality in our world, we are called to embrace each person as our sister or brother. Though our circumstances may differ, we are all in need and we are all blessed.

Krystyna Higgins, Fredericton, NB

ENTRANCE ANTIPHON

I am the salvation of the people, says the Lord. Should they cry to me in any distress, I will hear them, and I will be their Lord for ever.

INTRODUCTORY RITES *(p. 5)*

COLLECT

O God, who founded all the commands of your sacred Law upon love of you and of our neighbour, grant that, by keeping your precepts, we may merit to attain eternal life. Through our Lord Jesus Christ, your Son, who lives and reigns with you in the unity of the Holy Spirit, one God, for ever and ever. **Amen.**

FIRST READING *(Amos 8.4-7)*

Hear this, you that trample on the needy, and bring to ruin the poor of the land, saying, "When will the new moon be over so that we may sell grain; and the Sabbath, so that we may offer wheat for sale? We will measure out less and charge more, and tamper with the scales, buying the poor for silver and the needy for a pair of sandals, and selling the sweepings of the wheat."

The Lord has sworn by the pride of Jacob: "Surely I will never forget any of their deeds."

The word of the Lord. **Thanks be to God.**

RESPONSORIAL PSALM *(Psalm 113)*

℟. **Praise the Lord who lifts up the needy.**
or **Alleluia!**

Praise, O servants of the · **Lord;**
praise the name of the · **Lord.**
Blessed be the name of the · **Lord**
from this time on and for-·**ever**-more. ℟.

The Lord is high above all · **nations,**
and his glory above the · **heavens.**
Who is like the Lord our God, who is
seated on · **high,**
who looks far down on the heavens
· **and_the** earth? ℟.

The Lord raises the poor from the · **dust,**
and lifts the needy from the · **ash_heap,**
to make them sit with · **princes,**
with the princes · **of_his** people. ℟.

To hear the Sunday Psalms, go to www.livingwithchrist.ca and select the psalm button at the bottom of the home page.

SECOND READING *(1 Timothy 2.1-7)*
Beloved: I urge that supplications, prayers, intercessions, and thanksgivings be made for everyone, for kings and all who are in high positions,

so that we may lead a quiet and peaceable life in all godliness and dignity. This is right and is acceptable in the sight of God our Saviour, who desires everyone to be saved and to come to the knowledge of the truth.

For there is one God; there is also one mediator between God and the human race, the man Christ Jesus, who gave himself a ransom for all; this was attested at the right time.

For this I was appointed a herald and an apostle, a teacher of the Gentiles in faith and truth. I am telling the truth, I am not lying.

The word of the Lord. **Thanks be to God.**

GOSPEL ACCLAMATION *(2 Corinthians 8.9)*

Alleluia. Alleluia. Though Jesus Christ was rich, yet he became poor, so that by his poverty you might become rich. **Alleluia.**

GOSPEL *(Luke 16.1-13)*

The shorter version begins at the asterisks.

The Lord be with you. **And with your spirit.**
A reading from the holy Gospel according to Luke. **Glory to you, O Lord.**

Jesus said to the disciples, "There was a rich man who had a manager, and charges were brought to him that the manager was squandering his property. So the rich man summoned him and said to him, 'What is this that I hear about you? Give me an accounting of your management, because you cannot be my manager any longer.'

"Then the manager said to himself, 'What will I do, now that my master is taking the position away from me? I am not strong enough to dig, and

I am ashamed to beg. I have decided what to do so that, when I am dismissed as manager, people may welcome me into their homes.'

"So, summoning his master's debtors one by one, he asked the first, 'How much do you owe my master?' He answered, 'A hundred jugs of olive oil.' He said to him, 'Take your bill, sit down quickly, and make it fifty.' Then he asked another, 'And how much do you owe?' He replied, 'A hundred containers of wheat.' He said to him, 'Take your bill and make it eighty.'

"And his master commended the dishonest manager because he had acted shrewdly; for the children of this age are more shrewd in dealing with their own generation than are the children of light.

"And I tell you, make friends for yourselves by means of dishonest wealth so that when it is gone, they may welcome you into the eternal homes.

* * *

"Whoever is faithful in a very little is faithful also in much; and whoever is dishonest in a very little is dishonest also in much. If then you have not been faithful with the dishonest wealth, who will entrust to you the true riches? And if you have not been faithful with what belongs to another, who will give you what is your own?

"No slave can serve two masters; for a slave will either hate the one and love the other, or be devoted to the one and despise the other. You cannot serve God and wealth."

The Gospel of the Lord. **Praise to you, Lord Jesus Christ.**

PROFESSION OF FAITH *(p. 11)*

PRAYER OF THE FAITHFUL

The following intentions are suggestions only. There are more suggestions at www.livingwithchrist.ca

℟. **Lord, hear our prayer.**

For the Church in its prophetic mission to speak for the voiceless and denounce injustice and exploitation, we pray to the Lord: ℟.

For leaders of nations who have the power to ease the burden of the poor, we pray to the Lord: ℟.

For all those deprived of basic necessities and the people responding to their need, we pray to the Lord: ℟.

For this community, on its journey of faith, we pray to the Lord: ℟.

PREPARATION OF THE GIFTS *(p. 14)*

PRAYER OVER THE OFFERINGS

Receive with favour, O Lord, we pray, the offerings of your people, that what they profess with devotion and faith may be theirs through these heavenly mysteries. Through Christ our Lord. **Amen.**

PREFACE *(Sundays in Ordinary Time, p. 28)*

COMMUNION ANTIPHON *(Psalm 118.4-5)*
You have laid down your precepts to be carefully kept; may my ways be firm in keeping your statutes.

or (John 10.14)
I am the Good Shepherd, says the Lord; I know my sheep, and mine know me.

PRAYER AFTER COMMUNION
Graciously raise up, O Lord, those you renew with this Sacrament, that we may come to possess your redemption both in mystery and in the manner of our life. Through Christ our Lord. **Amen.**

BLESSING AND DISMISSAL *(p. 70)*

September 25

The prophet Amos is the great champion of the poor and he is quite serious about the complacent folk who pamper themselves at the expense of others, having apparently lost interest in the sufferings of their fellow human beings. The idle rich are the target of the prophet's wrath because their blatant consumption of delicacies is always at the expense of those who lack bare necessities.

That same theme continues in today's gospel, where Luke presents a vivid study in contrasts. The rich man, called Dives in the Latin Bible, was consumed in self-centred living. He had everything in this life but no compassion for the poor or anyone else but himself. When Lazarus and Dives were in this life, there was no chasm between them. The rich man could have gone out and helped Lazarus any time. But in eternal life there is a great chasm separating heaven and hell.

Today's gospel is not just about money or wealth. Almsgiving is good, but involvement is better. Our focus must be on the well-being of the poor and downtrodden. It is in giving that we receive, and God loves cheerful givers. Let us consider what we are depending on. Do we think being rich means we are right with God? It is wiser to think ahead to eternity!

Fr. Thomas Rosica, CSB, Toronto, ON

National Collection for the Needs of the Church in Canada

ENTRANCE ANTIPHON *(Daniel 3.31, 29, 30, 43, 42)*
All that you have done to us, O Lord, you have done with true judgment, for we have sinned against you and not obeyed your commandments. But give glory to your name and deal with us according to the bounty of your mercy.

INTRODUCTORY RITES *(p. 5)*

COLLECT
O God, who manifest your almighty power above all by pardoning and showing mercy, bestow, we pray, your grace abundantly upon us and make those hastening to attain your promises heirs to the treasures of heaven. Through our Lord Jesus Christ, your Son, who lives and reigns with you in the unity of the Holy Spirit, one God, for ever and ever. **Amen.**

FIRST READING *(Amos 6.1a, 4-7)*
Thus says the Lord, the God of hosts: "Alas for those who are at ease in Zion, and for those who feel secure on Mount Samaria!

"Alas for those who lie on beds of ivory, and lounge on their couches, and eat lambs from the flock, and calves from the stall; who sing idle songs to the sound of the harp, and like David improvise on instruments of music; who drink wine from bowls, and anoint themselves with the finest oils, but are not grieved over the ruin of Joseph!

"Therefore they shall now be the first to go into exile, and the revelry of those who lie in ease shall pass away."

The word of the Lord. **Thanks be to God.**

RESPONSORIAL PSALM *(Psalm 146)*

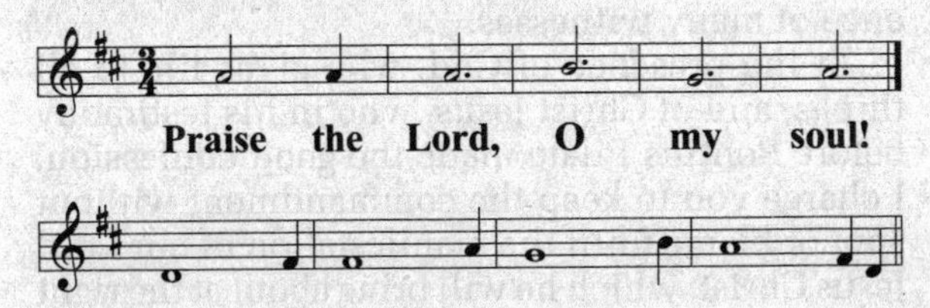

℟. **Praise the Lord, O my soul!**
or **Alleluia!**

It is the Lord who keeps faith for·-**ever,**
who executes justice for the op·-**pressed;**
who gives food to the · **hungry.**
The Lord sets the · **prisoners** free. ℟.

The Lord opens the eyes of the · **blind**
and lifts up those who are bowed · **down;**
the Lord loves the · **righteous**
and watches over · **the** strangers. ℟.

The Lord upholds the orphan and the · **widow,**
but the way of the wicked he brings to · **ruin.**
The Lord will reign for·-**ever,**
your God, O Zion, for all · **gener**-ations. ℟.

To hear the Sunday Psalms, go to www.livingwithchrist.ca and select the psalm button at the bottom of the home page.

SECOND READING *(1 Timothy 6.11-16)*

As for you, man of God; pursue righteousness, godliness, faith, love, endurance, gentleness. Fight the good fight of the faith; take hold of the eternal life, to which you were called and for which you made the good confession in the presence of many witnesses.

In the presence of God, who gives life to all things, and of Christ Jesus, who in his testimony before Pontius Pilate made the good confession, I charge you to keep the commandment without spot or blame until the manifestation of our Lord Jesus Christ, which he will bring about at the right time. He is the blessed and only Sovereign, the King of kings and Lord of lords.

It is he alone who has immortality and dwells in unapproachable light, whom no human being has ever seen or can see; to him be honour and eternal dominion. Amen.

The word of the Lord. **Thanks be to God.**

GOSPEL ACCLAMATION *(2 Corinthians 8.9)*

Alleluia. Alleluia. Though Jesus Christ was rich, yet he became poor, so that by his poverty you might become rich. **Alleluia.**

GOSPEL *(Luke 16.19-31)*

The Lord be with you. **And with your spirit.** A reading from the holy Gospel according to Luke. **Glory to you, O Lord.**

Jesus told this parable to those among the Pharisees who loved money: "There was a rich man who was dressed in purple and fine linen and who feasted sumptuously every day. And at his gate lay a poor man named Lazarus, covered with sores, who longed to satisfy his hunger with what fell from the rich man's table; even the dogs would come and lick his sores.

"The poor man died and was carried away by the Angels to be with Abraham. The rich man also died and was buried. In Hades, where he was being tormented, he looked up and saw Abraham far away with Lazarus by his side. He called out, 'Father Abraham, have mercy on me, and send Lazarus to dip the tip of his finger in water and cool my tongue; for I am in agony in these flames.'

"But Abraham said, 'Child, remember that during your lifetime you received your good things, and Lazarus in like manner evil things; but now he is comforted here, and you are in agony. Besides all this, between you and us a great chasm has been fixed, so that those who might want to pass from here to you cannot do so, and no one can cross from there to us.'

"The man who had been rich said, 'Then, father, I beg you to send Lazarus to my father's house — for I have five brothers — that he may warn them, so that they will not also come into this place of torment.'

"Abraham replied, 'They have Moses and the Prophets; they should listen to them.' He said, 'No, father Abraham; but if someone goes to them from the dead, they will repent.' Abraham said to him, 'If they do not listen to Moses and the Prophets, neither will they be convinced even if someone rises from the dead.'"

The Gospel of the Lord. **Praise to you, Lord Jesus Christ.**

PROFESSION OF FAITH *(p. 11)*

PRAYER OF THE FAITHFUL

The following intentions are suggestions only. There are more suggestions at www.livingwithchrist.ca

℟. **Lord, hear our prayer.**

For the pilgrim Church, willing partner in the building of God's kingdom, we pray to the Lord: ℟.

For a growing awareness of the gulf that exists between the 'haves' and the 'have-nots' and for the courage and the perseverance to bridge that gulf, we pray to the Lord: ℟.

For the hungry, both near and far, who seek a place of dignity at our table, we pray to the Lord: ℟.

For us, God's People, seeking to serve even as we are aware of our own needs and concerns, we pray to the Lord: ℟.

PREPARATION OF THE GIFTS *(p. 14)*

PRAYER OVER THE OFFERINGS

Grant us, O merciful God, that this our offering may find acceptance with you and that through it the wellspring of all blessing may be laid open before us. Through Christ our Lord. **Amen.**

PREFACE *(Sundays in Ordinary Time, p. 28)*

COMMUNION ANTIPHON *(Cf. Psalm 118.49-50)*
Remember your word to your servant, O Lord, by which you have given me hope. This is my comfort when I am brought low.

or (1 John 3.16)

By this we came to know the love of God: that Christ laid down his life for us; so we ought to lay down our lives for one another.

PRAYER AFTER COMMUNION
May this heavenly mystery, O Lord, restore us in mind and body, that we may be co-heirs in glory with Christ, to whose suffering we are united whenever we proclaim his Death. Who lives and reigns for ever and ever. **Amen.**

BLESSING AND DISMISSAL *(p. 70)*

October Saints' Days

The following saints are traditionally remembered in October in Canada.

1	Saint Thérèse of the Child Jesus
2	The Holy Guardian Angels
4	Saint Francis of Assisi
6	Saint Bruno Blessed Marie-Rose Durocher
7	Our Lady of the Rosary
9	Saint Denis and Companions Saint John Leonardi
14	Saint Callistus I
15	Saint Teresa of Jesus
16	Saint Marguerite d'Youville
17	Saint Ignatius of Antioch
18	Saint Luke
19	Saint Paul of the Cross
20	Saint Hedwig Saint Margaret Mary Alacoque
23	Saint John of Capistrano
24	Saint Anthony Mary Claret
28	Saints Simon and Jude

October 2

Today is filled with voices challenging God. The verse from Habakkuk, for example, opens with "O Lord, how long shall I cry for help, and you will not listen?" Habakkuk wants to know why bad things happen to good people. And in the gospel, the apostles — even though they have witnessed Jesus actively at work — demand, "Increase our faith!"

The apostles ask for their faith to be increased because they want proof that Jesus is who he says he is — they want to see a miracle. It's telling that Jesus doesn't reply "Okay" and light the nearest bush on fire; nor does he say, "Get lost." Instead, he informs them, "If you had faith the size of a mustard seed, you could say to this mulberry tree, 'Be uprooted and planted in the sea,' and it would obey you."

Faith, like love, isn't something that is; it's something that you do every day. As the reading from Timothy reminds us, the gift of God is within us; with self-discipline and love we can see our belief grow as we engage in the work God asks of us. A miracle doesn't have to be inexplicable. Sometimes a miracle is as small as a homeless person getting a free meal, or an unexpected compliment to brighten someone's day. Miracles can occur when we choose to do more than simply what we ought to do.

Gillian Robinson, Toronto, ON

ENTRANCE ANTIPHON *(Cf. Esther 4.17)*
Within your will, O Lord, all things are established, and there is none that can resist your will. For you have made all things, the heaven and the earth, and all that is held within the circle of heaven; you are the Lord of all.

INTRODUCTORY RITES *(p. 5)*

COLLECT
Almighty ever-living God, who in the abundance of your kindness surpass the merits and the desires of those who entreat you, pour out your mercy upon us to pardon what conscience dreads and to give what prayer does not dare to ask. Through our Lord Jesus Christ, your Son, who lives and reigns with you in the unity of the Holy Spirit, one God, for ever and ever. **Amen.**

FIRST READING *(Habakkuk 1.2-3; 2.2-4)*
"O Lord, how long shall I cry for help,
and you will not listen?
Or cry to you 'Violence!'
and you will not save?
Why do you make me see wrongdoing
and look at trouble?
Destruction and violence are before me;
strife and contention arise."

Then the Lord answered me and said:
"Write the vision;
make it plain on tablets,
so that a runner may read it.
For there is still a vision for the appointed time;

it speaks of the end, and does not lie.
If it seems to tarry, wait for it;
it will surely come, it will not delay.
Look at the proud person!
Their spirit is not right in them,
but the righteous person lives by their faith."

The word of the Lord. **Thanks be to God.**

RESPONSORIAL PSALM *(Psalm 95)*

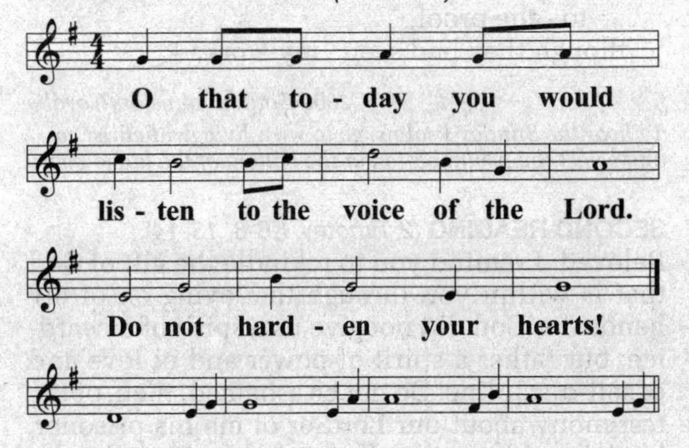

℟. **O that today you would listen to the voice of the Lord. Do not harden your hearts!**

O come, let us sing to · **the** Lord;
let us make a joyful noise to the rock of
our · **sal**-vation!
Let us come into his presence with
· **thanks**-giving;
let us make a joyful noise to him with
songs · **of** praise! ℟.

O come, let us worship and · **bow** down,
let us kneel before the Lord, · **our** Maker!
For he is our God, and we are the people
 of · **his** pasture,
and the sheep of · **his** hand. ℟.

O that today you would listen to · **his** voice!
Do not harden your hearts, as at Meribah,
 as on the day at Massah in · **the** wilderness,
when your ancestors tested me, and put me
 to · **the** proof,
though they had seen · **my** work. ℟.

To hear the Sunday Psalms, go to www.livingwithchrist.ca and select the psalm button at the bottom of the home page.

SECOND READING *(2 Timothy 1.6-8, 13-14)*

Beloved: I remind you to rekindle the gift of God that is within you through the laying on of my hands; for God did not give us a spirit of cowardice, but rather a spirit of power and of love and of self-discipline. Do not be ashamed, then, of the testimony about our Lord or of me his prisoner, but join with me in suffering for the Gospel, relying on the power of God.

Hold to the standard of sound teaching that you have heard from me, in the faith and love that are in Christ Jesus. Guard the good treasure entrusted to you, with the help of the Holy Spirit living in us.

The word of the Lord. **Thanks be to God.**

GOSPEL ACCLAMATION *(1 Peter 1.25)*
Alleluia. Alleluia. The word of the Lord endures for ever; that word is the good news announced to you. **Alleluia.**

GOSPEL *(Luke 17.5-10)*
The Lord be with you. **And with your spirit.** A reading from the holy Gospel according to Luke. **Glory to you, O Lord.**

The Apostles said to the Lord, "Increase our faith!" The Lord replied, "If you had faith the size of a mustard seed, you could say to this mulberry tree, 'Be uprooted and planted in the sea,' and it would obey you.

"Who among you would say to your slave who has just come in from ploughing or tending sheep in the field, 'Come here at once and take your place at the table'? Would you not rather say to him, 'Prepare supper for me, put on your apron and serve me while I eat and drink; later you may eat and drink'? Do you thank the slave for doing what was commanded? So you also, when you have done all that you were ordered to do, say, 'We are worthless slaves; we have done only what we ought to have done!'"

The Gospel of the Lord. **Praise to you, Lord Jesus Christ.**

PROFESSION OF FAITH *(p. 11)*

PRAYER OF THE FAITHFUL

The following intentions are suggestions only. There are more suggestions at www.livingwithchrist.ca

℟. **Lord, hear our prayer.**

For all leaders in the Church, in their daily efforts to humbly and faithfully serve the People of God, we pray to the Lord: ℟.

For an abiding faithfulness to the gospel message of justice and peace, we pray to the Lord: ℟.

For those who cannot pray for themselves and for those most in need of our prayers, we pray to the Lord: ℟.

For this community, praying for a deepening of the grace of humility among us, we pray to the Lord: ℟.

PREPARATION OF THE GIFTS *(p. 14)*

PRAYER OVER THE OFFERINGS

Accept, O Lord, we pray, the sacrifices instituted by your commands and, through the sacred mysteries, which we celebrate with dutiful service, graciously complete the sanctifying work by which you are pleased to redeem us. Through Christ our Lord. **Amen.**

PREFACE *(Sundays in Ordinary Time, p. 28)*

COMMUNION ANTIPHON *(Lamentations 3.25)*
The Lord is good to those who hope in him, to the soul that seeks him.

or (Cf. 1 Corinthians 10.17)

Though many, we are one bread, one body, for we all partake of the one Bread and one Chalice.

PRAYER AFTER COMMUNION
Grant us, almighty God, that we may be refreshed and nourished by the Sacrament which we have received, so as to be transformed into what we consume. Through Christ our Lord. **Amen.**

BLESSING AND DISMISSAL *(p. 70)*

October 9

There are a lot of 'peripheries' in today's gospel. Pope Francis often uses the word to translate the margins of society to which he urges us to take Christ's compassion. Jesus was going through the region between Samaria and Galilee, whose populations of Samaritans and Jews were usually bitter enemies. Such frontiers were fraught with ethnic and religious tensions.

Lepers were also people of the 'periphery,' living on the edges of communities, isolated for fear of contagion. Their disease had allied ancient enemies who knew one thing. The Master who approached did not fear those on the margins, and indiscriminately lavished God's mercy and healing on them. The lepers asked for mercy. Jesus offered it, and then wondered at the gratitude expressed only by one — the hated Samaritan. To all, Jesus had given life: he had re-created, healed and restored them to family, friends, community.

Jesus offers life restored to us too. Perhaps we imagine ourselves far from the margins, little in need of mercy. But in moments of utter honesty, we recognize that we too are marginalized. We need healing. Jesus invites us to trust his word of power, and to surrender ourselves to God to be transformed and restored by his Spirit in this Eucharist so that, brimming with gratitude and joy, we may return to the margins as bearers of God's mercy.

Bernadette Gasslein, Edmonton, AB

ENTRANCE ANTIPHON *(Psalm 129.3-4)*
If you, O Lord, should mark iniquities, Lord, who could stand? But with you is found forgiveness, O God of Israel.

INTRODUCTORY RITES *(p. 5)*

COLLECT
May your grace, O Lord, we pray, at all times go before us and follow after and make us always determined to carry out good works. Through our Lord Jesus Christ, your Son, who lives and reigns with you in the unity of the Holy Spirit, one God, for ever and ever. **Amen.**

FIRST READING *(2 Kings 5.14-17)*
Naaman the Syrian went down and immersed himself seven times in the Jordan, according to the word of the man of God; his flesh was restored like the flesh of a young boy, and he was clean.

Then he returned to the man of God, he and all his company; Naaman came and stood before Elisha and said, "Now I know that there is no God in all the earth except in Israel; please accept a present from your servant."

But Elisha said, "As the Lord lives, whom I serve, I will accept nothing!" Naaman urged Elisha to accept, but he refused.

Then Naaman said, "If not, please let two mule-loads of earth be given to your servant; for your servant will no longer offer burnt offering or sacrifice to any god except the Lord."

The word of the Lord. **Thanks be to God.**

RESPONSORIAL PSALM *(Psalm 98)*

℟. **The Lord has revealed his victory**
in the sight of the nations.

O sing to the Lord · **a** new song,
for he has done · **marvel**-lous things.
His right hand and his · **ho**-ly arm
have · **brought** him victory. ℟.

The Lord has made · **known** his victory;
he has revealed his vindication in the
· **sight_of** the nations.
He has remembered his · **stead**-fast love
and faithfulness to the · **house** of Israel. ℟.

All the ends of the · **earth** have seen
the victory · **of** our God.
Make a joyful noise to the Lord, · **all** the earth;
break forth into joyous · **song_and** sing
praises. ℟.

To hear the Sunday Psalms, go to www.livingwithchrist.ca and select the psalm button at the bottom of the home page.

SECOND READING *(2 Timothy 2.8-13)*
Beloved: Remember Jesus Christ, raised from the dead, a descendant of David — that is my Gospel, for which I suffer hardship, even to the point of being chained like a criminal. But the word of God is not chained.

Therefore I endure everything for the sake of the elect, so that they may also obtain the salvation that is in Christ Jesus, with eternal glory.

The saying is sure: If we have died with him, we will also live with him; if we endure, we will also reign with him; if we deny him, he will also deny us; if we are faithless, he remains faithful — for he cannot deny himself.

The word of the Lord. **Thanks be to God.**

GOSPEL ACCLAMATION *(1 Thessalonians 5.18)*
Alleluia. Alleluia. Give thanks in all circumstances; for this is the will of God in Christ Jesus for you. **Alleluia.**

GOSPEL *(Luke 17.11-19)*
The Lord be with you. **And with your spirit.** A reading from the holy Gospel according to Luke. **Glory to you, O Lord.**

On the way to Jerusalem Jesus was going through the region between Samaria and Galilee.

As he entered a village, ten lepers approached him. Keeping their distance, they called out, saying, "Jesus, Master, have mercy on us!"

When Jesus saw them, he said to them, "Go and show yourselves to the priests." And as they went, they were made clean. Then one of them, when he saw that he was healed, turned back, praising God with a loud voice. He prostrated himself at Jesus' feet and thanked him. And he was a Samaritan.

Then Jesus asked, "Were not ten made clean? But the other nine, where are they? Was none of them found to return and give praise to God except this foreigner?"

Then Jesus said to the Samaritan, "Get up and go on your way; your faith has made you well."

The Gospel of the Lord. **Praise to you, Lord Jesus Christ.**

PROFESSION OF FAITH *(p. 11)*

PRAYER OF THE FAITHFUL

The following intentions are suggestions only. There are more suggestions at www.livingwithchrist.ca

℟. **Lord, hear our prayer.**

For the People of God, called to the tender loving care of the human family, we pray to the Lord: ℟.

For openness and renewed trust among the world's nations and religious traditions we pray to the Lord: ℟.

For the sick, especially those who feel isolated because of their illness, we pray to the Lord: ℟.

For hearts filled with gratitude and generosity in this harvest season, we pray to the Lord: ℟.

PREPARATION OF THE GIFTS *(p. 14)*

PRAYER OVER THE OFFERINGS

Accept, O Lord, the prayers of your faithful with the sacrificial offerings, that, through these acts of devotedness, we may pass over to the glory of heaven. Through Christ our Lord. **Amen.**

PREFACE *(Sundays in Ordinary Time, p. 28)*

COMMUNION ANTIPHON *(Cf. Psalm 33.11)*

The rich suffer want and go hungry, but those who seek the Lord lack no blessing.

or (1 John 3.2)

When the Lord appears, we shall be like him, for we shall see him as he is.

PRAYER AFTER COMMUNION

We entreat your majesty most humbly, O Lord, that, as you feed us with the nourishment which comes from the most holy Body and Blood of your Son, so you may make us sharers of his divine nature. Who lives and reigns for ever and ever. **Amen.**

BLESSING AND DISMISSAL *(p. 70)*

October 16

At first glance, the meaning of Jesus' parables is not clear to us. This Sunday's gospel, however, doesn't require us to peel back layers of metaphors to get at its meaning. The opening sentence is quite clear — Jesus reminds us of our need to pray always and not to lose heart.

The challenge for us is figuring out how to pray when we do lose heart, when we do give up or are tempted to give up because we don't get what we have been praying for. The golden nugget of the parable is revealed to us at the end, when Jesus asks whether he will find faith on earth when justice has been granted to us.

We are being reminded that prayer cannot exist without our faith: a faith that is deeply rooted in our loving relationship with our Father. Our faith in God's love for us gives us the strength and the courage to be persistent with our prayers. We trust in God's protection because we know that our help is "from the Lord, who made heaven and earth."

Let us not lose heart in our prayer life, but draw on St Paul's "utmost patience," so that through our faith we will be open to the Holy Spirit working through our prayers, always knowing that "the Lord is our keeper."

Julie Cachia, Toronto, ON

ENTRANCE ANTIPHON *(Cf. Psalm 16.6, 8)*
To you I call; for you will surely heed me, O God; turn your ear to me; hear my words. Guard me as the apple of your eye; in the shadow of your wings protect me.

INTRODUCTORY RITES *(p. 5)*

COLLECT
Almighty ever-living God, grant that we may always conform our will to yours and serve your majesty in sincerity of heart. Through our Lord Jesus Christ, your Son, who lives and reigns with you in the unity of the Holy Spirit, one God, for ever and ever. **Amen.**

FIRST READING *(Exodus 17.8-13)*
Amalek came and fought with Israel at Rephidim. Moses said to Joshua, "Choose some men for us and go out, fight with Amalek. Tomorrow I will stand on the top of the hill with the staff of God in my hand."

So Joshua did as Moses told him, and fought with Amalek, while Moses, Aaron, and Hur went up to the top of the hill.

Whenever Moses held up his hands, Israel prevailed; and whenever he lowered his hands, Amalek prevailed. But Moses' hands grew weary; so they took a stone and put it under him, and he sat on it. Aaron and Hur held up his hands, one on one side, and the other on the other side; so his hands were steady until the sun set.

And Joshua defeated Amalek and his people with the sword.

The word of the Lord. **Thanks be to God.**

RESPONSORIAL PSALM *(Psalm 121)*

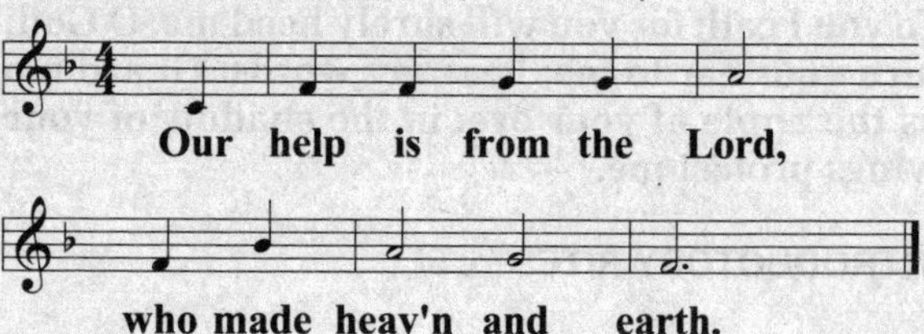

℞. **Our help is from the Lord,**
who made heaven and earth.

I lift up my eyes to the · **hills —**
from where will my help · **come?**
My help comes from the · **Lord,**
who made heaven · **and** earth. ℞.

The Lord will not let your foot be · **moved;**
he who keeps you will not · **slumber.**
He who keeps · **Israel**
will neither slumber · **nor** sleep. ℞.

The Lord is your · **keeper;**
the Lord is your shade at your right · **hand.**
The sun shall not strike you by · **day,**
nor the moon · **by** night. ℞.

The Lord will keep you from all · **evil;**
he will keep your · **life.**
The Lord will keep your going out and your
coming · **in**
from this time on and for·-**ever**-more. ℞.

SECOND READING *(2 Timothy 3.14 – 4.2)*
Beloved: Continue in what you have learned and firmly believed, knowing from whom you learned it, and how from childhood you have known the sacred writings that are able to instruct you for salvation through faith in Christ Jesus.

All Scripture is inspired by God and is useful for teaching, for reproof, for correction, and for training in righteousness, so that the one who belongs to God may be proficient, equipped for every good work.

In the presence of God and of Christ Jesus, who is to judge the living and the dead, and in view of his appearing and his kingdom, I solemnly urge you: proclaim the message; be persistent whether the time is favourable or unfavourable; convince, rebuke, and encourage, with the utmost patience in teaching.

The word of the Lord. **Thanks be to God.**

GOSPEL ACCLAMATION *(Hebrews 4.12)*
Alleluia. Alleluia. The word of God is living and active; it judges the thoughts and intentions of the heart. **Alleluia.**

GOSPEL *(Luke 18.1-8)*
The Lord be with you. **And with your spirit.** A reading from the holy Gospel according to Luke. **Glory to you, O Lord.**

Jesus told the disciples a parable about their need to pray always and not to lose heart.

He said, "In a certain city there was a judge who neither feared God nor had respect for any human being. In that city there was a widow who kept coming to him and saying, 'Grant me justice against my opponent.'

"For a while the judge refused; but later he said to himself, 'Though I have no fear of God and no respect for any human being, yet because this widow keeps bothering me, I will grant her justice, so that she may not wear me out by continually coming.'"

And the Lord said, "Listen to what the unjust judge says. Will not God grant justice to his chosen ones who cry to him day and night? Will he delay long in helping them? I tell you, God will quickly grant justice to them. And yet, when the Son of Man comes, will he find faith on earth?"

The Gospel of the Lord. **Praise to you, Lord Jesus Christ.**

PROFESSION OF FAITH *(p. 11)*

PRAYER OF THE FAITHFUL

The following intentions are suggestions only. There are more suggestions at www.livingwithchrist.ca

℟. **Lord, hear our prayer.**

For Church leaders, as they care for all people in faith and trust, we pray to the Lord: ℟.

For world leaders willing to listen to and learn from one another, we pray to the Lord: ℟.

For the needs of the weakest members of societies around the world, we pray to the Lord: ℟.

For this community, praying for a deepening of the grace of humility among us, we pray to the Lord: ℟.

PREPARATION OF THE GIFTS *(p. 14)*

PRAYER OVER THE OFFERINGS
Grant us, Lord, we pray, a sincere respect for your gifts, that, through the purifying action of your grace, we may be cleansed by the very mysteries we serve. Through Christ our Lord. **Amen.**

PREFACE *(Sundays in Ordinary Time, p. 28)*

COMMUNION ANTIPHON *(Cf. Psalm 32.18-19)*
Behold, the eyes of the Lord are on those who fear him, who hope in his merciful love, to rescue their souls from death, to keep them alive in famine.

or (Mark 10.45)

The Son of Man has come to give his life as a ransom for many.

PRAYER AFTER COMMUNION
Grant, O Lord, we pray, that, benefiting from participation in heavenly things, we may be helped by what you give in this present age and prepared for the gifts that are eternal. Through Christ our Lord. **Amen.**

BLESSING AND DISMISSAL *(p. 70)*

October 23

World Mission Sunday

"Who am I to judge?" "I am a sinner." Think about how these two quotes from Pope Francis apply to today's gospel and to your life.

The Church does not close itself to one and open to the other. The Church is called the house of the Father with doors wide open to everyone, including those the Pharisee casually dismisses. The Lord looks at the heart and is always searching for us, patiently waiting for us to respond and to repent. Those who welcome the message experience a sense of the sacred. Our mission as followers of Jesus is to believe and live a life beyond our sensory experiences of the commercial world and invite others to get to know and experience the Divine.

Our affluent society dulls our sensitivity to the transcendental world of the Divine. Some people will say that faith is an illusion. We must stay positive about our faith: promote our faith. People hunger for the sacred. We shouldn't deprive ourselves of that sense of the Divine, nor deprive others of experiencing the Divine in their lives.

Let us embrace Mission Sunday's call to spread the Good News to invite and help family, friends and others, to satisfy their hunger for the sacred and to enable them to live in union with Jesus, the Son of the living God.

Friar Ed Debono, OFM Conv, Kingston, ON

ENTRANCE ANTIPHON *(Cf. Psalm 104.3-4)*
Let the hearts that seek the Lord rejoice; turn to the Lord and his strength; constantly seek his face.

INTRODUCTORY RITES *(p. 5)*

COLLECT
Almighty ever-living God, increase our faith, hope and charity, and make us love what you command, so that we may merit what you promise. Through our Lord Jesus Christ, your Son, who lives and reigns with you in the unity of the Holy Spirit, one God, for ever and ever. **Amen.**

FIRST READING *(Sirach 35.15-17, 20-22)*
The Lord is the judge, and with him there is no partiality. He will not show partiality to the poor but he will listen to the prayer of one who is wronged. The Lord will not ignore the supplication of the orphan, or the widow when she pours out her complaint.

The person whose service is pleasing to the Lord will be accepted, and their prayer will reach to the clouds.

The prayer of the humble pierces the clouds, and it will not rest until it reaches its goal; it will not desist until the Most High responds and does justice for the righteous, and executes judgment. Indeed, the Lord will not delay.

The word of the Lord. **Thanks be to God.**

RESPONSORIAL PSALM *(Psalm 34)*

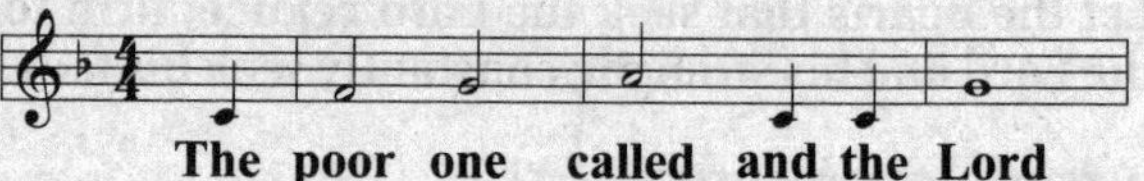

℟. **The poor one called and the Lord heard.**

I will bless the Lord at all · **times;**
his praise shall continually be in · **my** mouth.
My soul makes its boast in the · **Lord;**
let the humble hear and · **be** glad. ℟.

The face of the Lord is against · **evildoers,**
to cut off the remembrance of them ·
from_the earth.
When the righteous cry for help, the Lord
· **hears,**
and rescues them from all · **their** troubles. ℟.

The Lord is near to the broken·-**hearted,**
and saves the crushed · **in** spirit.
The Lord redeems the life of his · **servants;**
none of those who take refuge in him will be
· **con**-demned. ℟.

To hear the Sunday Psalms, go to www.livingwithchrist.ca and select the psalm button at the bottom of the home page.

SECOND READING *(2 Timothy 4.6-8, 16-18)*
Beloved: I am already being poured out as a libation, and the time of my departure has come. I have fought the good fight, I have finished the race, I have kept the faith.

From now on there is reserved for me the crown of righteousness, which the Lord, the righteous judge, will give me on that day, and not only to me but also to all who have longed for his appearing.

At my first defence no one came to my support, but all deserted me. May it not be counted against them!

But the Lord stood by me and gave me strength, so that through me the message might be fully proclaimed and all the Gentiles might hear it. So I was rescued from the lion's mouth.

The Lord will rescue me from every evil attack and save me for his heavenly kingdom. To him be the glory forever and ever. Amen.

The word of the Lord. **Thanks be to God.**

GOSPEL ACCLAMATION *(2 Corinthians 5.19)*
Alleluia. Alleluia. In Christ God was reconciling the world to himself, and entrusting the message of reconciliation to us. **Alleluia.**

GOSPEL *(Luke 18.9-14)*
The Lord be with you. **And with your spirit.**
A reading from the holy Gospel according to Luke. **Glory to you, O Lord.**

Jesus told this parable to some who trusted in themselves that they were righteous, and regarded others with contempt:

"Two men went up to the temple to pray, one a Pharisee and the other a tax collector. The Pharisee, standing by himself, was praying thus, 'God, I thank you that I am not like other people: thieves, rogues, adulterers, or even like this tax collector. I fast twice a week; I give a tenth of all my income.'

"But the tax collector, standing far off, would not even look up to heaven, but was beating his breast and saying, 'God, be merciful to me, a sinner!'

"I tell you, this man went down to his home justified rather than the other; for whoever exalts himself will be humbled, but whoever humbles himself will be exalted."

The Gospel of the Lord. **Praise to you, Lord Jesus Christ.**

PROFESSION OF FAITH *(p. 11)*

PRAYER OF THE FAITHFUL

The following intentions are suggestions only. There are more suggestions at www.livingwithchrist.ca

℟. **Lord, hear our prayer.**

For the People of God, called to bring life and hope to our world, we pray to the Lord: ℟.

For responsible governments, ruling in peace and justice, we pray to the Lord: ℟.

For missionaries, men and women of faith who model Jesus in their everyday lives, we pray to the Lord: ℟.

For ourselves, called to bring life to the world around us, we pray to the Lord: ℟.

PREPARATION OF THE GIFTS *(p. 14)*

PRAYER OVER THE OFFERINGS

Look, we pray, O Lord, on the offerings we make to your majesty, that whatever is done by us in your service may be directed above all to your glory. Through Christ our Lord. **Amen.**

PREFACE *(Sundays in Ordinary Time, p. 28)*

COMMUNION ANTIPHON *(Cf. Psalm 19.6)*

We will ring out our joy at your saving help and exult in the name of our God.

or (Ephesians 5.2)

Christ loved us and gave himself up for us, as a fragrant offering to God.

PRAYER AFTER COMMUNION

May your Sacraments, O Lord, we pray, perfect in us what lies within them, that what we now celebrate in signs we may one day possess in truth. Through Christ our Lord. **Amen.**

BLESSING AND DISMISSAL *(p. 70)*

October 30

Saint Paul prays for the Thessalonians, and also for us, that God will make us worthy. Sometimes we think we deserve everything we want, so we need the reminder that everything is gift, and that it is only by God's gift that we are made worthy to be the children of God.

The Book of Wisdom explains why this is so astounding, acknowledging that we are part of a vast universe. When we say that God is great, that greatness comes from God's care for us, who are "the speck that tips the scales." Tiny though we are, we are offered divine love for free, like handfuls of candy. Too often we just don't get it, and we sit hungry in the midst of a rich feast of grace. And when we don't get it, it is good to hear Jesus in the gospel showing the lengths to which God will go to make us worthy: "the Son of Man came to seek out and to save the lost."

But why did Jesus call Zacchaeus? Weren't there other worthy tax collectors around? Jesus saw how Zacchaeus worked past his own limitations in order to have an encounter with Jesus. In ways large and small, our lives are filled with opportunities to do the same.

Glenn Byer, Toronto, ON

ENTRANCE ANTIPHON *(Cf. Psalm 37.22-23)*
Forsake me not, O Lord, my God; be not far from me! Make haste and come to my help, O Lord, my strong salvation!

INTRODUCTORY RITES *(p. 5)*

COLLECT
Almighty and merciful God, by whose gift your faithful offer you right and praiseworthy service, grant, we pray, that we may hasten without stumbling to receive the things you have promised. Through our Lord Jesus Christ, your Son, who lives and reigns with you in the unity of the Holy Spirit, one God, for ever and ever. **Amen.**

FIRST READING *(Wisdom 11.22 – 12.2)*
The whole world before you, O Lord,
is like a speck that tips the scales,
and like a drop of morning dew that falls on
the ground.
But you are merciful to all,
for you can do all things,
and you overlook people's sins,
so that they may repent.

Lord, you love all things that exist,
and detest none of the things that you have made,
for you would not have made anything if you
had hated it.
How would anything have endured
if you had not willed it?
Or how would anything not called forth by you
have been preserved?

You spare all things, for they are yours, O Lord,
you who love the living.

For your immortal spirit is in all things.
Therefore you correct little by little those
who trespass,
and you remind and warn them of the things
through which they sin,
so that they may be freed from wickedness
and put their trust in you, O Lord.

The word of the Lord. **Thanks be to God.**

RESPONSORIAL PSALM *(Psalm 145)*

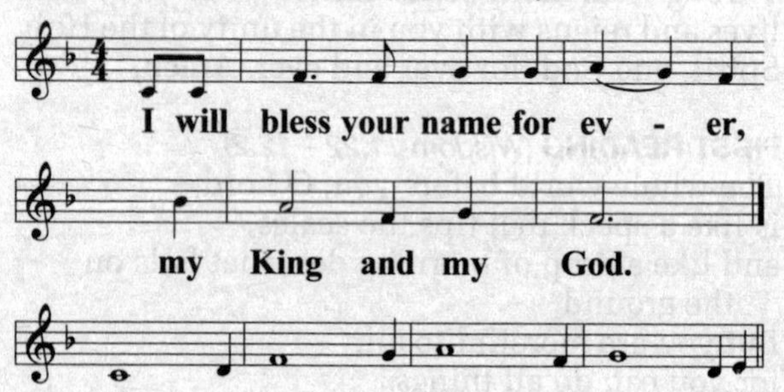

℟. **I will bless your name for ever,
my King and my God.**

I will extol you, my God and · **King,**
and bless your name forever and · **ever.**
Every day I will · **bless_you,**
and praise your name forever · **and** ever. ℟.

The Lord is gracious and · **merciful,**
slow to anger and abounding in steadfast · **love.**
The Lord is good to · **all,**
and his compassion is over all that he · **has** made. ℞.

All your works shall give thanks to you, O · **Lord,**
and all your faithful shall · **bless_you.**
They shall speak of the glory of your · **kingdom,**
and tell of · **your** power. ℞.

The Lord is faithful in all his · **words,**
and gracious in all his · **deeds.**
The Lord upholds all who are · **falling,**
and raises up all who are · **bowed** down. ℞.

To hear the Sunday Psalms, go to www.livingwithchrist.ca and select the psalm button at the bottom of the home page.

SECOND READING *(2 Thessalonians 1.11 – 2.2)*

Brothers and sisters: We always pray for you, asking that our God will make you worthy of his call and will fulfill by his power every good resolve and work of faith, so that the name of our Lord Jesus may be glorified in you, and you in him, according to the grace of our God and the Lord Jesus Christ.

As to the coming of our Lord Jesus Christ and our being gathered together to him, we beg you, brothers and sisters, not to be quickly shaken in mind or alarmed, either by spirit or by word or by letter, as though from us, to the effect that the day of the Lord is already here.

The word of the Lord. **Thanks be to God.**

GOSPEL ACCLAMATION *(John 3.16)*
Alleluia. Alleluia. God so loved the world that he gave his only-begotten Son, that everyone who believes in him may have eternal life. **Alleluia.**

GOSPEL *(Luke 19.1-10)*
The Lord be with you. **And with your spirit.** A reading from the holy Gospel according to Luke. **Glory to you, O Lord.**

Jesus entered Jericho and was passing through it. A man was there named Zacchaeus; he was a chief tax collector and was rich. He was trying to see who Jesus was, but on account of the crowd he could not, because he was short in stature.

So he ran ahead and climbed a sycamore tree to see Jesus, because he was going to pass that way. When Jesus came to the place, he looked up and said to him, "Zacchaeus, hurry and come down; for I must stay at your house today."

So Zacchaeus hurried down and was happy to welcome Jesus. All who saw it began to grumble and said, "He has gone to be the guest of one who is a sinner."

Zacchaeus stood there and said to the Lord, "Look, half of my possessions, Lord, I will give to the poor; and if I have defrauded anyone of anything, I will pay back four times as much."

Then Jesus said of him, "Today salvation has come to this house, because Zacchaeus too is a son of Abraham. For the Son of Man came to seek out and to save the lost."

The Gospel of the Lord. **Praise to you, Lord Jesus Christ.**

PROFESSION OF FAITH *(p. 11)*

PRAYER OF THE FAITHFUL

The following intentions are suggestions only. There are more suggestions at www.livingwithchrist.ca

℟. **Lord, hear our prayer.**

For Church leaders, called to be models of humble awareness of our need for God, we pray to the Lord: ℟.

For a spirit of wisdom for the leaders of nations, we pray to the Lord: ℟.

For victims of famine and war, and for all those who reach out to alleviate their suffering, we pray to the Lord: ℟.

For this Christian community, called to let Christ's light shine for all those around us, we pray to the Lord: ℟.

PREPARATION OF THE GIFTS *(p. 14)*

PRAYER OVER THE OFFERINGS

May these sacrificial offerings, O Lord, become for you a pure oblation, and for us a holy outpouring of your mercy. Through Christ our Lord. **Amen.**

PREFACE *(Sundays in Ordinary Time, p. 28)*

COMMUNION ANTIPHON *(Cf. Psalm 15.11)*

You will show me the path of life, the fullness of joy in your presence, O Lord.

or (John 6.58)
Just as the living Father sent me and I have life because of the Father, so whoever feeds on me shall have life because of me, says the Lord.

PRAYER AFTER COMMUNION

May the working of your power, O Lord, increase in us, we pray, so that, renewed by these heavenly Sacraments, we may be prepared by your gift for receiving what they promise. Through Christ our Lord. **Amen.**

BLESSING AND DISMISSAL *(p. 70)*

November Saints' Days

The following saints are traditionally remembered in November in Canada.

1 All Saints
2 All Souls' Day
3 Saint Martin de Porres
4 Saint Charles Borromeo
10 Saint Leo the Great
11 Saint Martin of Tours
12 Saint Josaphat
15 Saint Albert the Great
16 Saint Margaret of Scotland
Saint Gertrude
17 Saint Elizabeth of Hungary
22 Saint Cecilia
23 Saint Clement I
Saint Columban
24 Saint Andrew Düng-Lac and Companions
25 Saint Catherine of Alexandria
30 Saint Andrew

November 6

The Sadducees rejected resurrection because it was not in the Pentateuch, the only books they considered Scripture. They tried to discredit Jesus through a Leviticus law requiring that if a man died without children, his brother would marry the widow and their first son would be considered the dead man's son. But what if the second brother died childless, and a third, up to a seventh brother? Which of the seven would be her husband when they rose from the dead? Surely the idea of resurrection was problematic.

But Jesus rejected their premise. Resurrected life was not the same as our pre-resurrection life. The resurrection transforms us into a different state of being, where things like marriage no longer occur. Jesus also addressed their view that resurrection was not in the Torah. In Exodus, God spoke to Moses as the God of Abraham, Isaac and Jacob, all of whom were long dead by Moses' time. But God is the God of the living, so those three must still be alive in some way.

Jesus himself is the basis for our own resurrection. He lived a human life like each of us and, just as we will, he died. But he rose from the dead three days later. This is the central mystery we celebrate in the Eucharist, and our hope for the future.

John L. McLaughlin, Toronto, ON

ENTRANCE ANTIPHON *(Cf. Psalm 87.3)*
Let my prayer come into your presence. Incline your ear to my cry for help, O Lord.

INTRODUCTORY RITES *(p. 5)*

COLLECT
Almighty and merciful God, graciously keep from us all adversity, so that, unhindered in mind and body alike, we may pursue in freedom of heart the things that are yours. Through our Lord Jesus Christ, your Son, who lives and reigns with you in the unity of the Holy Spirit, one God, for ever and ever. **Amen.**

FIRST READING *(2 Maccabees 7.1-2, 7, 9-14)*
It happened that seven brothers and their mother were arrested and were being compelled by King Antiochus, under torture with whips and thongs, to partake of unlawful swine's flesh. One of the brothers, speaking for all, said, "What do you intend to ask and learn from us? For we are ready to die rather than transgress the laws of our ancestors."

After the first brother had died, they brought forward the second for their sport. And when he was at his last breath, he said to King, "You accursed wretch, you dismiss us from this present life, but the King of the universe will raise us up to an everlasting renewal of life, because we have died for his laws."

After him, the third was the victim of their sport. When it was demanded, he quickly put out his tongue and courageously stretched forth his hands, and said nobly, "I got these from Heaven, and because of God's laws I disdain them, and from God I hope to get them back again."

As a result the king himself and those with him were astonished at the young man's spirit, for he regarded his sufferings as nothing.

After the third brother too had died, they maltreated and tortured the fourth in the same way. When he was near death, he said to his torturers, "One cannot but choose to die at the hands of humans and to cherish the hope God gives of being raised by him. But for you, there will be no resurrection to life!"

The word of the Lord. **Thanks be to God.**

RESPONSORIAL PSALM *(Psalm 17)*

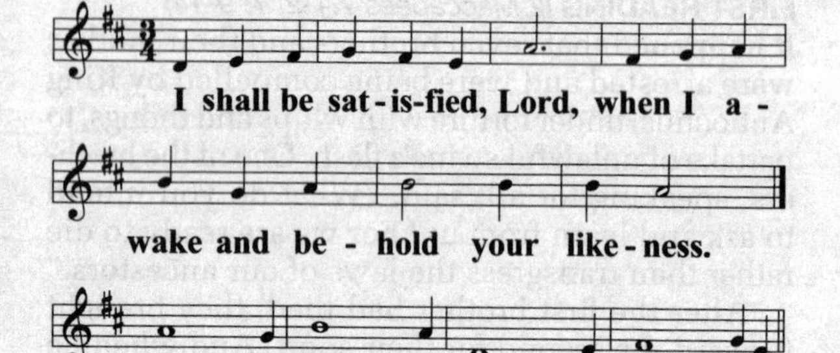

℟. **I shall be satisfied, Lord, when I awake and behold your likeness.**

Hear a just cause, O · **Lord;**
attend to my · **cry;**
give ear to my · **prayer**
from lips free of · **de**-ceit. ℟.

My steps have held fast to your · **paths;**
my feet have not · **slipped.**
I call upon you, for you will answer me,
O · **God;**
incline your ear to me, hear · **my** words. ℟.

Guard me as the apple of the · **eye;**
hide me in the shadow of your · **wings,**
As for me, I shall behold your face in
· **righteousness;**
when I awake I shall be satisfied,
beholding · **your** likeness. ℟.

To hear the Sunday Psalms, go to www.livingwithchrist.ca and select the psalm button at the bottom of the home page.

SECOND READING *(2 Thessalonians 2.16 – 3.5)*
Brothers and sisters: May our Lord Jesus Christ himself and God our Father, who loved us and through grace gave us eternal comfort and good hope, comfort your hearts and strengthen them in every good work and word.

Brothers and sisters, pray for us, so that the word of the Lord may spread rapidly and be glorified everywhere, just as it is among you, and that we may be rescued from wicked and evil people; for not all have faith.

But the Lord is faithful; he will strengthen you and guard you from the evil one. And we have confidence in the Lord concerning you, that you are doing and will go on doing the things that we command. May the Lord direct your hearts to the love of God and to the steadfastness of Christ.

The word of the Lord. **Thanks be to God.**

GOSPEL ACCLAMATION *(Revelation 1.5-6)*
Alleluia. Alleluia. Jesus Christ is the firstborn of the dead; to him be glory and dominion for ever and ever. **Alleluia.**

GOSPEL *(Luke 20.27-38)*
For the shorter version, omit the indented part.
The Lord be with you. **And with your spirit.**
A reading from the holy Gospel according to Luke. **Glory to you, O Lord.**

Some Sadducees, those who say there is no resurrection, came to Jesus.

> and asked him a question, "Teacher, Moses wrote for us that if a man's brother dies, leaving a wife but no children, the man shall marry the widow and raise up children for his brother. Now there were seven brothers; the first married, and died childless; then the second and the third married her, and so in the same way all seven died childless.
>
> Finally the woman also died. In the resurrection, therefore, whose wife will the woman be? — for the seven had married her."

Jesus said to them, "The children of this age marry and are given in marriage; but those who are considered worthy of a place in that age and in the resurrection from the dead neither marry nor are given in marriage. Indeed they cannot die any more, because they are like Angels and are sons and daughters of God, being children of the resurrection.

"And the fact that the dead are raised Moses himself showed in the story about the bush, where he speaks of the Lord as the God of Abraham, the God of Isaac, and the God of Jacob. Now he is God not of the dead, but of the living; for to him all of them are alive."

The Gospel of the Lord. **Praise to you, Lord Jesus Christ.**

PROFESSION OF FAITH *(p. 11)*

PRAYER OF THE FAITHFUL

The following intentions are suggestions only. There are more suggestions at www.livingwithchrist.ca

℟. **Lord, hear our prayer.**

For Church leaders, shepherding us in our witness to Christ in the world, we pray to the Lord: ℟.

For courage, mercy and patience in the hearts of our leaders, we pray to the Lord: ℟.

For the dying and those who care for them, and for all who grieve, we pray to the Lord: ℟.

For this community, celebrating Eucharist in hope of the resurrection, we pray to the Lord: ℟.

PREPARATION OF THE GIFTS *(p. 14)*

PRAYER OVER THE OFFERINGS

Look with favour, we pray, O Lord, upon the sacrificial gifts offered here, that, celebrating in mystery the Passion of your Son, we may honour it with loving devotion. Through Christ our Lord. **Amen.**

PREFACE *(Sundays in Ordinary Time, p. 28)*

COMMUNION ANTIPHON *(Cf. Psalm 22.1-2)*
The Lord is my shepherd; there is nothing I shall want. Fresh and green are the pastures where he gives me repose, near restful waters he leads me.
or (Cf. Luke 24.35)
The disciples recognized the Lord Jesus in the breaking of bread.

PRAYER AFTER COMMUNION
Nourished by this sacred gift, O Lord, we give you thanks and beseech your mercy, that, by the pouring forth of your Spirit, the grace of integrity may endure in those your heavenly power has entered. Through Christ our Lord. **Amen.**

BLESSING AND DISMISSAL *(p. 70)*

November 13

When I was much younger, we used to play a game called Truth or Dare. If you didn't want to answer your opponent's question truthfully, you had to accept a dare. Today, Jesus turns the game inside out and challenges his followers to tell their truth by accepting his dare. Jesus asks, Do you dare to be publicly Christian? How? What are your limits on doing so? What consequences are you willing to risk? Jesus does not promise us the proverbial rose garden. Rose gardens, like nations and kingdoms, will surely pass away. Jesus simply promises his presence, his words and his wisdom. These will never pass away. Here is where the good news lies today for us who accept his challenge.

This is a good time to start preparing for the new church year ahead, asking ourselves how we will be boldly Christian in 2017. Pope Francis offers an example. In his quiet, gentle way, he calls us to examine the lines we have drawn in the sand — and to take one small step past them.

Two of the great dismissals at the end of Mass graciously instruct us, "Go and announce the Gospel of the Lord" or "Go in peace, glorifying the Lord by your life." Perhaps one should boldly declare, "The living God is with you. Don't just sit there: do something. Change the world!"

Margaret Bick, Toronto, ON

ENTRANCE ANTIPHON *(Jeremiah 29.11, 12, 14)*
The Lord said: I think thoughts of peace and not of affliction. You will call upon me, and I will answer you, and I will lead back your captives from every place.

INTRODUCTORY RITES *(p. 5)*

COLLECT
Grant us, we pray, O Lord our God, the constant gladness of being devoted to you, for it is full and lasting happiness to serve with constancy the author of all that is good. Through our Lord Jesus Christ, your Son, who lives and reigns with you in the unity of the Holy Spirit, one God, for ever and ever. **Amen.**

FIRST READING *(Malachi 4.1-2)*
"See, the day is coming, burning like an oven,
when all the arrogant and all evildoers will
  be stubble;
the day that comes shall burn them up," says
  the Lord of hosts,
"so that it will leave them neither root nor branch.

"But for you who revere my name
the sun of righteousness shall rise,
with healing in its wings."

The word of the Lord. **Thanks be to God.**

RESPONSORIAL PSALM *(Psalm 98)*

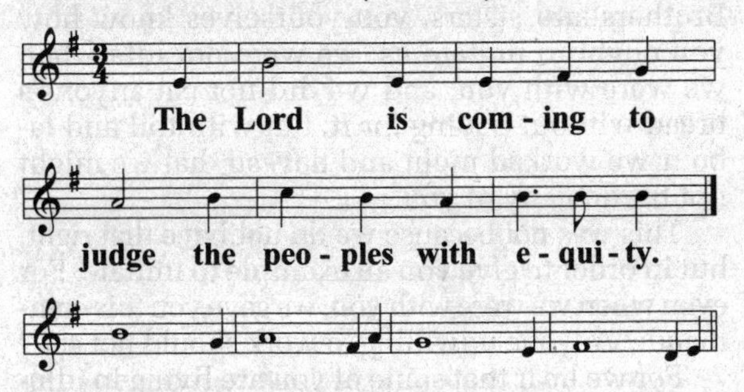

℟. **The Lord is coming to judge the peoples with equity.**

Sing praises to the Lord with the · **lyre,**
with the lyre and the sound · **of** melody.
With trumpets and the sound of the · **horn**
make a joyful noise before the King,
· **the** Lord. ℟.

Let the sea roar, and all that · **fills_it;**
the world and those · **who** live_in_it.
Let the floods clap their · **hands;**
let the hills sing together for joy at the
presence · **of_the** Lord. ℟.

For the Lord is · **coming,**
coming to judge · **the** earth.
He will judge the world with · **righteousness,**
and the peoples · **with** equity. ℟.

To hear the Sunday Psalms, go to www.livingwithchrist.ca and select the psalm button at the bottom of the home page.

SECOND READING *(2 Thessalonians 3.7-12)*
Brothers and sisters, you yourselves know how you ought to imitate us; we were not idle when we were with you, and we did not eat anyone's bread without paying for it; but with toil and labour we worked night and day, so that we might not burden any of you.

This was not because we do not have that right, but in order to give you an example to imitate. For even when we were with you, we gave you this command: "Anyone unwilling to work should not eat."

For we hear that some of you are living in idleness, mere busybodies, not doing any work. Now such persons we command and exhort in the Lord Jesus Christ to do their work quietly and to earn their own living.

The word of the Lord. **Thanks be to God.**

GOSPEL ACCLAMATION *(Luke 21.28)*
Alleluia. Alleluia. Stand up and raise your heads, because your redemption is drawing near. **Alleluia.**

GOSPEL *(Luke 21.5-19)*
The Lord be with you. **And with your spirit.** A reading from the holy Gospel according to Luke. **Glory to you, O Lord.**

When some were speaking about the temple, how it was adorned with beautiful stones and gifts dedicated to God, Jesus said, "As for these things that you see, the days will come when not one stone will be left upon another; all will be thrown down."

They asked him, "Teacher, when will this be, and what will be the sign that this is about to take place?"

And Jesus said, "Beware that you are not led astray; for many will come in my name and say, 'I am he!' and, 'The time is near!' Do not go after them.

"When you hear of wars and insurrections, do not be terrified; for these things must take place first, but the end will not follow immediately."

Then Jesus said to them, "Nation will rise against nation, and kingdom against kingdom; there will be great earthquakes, and in various places famines and plagues; and there will be dreadful portents and great signs from heaven.

"But before all this occurs, they will arrest you and persecute you; they will hand you over to synagogues and prisons, and you will be brought before kings and governors because of my name.

"This will give you an opportunity to testify. So make up your minds not to prepare your defence in advance; for I will give you words and a wisdom that none of your opponents will be able to withstand or contradict.

"You will be betrayed even by parents, by brothers and sisters, and by relatives and friends; and they will put some of you to death. You will be hated by all because of my name. But not a hair of your head will perish. By your endurance you will gain your souls."

The Gospel of the Lord. **Praise to you, Lord Jesus Christ.**

PROFESSION OF FAITH *(p. 11)*

PRAYER OF THE FAITHFUL

The following intentions are suggestions only. There are more suggestions at www.livingwithchrist.ca

℟. **Lord, hear our prayer.**

For all Christians, empowered to bring God's blessings into the whole creation, we pray to the Lord: ℟.

For the world, created to share in the love of God and enjoy peace, we pray to the Lord: ℟.

For those who cry and mourn, waiting for the renewal of all things in creation, we pray to the Lord: ℟.

For God's People gathered here, called to wait, watch and hope, we pray to the Lord: ℟.

PREPARATION OF THE GIFTS *(p. 14)*

PRAYER OVER THE OFFERINGS

Grant, O Lord, we pray, that what we offer in the sight of your majesty may obtain for us the grace of being devoted to you and gain us the prize of everlasting happiness. Through Christ our Lord. **Amen.**

PREFACE *(Sundays in Ordinary Time, p. 28)*

COMMUNION ANTIPHON *(Psalm 72.28)*

To be near God is my happiness, to place my hope in God the Lord.

or (Mark 11.23-24)

Amen, I say to you: Whatever you ask in prayer, believe that you will receive, and it shall be given to you, says the Lord.

PRAYER AFTER COMMUNION

We have partaken of the gifts of this sacred mystery, humbly imploring, O Lord, that what your Son commanded us to do in memory of him may bring us growth in charity. Through Christ our Lord. **Amen.**

BLESSING AND DISMISSAL *(p. 70)*

November 20

People have mixed feelings about kings and queens these days. Modern monarchs usually enjoy privileged lives and are far wealthier than their subjects. Because they are often figureheads, they may seem irrelevant to us, as if they are from another world.

But in Jesus' day, the king was all-important. He had great authority over the people's lives and commanded deep respect. He held the power and he was anointed, the chosen one. Those who followed Jesus saw him as their king, yet others protested this use of the term. Even as he hung on the cross, the debate continued. The religious leaders and soldiers scoffed at him and mocked him. One of the criminals crucified with him derided Jesus. But the other criminal got the last word. He spoke from the heart, in faith and humility: "Jesus, remember me when you come into your kingdom."

This refrain is often sung during the Triduum, when we recall Jesus' passion, death and resurrection. And today, as we celebrate Christ the King, these words of faith and hope and trust echo in our hearts once again.

This king is not about power or wealth. This king is "the image of the invisible God, the firstborn of all creation." For Christians, what could be more relevant?

Anne Louise Mahoney, Ottawa, ON

ENTRANCE ANTIPHON *(Revelation 5.12; 1.6)*
How worthy is the Lamb who was slain, to receive power and divinity, and wisdom and strength and honour. To him belong glory and power for ever and ever.

INTRODUCTORY RITES *(p. 5)*

COLLECT
Almighty ever-living God, whose will is to restore all things in your beloved Son, the King of the universe, grant, we pray, that the whole creation, set free from slavery, may render your majesty service and ceaselessly proclaim your praise. Through our Lord Jesus Christ, your Son, who lives and reigns with you in the unity of the Holy Spirit, one God, for ever and ever. **Amen.**

FIRST READING *(2 Samuel 5.1-3)*
All the tribes of Israel came to David at Hebron, and said, "Look, we are your bone and flesh. For some time, while Saul was king over us, it was you who led out Israel and brought it in. The Lord said to you: 'It is you who shall be shepherd of my people Israel, you who shall be ruler over Israel.'"

So all the elders of Israel came to the king at Hebron; and King David made a covenant with them at Hebron before the Lord, and they anointed David king over Israel.

The word of the Lord. **Thanks be to God.**

RESPONSORIAL PSALM *(Psalm 122)*

℟. **Let us go rejoicing to the house of the Lord.**

I was glad when they said · **to** me,
"Let us go to the house of · **the** Lord!"
Our feet · **are** standing
within your gates, O · **Je**-rusalem. ℟.

Jerusalem — built as · **a** city
that is bound firmly · **to**-gether.
To it the tribes · **go** up,
the tribes · **of_the** Lord. ℟.

As it was decreed · **for** Israel,
to give thanks to the name of · **the** Lord.
For there the thrones for judgment
· **were_set** up,
the thrones of the · **house_of** David. ℟.

To hear the Sunday Psalms, go to www.livingwithchrist.ca and select the psalm button at the bottom of the home page.

SECOND READING *(Colossians 1.12-20)*

Brothers and sisters: Give thanks to the Father, who has enabled you to share in the inheritance of the saints in the light. The Father has rescued us from the power of darkness and transferred us into the kingdom of his beloved Son, in whom we have redemption, the forgiveness of sins.

Christ is the image of the invisible God, the firstborn of all creation; for in him all things in heaven and on earth were created, things visible and invisible, whether thrones or dominions or rulers or powers — all things have been created through him and for him. Christ is before all things, and in him all things hold together.

He is the head of the body, the Church; he is the beginning, the firstborn from the dead, so that he might come to have first place in everything. For in Christ all the fullness of God was pleased to dwell, and through him God was pleased to reconcile to himself all things, whether on earth or in heaven, by making peace through the blood of his Cross.

The word of the Lord. **Thanks be to God.**

GOSPEL ACCLAMATION *(Mark 11.10)*

Alleluia. Alleluia. Blessed is the one who comes in the name of the Lord; blessed is the coming kingdom of our father David. **Alleluia.**

GOSPEL *(Luke 23.35-43)*

The Lord be with you. **And with your spirit.** A reading from the holy Gospel according to Luke. **Glory to you, O Lord.**

The leaders scoffed at Jesus saying, "He saved others; let him save himself if he is the Christ of God, his chosen one!" The soldiers also mocked Jesus, coming up and offering him sour wine, and saying, "If you are the King of the Jews, save yourself!" There was also an inscription over him, "This is the King of the Jews."

One of the criminals who were hanged there kept deriding him and saying, "Are you not the Christ? Save yourself and us!"

But the other rebuked him, saying, "Do you not fear God, since you are under the same sentence of condemnation? And we indeed have been condemned justly, for we are getting what we deserve for our deeds, but this man has done nothing wrong." Then he said, "Jesus, remember me when you come into your kingdom." Jesus replied, "Truly I tell you, today you will be with me in Paradise."

The Gospel of the Lord. **Praise to you, Lord Jesus Christ.**

PROFESSION OF FAITH *(p. 11)*

PRAYER OF THE FAITHFUL

The following intentions are suggestions only. There are more suggestions at www.livingwithchrist.ca

℟. **Lord, hear our prayer.**

For the Church, as we prepare for the coming of Jesus, we pray to the Lord: ℟.

For world leaders who model Jesus' message of compassion and inclusion, we pray to the Lord: ℟.

For those who find this time of year lonely, stressful and difficult, we pray to the Lord: ℟.

For this community, striving to make the kingdom of God a reality among us, we pray to the Lord: ℟.

PREPARATION OF THE GIFTS *(p. 14)*

PRAYER OVER THE OFFERINGS
As we offer you, O Lord, the sacrifice by which the human race is reconciled to you, we humbly pray that your Son himself may bestow on all nations the gifts of unity and peace. Through Christ our Lord. **Amen.**

PREFACE *(Christ the King, p. 32)*

COMMUNION ANTIPHON *(Psalm 28.10-11)*
The Lord sits as King for ever. The Lord will bless his people with peace.

PRAYER AFTER COMMUNION
Having received the food of immortality, we ask, O Lord, that, glorying in obedience to the commands of Christ, the King of the universe, we may live with him eternally in his heavenly Kingdom. Who lives and reigns for ever and ever. **Amen.**

BLESSING AND DISMISSAL *(p. 70)*

YEAR C: THE YEAR OF LUKE

With the beginning of Advent, the Church moves into a new liturgical year. In 2015-2016, we observe Year C, in what is a three-year cycle, with the majority of the Sunday gospel readings taken from the Gospel of Luke.

More than other evangelists, Luke stresses the "world-affirming" dimension of Jesus' ministry; he locates Jesus not only within the salvation history of God's chosen people but within the history of the whole human race. Thus, Luke refers both to the leaders of Israel and to figures like the Caesars (Augustus and Tiberius) who played key roles on the world stage, where Jesus of Nazareth belongs.

Luke's Gospel highlights God's designs as the reversal of human values and expectations.

God demonstrated a preferential love for the poor, the afflicted and the outcast as the starting point for summoning all humanity to salvation.

Luke underlines the importance of faith and of prayer, giving prominence to the Holy Spirit's role in the life of Jesus and his disciples. [...] Luke shows that conversion implies a change in one's behaviour, and he accentuates the presence and contribution of women among Jesus' disciples.

Above all, Luke emphasizes the orderly transition from the ministry of Jesus to the mission of the Twelve Apostles. The evangelist shows that God blessed the transition from early Church patterns in the apostolic era to later structures governed by elders appointed in apostolic succession. Though many of the early Church's struggles might appear to have been chaotic, the development of the Church came about following a divinely ordained plan so that people's faith might be firmly grounded (Luke 1.1-4).

During this liturgical year, we will see how Luke explores dimensions in the disciples' experiences with Jesus that get below surface appearances. One example is Peter's sense of unworthiness at his call (Luke 5.1-11). Another is a forgiven woman's love overflowing into tears that bathed the feet of Jesus (7.36-50). Others still are a cleansed leper's joy that had to say "thank you" (17.11-19), and the recollection by the Emmaus disciples that their hearts burned within them as Jesus opened the meaning of the Scriptures to them (24.13-35).

These themes and others are found in parables and narratives unique to the Third Gospel.

Archbishop Terrence Prendergast, SJ, *Living God's Word: Reflections on the Sunday Readings for Year C* (Toronto: Novalis, 2012), pp. 14-15.

PAPAL PRAYER INTENTIONS 2016

JANUARY

That sincere dialogue among men and women of different faiths may produce the fruits of peace and justice.

That by means of dialogue and fraternal charity and with the grace of the Holy Spirit, Christians may overcome divisions.

FEBRUARY

That we may take good care of creation — a gift freely given — cultivating and protecting it for future generations.

That opportunities may increase for dialogue and encounter between the Christian faith and the peoples of Asia.

MARCH

That families in need may receive the necessary support and that children may grow up in healthy and peaceful environments.

That those Christians who, on account of their faith, are discriminated against or are being persecuted, may remain strong and faithful to the Gospel, thanks to the incessant prayer of the Church.

APRIL

That small farmers may receive a just reward for their precious labour.

That Christians in Africa may give witness to love and faith in Jesus Christ amid political-religious conflicts.

MAY

That in every country of the world, women may be honoured and respected and that their essential contribution to society may be highly esteemed.

That families, communities, and groups may pray the Holy Rosary for evangelization and peace.

JUNE

That the aged, marginalized, and those who have no one may find — even within the huge cities of the world — opportunities for encounter and solidarity.

That seminarians and men and women entering religious life may have mentors who live the joy of the Gospel and prepare them wisely for their mission.

JULY

That indigenous peoples, whose identity and very existence are threatened, will be shown due respect.

That the Church in Latin America and the Caribbean, by means of her mission to the continent, may announce the Gospel with renewed vigour and enthusiasm.

AUGUST

That sports may be an opportunity for friendly encounters between peoples and may contribute to peace in the world.

That Christians may live the Gospel, giving witness to faith, honesty and love of neighbour.

SEPTEMBER

That each may contribute to the common good and to the building of a society that places the human person at the centre.

That by participating in the Sacraments and meditating on Scripture, Christians may become more aware of their mission to evangelize.

OCTOBER

That journalists, in carrying out their work, may always be motivated by respect for truth and a strong sense of ethics.

That World Mission Day may renew within all Christian communities the joy of the Gospel and the responsibility to announce it.

NOVEMBER

That the countries which take in a great number of displaced persons and refugees may find support for their efforts which show solidarity.

That within parishes, priests and lay people may collaborate in service to the community without giving in to the temptation of discouragement.

DECEMBER

That the scandal of child-soldiers may be eliminated the world over.

That the peoples of Europe may rediscover the beauty, goodness and truth of the Gospel which gives joy and hope to life.

TRADITIONAL PRAYERS

HAIL MARY

Hail Mary, full of grace, the Lord is with thee. Blessed art thou among women and blessed is the fruit of thy womb, Jesus.

Holy Mary, Mother of God, pray for us sinners, now and at the hour of our death. Amen.

GLORY BE TO THE FATHER

Glory be to the Father, and to the Son, and to the Holy Spirit. As it was in the beginning, is now, and ever shall be, world without end. Amen.

COME, HOLY SPIRIT

Come, Holy Spirit, fill the hearts of your faithful and kindle in them the fire of your love. Send forth your Spirit, O Lord, and renew the face of the earth. Amen.

ACT OF FAITH

O my God, I firmly believe that you are one God in three divine Persons, Father, Son, and Holy Spirit. I believe that your divine Son became man, died for our sins, and that he will come to judge the living and the dead. I believe these and all the truths which the holy Catholic Church teaches, because you have revealed them, who can neither deceive nor be deceived. Amen.

ACT OF HOPE

O my God, relying on your almighty power and infinite mercy and promises, I hope to obtain pardon of my sins, the help of your grace, and life everlasting through the merits of Jesus Christ, my Lord and Redeemer. Amen.

ACT OF LOVE

O my God, I love you above all things, with my whole heart and soul, because you are all good and worthy of all love. I love my neighbour as myself for the love of you. I forgive all who have injured me, and ask pardon of all whom I have injured. Amen.

DIVINE PRAISES

Blessed be God.
Blessed be his holy name.

Blessed be Jesus Christ, true God and true man.
Blessed be the name of Jesus.
Blessed be his most sacred heart.
Blessed be his most precious blood.
Blessed be Jesus in the sacrament of the altar.

Blessed be the Holy Spirit, the Paraclete.

Blessed be the Mother of God, Mary most holy.
Blessed be her holy and immaculate conception.
Blessed be her glorious assumption.
Blessed be the name of Mary, virgin and mother.

Blessed be Saint Joseph, her most chaste spouse.
Blessed be God in his angels and in his saints.

ANGELUS

The angel of the Lord declared unto Mary, and she conceived of the Holy Spirit. *Hail Mary...*

Behold, the handmaid of the Lord; be it done to me according to your word. *Hail Mary...*

And the word was made flesh, and dwelt among us. *Hail Mary...*

Pray for us, O holy Mother of God; that we may be made worthy of the promises of Christ.

Pour forth, we beseech you, O Lord, your grace into our hearts that we, to whom the incarnation of your Son was made known by the message of an angel, may by his passion and cross be brought to the glory of his resurrection. We ask this through the same Christ, our Lord. Amen.

REGINA CAELI

O Queen of heaven, rejoice, alleluia!
For he whom you chose to bear, alleluia!
Is risen as he said, alleluia!
Pray for us to God, alleluia!
Rejoice and be glad, O Virgin Mary, alleluia!
For the Lord is truly risen, alleluia!

O God, by the resurrection of your Son, our Lord, you were pleased to make glad the whole world. Grant, we beseech you, that through the intercession of the Virgin Mary, his mother, we may attain the joys of everlasting life, through the same Christ our Lord. Amen.

THE ROSARY

In the Rosary we focus on 20 events or mysteries in the life and death of Jesus and meditate on how we share with Mary in the redemptive work of Christ. Reading a pertinent passage from the Bible helps to deepen meditation on a particular mystery. The scriptural references given here are not exhaustive. In many instances, other biblical texts are equally suitable for meditation.

~ Begin the Rosary at the crucifix by praying the Apostles' Creed (p. 13)
~ At each large bead, pray the Lord's Prayer
~ At each small bead, pray the Hail Mary
~ At the first three beads it is customary to pray a Hail Mary for each of the gifts of faith, hope, and love
~ For each mystery, begin with the Lord's Prayer, then recite the Hail Mary ten times, and end with Glory Be to the Father.

The Five Joyful Mysteries:

The Annunciation (Luke 1.26-38)
The Visitation (Luke 1.39-56)
The Nativity (Luke 2.1-20)
The Presentation (Luke 2.22-38)
The Finding in the Temple (Luke 2.41-52)

The Five Mysteries of Light:

The Baptism in the Jordan (Matthew 3.13-17)
The Wedding at Cana (John 2.1-12)
The Proclamation of the Kingdom (Mark 1.15)
The Transfiguration (Luke 9.28-36)
The First Eucharist (Matthew 26.26-29)

The Five Sorrowful Mysteries:

The Agony in the Garden (Matthew 26.36-56)
The Scourging at the Pillar (Matthew 27.20-26)
The Crowning with Thorns (Matthew 27.27-30)
The Carrying of the Cross (Matthew 27.31-33)
The Crucifixion (Matthew 27.34-60)

The Five Glorious Mysteries:

The Resurrection (John 20.1-18)
The Ascension (Acts 1.9-11)
The Descent of the Holy Spirit (John 20.19-23)
The Assumption of Mary (John 11.26)
The Crowning of Mary (Philippians 2.1-11)

THE WAY OF THE CROSS

(Revised version: The Sacred Congregation for Divine Worship recommends that the traditional Stations be revised to emphasize that the sufferings and resurrection of Christ are one redemptive mystery.)

OPENING PRAYER

Lord Jesus, all of your life led up to the Way of the Cross. In this final journey you lay down your life for your friends.

Jesus, you consider us your friends. You walk side by side with us on the journey of life. You know its joys and hopes, its suffering and pain. Today we want to walk side by side with you on your way to the Cross. Your suffering, your death, your rising from the dead give meaning to our lives. The way of the Cross is the way of life.

Lord, as you took the bread, your body, take us, bless us, break us, give us to others, so that in you we may be instruments of salvation for the world. **Amen.**

1. THE LAST SUPPER

Jesus said to them, "I have wanted so much to eat this Passover meal with you before I suffer! For I tell you, I will never eat it until it is given its full meaning in the Kingdom of God."

Then Jesus took a cup, gave thanks to God, and said, "Take this and share it among yourselves. I tell you that from now on I will not drink this wine until the Kingdom of God comes."

Then he took a loaf of bread, gave thanks to God, broke it, and gave it to them, saying, "This is my body, which is given for you. Do this in memory of me." In the same way, he gave them the cup after supper, saying, "This cup is God's new covenant sealed with my blood, which is poured out for you." *(Luke 22.15-20)*

Jesus, you love us. Make us realize we are a covenant people, make our eucharists moments when we feel your friendship, so that we may live this out for all humankind.

2. IN THE GARDEN OF GETHSEMANE

Then Jesus went with his disciples to a place called Gethsemane, and said to them, "Sit here while I go over there and pray." He took with him Peter and the two sons of Zebedee. Grief and anguish came over him, and he said to them, "The sorrow in my heart is so great that it almost crushes me. Stay here and keep watch with me." *(Matthew 26.36-38)*

Jesus, you love us. Comfort us in times of distress. Help us to see beyond ourselves; help us to overcome the feeling of senseless chaos; help us to see the joy and hope of those who truly suffer and who truly believe. Remind us of your covenant of friendship with us.

3. BEFORE THE SANHEDRIN

Jesus was taken to the High Priest's house, where the chief priests, the elders, and the teachers of the Law were gathering. Peter followed at a distance and went into the courtyard, where he sat down with the guards, keeping himself warm by the fire. The chief priests and the whole Council tried to find some evidence against Jesus in order to put him to death, but they could not find any. *(Mark 14.53-55)*

Jesus, you love us. Help us live out your covenant of friendship; give us strength to stand against authorities who exercise power for evil. Make us nonviolent, but strong in this struggle for humankind. Jesus, strengthen us.

4. BEFORE PONTIUS PILATE

Early in the morning Jesus was taken from Caiaphas' house to the governor's palace. The Jewish authorities did not go inside the palace, for they wanted to keep themselves ritually clean in order to be able to eat the Passover meal. So Pilate went outside to them and asked, "What do you accuse this man of?" Their answer was, "We would not have brought him to you if he had not committed a crime." *(John 18.28-30)*

Jesus, you love us. You stand with the victims in this world. Is that one meaning of the covenant for us: that we too should side with the oppressed against the oppressor? Lord, this is hard for us, teach us how to side with the oppressed, with the victims.

5. THE WHIPPING AND CROWNING WITH THORNS

Then Pilate took Jesus and had him whipped. The soldiers made a crown of thorny branches, put it on his head, then put a purple robe on him. They came to him and said, "Long live the King of the Jews!" and slapped him. *(John 19.1-3)*

Jesus, you love us. Turn our sympathies to the poor victims of desperate soldiers all over the world. Empower us to stop the sale of arms to ruthless armies. Show us the way to curb senseless attacks by states against their own people. Jesus, teach us how to resist evil.

6. THE CARRYING OF THE CROSS

So they took charge of Jesus. He went out, carrying his cross, and came to the 'Place of the Skull,' as it is called. (In Hebrew it is called 'Golgotha.') *(John 19.16-17)*

Jesus, you love us. Your love for us affirms the goodness of our humanity. We are the friends for whom you suffered. Teach us to respect others, not to dismiss or diminish them as less human.

7. SIMON OF CYRENE

On the way they met a man named Simon, who was coming into the city from the country. The soldiers forced him to carry Jesus' cross. *(Mark 15.21)*

Jesus, you love us. We don't like carrying crosses, but many times our cross is of our own making. It is a self-centred cross. Help us find the true cross in the lives of the poor. Help us to help carry their burden. Jesus, help us!

8. THE WOMEN OF JERUSALEM

A large crowd of people followed him; among them were some women who were weeping and wailing for him. Jesus turned to them and said, "Women of Jerusalem! Do not cry for me, but for yourselves and your children. For the days are coming when people will say, 'How lucky are the women who never had children, who never bore babies, who never nursed them!' " *(Luke 23.27-31)*

Jesus, you love us. Allow us to comfort the grieving women of our time. But even more, enable us to prevent their grief, which so often could be avoided. Help us to break down the human systems which starve and kill. Jesus, make us angry about this unnecessary grief and suffering. Teach us to weep, knowing all the time that tears are never enough.

9. THE STRIPPING AND CRUCIFIXION

They came to a place called Golgotha, which means 'Place of the Skull.' There they offered Jesus wine mixed with a bitter substance; but after tasting it, he would not drink it.

They crucified him and then divided his clothes among them by throwing dice. *(Matthew 27.33-35)*

Jesus, you love us. Stripped naked, nailed to the cross, you have given your all for us. Jesus, help us break the bonds of our selfishness and materialism. Show us how we can give our life for others, in your covenant.

10. THE SECOND THIEF

One of the criminals hanging there hurled insults at him: "Aren't you the Messiah? Save yourself and us!"

The other one, however, rebuked him, saying, "Don't you fear God? You received the same sentence he did. Ours, however, is only right because we are getting what we deserve; but he has done no wrong." And he said to Jesus, "Remember me, Jesus, when you come as King!"

Jesus said to him, "I promise you that today you will be in Paradise with me." *(Luke 23.39-43)*

Jesus, you love us. Impress on us that the lives we live, the work we do, have consequences for others. Awaken our awareness to real evil and real faith. Help us honour your covenant of friendship in our lives.

11. MARY AND JOHN

Standing close to Jesus' cross were his mother, his mother's sister, Mary the wife of Clopas, and Mary Magdalene. Jesus saw his mother and the disciple he loved standing there; so he said to his mother, "He is your son."

Then he said to the disciple, "She is your mother." From that time the disciple took her to live in his home. *(John 19.25-27)*

Jesus, you love us. You gave us your mother Mary as our own mother. Touch our hearts with her sorrow at your death. Lift our eyes so we may see in her the beauty of your covenant; the beauty of her gift of herself to you and to us.

12. DEATH ON THE CROSS

But when they came to Jesus, they saw that he was already dead, so they did not break his legs. One of the soldiers, however, plunged his spear into Jesus' side, and at once blood and water poured out. *(John 19.33-34)*

Jesus, you love us. Teach us your way. Give us the wisdom to recognize evil. Give us the courage to confront it, to struggle against it, so that we may truly be your friends.

13. THE NEW SEPULCHRE

When it was evening, a rich man from Arimathea arrived; his name was Joseph, and he also was a disciple of Jesus. He went to Pilate and asked for the body of Jesus. Pilate gave orders for the body to be given to Joseph. So Joseph took it, wrapped it in a new linen sheet, and placed it in his own tomb which he had just recently dug out of solid rock. Then he rolled a large stone across the entrance to the tomb and went away. *(Matthew 27.57-60)*

Jesus, you love us. Help us to distinguish justice and charity. Sometimes it is easier to do charity than to do justice. Let us know which should be our response and when, in our lives. Give us the grace to act charitably and justly.

14. THE RESURRECTION

Very early on Sunday morning the women went to the tomb, carrying the spices they had prepared. They found the stone rolled away from the entrance to the tomb, so they went in; but they did not find the body of the Lord Jesus. *(Luke 24.1-3)*

Jesus, you love us. You have returned from the dead to be with us. Be our promise, our hope that all evil will be overcome. Bless us with full life for all humankind, under your covenant.

FINAL PRAYER

We know that Christ has been raised from death and will never die again — death will no longer rule over him. And so, because he died, sin has no power over him; and now he lives his life in fellowship with God. In the same way, you are to think of yourselves as dead, so far as sin is concerned, but living in fellowship with God through Christ Jesus. *(Romans 6.9-11)*

Father, your only Son gave up his life for us, his friends. Help us understand the meaning of that friendship. Help us grow in that friendship.

We are a weak and distracted people. Often we neglect you, but you never abandon us. You love us. Make us a less selfish and a more caring people. Help us to share the crosses of others, as Simon did. Show us how to live your covenant of friendship day by day with the victims and the poor of this world. Father, we depend on you.

We pray this through Jesus, the Christ, your Son who has risen from the dead. Amen.

PRAYING WITH THE EUCHARIST

ANIMA CHRISTI

Soul of Christ, be my sanctification;
Body of Christ, be my salvation;
Blood of Christ, fill all my veins;
Water of Christ's side, wash out my stains;
Passion of Christ, my comfort be;
O good Jesus, listen to me;
In Thy wounds I fain would hide;
Ne'er to be parted from Thy side;
Guard me, should the foe assail me;
Call me when my life shall fail me;
Bid me come to Thee above,
With Thy saints to sing Thy love,
World without end. Amen.

* * *

My Lord, I offer Thee myself in turn as a sacrifice of thanksgiving. Thou hast died for me, and I in turn make myself over to Thee. I am not my own. Thou hast bought me; I will by my own act and deed complete the purchase. My wish is to be separated from everything of this world; to cleanse myself simply from sin; to put away from me even what is innocent, if used for its own sake, and not for Thine. I put away reputation and honour, and influence, and power, for my praise and strength shall be in Thee. Enable me to carry on what I profess. Amen.

Blessed John Henry Newman

I believe Thou art present in the Blessed Sacrament, O Jesus. I love Thee and desire Thee. Come into my heart. I embrace Thee, O never leave me. I beseech Thee, O Lord Jesus, may the burning and most sweet power of Thy love absorb my mind, that I may die through love of Thy love, Who wast graciously pleased to die through love of my love.

Saint Francis of Assisi

***

Lord Jesus, Who in the Eucharist make your dwelling among us and become our traveling companion, sustain our Christian communities so that they may be ever more open to listening and accepting your Word. May they draw from the Eucharist a renewed commitment to spreading in society, by the proclamation of your Gospel, the signs and deeds of an attentive and active charity.

Saint John Paul II

AN ACT OF SPIRITUAL COMMUNION

My Jesus, I believe that you are present in the most Blessed Sacrament. I love You above all things and I desire to receive You into my soul. Since I cannot now receive You sacramentally, come at least spiritually into my heart. I embrace You as if You have already come, and unite myself wholly to You. Never permit me to be separated from You. Amen.

Saint Alphonsus Liguori

INSPIRATION FROM THE SAINTS

LIVING HOPE

Consult not your fears but your hopes and your dreams. Think not about your frustrations, but about your unfulfilled potential. Concern yourself not with what you tried and failed in, but with what it is still possible for you to do.

Saint John XXIII

SEEKING JESUS

It is Jesus that you seek when you dream of happiness; He is waiting for you when nothing else you find satisfies you; He is the beauty to which you are so attracted; it is He who provoked you with that thirst for fullness that will not let you settle for compromise; it is He who urges you to shed the masks of a false life; it is He who reads in your heart your most genuine choices, the choices that others try to stifle.

It is Jesus who stirs in you the desire to do something great with your lives, the will to follow an ideal, the refusal to allow yourselves to be ground down by mediocrity, the courage to commit yourselves humbly and patiently to improving yourselves and society, making the world more human.

Saint John Paul II, World Youth Day, August 19, 2000

GOD'S HANDIWORK

It is with the smallest brushes that the artist paints the most exquisitely beautiful pictures.

Saint André Bessette.

PRAYER OF ST. THOMAS AQUINAS

Grant me, O Lord my God,
a mind to know you,
a heart to seek you,
wisdom to find you,
conduct pleasing to you,
faithful perseverance in waiting for you,
and a hope of finally embracing you.

Saint Thomas Aquinas

DOING GOD'S WILL

Lord Jesus, teach me to be generous;
teach me to serve you as you deserve;
to give and not count the cost,
to fight and not heed the wounds,
to toil and not seek for rest,
to labour and not to seek reward,
except that of knowing that I do your will.

Saint Ignatius Loyola

* * *

Give me, Lord, a full faith, a firm hope and a fervent love, a love for you incomparably above the love of myself. These things, good Lord, that I pray for, give me your grace also to labour for.

Saint Thomas More

THE PEACE PRAYER OF ST. FRANCIS

Lord, make me an instrument of your peace.
Where there is hatred let me sow love;
where there is injury, pardon;
where there is doubt, faith;
where there is despair, hope;
where there is darkness, light;
and where there is sadness, joy.

Divine Master,
grant that I may not so much seek
to be consoled as to console,
to be understood as to understand,
to be loved as to love.

For it is in giving that we receive,
in pardoning that we are pardoned,
and in dying that we are brought to eternal life.

Unknown, ca. 1915

IN SERVICE TO GOD

Govern everything by your wisdom, O Lord,
so that my soul may always be serving you
in the way you will
and not as I choose.
Let me die to myself so that I may serve you;
let me live to you who are life itself.

Saint Teresa of Avila

God doesn't ask for the impossible, but wants everyone to offer their good intentions, their day's work, and some prayers: that will help them a lot. The best Way of the Cross is when people accept willingly the crosses that are sent to them.

Saint André Bessette

The lover gives her life gladly for the beloved. She does not know her own interests or even her own needs. Sickness and health, prosperity and adversity, life and death, consolation and desolation are alike to her.

Saint Marguerite Bourgeoys

Give something, however small, to the one in need. For it is not small to one who has nothing. Neither is it small to God, if we have given what we could.

Saint Gregory Nazianzen

The Eucharist is the heart of the Christian religion. It is an ineffable mystery that embraces the untold depths of divine love, and in which God bestows upon us all blessings and graces.

Saint Francis de Sales

PRAYERS FOR CEMETERY VISITS

PSALM 23 – THE DIVINE SHEPHERD

The Lord is my shepherd, I shall not want.
He makes me lie down in green pastures;
he leads me beside still waters;
he restores my soul.
He leads me in right paths
for his name's sake.

Even though I walk through the darkest valley,
I fear no evil;
for you are with me;
your rod and your staff —
they comfort me.

You prepare a table before me
in the presence of my enemies;
you anoint my head with oil;
my cup overflows.

Surely goodness and mercy shall follow me
all the days of my life,
and I shall dwell in the house of the Lord
my whole life long.

ETERNAL REST

Eternal rest grant unto them, O Lord,
and let perpetual light shine upon them.
May the souls of the faithful departed,
through the mercy of God,
rest in peace. Amen.

DE PROFUNDIS *(Psalm 130)*
Out of the depths I cry to You, O Lord;
Lord, hear my voice.
Let Your ears be attentive
to my voice in supplication.
If You, O Lord, mark iniquities,
Lord, who can stand?
But with You is forgiveness,
that You may be revered.

I trust in the Lord;
my soul trusts in His word.
My soul waits for the Lord
more than sentinels wait for the dawn.
More than sentinels wait for the dawn,
let Israel wait for the Lord,

For with the Lord is kindness
and with Him is plenteous redemption;
And He will redeem Israel
from all their iniquities.

* * *

Lord, support us all the day long,
until the shadows lengthen
and the evening comes,
and the busy world is hushed
and the fever of life is over
and our work is done.
Then in thy mercy grant us
a safe lodging,
and a holy rest,
and peace at the last.

Blessed John Henry Newman

WHEN TO PRAY

It's sometimes said that the only person who prays well is the one who prays often. If prayer is understood, however, as something undertaken only during times of quiet and calm, then family life is the last place to find it. The good news is that prayer is easily folded into the rhythm of our days, weeks, months, and years, no matter how offbeat these times may be. Although it may not help solve the problem of overstuffed schedules, prayer helps us shape the time we've been given.

In his book *Pray All Ways,* Father Edward Hays describes how Jesus calls us into a living communion with God. To do so means threading prayer into each day as well as into the seasons of both nature and worship. Jesus is an ideal model for such prayer. As a faithful Jew, he observed the prayers of his people through the marking of holy days and festivals. Thus, he prayed in the synagogue and temple and at the Passover meal that we call the Last Supper. He prayed before sharing food with others and before performing miracles and healings. He prayed during his hour of agony in the Garden of Gethsemane and in his solitary time in the desert. And, in an especially heartening message for those with busy lives, he said that prayers needn't be long or formal. Simply "show up," as one contemplative puts it, and you will find God waiting to listen.

Until we learn to pray always and in all ways, says Fr. Hays, we are in danger of replacing prayer with busyness and even with "small act of kindness." The tasks that we undertake and the service we provide to others are certainly important, but if they are separated from a prayerful heart, they can grow empty and fruitless. The great German mystic Hildegard of Bingen once noted that there was nothing sadder than a drooping soul. The only way to keep it alive and vibrant is by watering it regularly with the replenishing waters of prayer.

Kathy Hendricks, *Prayers and Rituals for the Home: Celebrating the Life and Times of Your Family* (Toronto: Novalis, 2014), pp. 51-52.

Acquire the habit of speaking to God
as if you were alone with him.
Speak with familiarity and confidence
as to your dearest and most loving friend.
Speak of your likes, your plans,
your troubles, your joys, your fears.
In return, God will speak to you —
not that you will hear audible words
in your ears, but words that you will
clearly understand in your heart.

– *Saint Alphonsus Liguori*

PRAYER IN THE MORNING

INVITATION TO PRAYER

Lord, open our lips.
And we shall proclaim your praise.
Glory to God in the highest.
And peace to God's people on earth.

HYMN OF PRAISE *(Optional)*

PSALM OF PRAISE

Psalm 63 and/or another psalm of praise, followed by a moment of silence.

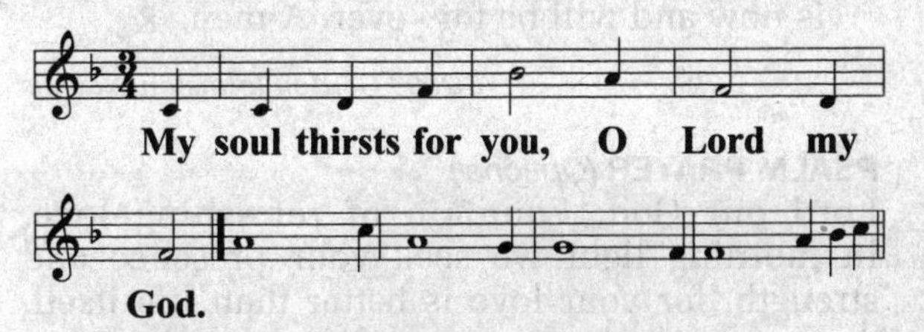

℟. **My soul thirsts for you, O Lord my God.**

O God, you are my God, I · **seek_you**,
my soul · **thirsts_for_you;**
my flesh · **faints_for_you,**
as in a dry and weary land
where there · **is** no water. ℟.

So I have looked upon you in the · **sanctuary,**
beholding your power and · **glory.**
Because your steadfast love is better than · **life,**
my · **lips** will praise_you. ℟.

So I will bless you as long as I · **live;**
I will lift up my hands and call on your · **name.**
My soul is satisfied as with a rich · **feast,**
and my mouth praises you
with · **joy-**ful lips. ℟.

For you have been my · **help**,
and in the shadow of your wings I sing for · **joy**.
My soul · **clings_to_you;**
your right · **hand** up-holds_me. ℟.

Glory to the Father, and to the · **Son,**
and to the Holy · **Spirit.**
As it was in the be-·**ginning,**
is now and will be for · **ever.** A-men. ℟.

PSALM PRAYER *(Optional)*

Lord our God, Fountain of refreshing love, in morning light we seek your presence and strength, for your love is better than life itself. Accept our prayers with uplifted hands as we proclaim your praise in songs of joy. Satisfy our longing hearts and renew our thirsting spirits that our worship may give you glory and our lives be poured out in loving service.

Glory and praise to you, loving God, through our Lord Jesus Christ, your Son, who lives and reigns with you in the unity of the Holy Spirit, God for ever and ever. **Amen.**

WORD OF GOD

Appropriate verse(s) selected beforehand from the readings of the day, followed by a moment of silence.

CANTICLE OF ZECHARIAH

1. Blessed be the God of Israel,
Who comes to set us free,
Who visits and redeems us,
And grants us liberty.
The prophets spoke of mercy,
Of freedom and release;
God shall fulfill the promise
To bring our people peace.

2. Now from the house of David
A child of grace is giv'n;
A Saviour comes among us
To raise us up to heaven.
Before him goes the herald,
Forerunner in the way:
The prophet of salvation,
The messenger of Day.

3. Where once were fear and darkness
The sun begins to rise,
The dawning of forgiveness
Upon the sinners' eyes,
To guide the feet of pilgrims
Along the paths of peace:
O bless our God and Saviour
With songs that never cease!

Text: Michael Perry, *©1973 Hope Publishing Co.*
Tune: MERLE'S TUNE, *76.76.D.; ©1983 Hope Publishing Co.*

Music: *CBW III* 13E

PETITIONS

These reflect the needs of the Church, the world, the suffering, and the local community. Weekly suggestions are available at www.livingwithchrist.ca

OUR FATHER...

CONCLUDING PRAYER

God of glory and compassion, at your touch the wilderness blossoms, broken lives are made whole, and fearful hearts grow strong in faith. Open our eyes to your presence and awaken our hearts to sing your praise. To all who long for your Son's return grant perseverance and patience, that we may announce in word and deed the good news of the kingdom.

We ask this through our Lord Jesus Christ, your Son, who lives and reigns with you in the unity of the Holy Spirit, God for ever and ever. **Amen.**

BLESSING

May the Lord almighty order our days and our deeds in lasting peace. **Amen.**

Let us offer each other a sign of Christ's peace.

The celebration ends with the exchange of peace.

***

For a fuller version of the Liturgy of the Hours, consult the Living with Christ *missalette.*

PRAYER IN THE EVENING

The paschal candle is lit and carried in procession. During Advent, the Advent wreath may be lit instead. If you plan to use Psalm 141, prepare the thurible beforehand so that incense may be burned during the singing of the psalm.

INVITATION TO PRAYER

God, come to our assistance.
Lord, make haste to help us.
Glory to the Father, and to the Son, and to the Holy Spirit.
As it was in the beginning, is now, and will be forever. Amen.

HYMN OF PRAISE *(Optional)*

PSALM OF PRAISE

Psalm 141 and/or another psalm of praise, followed by a moment of silence.

℟. **Let my prayer arise like incense before you.**

I call upon you, O Lord: come quickly to · **me;**
give ear to my voice when I call to · **you.**
Let my prayer be counted as incense be·-**fore_you.**
and the lifting up of my hands as
an eve·-**ning** sacrifice. ℟.

Set a guard over my mouth, O · **Lord;**
keep watch over the door of my · **lips.**
But my eyes are turned toward you,
O God, my · **Lord;**
in you I seek refuge; do not leave me
· **de-**fenceless. ℟.

Glory to the Father, and to the · **Son,**
and to the Holy · **Spirit.**
As it was in the be·-**ginning,**
is now and will be for ever. · **A**-men. ℟.

PSALM PRAYER *(Optional)*

Loving God, creator of light and life, may our prayers ascend to you like the fragrance of incense. Purify our hearts to sing your praise in the company of your saints in glory.

We ask this through Christ our Lord. **Amen.**

WORD OF GOD

Appropriate verse(s) selected beforehand from the readings of the day, followed by a moment of silence.

CANTICLE OF MARY

1. My soul proclaims the Lord my God.
My spirit sings God's praise,
Who looks on me and lifts me up,
That gladness fill my days.
2. All nations now will share my joy,
For gifts God has outpoured.
This lowly one has been made great
I magnify the Lord.

3. For those who fear the Holy One,
   God's mercy will not die,
   Whose strong right arm puts down the proud,
   And lifts the lowly high.
4. God fills the hungry with good things,
   And sends the rich away.
   The promise made to Abraham,
   Is filled to endless day.
5. Then let all nations praise our God,
   The Father and the Son,
   The Spirit blest who lives in us,
   While endless ages run.

Text: Anne Carter, ©*1988 Religious of the Sacred Heart.*
Tune: HEATHER DEW **Music:** *CBW III* 592, 617; *CBW II 74,* 589

PETITIONS

These reflect the needs of the Church, the world, the suffering, and the local community. Weekly suggestions are available at www.livingwithchrist.ca

OUR FATHER...

CONCLUDING PRAYER

Creator of the universe, watch over us and keep us in the light of your presence. May our praise continually blend with that of all creation, until we come together to the eternal joys which you promise in your love.

We ask this through our Lord Jesus Christ, your Son, who lives and reigns with you in the unity of the Holy Spirit, God for ever and ever. **Amen.**

BLESSING

May God the Father almighty bless and keep us. **Amen.**

May Jesus Christ, his only Son, our Lord, graciously smile upon us. **Amen.**

May the Holy Spirit, the Lord and giver of life, grant us peace. **Amen.**

Let us offer each other a sign of Christ's peace.

The celebration ends with the exchange of peace.

***

For a fuller version of the Liturgy of the Hours, consult the Living with Christ missalette.

CELEBRATING THE SACRAMENT OF RECONCILIATION

When ready to celebrate the sacrament of Reconciliation (Confession), the following steps are involved.

BEFOREHAND

Examination of Conscience:
Pray to the Holy Spirit for light and strength, examine your conscience in the light of the Scriptures and the Commandments since your last confession and become truly sorry for your sins.

GOING TO CONFESSION

Welcome:
The priest welcomes you, the penitent. It is helpful if you indicate the time of your last Confession and anything else that will help the priest hearing your confession.

Scripture:
A short passage of Scripture may be read.

Confession:
Confess your sins and listen to the advice of the priest.

Penance:
The priest proposes a good action or prayer to help make up for sin and deepen virtue.

Prayer of Sorrow (Act of Contrition):
Pray expressing personal sorrow and asking for forgiveness.

Absolution:
The priest grants absolution in the name of God and the Church.

Praise of God and Dismissal:
The priest invites you to praise God and dismisses you with the command to go in peace.

AFTERWARD
Spend some time in thanking God for forgiving us and restoring us to full life in Christ.

EXAMINATION OF CONSCIENCE

Do I centre my life on God, on fidelity to the Gospel and the Commandments? Do I set aside time for personal prayer?

Do I keep Sunday by participating in the Eucharist?

Is Sunday a day of prayer and rest? Do I observe the penitential practices of the Church? Do I keep Lent as a time of prayer and sacrifice?

Do I behave as a Christian in daily and public life? Is my faith reflected in my employment?

Have I taken property of others including my employer?

Am I envious of what others have? Do I share my goods and time with those in need? Do I respect the reputation of others?

Do I care for my family? Do I model Christian life for my family: parents, wife, husband, children?

Do I exercise authority with genuine concern and responsibility? Do I give others the same respect that I expect for myself?

Have I dishonoured my body by thoughts or actions incompatible with Christian life? Am I faithful to my marriage? Do I set an example of committed single living?

Do I live out my commitments to my spouse and my children to the best of my ability and reflect God's love and faithfulness?

How do I deal with the difficulties, failures and disappointments of life?

Do I tend to the spiritual, physical and medical needs of my body? Can others see the grace of Baptism at work in my life?

ACT OF CONTRITION

My God,
I am sorry for my sins with all my heart.
In choosing to do wrong
and failing to do good,
I have sinned against you
whom I should love above all things.
I firmly intend, with your help,
to do penance,
to sin no more,
and to avoid whatever leads me to sin.
Our Saviour Jesus Christ
suffered and died for us.
In his name, my God, have mercy.

Excerpted from *Celebrating Reconcilation*
(Ottawa: Concacan Inc., 2006).

KYRIE – PENITENTIAL ACT, FORM 1

Presider/Cantor — Assembly

Lord, have mer-cy. Lord, have mer-cy.

Text and setting: *Excerpts from Chants of the Roman Missal*

KYRIE – PENITENTIAL ACT, FORM 2

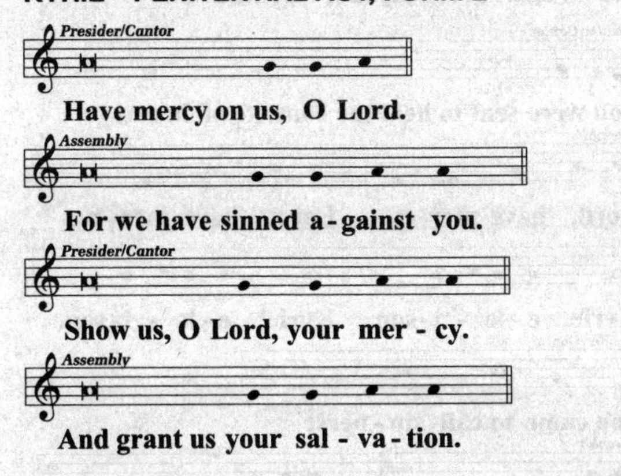

KYRIE – PENITENTIAL ACT, FORM 3

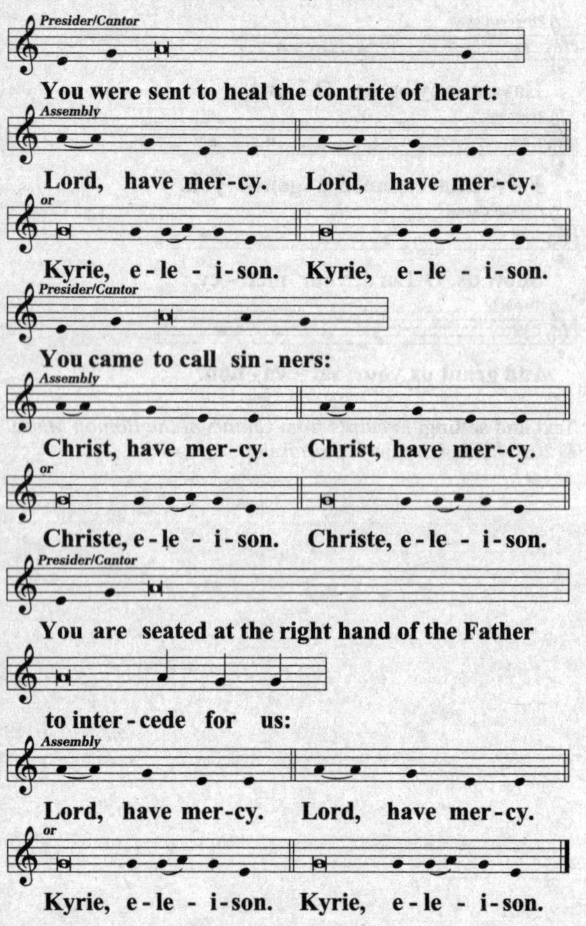

GLORIA

Glory to God in the high - est,
and on earth peace to people of good will.
We praise you, we bless you, we a - dore you,
we glo - ri - fy you,
we give you thanks for your great glo - ry,
Lord God, heav - en - ly King,
O God, al - might - y Fa - ther.
Lord Je - sus Christ, Only Be - got - ten Son,
Lord God, Lamb of God, Son of the Fa - ther,
you take away the sins of the world,
have mer - cy on us;

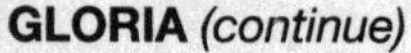

GLORIA *(continue)*

Music: *Anonymous.* **Text:** *Excerpts from Chants of the Roman Missal © 2010 ICEL. Used with permission.*

HOLY, HOLY, HOLY

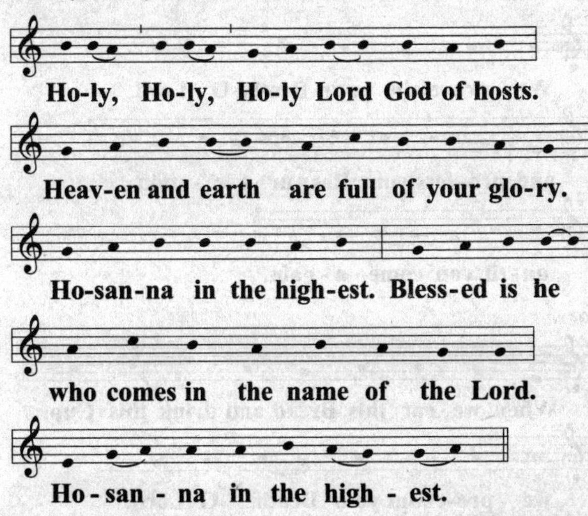

Text and setting: *Excerpts from Chants of the Roman Missal*

MEMORIAL ACCLAMATIONS

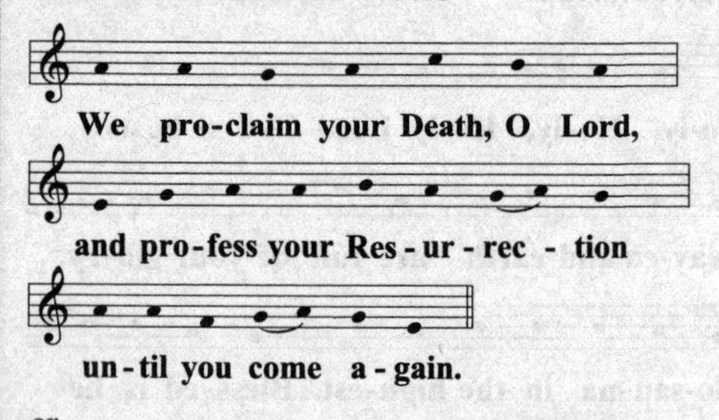

or

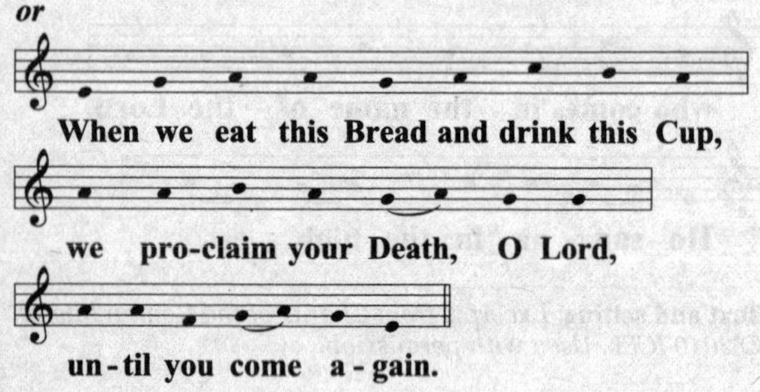

or

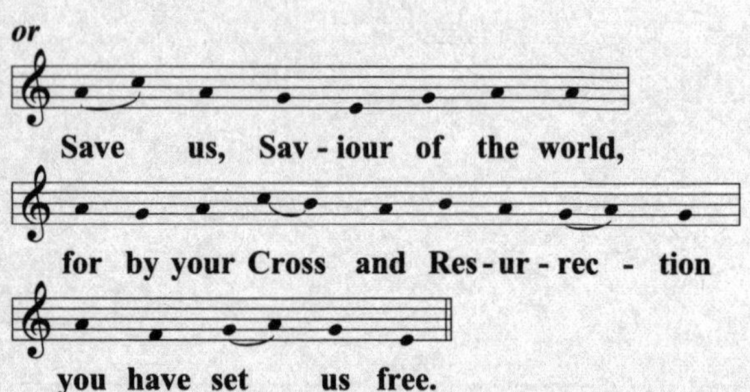

Text and setting: *Excerpts from Chants of the Roman Missal*

LAMB OF GOD

Text and setting: *Excerpts from Chants of the Roman Missal*

Hymns

ON JORDAN'S BANK

1. On Jordan's bank the Baptist's cry
Announces that the Lord is nigh;
Awake and hearken, for he brings
Glad tidings of the King of kings!

2. Then cleansed be ev'ry life from sin;
Make straight the way for God within;
And let us all our hearts prepare
For Christ to come and enter there.

3. We hail you as our Saviour, Lord,
Our refuge and our great reward;
Without your grace we waste away
Like flow'rs that wither and decay.

4. Stretch forth your hand, our health restore,
And make us rise to fall no more;
O, let your face upon us shine
And fill the world with love divine.

Text: *Jordanis oras praevis,* Charles Coffin, 1676-1749; tr. st. 1-3 John Chandler, 1806-76; st. 4 unknown; alt.
Tune: WINCHESTER NEW, LM **Music:** CBW II 443; CBW III 350

O COME, O COME EMMANUEL

1. O come, O come, Emmanuel,
   And ransom captive Israel
   That mourns in lonely exile here
   Until the Son of God appear.

Ref: Rejoice! Rejoice! Emmanuel
shall come to you, O Israel.

2. O come, O Wisdom from on high,
   Who order all things mightily;
   To us the path of knowledge show,
   And teach us in your ways to go.

3. O come, O come, great Lord of might,
   Who to your tribes on Sinai's height
   In ancient times once gave the law,
   In cloud, and majesty, and awe.

4. O come, O rod of Jesse's stem,
   From ev'ry foe deliver them
   That trust your mighty pow'r to save,
   and give them vict'ry o'er the grave.

5. O come, O key of David, come
   And open wide our heav'nly home;
   Make safe the way that leads on high,
   And close the path to misery.

6. O come, O Dayspring from on high,
   And cheer us by your drawing nigh;
   Disperse the gloomy clouds of night,
   And death's dark shadow put to flight.

7. O come, Desire of nations, bind
   In one the hearts of humankind;
   O bid our sad divisions cease,
   And be for us our king of peace.

Text: *Veni, veni Emmanuel;* Latin 9th c.; tr. by John Mason Neale, 1818-1866, alt. **Tune:** VENI, VENI EMMANUEL **Music:** CBW II 440; CBW III 312

O COME, DIVINE MESSIAH!

1. O come, divine Messiah!
   The world in silence waits the day
   When hope shall sing its triumph,
   And sadness flee away.

Ref: Sweet Saviour, haste;
Come, come to earth:
Dispel the night, and show thy face,
And bid us hail the dawn of grace.
O come, divine Messiah,
The world in silence waits the day
When hope shall sing its triumph,
And sadness flee away.

2. O thou, whom nations sighed for,
   Whom priests and prophets long foretold,
   Wilt break the captive fetters,
   Redeem the long-lost fold.

3. Shalt come in peace and meekness,
   And lowly will your cradle be:
   All clothed in human weakness
   Shall we thy God-head see.

Text: Abbé Pellegrin, 1663-1745; tr. Sr. Mary of St. Philip
Tune: VENEZ DIVIN MESSIE, 78.76.888 **Music:** CBW II 441; CBW III 310

THE FIRST NOWELL

1. The first Nowell the angel did say
Was to certain poor shepherds in fields as they lay;
In fields where they lay, keeping their sheep,
On a cold winter's night that was so deep.

Ref: Nowell, Nowell, Nowell, Nowell,
born is the King of Israel.

2. They lookéd up and saw a star
Shining in the east, beyond them far,
And to the earth it gave great light
And so it continued both day and night.

3. And by the light of that same star
Three wise men came from country far;
To seek for a king was their intent,
And to follow the star wherever it went.

4. This star drew nigh to the northwest,
O'er Bethlehem it took its rest,
And there it did both stop and stay
Right over the place where Jesus lay.

5. Then entered in those wise men three,
Full reverently upon their knee,
And offered there in his presence,
Their gold and myrrh and frankincense.

6. Then let us all with one accord
Sing praises to our heav'nly Lord:
Who with the Father we adore
And Spirit blest for evermore.

Text: English Carol, 17th c. **Tune:** THE FIRST NOWELL, Irregular **Music:** CBW II 460; CBW III 344

WHAT CHILD IS THIS

1. What Child is this, who laid to rest,
   On Mary's lap is sleeping?
   Whom angels greet with anthems sweet,
   While shepherds watch are keeping?

Ref: This, this is Christ the King,
   Whom shepherds guard and angels sing:
   Haste, haste to bring him laud,
   The babe, the son of Mary.

2. Why lies he in such mean estate
   Where ox and ass are feeding?
   Good Christian, fear: for sinners here
   The silent Word is pleading.

3. So bring him incense, gold, and myrrh,
   Come, peasant, king to own him,
   The King of kings salvation brings,
   Let loving hearts enthrone him.

Text: William Chatterton Dix, 1837-1898 **Tune:** GREENSLEEVES, 87 87 with refrain **Music:** CBW II 461; CBW III 338

GOOD CHRISTIAN FRIENDS, REJOICE

Good Christian friends, rejoice
With heart and soul and voice;

1. O give heed to what we say:
   Jesus Christ was born today!
   Ox and ass before him bow,
   and he is in the manger now.
   Christ is born today!
   Christ is born today!

2. Now you hear of endless bliss:
   Jesus Christ was born for this!
   He has opened heaven's door,
   And we are blest for ever more.
   Christ was born for this!
   Christ was born for this!

3. Now you need not fear the grave:
   Jesus Christ was born to save!
   Calls you one and calls you all
   To gain his everlasting hall.
   Christ was born to save!
   Christ was born to save!

Text: *In dulci jubilo;* Latin and German, 14th c., tr. John Mason Neale, 1818-1866, alt. **Tune:** IN DULCI JUBILO; 66 77 77 55 **Music:** *CBW II 465; CBW III 322*

O COME, ALL YE FAITHFUL

1. O come, all ye faithful, joyful and triumphant,
   O come ye, o come ye to Bethlehem;
   Come and behold him, born the king of angels.

Ref: O come, let us adore him,
O come, let us adore him,
O come, let us adore him, Christ, the Lord!

2. Sing, choirs of angels, sing in exultation,
   Sing, all ye citizens of heav'n above!
   Glory to God in the highest.

3. Yea, Lord, we greet thee, born this happy morning,
   Jesus, to thee be glory giv'n;
   Word of the Father, now in flesh appearing.

Text: *Adeste, fideles;* John F. Wade, c. 1711-1786; tr. Frederick Oakley, 1802-80, alt. **Tune:** ADESTE, FIDELES, Irregular with refrain; John F. Wade, c. 1711-1786 **Music:** CBW II 458; CBW III 329

TAKE UP YOUR CROSS

1. Take up your cross, the Saviour said,
   If you would my disciple be;
   Take up your cross with willing heart,
   And humbly follow after me.

2. Take up your cross, let not its weight
   Fill your weak spirit with alarm;
   His strength shall bear your spirit up,
   And brace your heart and nerve your arm.

3. Take up your cross, heed not the shame,
   And let your foolish heart be still;
   The Lord for you accepted death
   Upon a cross, on Calvary's hill.

4. Take up your cross, then, in his strength,
   And calmly every danger brave:
   It guides you to abundant life,
   And leads to vict'ry o'er the grave.

5. Take up your cross, and follow Christ,
   Nor think till death to lay it down;
   For only those who bear the cross
   May hope to wear the glorious crown.

Text: Charles W. Everest, 1814-1877, alt. **Tune:** ERHALT UNS, HERR, LM **Music:** CBW II 481; CBW III 352

O SACRED HEAD SURROUNDED

1. O sacred head surrounded
By crown of piercing thorn.
O bleeding head, so wounded
Reviled and put to scorn.
The pow'r of death comes o'er you,
The glow of life decays,
Yet angel hosts adore you,
And tremble as they gaze.

2. In this your bitter passion,
Good Shepherd, think of me
With your most sweet compassion,
Unworthy though I be:
Beneath your cross abiding
For ever would I rest,
In your dear love confiding,
And with your presence blest.

3. Christ Jesus, we adore you,
Our thorn-crowned Lord and King.
We bow our heads before you,
And to your cross we cling.
Lord, give us strength to bear it
With patience and with love,
That we may truly merit
A glorious crown above.

Text: Bernard of Clairvaux, v. 1, tr. Henry W. Baker, 1821-77; v. 2 & 3, tr. Arthur T. Russell, 1806-74, alt. **Tune:** PASSION CHORALE; 76 76 D; Hans Leo Hassler, 1564-1612
Music: CBW 11 491; CBW III 377

LORD, WHO THROUGHOUT THESE FORTY DAYS

1. Lord, who throughout these forty days
For us did fast and pray,
Teach us to overcome our sins
And close by you to stay.

2. As you with Satan did contend
And did the vict'ry win,
O give us strength in you to fight,
In you to conquer sin.

3. As you did hunger and did thirst,
So teach us, gracious Lord,
To die to self and so to live
By your most holy word.

4. And through these days of penitence,
and through your passion-tide,
For evermore, in life and death,
O Lord, with us abide.

5. Abide with us, that through this life
Of doubts and hopes and pain
An Easter of unending joy
We may at last attain.

Text: Claudia F. Hernaman, 1838-98, in her *A Child's Book of Praise,* 1873, alt. **Tune:** ST. FLAVIAN, CM; adapted from Day's Psalter, 1562 **Music:** CBW II 482; CBW III 367

WHEN I BEHOLD THE WONDROUS CROSS

1. When I behold the wondrous cross
On which the prince of glory died,
My richest gain I count but loss
And pour contempt on all my pride.

2. Forbid it, Lord, that I should boast
Save in the death of Christ, my God;
The vain things that attract me most,
I sacrifice them to his blood.

3. See, from his head, his hands, his feet,
Sorrow and love flow mingled down.
Did e'er such love and sorrow meet,
Or thorns compose so rich a crown?

4. Were all the realms of nature mine,
It would be off'ring far too small;
Love so amazing, so divine,
Demands my soul, my life, my all!

Text: Isaac Watts, 1674-1748, alt. **Tune:** ROCKINGHAM, LM
Music: CBW II 489; CBW III 382

O SONS AND DAUGHTERS

Ref: Alleluia, alleluia, alleluia!

1. O sons and daughters, let us sing!
The king of heav'n, our glorious king,
From death today rose triumphing. Alleluia!

2. That Easter morn, at break of day,
The faithful women went their way,
To seek the tomb where Jesus lay. Alleluia!

3. An angel clothed in white they see,
Who sat and spoke unto the three,
"Your Lord has gone to Galilee." Alleluia!

4. That night th'apostles met in fear;
And Christ did in their midst appear,
And said, "My peace be with you here." Alleluia!

5. How blest are they who have not seen,
And yet whose faith has constant been,
For they eternal life shall win. Alleluia!

6. On this most holy day of days,
To God your hearts and voices raise,
In laud and jubilee and praise. Alleluia!

Text: Jean Tisserand, †1494; tr. John Mason Neale, 1818-66, alt.
Tune: O FILII ET FILIAE 8 8 8 4 with Alleluias
Music: CBW II 506; CBW III 404

JESUS CHRIST IS RIS'N TODAY

1. Jesus Christ is ris'n today, Alleluia!
   Our triumphant holy day, Alleluia!
   Who did once upon the cross, Alleluia!
   Suffer to redeem our loss. Alleluia!

2. Hymns of praise then let us sing, Alleluia!
   Unto Christ our heav'nly king, Alleluia!
   Who endured the cross and grave, Alleluia!
   Sinners to redeem and save. Alleluia!

3. But the pains which he endured, Alleluia!
   Our salvation have procured; Alleluia!
   Now above the sky he's king, Alleluia!
   Where the angels ever sing. Alleluia!

4. Sing we to our God above, Alleluia!
   Praise eternal as his love, Alleluia!
   Praise him, now his might confess, Alleluia!
   Father, Son and Spirit bless. Alleluia!

Text: Lyra Davidica, 1708, alt. & others **Tune:** EASTER HYMN; 77 77 with Alleluias **Music:** CBW II 500; CBW III 389

SING WITH ALL THE SAINTS IN GLORY

1. Sing with all the saints in glory,
   Sing the resurrection song!
   Death and sorrow, earth's dark story,
   To the former days belong.
   All around the clouds are breaking,
   Soon the storms of time shall cease;
   In God's likeness we awaken,
   Knowing everlasting peace.

2. O what glory, far exceeding
   All that eye has yet perceived!
   Holiest hearts for ages pleading,
   Never that full joy conceived.

God has promised, Christ prepares it,
There on high our welcome waits;
Ev'ry humble spirit shares it,
Christ has passed th'eternal gates.

3. Life eternal! heav'n rejoices:
Jesus lives who once was dead;
Shout with joy, O deathless voices!
Child of God, lift up your head!
Patriarchs from distant ages,
Saints all longing for their heaven,
Prophets, psalmists, seers, and sages,
All await the glory giv'n.

Text: 1 Cor 15.20; William J. Irons, 1812-1883, alt.
Tune: HYMN TO JOY, 87 87 D **Music:** CBW III 406

THE STRIFE IS O'ER

Ref: Alleluia, alleluia, alleluia!

1. The strife is o'er, the battle done;
Now is the victor's triumph won;
O let the song of praise be sung! Alleluia!

2. The pow'rs of sin have done their worst;
But Jesus has his foes dispersed;
Let shouts of joy and praise out-burst! Alleluia!

3. Lord, by the stripes which wounded you,
From death's sting free your servants too,
That we may live and sing to you. Alleluia!

4. On the third morn you rose again,
Glorious in majesty to reign;
O let us swell the joyful strain! Alleluia!

Text: *Finita iam sunt praelia,* Latin 12th c.; *Symphonia Sirenum Selectarum,* Cologne, 1695; tr. Francis Pott, 1832-1909, alt. **Tune:** VICTORY, 8 8 8 with Alleluias **Music:** CBW II 503; CBW III 395

THAT EASTER DAY WITH JOY WAS BRIGHT

1. That Easter day with joy was bright,
The sun shone out with fairer light,
Alleluia, alleluia!
When to their longing eyes restored,
The glad apostles saw their Lord.

Ref: Alleluia, alleluia, alleluia, alleluia, alleluia!

2. His risen flesh with radiance glowed;
His wounded hands and feet he showed;
Alleluia, alleluia!
Those scars their solemn witness gave
That Christ was risen from the grave.

3. O Jesus, in your gentleness,
With constant love our hearts possess;
Alleluia, alleluia!
To you our lips will ever raise
The tribute of our grateful praise.

4. O Lord of all, with us abide
In this our joyful Eastertide;
Alleluia, alleluia!
From ev'ry weapon death can wield
Your own redeemed for ever shield.

5. All praise to you, O risen Lord,
Now by both heav'n and earth adored;
Alleluia, alleluia!
To God the Father equal praise,
And Spirit blest our songs we raise.

Text: *Claro paschali gaudio;* Latin 5th c; tr. By John Mason Neal, 1818-1866; alt. **Tune:** LASST UNS ERFREUEN, LM with Alleluias **Music:** CBW II 507; CBW III 392

HAIL, HOLY QUEEN, ENTHRONED ABOVE

1. Hail, holy Queen, enthroned above, O Maria!
   Hail, Queen of mercy and of love, O Maria!

Ref: Triumph, all you cherubim,
sing with us, you seraphim,
Heav'n and earth resound the hymn:
Salve, salve, salve, Regina!

2. Our life, our sweetness here below, O Maria!
   Our hope in sorrow and in woe, O Maria!

3. We honour you for Christ, your son, O Maria!
   Who has for us redemption won, O Maria!

Text: *Salve, Regina, mater misericordiae,* c. 1080; tr. from the *Roman Hymnal,* 1884 **Tune:** SALVE, REGINA COELITUM, 84 84 with refrain **Music:** CBW II 610; CBW III 457

IMMACULATE MARY

1. Immaculate Mary, your praises we sing,
   You reign now in heaven with Jesus our king.

Ref: Ave, Ave, Ave, Maria!
Ave, Ave, Ave, Maria!

2. In heaven, the blessed your glory proclaim;
   On earth, we your children invoke your fair name.

3. Your name is our power, your virtues our light;
   Your love is our comfort, your pleading our might.

4. We pray for our mother the Church upon earth,
   And bless, dearest lady, the land of our birth.

Text: Anon., in *Parochial Hymn Book,* Boston, 1897, rev. version of "Hail, Virgin of Virgins," by Jeremiah Cummings, 1814-1866, in his *Songs for Catholic Schools,* 1860, alt. **Tune:** LOURDES HYMN, 11 11 **Music:** CBW II 611: CBW III 463A

HOLY GOD, WE PRAISE YOUR NAME

1. Holy God, we praise your name;
Lord of all, we bow before you.
All on earth your sceptre claim;
All in heav'n above adore you.
Infinite your vast domain;
Everlasting is your reign.

2. Hark, the glad celestial hymn
Angel choirs above are raising:
Cherubim and seraphim,
In unceasing chorus praising,
Fill the heav'ns with sweet accord:
"Holy, holy, holy Lord!"

3. Lo, the apostolic train
Joins your sacred name to hallow;
Prophets swell the glad refrain,
And the white-robed martyrs follow;
And from morn to set of sun,
Through the church the song goes on.

4. Holy Father, holy Son,
Holy Spirit, three we name you,
Though in essence only one;
Undivided God, we claim you,
And, adoring, bend the knee
While we own the mystery.

Text: *Te Deum laudamus; tr.* Clarence Walworth, 1820-1900, in *Catholic Psalmist,* 1858, alt. **Tune:** GROSSER GOTT, 7 8 7 8 77 **Music:** CBW II 631; CBW III 555

ALL PEOPLE THAT ON EARTH DO DWELL

1. All people that on earth do dwell,
Sing to the Lord with cheerful voice;
Him serve with mirth, his praise forth tell,
Come we before him and rejoice.

2. Know that the Lord is God indeed;
Without our aid he did us make;
We are his folk, he does us feed,
And for his sheep he does us take.

3. O enter then his gates with praise;
Approach with joy his courts unto;
Praise, laud, and bless his name always,
For it is seemly so to do.

4. For why? The Lord our God is good:
His mercy is for ever sure;
His truth at all times firmly stood,
And shall from age to age endure.

5. To Father, Son, and Holy Ghost,
The God whom heav'n and earth adore,
From us and from the angel host
Be praise and glory evermore.

6. Praise God, from whom all blessings flow,
Praise him, all creatures here below;
Praise him above, you heav'nly host;
Praise Father, Son, and Holy Ghost.

Text: Psalm 100; William Kethe, d. c. 1594; v. 6: Thomas Ken, 1637-1711 **Tune:** OLD HUNDREDTH, LM 8 8 8 8
Music: CBW II 621; CBW III 578

O GOD, OUR HELP IN AGES PAST

1. Our God, our help in ages past,
Our hope for years to come,
Our shelter from the stormy blast,
And our eternal home.

2. Beneath the shadow of your throne,
Your saints have dwelt secure;
Sufficient is your arm alone,
And our defence is sure.

3. Before the hills in order stood,
Or earth received its frame,
From everlasting you are God,
To endless years the same.

4. A thousand ages in your sight
Are like an ev'ning gone,
Short as the watch that ends the night
Before the rising sun.

5. Time, like an ever-rolling stream,
Bears all our lives away;
Thy fly, forgotten, as a dream
Dies at the op'ning day.

6. O God, our help in ages past,
Our hope for years to come,
Be now our guide while life shall last,
And our eternal home.

Text: Psalm 90; Isaac Watts, 1674-1748, alt.
Tune: ST. ANNE, CM **Music:** CBW II 640; CBW III 644

COME, HOLY SPIRIT

1. Come, Holy Spirit, Creator blest,
And in our hearts take up your rest;
Come with your grace and heav'nly aid
To fill the hearts which you have made.

2. O Comforter, to you we cry,
The heav'nly gift of God most high;
The fount of life and fire of love,
And sweet anointing from above.

3. To ev'ry sense your light impart,
And shed your love in ev'ry heart.
To our weak flesh your strength supply:
Unfailing courage from on high.

4. O grant that we through you may come
To know the Father and the Son,
And hold with firm, unchanging faith
That you are Spirit of them both.

5. Now let us praise Father and Son,
And Holy Spirit, with them one;
And may the Son on us bestow
The gifts that from the Spirit flow.

Text: *Veni, Creator Spiritus,* anon., 9th c.; tr. by Edward Caswall, 1814-1878, et al.; alt. **Tune:** LAMBILOTTE, LM
Music: CBW II 516; CBW III 416

ALLELUIA! SING TO JESUS!

1. Alleluia! Sing to Jesus!
His the sceptre, his the throne;
Alleluia! His the triumph,
His the victory alone;
Hark! The songs of peaceful Sion
Thunder like a mighty flood;
Jesus out of ev'ry nation
Has redeemed us by his blood.

2. Alleluia! Not as orphans
Are we left in sorrow now;
Alleluia! He is near us,
Faith believes, nor questions how:
Though the cloud from sight received him
When the forty days were o'er,
Shall our hearts forget his promise,
"I am with you evermore"?

3. Alleluia! Bread of heaven,
Here on earth our food and stay;
Alleluia! Here the sinful
Turn to you from day to day:
Intercessor, friend of sinners,
Earth's Redeemer, plead for us
Where the voices of the blessed
Join the chant victorious.

4. Alleluia! King eternal,
you are Lord of lords alone.
Alleluia! Born of Mary,
Earth your footstool, heav'n your throne:
You within the veil have entered,
Robed in flesh, our great high priest;
You on earth, both priest and victim.
In the eucharistic feast.

Text: William Chatteron Dix, 1837-1898; alt.
Tune: HYFRYDOL, 87 87 D **Music:** CBW II 536; CBW III 426

FOR ALL THE SAINTS

1. For all the saints,
   Who from their labours rest,
   Who their great faith
   To all the world confessed,
   Your name, O Jesus,
   Be forever blest. Alleluia, alleluia.

2. You were their rock,
   Their fortress and their might,
   Their strength and solace
   In the well-fought fight,
   And in the darkness
   their unfailing light. Alleluia, alleluia.

3. O blest communion,
   Family divine,
   We live and struggle,
   You in glory shine;
   Yet all are one
   within God's great design. Alleluia, alleluia.

4. And when the strife
   Is fierce, the conflict long,
   Then from the distance
   Sounds the trumpet song,
   And hearts are bold again,
   And courage strong. Alleluia, alleluia.

Text: William How, 1823-1897 **Tune:** SINE NOMINE, 10 10 10 with Alleluias **Music:** CBW II 617; CBW III 449.

Music Index

SERVICE MUSIC

Eucharistic Chants 644

HYMNS

All People That on Earth Do Dwell 667
Alleluia! Sing to Jesus! 670
Come, Holy Spirit 669
For All the Saints 671
Good Christian Friends, Rejoice 656
Hail, Holy Queen, Enthroned Above 665
Hail Our Saviour's Glorious Body 276
Holy God, We Praise Your Name 666
Immaculate Mary 665
Jesus Christ Is Ris'n Today 662
Lord, Who Throughout These Forty Days 660
O Come, All Ye Faithful 657
O Come, Divine Messiah! 654
O Come, O Come Emmanuel 653
O God, Our Help in Ages Past 668
O Sacred Head Surrounded 659
O Sons and Daughters 661
On Jordan's Bank 652
Pange Lingua / Tantum Ergo 276
Sing with All the Saints in Glory 662
Take Up Your Cross 658
That Easter Day with Joy Was Bright 664
The First Nowell 655
The Strife Is O'er 663
What Child Is This 656
When I Behold the Wondrous Cross 660